Atypical Infant Development

Edited by
Marci J. Hanson, Ph.D.
Department of Special Education
San Francisco State University

University Park Press
Baltimore

UNIVERSITY PARK PRESS
International Publishers in Medicine and Human Services
300 North Charles Street
Baltimore, Maryland 21201

Typeset by Maryland Composition Company, Inc.
Design by S. Stoneham, Studio 1812, Baltimore
Manufactured in the United States of America by
The Maple Press Company

Library of Congress Cataloging in Publication Data
Main entry under title:

Atypical infant development.

Includes index.
1. Developmentally disabled children.   2. Infants—
Growth.   3. Infant health services.   4. Developmentally
disabled children—Education.   5. Developmentally
disabled chidren—Services for.   I. Hanson, Marci J.
RJ135.A88   1983   618.92   83-14741
ISBN 0-8391-1884-8

Atypical Infant Development

Contents

v

Contributors

Bonnie J. Breitmayer, Ph.D.
Research Training Program
  Fellow
Frank Porter Graham Child
  Development Center
Highway 54, Bypass West 071A
Chapel Hill, North Carolina
  27514

William A. Bricker, Ph.D.
Professor
Department of Special
  Education
Kent State University
Kent, Ohio 44242

Lucy S. Crain, M.D., M.P.H.
Associate Clinical Professor
Departments of Pediatrics and
  Family and Community
  Medicine
Director of Pediatric Disabilities
  Clinic
University of California, San
  Francisco, Medical Center
400 Parnassus Avenue, 205A
San Francisco, California 94143

Linda Fetters, M.S., R.P.T.
Doctoral Candidate
Department of Psychology
Brandeis University
Waltham, Massachusetts 02254

R. J. Gallagher, Ph.D.
Research Associate
Illinois Institute for
  Developmental Disabilities
University of Illinois–Chicago
1640 West Roosevelt Drive
Chicago, Illinois 60608

Barbara Davis Goldman, Ph.D.
Investigator
Frank Porter Graham Child
  Development Center
Highway 54, Bypass West 071A
Chapel Hill, North Carolina
  27514

Peter A. Gorski, M.D.
Director
Developmental and Behavioral
  Pediatrics
Mt. Zion Hospital and Medical
  Center
1600 Divisidero Street
San Francisco, California 94115

Mary Frances Hanline, M.A.
Doctoral Candidate
Department of Special
  Education
San Francisco State University
San Francisco, California 94132

Marci J. Hanson, Ph.D.
Associate Professor
Department of Special Education
San Francisco State University
1600 Holloway Avenue
San Francisco, California 94132

Jean A. Levin, Ph.D.
Department of Speech
  Pathology and Audiology
Kent State University
Kent, Ohio 44242

Michael Lewis, Ph.D.
Professor of Pediatrics
Rutgers Medical School
Academic Health Sciences,
  CN–19
New Brunswick, New Jersey
  08903

Patrick R. Macke, M.Ed.
Doctoral Candidate
Department of Special Education
Kent State University
Kent, Ohio 44242

Craig T. Ramey, Ph.D.
Professor, Department of
  Psychology
Director of Research
Frank Porter Graham Child
  Development Center
Highway 54, Bypass 071A
Chapel Hill, North Carolina
  27514

Mary K. Rothbart, Ph.D.
Professor
Department of Psychology
University of Oregon
Eugene, Oregon 97403

Robert Sheehan, Ph.D.
Assistant Professor
Department of Child
  Development and Family
  Services
Purdue University
West Lafayette, Indiana
  47907

To my students, who requested that I write this book

Foreword

This book explores the complex subject of evaluating and aiding the development of atypical and high-risk infants. Before proceeding, I would like to clarify a few working concepts and perhaps muddy some traditional orientations, which at one time appeared clear and reasonable.

Let me plainly specify the challenge to all students, investigators, parents, and clinical workers who seek to help optimize the course of infants born at risk for atypical development: To date, no reliable system exists for predicting which children will outgrow initial vulnerabilities nor for accurately forecasting the extent of ultimate disability based on earlier biological circumstances.

Yet, do not cringe or turn back upon learning so bluntly about the failings of our profession. Indeed, the unsolved mystery of recovery from initial stress to the newborn brain and nervous system bears much cause for optimistic study. Our understanding has grown beyond the pioneering era when investigators believed that by identifying perinatal biological tags or risk factors, a child's developmental prognosis could be accurately predicted. Instead, we find ourselves in the thick of an excitingly unsettled period in which researchers recognize the necessity of approaching our questions from prospective, longitudinal, and transdisciplinary perspectives. No one scientific field seems able to derive all the answers to the puzzle of influences upon the developmental course of infants born at risk.

Surely, then, we are gaining the realization that infants are more complex and responsive organisms than was initially credited. By definition, the concept of developmental risk implies change of condition over time. A child's central nervous system functions toward its most mature states of motor coordination, cognition, communication, and personal-social capacities over many years. During such unfinished stages of neurological and behavioral maturation, the organism remains responsive to the effects of medical as well as social events or conditions.

Moreover, we are learning how strong an impact the child has on his or her own course of development. Each human being carries a special style of behavior into interactions with others. These individual characteristics can be observed as early as the neonatal period. Such temperamental qualities as intensity, activity, mood, rhythmicity, adaptability, persistence, distractability, and sensory threshold seem unrelated to medical conditions or neurological function. Through expressing thoughts, emotions, or interests in their individual ways, atypical children (like all children) guide the responses of their caregivers toward them as persons and not just as diseases or vulnerabilities. Logically, then, certain approaches to social interaction or intervention will succeed with some children while getting not much more than frustrated standstill from different parents and children facing identical problems. Likewise, we need to have a better appreciation of the range of therapeutic opportunities indicated by understanding parents as people who also respond individually to the obstacles, demands, and variations concerned with supporting the optimal development of their child.

I wish merely to open the case for understanding the roles of biological, psychological, and social strengths and weaknesses toward coordinating a hopeful plan for intervening on behalf of infants who may be at risk for developmental difficulties. The succeeding chapters build a comprehensive base from which the interested student can approach challenges met in his or her own clinical or research setting. The accumulated expertise of the authors represents distinguished contributions of several disciplines including psychology, education, physical therapy, and medicine. By its penetrating and honest example, this volume draws at least two lessons to all interested professionals:

1. Failure to fit real-life experiences into unidirectional theories of development may in fact reveal important clues toward better understanding the multivariable time-linked influences upon atypical infant development.
2. Chances are great that new advances on behalf of infants at risk will come as professionals discover how to utilize and combine the valuable insights possible when a number of related disciplines concertedly tackle the future.

This volume reflects a profound dedication to learning how to promote optimal development in at-risk and handicapped infants as early as possible. Infancy encompasces the most rapid changes in growth, neurological maturation, and behavioral competence. With the fine contributions presented in this book, we gain fresh inspiration and optimism for our work.

Peter A. Gorski, M.D.

Preface

Care for infants born disabled or at risk for subsequent developmental delay has moved from a focus solely on infant survival and medical treatment to concerns about long-range developmental outcomes for these babies. A recognition of the support needs of the families of these children and a general acceptance of the importance of early intervention to achieve optimal developmental results has led to an increase in the type and number of services available for infants. With no other age group perhaps is the need for a variety of services delivered by different disciplines more apparent. This volume, thus, represents the collective expertise of diverse disciplines, among them special education, psychology, physical therapy, and medicine. It attempts to draw together research findings and clinical applications of importance to those involved in identifying and treating atypical infants.

The audience for this volume is similarly diverse. The text is aimed primarily at the preservice level to be used as primary reading for students receiving early childhood training in departments of special education and developmental psychology and in medical settings. Although the major focus is on early childhood special education, the text is equally useful for other professionals studying early atypical development—physical and occupational therapists, communication specialists, nurses, and physicians. The information in this volume also speaks to the needs and interests of parents and professionals in the field. It can be used as a current reference for those involved in policy making and infant program planning and implementation.

The care and treatment of atypical infants requires a multifaceted service delivery model. The needs of these infants can be met only through a collaborative and concerted interdisciplinary effort carried out by professionals trained in this orientation. We have endeavored to provide this focus in *Atypical Infant Development* and hope that this volume assists teachers, clinicians, parents, and researchers in their planning for infants born disabled or at risk.

Marci J. Hanson, Ph.D.

Introduction

Marci J. Hanson

Arlette is a 4-year-old child with Down syndrome. She attends a pre-school program in a local public school where at least half of her academic training is in an integrated program that includes disabled and nondisabled children. Her mother attributes the great strides Arlette has made to her participation in an early intervention program from the age of 4 months. Through this program Arlette's mother learned to care for, play, and interact with Arlette in an enjoyable and educationally beneficial fashion. She feels that the program has helped her as well as Arlette. Since she speaks only Spanish, finding and coordinating services for Arlette has been particularly difficult. Through the early intervention program she was assisted in making other community contacts, assisted in teaching her child, and also placed in contact with other parents with whom she could share information and provide mutual support.

Demiko's parents report that he was a healthy, active baby until he developed spinal meningitis at 10 months of age. This disease left him with visual and hearing impairments and spasticity in his legs and arms. His parents are actively involved with the team members of the early intervention program—special education teacher, physical and occupational therapists, communication specialist—in designing and implementing training programs for Demiko. Although his disabilities are major, Demiko's parents are teaching Demiko to become more active, to reach and grasp objects, to feed himself independently, and to communicate with them. They feel the early intervention program has been a turning point for them—a factor that allowed them to cope with the range of Demiko's problems so that they could continue to care for him at home.

Justin was born prematurely at just 26 weeks gestational age. The severe complications at birth necessitated hospitalization for 3 months. Shortly after his first birthday he was referred by a pediatrician to the early intervention program having been diagnosed as exhibiting spastic diplegia, visual impairments, and general developmental delay. At age 2½ he is learning to pull to standing position, independently feed himself, use the toilet, discriminate among objects in his environment, and label objects and events. Because of his developmental progress his parents plan to enroll him in a regular preschool at age 3 where he will continue his academic and social learning; he will receive extra physical therapy services for his motor impairments.

These families all participated in an early intervention program for developmentally delayed infants and toddlers. All children described have had considerable medical and educational service demands from birth. In addition, their births have precipitated additional needs for their families—the need for accurate information about the disabling conditions, the need for support in coping with the stress, and the need for locating and coordinating services for their children.

These descriptions underscore the range of service delivery requirements for atypical infants and their families. Furthermore, they demonstrate that professionals in the social and health sciences must work together to tackle the complex issues of overcoming and remediating the effects of early disabling conditions.

This volume draws together information—both scientific findings and clinical applications—from the variety of professions involved with the study and treatment of young atypical children. Its purpose as such is for use as a reference for concerned professionals and parents. The studies reviewed highlight the recentness of this field of inquiry and remind us of the work yet to be done in order to solve adequately the challenges posed by young children who are disabled or at risk for developmental delay.

Contributors to this volume come from the fields of special education, psychology, pediatrics, and physical therapy. All have had considerable experience in interdisciplinary service settings. It is our intent that this volume will facilitate communication between professional groups concerned with young atypical children and thus lead to a better understanding of the development and treatment of these children.

Several assumptions have been made by the authors from the outset:

1. The interaction of the young child within the larger environment plays a powerful role in the child's developmental outcome. Thus, no matter how major the biological insults the child has endured, long-range outcomes can be gauged only through continuous assessment and analysis of the quality of the child's interaction within the environment. All children can learn; our challenge is to provide optimal experiences.

2. Based upon the first assumption, this volume has an educational focus. This focus, however, is generic, encompassing the wide range of services and special needs of atypical children. As such, this perspective is not the unique domain of any single professional group which may be involved in the care and treatment of young children; rather it emphasizes collaborative efforts among a variety of service fields.

The theme of this text, thus, centers around the complex developmental issues and comprehensive interdisciplinary service needs of young children at risk and their families.

Before introducing the specific content of chapters, it is necessary to define the population here referred to as "atypical infants." For purposes of this discussion the term *infant* includes children from birth to 3 years because current early intervention practices tend to refer to service for both infants and toddlers as "infant" programs.

Tjossem's (1976) categories of risk—environmental, biological, and established—define clusters of factors that produce atypical development. Although many young children are at extreme risk because of environmental factors associated with conditions such as deprivation and abuse, the discussion in this volume more specifically focuses on the categories of biological (e.g., birth trauma and prematurity) and established risks (e.g., congenital syndromes such as Down syndrome and identifiable impairment with nonspecific etiology such as visual impairment). As is reflected, however, in the ensuing discussion, environmental factors also play a major role in identifying, understanding, and planning for the child with an obvious biologically based risk condition. Although treatment approaches aimed exclusively at children at environmental risk are not addressed in this volume, the complex interaction of factors producing atypical development are considered from an interdisciplinary perspective.

This text is organized around four topics: developmental principles, identification and assessment, developmental issues, and early intervention. To provide the reader an introduction to these topics, the content of each chapter is briefly described in the following review.

DEVELOPMENTAL PRINCIPLES

Lewis in the first chapter presents five principles of development, which are of both theoretical and pragmatic importance. These tenets include those that view: the infant as a competent organism, as a social organism, and as an active organism; development as proceeding from undifferentiated to differentiated abilities, and development as an interactive process between the infant's status and the environment at any point in time. Lewis discusses each of these principles and examines each in light of implications for the assessment and education of young children with special needs.

IDENTIFICATION AND ASSESSMENT

Any discussion of atypical infant development centers on the identification and definition of those factors which account for the at-risk status of these babies. Crain (Chapter 2) begins this discussion with a thorough examination of prenatal causes or risk factors. These factors include maternal status, teratogens, infectious agents, genetic and chromosomal abnormalities, and trauma. Gorski continues this review in Chapter 3 by describing perinatal (at or around the time of birth) conditions which contribute to at-risk status. He proceeds to an analysis of neonatal screening and assessment devices used to identify at-risk newborns in the neonatal nursery.

Sheehan and Gallagher (Chapter 4) expand the topic of identification to a broader consideration of infant assessment. They describe the purposes and uses of infant assessments (screening, program planning, and evaluation of intervention) and provide a classification of contemporary infant behavior measures.

DEVELOPMENTAL ISSUES

The potential effects of disability cannot be fully understood without a knowledge of the normal course of development. This section, thus, presents descriptions of developmental trends and markers in various behavioral domains and relates how conditions posing developmental risk to the infant may alter the developmental course. In each developmental area implications for assessment and intervention efforts are considered.

Hanson and Hanline (Chapter 5) introduce this section with an outline of the typical infant's sensory-perceptual development and information processing skills, and a review of sensorimotor development. They follow with descriptive information on the developmental effects of specific disabilities and a consideration of developmental outcomes for disabled children.

In Chapter 6, Hanson discusses one of the most crucial factors in the young child's development—the parent-infant interactional system. The challenges faced by parents of atypical infants are explored and implications for intervention are derived.

The remaining chapters in this section are devoted to issues within specific developmental areas. In Chapter 7, Rothbart discusses the course of normal social development and the importance of the social/affective system in determining the atypical infant's ability to adapt to the environment. Ramey, Breitmayer, and Goldman in Chapter 8 review learning and cognition during infancy from four theoretical approaches—psychometric, constructivist, behavioral, and information processing—and analyze assessment and intervention practices. The interrelationships between cognitive and language development are described further by Bricker, Levin, and Macke in Chapter 9. They review prelinguistic and early language developmental goals and draw implications for devising speech and language intervention strategies. Finally, developmental issues in the area of motor development are discussed by Fetters (Chapter 10). She reviews normal motor developmental sequences and defines guidelines for assessment and intervention in this area.

EARLY INTERVENTION

Over the past decade considerable information has been amassed defining early intervention service delivery models and documenting the short- and long-term effects of these programs. In the final section Hanson defines exemplary practices in the field in light of this experience (Chapter 11) and reviews studies on the efficacy of early intervention (Chapter 12). The primary focus is from an educational model that emphasizes coordination of health, social, and educational services to meet the comprehensive needs of the atypical infant population.

The provision of services to young atypical children and their families necessitates coordinated planning and implementation efforts across fields. We, thus, have the opportunity to exchange information and collaborate with one another in order to address this complex task. This text is dedicated to that effort.

REFERENCE

Tjossem, T. D. (Ed.) *Intervention Strategies for High-Risk Infants and Young Children.* Baltimore: University Park Press, 1976.

Atypical Infant Development

SECTION I
DEVELOPMENTAL PRINCIPLES

Research on early development has supplied a useful structure for viewing infant development. Lewis (Chapter 1) provides the foundation for this volume by reviewing five tenets that have been distilled from the literature. These tenets are applicable not only when development proceeds according to the normal course but also when developmental deviations occur. Lewis discusses the principles that view the infant as a competent organism, the infant  as a social organism, the infant as an active organism, the infant's development as proceeding from undifferentiated to differentiated abilities, and the infant's development as an interactive process between the infant's status and the environment in which the infant is placed. Although these tenets are derived from research on typical infant development, they provide a useful framework for examining developmental deviations and designing appropriate assessment and intervention techniques for young children at risk.

An exploration of the causes, characteristics, and treatments for developmental disorders can advance only from a firm knowledge of child development. Lewis provides the underpinning for this exploration, and in so doing introduces issues and implications for identifying infants at risk and assisting these infants to achieve optimal development.

CHAPTER 1

Developmental Principles and Their Implications for At-Risk and Handicapped Infants

Michael Lewis

In the last two decades several important tenets concerning early development have emerged from the research literature. These are noteworthy both as theoretical guideposts and for their heuristic value in designing education and intervention programs for exceptional children. Among the most important of these principles are those that view:

1. The infant as a competent organism
2. The infant as a social organism
3. The infant as an active organism
4. The infant's development as proceeding from undifferentiated to differentiated abilities
5. The infant's development as an interactive process between the infant's status at any point in time and the environment in which the infant is immersed.

Each of these tenets is examined, along with a summary of the relevant research that supports the principle. The implications for the assessment and education of exceptional children is considered.

THE INFANT AS A COMPETENT ORGANISM

Research on early child development since the mid-1950s is best characterized by the statement, "Infants are competent organisms." The data overwhelmingly demonstrate that the abilities of infants, even at birth, are more complex than adults had ever anticipated. Research has repeatedly shown that a wide variety of skills emerge in the infant much earlier than was previously thought (Mussen, 1970; Osofsky, 1979).

Several important issues in the sociology of science emerge, however, when we consider the historical record of this altered view of the infant. In his classic, *The Principles of Psychology*, William James (1890) concluded that the infant was a buzzing, blooming mass of confusion. At the same time, Preyer (1888) and Darwin (1872) were demonstrating that young infants had considerable abilities, including the ability to pay attention to visual stimuli and to detect unpleasant odors and tastes. Although both positions appeared equally tenable, I suspect that the reason for the popularity of James' view was related to the prevailing *zeitgeist*, which at the turn of the century was that human behavior was primarily determined by experience. The notion of a capable infant would have required the acceptance of biologically based organizational principles, or instincts, which were foreign to the prevailing world view and counter to the belief in the unlimited capacities of all individuals (Dewey, 1959).

James' view predominated until the late 1950s when research on infant development revealed once again the sensory, motor, and cognitive learning capacities of infants. In a set of landmark studies, Robert Fantz (1958, 1961, 1963, 1964) demonstrated that newborn infants, in fact, could see and could process information, and they even had visual preferences. For example, when Fantz (1964) gave newborns a choice between simple and complex visual patterns, the infants preferred the more complex. Until this time, there had been almost no research on infants' visual perception. Indeed, newborns were believed to be functionally blind until 6 weeks of age. By demonstrating that the limited visual ability of infants did not render them insensate, Fantz opened the door to research explorations, not only in the area of infants' sensory abilities but also in motivation and learning. These developments soon made infancy studies the center of research in development.

It is impossible to detail all of the sensory capabilities that have been discovered in young infants.[1] While research on the infant's visual system predominates, research on auditory (Berg et al., 1971; Graham and Clifton, 1966), olfactory and gustatory (Engen, Lipsitt, and Kaye, 1963; Engen, Lipsitt, and Peck, 1974) abilities yields similar findings: From the beginning of life infants are processing environmental information in all modalities. Although some systems

---

[1] For reviews of this literature, the reader is referred to Cohen and Salapetek (1975).

are immature when compared with analogous systems in adults, the evidence is overwhelming that infants are not insensate creatures, but are organisms which begin to interact with their environments at birth or even before (Sontag et al., 1969). It is clear that James' description of infants was off the mark. Infants' early abilities and competencies suggest there are at least some biologically based organizational principles (Bower, 1974).

The elaborate organizational properties of infants' sensory systems are a topic of current research interest (Lipsitt, 1976; Meltzoff and Moore, 1977; Papousek and Papousek, 1981). Recently investigators have examined sensory integration, or the ability of young children to integrate informational input from two different systems (Meltzoff, 1981; Spelke, 1976; Rose et al., 1979). Although it has been amply demonstrated that this ability exists as early as 1 month of age, it is still unknown whether this ability can be attributed to predetermined sensory organizational properties, such as those suggested by Bower (1974) or the Gestalt psychologists, or whether infants must learn to integrate information (Piaget, 1952).

Research on the intellectual ability of infants corroborates the basic findings of studies on infant sensory abilities. Infant intelligence tests, in addition to traditional tests of learning, showed that young infants were capable of altering their behavior in accord with the demand characteristics of their environment, the basic definition of intelligence (Siqueland and DeLucia, 1969). Instrumental conditioning studies (Lipsitt, 1963; Papousek, 1967) and habituation studies (Cohen, 1972; Fantz, 1964; Lewis, 1969) revealed that young infants were quite capable of learning new tasks, solving complex problems, and altering their behavior in response to environmental change. Siqueland and DeLucia (1969), for example, showed that infants could learn to change the brightness of a slide by sucking a specially designed pacifier that controlled the slide. Even more striking were the reports that by 3 months of age infants were able to manipulate physical aspects of their environments through simple motor acts. Watson (1966), for one, showed that infants could control the movement of an overhead mobile by turning their heads.

While empirical evidence of early infant learning was being gathered, Piaget's (1952) theory of sensorimotor intelligence provided a theoretical framework for data on the early growth of intelligence. Piaget's theory also provided the impetus for a series of studies on object permanence and means-ends behavior (Uzgiris and Hunt, 1975) that emphasized the cognitive competence of infants. Studies of other cognitive abilities, including memory, information retrieval, and attention underscored the existence of a complex information processing ability in infants (Cohen and Gelber, 1975; Fagan, 1975; Lewis et al., 1969; McCall, 1971).

These studies of general cognitive ability contributed to the growth of our understanding about children's knowledge of their world, particularly their social knowledge. Although this discussion will be expanded in a later section, the competence of infants cannot be fully appreciated without a word about their social competencies. The knowledge of infants about others and themselves, and their interactions with others have emerged as a new frontier in the rapidly burgeoning domain of social skills (Lewis and Brooks-Gunn, 1979). Infants as young as 3 months old are capable of differentiating strangers and familiar persons (Bronson, 1972). From the earliest months the interactions of infants with the social world become increasingly complex and vary as a function of the person with whom they are interacting (Ban and Lewis, 1974; Lewis et al., 1975).

It is clear that from the opening days or weeks of life, infants already have sensory and cognitive skills that enable them to acquire vast amounts of information about their world, which in turn enables them to develop still more complex skills. Thus, despite their relatively limited motor abilities, the sensory and cognitive skills of very young infants appear vast and far beyond those imagined by the early researchers. Moreover, the notion of the competent infant now incorporates a wide set of diverse abilities, including social and emotional as well as cognitive and perceptual skills (Lewis and Michalson, 1983). This changing view of human development has had a profound influence in our times, affecting not only our expectations about infants and their individual differences, but also our theories of and practices in assessment and education.

With the discoveries of the complex skills of very young infants, it becomes possible to devise new assessment protocols. Most measures of infant ability depend on an evaluation of the infant's motor skills, yet two decades of research indicate that motor ability is unrelated to other areas of development. Infant IQ scales based on motor development have limited use in predicting later development (Lewis and McGurk, 1972; McCall et al., 1972). In the long list of newly uncovered infant abilities, we should now be creating screening and assessment instruments related to cognitive or linguistic growth. Although many clinicians use instruments other than the standard scales (e.g., Bayley, 1969), their assessment procedures have not kept pace with the new discoveries of the infant's abilities nor have they looked at the multiple domains of functioning. The utilization of both developmental theory and empirical findings in the construction of assessment instruments is essential (Lewis and Brooks-Gunn, 1982).

Still another consequence of the last decades of research is the realization that the competencies of the newborn organism are diverse and multidetermined. Infants' competencies exist in all developmental domains including social, perceptual, emotional, and cognitive. In any analysis of development, the utilization of multiple domains for assessment and screening and an increased sensitivity to the array of competencies children exhibit are necessary.

For the general public, the notion of a competent infant has resulted in new educational policies. Implicit changes are apparent, not as educational programs, but as subtle attitude and behavior changes. Before the discovery of infants' sensory capacities, for example, they were placed in rather sterile surroundings—plain white sheets were used and few toys were provided. Knowing that newborns see has changed our manufacturing habits and buying preferences. Patterned sheets and toys varying in color, size, texture, and shape now surround the infant soon after birth. The infant mobile is a particular case. Prior to the 1960s the use of mobiles was absent, they began to appear in homes as a function of our knowledge of infants' ability.

More explicit educational programs also have resulted from the research effort. Infant education is itself a concept that has only become popular in the past 20 years. Educational programs have been shown to exert an important effect on children's later development (Lazar and Darlington, 1982). For infants at risk for dysfunction as well as for infants with a known handicap, these advances are of utmost importance. Assessment devices will ultimately be able to target the areas of dysfunction forcing us to initiate new education practices. Although such developments are still in the making, the tests now being constructed provide an increasingly focused diagnostic ability. In light of this development, the tailoring of programs and environments to meet the needs of such infants should become more efficient and effective. In educational programs it may be more important to strengthen abilities rather than concentrating on dysfunctions. Perception of the wide range of potential competencies allow for such consideration.

THE INFANT AS A SOCIAL ORGANISM

Until recently the infant's social competence has tended to take second place to motor and cognitive ability in studies of child development. For example, when the merits of Head Start were first presented to Congress, it was argued that the way to ameliorate social ills such as juvenile delinquency and school failure was to increase the intellectual ability of disadvantaged children. In other words,

Head Start was an attempt to alter the course of children's lives by altering their intellectual capabilities. Social skills were neglected in favor of intellectual ability. In the past, social skills tended to take this role vis-à-vis intellectual ability. Interpersonal relationships, specifically the infant's relationship to the mother were originally considered to be not a primary drive (i.e., a biological need) but a derived need or drive (Harlow, 1959). Originally conceived by learning theorists as a derivative of a primary drive such as hunger, the attachment between child and mother was not as important for the child's survival as feeding. The degree of satisfaction of the primary drive (i.e., hunger) was the degree to which the person who fed the child became a "secondary" reinforcer. Drive theorists found no biological role for love. To state the case more succinctly, love was derived from being fed. Although this view was not shared by all, it represented the mainstream of American psychology (Sears et al., 1957).

Bowlby (1951) attacked the notion of attachment as a secondary drive by arguing that infants' social needs were biologically based. If primary drives were drives whose lack of satisfaction resulted in the death of the organism, could it not be argued that the loss of the caregiver was also life threatening to the infant? In his monograph for the World Health Organization, Bowlby (1951) demonstrated this argument and thereby reestablished social development as a critical aspect in the life of the infant.

Especially in infancy and early childhood, the primary task of children is to adapt to their social environment. That this adaption is critical suggests that many skills and biological structures may be in its service. Much sensory processing seems keyed to this need. For example, it seems as if infants' discriminatory ability is greater for social than for nonsocial stimuli. By 12 weeks of age English-speaking children can distinguish between social stimuli such as the speech sounds "pa" and "ba" (Eimas et al., 1971). This discriminatory ability seems to be a function of social experience because infants who are not raised in an English-speaking environment are unable to distinguish these subtle differences. Moreover, although young infants are little interested in nonsocial stimuli, they are considerably more attentive as indexed by heart rate changes to social stimuli. Even brain structures seem more attuned to social than to nonsocial events. For instance, hemispheric differentiation for sound seems to be divided by social (speech sounds) and nonsocial (all other sounds) (Molfese et al., 1975; Molfese and Molfese, 1979).

Levis-Strauss (1966) has argued that all cognitive activity is essentially social in nature. Language and complex symbol systems constitute a social contract. The socialization process (i.e., the process of making children social) involves, to a large extent, the process of training children to use the adult forms of communication, thought, and conceptions of reality. Of equal importance to the social competence of children is the control of biological functions through social interactions. Important organizational processes, including the regulation of sleep-awake cycles, seem to result from the social interactions between caregivers and infants (Papousek and Papousek, 1981; Sanders, 1977).

Finally, there seems to be a strong decalage between social and nonsocial schema in the growth of knowledge. The amount of knowledge that children acquire about their social environment is incredibly vast and occurs rapidly. Lewis and Brooks-Gunn (1979) have shown that by 9 months infants already have some rudimentary knowledge about themselves. In a series of studies on self-recognition, they demonstrated that the infant's knowledge of self begins early and is manifested by the time the concept of object permanence emerges.

Moreover, children's knowledge about others is also highly developed quite early in life (Feinman and Lewis, 1983; Lewis et al., 1975). By 1 month, some infants and by 3 months, most infants have some understanding of the relationship between people's faces and voices (Aronson and Rosenbloom, 1971; Kuhl and Meltzoff, in press) Some time between 3 and 6 months of age children acquire knowledge about human faces, and by 7 months demonstrate discrimination of emotional expressions (Caron et al., 1982; Charlesworth and Kreutzer, 1973). By 3 to 4 months infants begin to respond differently to children and adults, and by 6 to 8 months they show differential fear responses to people on the basis of gender and age (Lewis and Brooks, 1974). By 6 to 8 months infants are surprised at the appearance of a small adult (i.e., a midget) and seem to understand that the height-facial feature integration is unusual (Brooks and Lewis, 1976). Recently, we have found that by ten months infants are using the same facial expression and tonal quality of their mothers in their interactions with strangers. Infants also are more friendly to strangers who are treated in a positive manner by their mothers (Feinman and Lewis, 1983).

Stern (1974), Brazelton et al. (1974), and others have shown that infants interact differentially with familiar persons and strangers as early as 5 weeks of age. Thus, data suggest that young infants can differentiate the social/nonsocial dimension and that the social domain seems to be at least as salient for infants as the nonsocial domain.

The implications of the infant's social nature are broad. From the point of view of evaluation one might argue that assessment of abilities should tap social skills as well as nonsocial ones. Because many social skills emerge early, they may be more complex and differentiated than cognitive or motor skills. Moreover, they may be more predictive of later abilities than are the cognitive ones. If one wishes to determine whether child A is dysfunctioning, it is necessary to locate skills that are differentiated early. For example, it is easier to detect a deficit in auditory processing using social (speech) sounds than using pure tones because pure tone differentiation is less advanced than speech sounds. This fact underscores a need to concentrate on items with social rather than nonsocial values on infant tests. In short our attention should be turned to the social domain in infant assessments because that is where *early differentiated* development seems to be located.

From an educational point of view, the importance for facilitating handicapped children's social knowledge and social behavior seem to be recognized. If adaptation to the social environment is important, then teaching social skills may be as important as the teaching of nonsocial skills. Moreover, because social may precede nonsocial skills in development, it is likely that by focusing on social skills we also improve the nonsocial ones.

THE INFANT AS AN ACTIVE ORGANISM

The infant had been characterized as both incompetent and inactive for many years. Long after the competence of infants had been established, it was still generally believed that infants were acted upon rather than active participants in their own development (Lerner, 1978). The view of a passive organism was derived from traditional learning models where the learner was believed slowly to acquire skills and information as a function of the number of learning trials and reinforcement schedule. Such a model lies at the heart of the traditional teacher-student relationship in which the teacher selects the information and passes it along to a receptive student. In this didactic model, the student is passive both with respect to the information and to its presentation schedule. Alternative models of the learner are possible, however, and it is on these models that we focus.

Infants interact with their environment not only to gain information but to test hypotheses already generated. In addition, infants are able to organize this information either through the development of schemata or through innate organizing capacities. Infants attend to their environments in a nonrandom fashion, and their motivation seems to be generated by their own need for mental activity. Organisms act on their environment in two ways: 1) to influence the actions of others; and 2) to process information and test hypotheses. Lewis and Rosenblum (1974) provided sufficient evidence that not only does the caregiver influence the infant's behavior, but also the infant has an effect on the caregiver, so that this active effect need not be focused upon here. Our attention is focused on the view of the infant as an active information processor.

A single example of the active nature of the infant highlights this concept. Lewis, Sullivan, and Brooks-Gunn (in press) and Lewis, Sullivan, and Michalson (in press) studied infants 10 to 24 weeks old under two conditions. In the experimental condition each infant could turn on an audiovisual event by pulling a string attached to the wrist. In a yoked control group identical audiovisual stimulation was administered, but it was not contingent on the infant's action. Of central importance to this study was whether the experimental infants would: 1) pay more attention to their environment and remain interested in the audiovisual event; and 2) show more enjoyment than the yoked control subjects. Our hypothesis was that organisms who remain active and perceive that they act on their environment will be more interested and happier, independent of the amount of stimulation.

The results of the study indicated that passive stimulation per se was not as important as active participation in the experimental situation, even for infants as young as 10 weeks. Experimental infants stayed in the situation significantly longer and showed more smiling and less fretting than the yoked controls. These results underscore the active nature of the processes underlying cognitive development, a view that Piaget (1952) endorsed in his notion of the acquisition of a means-end concept which he considered a vital aspect of early intellectual growth. These results also attest to the motivational effects of an active organism, that is, changes in infant state (Lewis, 1977; Lewis and Coates, 1980; Lewis and Goldberg, 1969).

This third tenet of infant development speaks to the types of intervention introduced to facilitate infant development and to our choice of assessment techniques. In terms of intervention, research findings suggest that stimulating handicapped, at-risk, or normal infants is insufficient. Effective stimulation must be interactive (Lewis, 1977) and must engage an active infant. Using this intervention model, Brinker and Lewis (1982a, 1982b) have begun to develop a contingent infant stimulation program, a "learning to learn" curric-

ulum (Lewis, 1967). Our home-based program is designed to stimulate the handicapped infant's interaction with its environment via
a microcomputer designed to increase the contingency between the
child's actions and environmental outcomes. Our preliminary data
and informal observations support our belief that contingency experiences are one of the early factors in the development of learning
strategies, even in handicapped infants.

The principle of the active organism also influences notions of
assessment. In most assessment procedures children are presented
a task that must be solved. This assessment procedure is based on
the passive learner/student model. Their responses are static. Children's ability to change an incorrect strategy is not tested nor is their
growth of knowledge considered. The criticism of such assessment
procedures is not new (Feuerstein, 1979). We have begun to explore
the ways in which our contingency intervention program might be
used to assess an infant's behavioral change in an attempt to provide
more dynamic process-oriented assessment.

DEVELOPMENT AS PROCEEDING FROM
UNDIFFERENTIATED TO DIFFERENTIATED SKILLS

The fourth principle has two aspects. Although some psychologists
would still argue for the concept of a general "g" factor, even in
infancy (Wilson, 1971), the general view is that the infant possesses
a set of skills (Lewis, 1976; McCall et al., 1977). The skills approach
can take many forms, including the slow unfolding of an increasingly
more complex set of skills (as in a geometric progression), the transformation of a key skill at different ages (McCall et al., 1977), or more
complex processing in which some skills are transformed, some are
created and others simply disappear. Despite the particulars of the
model, the concept is of an infant possessing multiple skills and
abilities which change with development. Whatever the size of the
infant's early set of skills, without doubt it increases over the life of
the child.

It is our belief that the infant's early competencies are interrelated and interdependent. Differentiation of the infant's various competencies occurs over time and the developmental process itself can
be characterized by this growing differentiation. Consider the structure of development as similar to a tree. The analogy begins with
the trunk where all functions—biological, social, and cognitive—
are one, each a part of the other. To affect one is to affect another.
At the next level are the main branches, in development these in-

clude emotional, physical, biological, and cognitive limbs. At this level the major developmental domains are more independent, but the skills subsumed by them are integrated and interactive. Finally, there are small branches and leaves at the highest level of differentiation. It is at this level that the independent and separate skills or competencies are located. Because groups of skills cluster around each other (i.e., are on the same branch), they can and often do interact.

One can better understand the status of the newborn as well as the patterns of growth through a model that depicts the integration and interaction of functions from a developmental perspective as well as the functional independence of skills as an end product of development. The assumption of the interaction of skills or what we have called a unified framework of development is a guiding principle in our view of the young child (Lewis and Cherry, 1977). Consider linguistic development as an example. At first, the child understands the meaning of linguistic acts only by attending to the specific contents of the acts (Ervin-Tripp and Mitchell-Kernan, 1977). That is, cognitive knowledge in general and linguistic knowledge in particular are embedded in a unified framework. Only with development do individual components become separated; at this point children are capable of understanding or producing language apart from its social context. This movement from an undifferentiated set of competencies to a large set of specific and separate capacities is the hallmark of early development.

In order to assess infants and to intervene in their development it is necessary to consider an interdependent set of competencies rather than a single set of independent skills. A major goal is to identify the relationships among seemingly separate competencies and to follow these relationships over the course of development whether the development is of normal or handicapped infants. We might ask, for example, what is the relationship between the development of social skills and cognitive development and does the abnormal development of a certain social skill, such as responsiveness to the mother, predict delays in the cognitive realm? If so, we need to know what the structures, schemata, or concepts common to those skills are.

Our assessment instruments should also detect signs of delayed development in the atypical differentiation of skills. Do at-risk or handicapped infants retain their undifferentiated social, cognitive, communication skills longer than normal infants and, if so, what are the symptoms of this lack of differentiation? A competency assessment profile needs to be developed that recognizes the interaction of basic skills. By looking at each infant's development in terms of a skill profile, we can more easily detect sets of competencies that are weak but that are related to other more developed skills of the infant. In addition, by using an assessment profile during intervention to monitor development across a wide range of skills, we can be alerted to potential dysfunctions in different areas of development.

Indeed, the major goal of any intervention effort is to identify deficits early and to intervene directly in order to reduce the likelihood of a dysfunctional interaction of skills, which might result in further impairment. By recognizing the impact on other areas of a dysfunction in one area of development, our intervention strategies should reduce the generalization of skill deficits. Furthermore, a flexibility in our intervention strategies must enable us to modify our intervention techniques according to the child's demonstrated pattern of strengths and weaknesses in various skills over time.

DEVELOPMENT AS AN INTERACTIVE PROCESS BETWEEN THE INFANT AND THE ENVIRONMENT

Perhaps the tenet regarding the interactive nature of development is the most critical tenet for understanding and intervening in the development of handicapped, at-risk, and normal infants. In order to understand this tenet, three contrasting models of development are described: the status model, the environmental model, and the interactional model (see Lewis, 1972).

Status Model

The status model, often called the medical model, is in essence a trait model. Its central feature is the belief that individuals can be characterized in terms of traits or attributes, which, once established, remain relatively stable over time. Thus, if subject A is assessed as superior in status to subject B at time (T), then it is assumed that subject A will continue to be superior in status to subject B at time $(T + 1)$. Regardless of the nature or the errors of our measurement system, the relative status of subject A vis-à-vis subject B is believed to be consistent over time. With respect to the development of handicapped infants, the status is based on the assumption that at some point in development every physical and biological insult will appear as a developmental dysfunction, *independent* of environmental influences. Various data, including differences in IQ of infants

(Lewis and McGurk, 1972) and of handicapped children and infants at risk (Broman et al., 1975), all demonstrate that the status model does not describe the data (Sameroff and Chandler, 1975). Although developmental delays caused by severe central nervous system insults may seem consistent over time, it is only at the most profound levels of dysfunction that this model can be said to apply.

Environmental Model

An alternative to the status model is the view that environmental factors: 1) are responsible for major individual differences in development; and 2) are capable of being used to modify most early individual differences. This environmental view of development pinpoints parental factors as the major influence on developmental processes and sees parents as being the primary means for intervening to alter a child's past experiences. According to this model, the best predictor of children's developmental outcome is the nature of the environment that they experience. Broman et al. (1975) examined data from over 55,000 subjects and found that all of the infant status measures indexed by such variables as head circumference, birthweight, and bleeding in the last trimester of pregnancy did not prove to be of much value in predicting IQ at 3½ years of age. Rather, environmental variables, particularly social class and mother's educational level, were better predictors of later intellectual functioning.

Interactional Model

Adherents of the interactional model propose that regardless of the type of measurement obtained, either of the subject's status or of the environment, the best predictor of later development must take into account both the child's status at the time (T) as well as the environment in which status is measured. This model views development as the consequence of the interaction between a prior state of the organism and the environment, which will result in a new status as well as a new environment (Lewis, 1972). The status of the organism at time (T) interacts with the environment at time (T) to produce a new status at time ($T + 1$). This interaction is thought to affect development from the point of conception throughout the life cycle. Sameroff and Chandler (1975) labeled this model a *transactional model* in recognition of the fact that the interaction between the organism and its environment is a continual process in which neither the organism's original status nor the environmental effects on that status can be separately assessed. Whether one chooses to call the model interactive or transactional, the focus of this view is the mutual interaction of the organism and environment on each other. Such a model is based on the implicit assumption of the plasticity of development and the possibility of change in normal as well as atypical development.

The distinctions among the three models can be highlighted using data gathered in our laboratory over the last 5 years. Bayley Mental Development Index (MDI) scores were collected on over 300 infants at 3 months and again at 12 months of age. In addition, mother-infant interaction data, in particular maternal responsivity to infant distress, were gathered when the infants were 3 months old. We were interested in what variables at 3 months best predict infant's cognitive status at 12 months. The hypothesis of the status model was that infants' MDI scores at 3 months would best predict their 12-month ability. The relevant correlation was $r = .30$, indicating a significant relationship between MDI scores at 3 and 12 months, but the correlation accounted for only 9% of the variance.

The environmental model posited that the infants' environment at 3 months (i.e., the mother-infant interaction) would be the best predictor of the 12 month MDI scores. The relevant correlation was $r = .30$, which was the same correlation as that obtained when measuring infants' early cognitive ability. Such findings indicate that the 12-month MDI scores are predicted as accurately using child measures as using measures of the child's environment or at least one aspect of the environment.

The interactional model was tested using a multiple regression technique that included both child status and environmental variables. A correlation of .60 was obtained, which accounted for 36% of the variance, or more than four times as much as was accounted for by predicting 12-month ability by either status or environment alone. Thus, by measuring both these variables, we are likely to increase our predictive ability inasmuch as developmental change involves both. Measurement errors and a general lack of knowledge may produce difficulties when we use either the child's status or the environment alone as predictors. The interactive model stresses that regardless of the specific measures used only by assessing both the child's status and the child's environment will we be able to portray the interactive nature of development and thereby predict development outcomes.

The interactional model is particularly relevant to assessing development in handicapped children because there are two specific problems that a dysfunctional child may suffer: the initial trauma itself and the responses of the environment to that trauma. If we can detect early trauma, then through various interventions, we may be able to eliminate the secondary sources of dysfunction, which are dysfunctional interactions. In this way we may be able to prevent or inhibit the development of dysfunctional structures, which often result from dysfunctional interactions.

The assumption that developmental dysfunction is the likely outcome of interactions between an infant experiencing an early biological trauma and the infant's social and physical environment underlies all aspects of the management of handicapped children. Such assessment must focus not only on biological variables of the child but also on variables in the child's social environment such as the ways in which a mother interacts with her handicapped or at-risk child. The interactional model also has implications for intervention strategies. Because primary biological deficits will affect all of the interactions between infants and their social and physical environment, intervention should begin as early as possible. The longer the lag between identifying a deficit and intervening, the more likely it is that dysfunctional interactions with the environment will result in impairments in other areas of development and exacerbation of the specific deficit. The interactional model also indicates a need to restructure the handicapped infant's environment in a way that will facilitate development by compensating for the infant's basic deficit.

SUMMARY

Although these five tenets of early development are largely based on research conducted with normal infants, they are general principles of development that seem to apply to handicapped infants as well. The tenets are quite general and are derived from a retrospective look at infant development. Nevertheless, they can be used to generate practical strategies for assessment and intervention. The benefits of these strategies to the development of handicapped children and their families emerge from an interface between theoretical issues and practical concerns, an interface that provides a basis for the continued study of the development of normal as well as handicapped children.

Chapter Outline

OVERVIEW: Developmental tenets important both as theoretical guideposts and for their heuristic value in designing intervention programs for exceptional children are presented. These tenets are those that view: the infant as a competent organism, the infant as a social organism, the infant as an active organism, the infant's development as proceeding from undifferentiated to differentiated abilities, and the infant's development as an interactive process between the infant's status at any point in time and the environment in which the infant is immersed.

I. THE INFANT AS A COMPETENT ORGANISM
    Research since the mid-1950s has characterized infants as competent organisms. The early sensory, motor, and cognitive/learning capacities of infants are reviewed. The complex abilities of infants are recognized in the development of infant educational programs.

II. THE INFANT AS A SOCIAL ORGANISM
    The importance of the infant's social adaptation to the environment and the infant's early abilities to process and select social stimuli are discussed. A focus on the infant's social nature is advocated for assessment and intervention.

III. THE INFANT AS AN ACTIVE ORGANISM
    Contrary to the traditional view of the infant as a passive organism, recent research has underscored the active nature of the infant. This principle of the active organism influences notions of assessment and intervention and suggests such processes must be interactive and engage an active infant.

IV. DEVELOPMENT AS PROCEEDING FROM UNDIFFERENTIATED TO DIFFERENTIATED SKILLS
    The structure of development is considered as analogous to the tree where all functions are integrated at the trunk but become increasingly differentiated as they branch. This model suggests the need to assess and intervene with infants by considering development as an interdependent set of competencies rather than single sets of independent skills.

V. DEVELOPMENT AS AN INTERACTIVE PROCESS
    BETWEEN THE INFANT AND THE ENVIRONMENT

Three models of development are contrasted: the status model, the environmental model, and the interactional model. The interactional model, by assessing both the child's status and the child's environment, portrays the interactive nature of development and thereby increases the ability to predict development outcome.

VI. SUMMARY

Though these five tenets are based largely on research with normal infants, they represent principles of development that can be used to generate strategies for assessing and intervening with atypical children.

REFERENCES

Aronson, E., and Rosenbloom, S. Space perception in early infancy: Perception within a common auditory-visual space. *Science*, 1971, *172*, 1161–1163.

Ban, P., and Lewis, M. Mothers and fathers, girls and boys: Attachment behavior in the year old child. *Merrill-Palmer Quarterly*, 1974, *20*, 195–204.

Bayley, N. *Bayley Scales of Infant Development*. New York: The Psychological Corporation, 1969.

Berg, W. K., Berg, W. K., and Graham, F. K. Infant heart rate response as a function of stimulus and state. *Psychophysiology*, 1971, *8*, 30–44.

Bower, T. G. R. *Development in Infancy*. San Francisco: W. H. Freeman, 1974.

Bowlby, J. *Maternal Care and Mental Health*. Geneva: World Health Organization/New York: Columbia University Press, 1951. (Abridged version published as *Child Care and the Growth of Love*. Harmondsworth: Penguin Books, 1965, 2nd Ed.)

Brazelton, T. B., Koslowski, B., and Main, M. The origins of reciprocity: The early mother-infant interaction. In M. Lewis and L. Rosenblum (Eds.), *The Effect of the Infant on Its Caregiver: The Origins of Behavior*, Vol. 1. New York: Wiley, 1974.

Brinker, R. P., and Lewis M. Contingency intervention in infancy. In T. Anderson and T. Cox (Eds.), *Curriculum Materials for High Risk and Handicapped Infants*. Chapel Hill, NC: Technical Assistance Development System, 1982a.

Brinker, R. P., and Lewis M. Discovering the competent handicapped infant: A process approach to assessment and intervention. *Topics in Early Childhood Special Education*, 1982b, *2*(2), 1–6.

Broman, S. H., Nichols, P. L., and Kennedy, W. A. *Preschool IQ: Prenatal and Early Development Correlates*. New York: Wiley, 1975.

Bronson, G. W. Infants' reactions to unfamiliar persons and novel objects. *Monographs of the Society for Research in Child Development*, 1972, *47* (3, Serial No. 148).

Brooks, J., and Lewis, M. Infants' responses to strangers: Midget, adult and child. *Child Development*, 1976, *47*, 323–332.

Caron, R. F., Caron, A. T., and Meyers, R. S. Abstraction of invariant face expressions in infancy. *Child Development*, 1982, *53*, 1008–1015.

Charlesworth, W. R., and Kruetzer, M. A. Facial expressions of infants and children. In P. Ekman (Ed.), *Darwin and Facial Expression: A Century of Research in Review*. New York: Academic Press, 1973.

Cohen, L. B. Attention-getting and attention-holding processes of infant visual preferences. *Child Development*, 1972, *43*, 869–879.

Cohen, L. B., and Gelber, E. R. Infant visual memory. In L. B. Cohen and P. Salapatek (Eds.), *Infant Perception: From Sensation to Cognition (Vol. 1)*. New York: Academic, 1975.

Cohen, L. B., and Salapatek, P. (Eds.). *Infant Perception: From Sensation to Cognition (Vols. 1 and 2)*. New York: Academic Press, 1975.

Darwin, C. R. *The Expression of Emotion in Man and Animals*. London: John Murrany, 1872.

Dewey, J. *Moral Principles in Education.* New York: Houghton Mifflin, 1959.

Eimas, P. D., Siqueland, E. R., Jusczyk, P., and Vigorito, H. Speech perception in infants. *Science,* 1971, *171,* 303–308.

Engen, T., Lipsitt, L. P., and Kaye, H. Olfactory responses and adaptation in the human neonate. *Journal of Comparative and Physiological Psychology,* 1963, 56, 73–77.

Engen, T., Lipsitt, L. P., and Peck, M. B. Ability of newborn infants to discriminate sapid substances. *Developmental Psychology,* 1974, *10,* 741–744.

Ervin-Tripp, S., and Mitchell-Kernan, C. (Eds.). *Language, Thought and Culture: Advances in the Study of Cognition.* New York: Academic Press, 1977.

Fagan, J. Infant recognition memory as a present and future index of cognitive abilities. In N. R. Ellis (Ed.), *Aberrant Development in Infancy: Human and Animal Studies.* Hillsdale, NJ: Erlbaum, 1975.

Fantz, R. L. Pattern vision in young infants. *Psychological Record,* 1958, *8,* 43–48.

Fantz, R. L. The origin of form perception. *Scientific American,* 1961, *204,* 66–72.

Fantz, R. L. Pattern vision in newborn infants. *Science,* 1963, *140,* 296–297.

Fantz, R. L. Visual experience in infants: Decreased attention to familiar patterns relative to novel ones. *Science,* 1964, *146,* 668–670.

Feinman, S., and Lewis, M. Social referencing at ten months: A second-order effect on infants' responses to strangers. *Child Development,* 1983, 54(1), 878–887.

Feuerstein, R. *The Dynamic Assessment of Retarded Performers: The Learning Potential Assessment Device, Theory, Instruments, and Techniques.* Baltimore: University Park Press, 1979. (Draft published as *Studies in Cognitive Modifiability,* Rept. 1, Hadassah-Wizo-Canada Research Institute, Jerusalem, 1972.)

Graham, F. K., and Clifton, R. K. Heart rate change as a component of the orienting response. *Psychological Bulletin,* 1966, *65,* 305–320.

Harlow, H. F. Love in infant monkeys. *Scientific American,* 1959, *200,* 68–74.

James, W. *The Principles of Psychology.* New York: Holt, 1890.

Kuhl, P. K., and Meltzoff, A. N. The bimodal perception of speech in infancy. *Nature,* in press.

Lazar, I. and Darlington, R. The lasting effects of early education: A report from the Consortium Longitudinal Series. *Monographs of the Society of Research in Child Development,* 1982, *47* (2–3 Serial No. 195).

Lerner, R. M. Nature, nurture and dynamic interactionism. *Human Development,* 1978, *21,* 1–20.

Levi-Strauss, C. *The Savage Mind.* Chicago: University of Chicago Press, 1966.

Lewis, M. Mother-infant interaction and cognitive development. A motivational construct. Paper presented at the National Institute of Child Health and Human Development Symposium on Issues in Human Development, November, 1967.

Lewis, M. Infants' responses to facial stimuli during the first year of life. *Developmental Psychology,* 1969, 1, 75–86.

Lewis, M. State as an infant-environment interaction: An analysis of mother-infant interaction as a function of sex. *Merrill-Palmer Quarterly*, 1972, *18*, 95–121.

Lewis, M. Infant intelligence tests: Their use and misuse. *Human Development*, 1973, *16*, 108–118.

Lewis, M. What do we mean when we say infant intelligence scores? A socio-political question. In M. Lewis (Ed.), *The Origins of Intelligence: Infancy and Early Childhood*. New York: Plenum Press, 1976.

Lewis, M. The busy, purposeful world of a baby. *Psychology Today*, 1977.

Lewis, M. The infant and its caregiver: The role of contingency. *Allied Health Behavioral Science*, 1978, *1* (4), 469–492.

Lewis, M., and Brooks, J. Self, other and fear: Infants' reactions to people. In M. Lewis and L. Rosenblum (Eds.), *The Origins of Fear: The Origins of Behavior* (Vol. 2). New York: Wiley, 1974.

Lewis, M., and Brooks-Gunn, J. *Social Cognition and the Acquisition of Self*. New York: Plenum. 1979.

Lewis, M., and Brooks-Gunn, J. Self, other and fear: The reactions of infants of people. In J. Belsky (Ed.), *The Beginning: Readings in Infancy*. New York: Columbia University Press, 1981.

Lewis, M., and Brooks-Gunn, J. Developmental models and assessment issues. In W. Frankenburg and A. Jandal (Eds.), *Identifying the Developmentally Delayed Child*. Baltimore: University Park Press, 1982.

Lewis, M., and Cherry, L. Social behavior & language acquisition. In M. Lewis and L. Rosenblum (Eds.), *Interaction, Conversation and the Development of Language: Origins of Behavior* (Vol. 5). New York: Wiley, 1977.

Lewis, M., and Coates, D. L. Mother-infant interactions and cognitive development in twelve-week-old infants. *Infant Behavior and Development*, 1980, *3*, 95–105.

Lewis, M., and Goldberg, S. The acquisition and violation of expectancy: An experimental paradysis. *Journal of Experimental Psychology*, 1969, *7*, 70–80.

Lewis, M., Goldberg, S., and Campbell, H. A developmental study of information processing within the first three years of life: Response decrement to a redundant signal. *Monographs of the Society for Research in Child Development*, 1969, *34*(9, Serial No. 133).

Lewis, M., and McGurk, H. Evaluation of infant intelligence: Infant intelligence scores—True or false? *Science*, 1972, *178*, 4066.

Lewis, M., and Michaelson, L. *Children's Emotions and Moods: Developmental Theory and Measurement*. New York: Plenum Press, 1983.

Lewis, M., and Rosenblum, L. (Eds.) *The Effect of the Infant on Its Caregiver: The Origins of Behavior* (Vol. 1). New York: Wiley, 1974.

Lewis, M., Sullivan, M. W., and Brooks-Gunn, J. The affective consequences of contingency learning in the first six-months of life. *Child Development*, in press.

Lewis, M., Sullivan, M. W., and Michalson, L. The cognitive-emotional fugue. In J. W. Kazan, C. Izard, and R. Zagonc (Eds.), *Emotion, Cognition and Behavior*. New York: Cambridge University Press, in press.

Lewis, M., Young, G., Brooks, J., and Michalson, L. The beginning of friendship. In M. Lewis and L. Rosenblum (Eds.), *Friendship and Peer Relations: The Origins of Behavior* (Vol. 4). New York: Wiley, 1975, 27–66.

Lipsitt, L. P. Learning in the first year of life. In L. P. Lipsitt and C. C. Spiker (Eds.), *Advances in Child Development and Behavior*, 1963, *1*, 147–195.

Lipsitt, L. P. (Ed.). *Developmental Psychobiology: The Significance of Infancy.* Hillsdale, NJ: Erlbaum, 1976.

McCall, R. B. Attention in the infant: Avenue to the study of cognitive development. In D. Walcher and D. L. Peters (Eds.), *Early Childhood: The Development of Self-regulatory Mechanisms.* New York: Academic Press, 1971, 107–140.

McCall, R. B., Eichorn, D. H., and Hogarty, P. S. Transitions in early mental development. *Monographs of the Society for Research in Child Development*, 1977, *42*(3).

McCall, R. B., Hogarty, P. S., and Hurlburt, N. Transitions in infant sensorimotor development and the prediction of childhood IQ. *American Psychologist*, 1972, *27*, 728–748.

Meltzoff, A. N. Imitation, intermodal coordination and representation in early infancy. In G. Butterworth (Ed.), *Infancy & Epistemology.* Brighton, England: Harvester Press, 1981.

Meltzoff, A. N., and Moore, M. K. Imitation of facial and manual gestures by human neonates. *Science*, 1977, *198*, 75–78.

Molfese, D. L., and Molfese, V. J. Hemispheric and stimulus differences as reflected in cortical responses of newborn infants' speech stimuli. *Developmental Psychology*, 1979, *15*, 505–511.

Molfese, D. L., Freeman, R. B., and Palermo, D. S. The ontogeny of brain lateralization for speech and nonspeech stimuli. *Brain and Language*, 1975, *2*, 356–368.

Mussen, J. (Ed.). *Carmichael's Manual of Child Psychology.* New York: Wiley, 1970.

Osofsky, J. (Ed.). *Handbook of Infant Development.* New York: Wiley, 1979.

Papousek, H. Experimental studies of appetitional behavior in human newborns and infants. In H. W. Stevenson, E. H. Hess, and H. L. Rheingold (Eds.), *Early Behavior: Comparative and Developmental Approaches.* New York: Wiley, 1967.

Papousek, H., and Papousek, M. The common in the uncommon child: Comments on the child's integrative capacities and on initiative parenting. In M. Lewis and L. A. Rosenblum (Eds.), *The Uncommon Child: The Genesis of Behavior* (Vol. 3). New York: Plenum, 1981.

Piaget, J. *The Origins of Intelligence in Children.* New York: Norton, 1952.

Preyer, W. *The Mind of the Child: Part 1. The Senses and the Will: Part 2. The Development of the Intellect.* (Translated by H. W. Brown). New York. Appleton, 1888/1889. (Reprinted ed., 1901.)

Rose, S. A., Gottfried, A. W., and Bridges, W. H. Effects of haptic cues on visual recognition memory in full term and preterm infants. *Infant Behavior and Development*, 1979, *2*, 55–67.

Sameroff, A. J., and Chandler, M. J. Reproductive risk and the continuum of caretaking casuality. In F. Horowitz (Ed.), *Review of Child Development Research* (Vol. 4). Chicago: University of Chicago Press, 1975.

Sanders, L. W. Infant and caretaking environment: Investigation and conceptualization of adaptive behavior in a system of increasing complexity. In E. J. Anthony (Ed.), *The Child Psychiatrist as Investigator.* New York: Plenum, 1977.

Sears, R. R., Maccoby, E. E., and Levin, H. *Patterns of Child Rearing.* New York: Row, Peterson, 1957.

Siqueland, E. R., and DeLucia, C. A. Visual reinforcement of nonnutritive sucking in human infant. *Science,* 1969, *165,* 1144–1146.

Sontag, L. W., Stelle, W. G., and Lewis, M. The fetal and maternal cardiac response to environmental stress. *Human Development,* 1969, *12,* 1–9.

Spelke, E. Infants intermodal perception of events. *Cognitive Psychology,* 1976, *8,* 553–560.

Stern, D. Mother and infant at play: The dyadic interaction involving facial, vocal and gaze behaviors. In M. Lewis and L. Rosenblum (Eds.), *The Effect of the Infant on Its Caregiver: The Origins of Behaviors* (Vol. 1). New York: Wiley, 1974.

Uzgiris, I. C., and Hunt, J. *Assessment in Infancy: Ordinal Scales of Psychological Development.* Urbana: University of Illinois Press, 1975.

Watson, J. S. The development and generalization on contingency awareness in early infancy: Some hypotheses. *Merrill-Palmer Quarterly,* 1966, *12,* 123–135.

Wilson, R. S., Brown, A. M., and Mathew, A. P. Emergence and persistence of behavioral differences in twins. *Child Development,* 1971, *42,* 1381–1398.

SECTION II
IDENTIFICATION AND ASSESSMENT

Given the difficulty in defining the parameters of behavior we are willing to consider as "normal," how do we then identify the infant who is at risk or disabled? A logical beginning is an examination of prenatal causes of disability or at-risk status. Crain (Chapter 2) provides an extensive review of these factors, which include maternal status, teratogenic variables, infectious agents, trauma, and genetic and chromosomal abnormalities. Gorski (Chapter 3) continues this discussion by describing perinatal conditions, which may adversely affect development. His account extends to an analysis of screening and assessment devices used to detect infants at risk and a review of attempts at intervention with these fragile newborns. He emphasizes the close relationship or interplay between the physiological and social/emotional characteristics of the child and the environment in which the child is situated in determining the child's developmental outcome.

Sheehan and Gallagher (Chapter 4) expand the topic of identification to a broader consideration of infant assessment. They describe the purposes or uses of infant assessment techniques: these include screening and/or diagnosis; program planning; and evaluation of intervention efforts. In addition, they present a system for classifying and evaluating contemporary infant assessment measures.

The provision of beneficial environments for infants at risk can proceed only from efficient, coordinated identification systems. Such systems must by necessity integrate information on the infant's physiological status, behavioral repertoire, and environment. This focus requires the collaboration of medical, social service, and educational personnel.

CHAPTER 2

Prenatal Causes of Atypical Development

Lucy S. Crain

As recently as the early 1960s, most of the causes of atypical infant development were unknown. However, during the past 20 years an explosion of new information in genetics, biochemistry, and dysmorphology has resulted in a more comprehensive and organized body of etiological information. Particularly significant is the development of noninvasive studies, such as sonography and computerized tomography (CT), which permit diagnoses that would have been impossible even a few years ago.

Certainly, all causes of atypical infant development, sensory impairment, and birth defects are not yet known. However, etiological explanations can be found in nearly 80% of children with significant developmental problems. Ironically, it is often more difficult to identify a cause for disability in children with borderline normal or mildly atypical development than in those with severe impairment. This may be so because findings in these cases are more subtle and do not constitute known patterns of malformation or defective development.

Identification of atypical development in a child is obviously important if the child is to be treated appropriately and to realize his/her maximal developmental potential. Attempted diagnosis of such atypical development is important in order to determine whether the condition is:

1. Chronic and incurable
2. Static and nonprogressive
3. Progressive and/or deteriorating
4. Genetically transmissible, for which siblings might also be at risk
5. Treatable, preventable, or even curable with appropriate therapeutic intervention.

A rational approach to the diagnostic evaluation of a child with

atypical development requires knowledge of both normal development and prenatal, perinatal, and postnatal factors that may cause
atypical or aberrant development (Smith and Simons, 1975). The
following discussion of such prenatal factors is by no means complete. As new data are acquired from research, additional causal
factors may be confirmed and suspected causal factors disproved.

EMBRYOLOGY AND DYSMORPHOLOGY

The time when a developing fetus is exposed to a disruptive factor
is of great importance in determining whether an adverse effect will
result. Major development occurs in the eye, ear, central nervous
system, heart, gastrointestinal system, and lungs within the 2 months
following conception. By the 16th gestational week, the gross appearance of the brain is well-established and myelination begins. By
the 28th week, the eyelids open, light can be perceived, and the
vascular components of the lungs are adequate for respiration. At
this point, the average fetus weighs about 1100 grams and is about
38.5-centimeters long.

While embryology is the systematic study of the developing em-
bryo, *dysmorphology* is the study of aberrant development of form
or structural defects, that is, malformations. A malformation is an
abnormality of form or structure that results from an intrinsic problem in tissue development. A malformation occurring early in gestation may lead to a complex sequence of additional malformations
because of absent or defective precursors of subsequent development. Malformation syndromes may result from chromosome abnormalities, mutant genes, teratogens, or unknown causes. These
and other causative agents are described in the following sections.

Teratogens

Teratogens are nongenetic, extraneous substances implicated in
causing malformations in the developing fetus (Table 2.1). Because
the suspicion of teratogenicity has been applied to so many substances in the past two decades, it is necessary to have reliable scientific methods for data collection and examination in order to determine which substances actually possess teratogenic properties. A
number of national and regional malformation registries have been
established for this purpose.

Fetal Alcohol Syndrome   Perhaps the most common specific
pattern of malformation due to a teratogen is the fetal alcohol syn-

Table 2.1.   Teratogens: A partial listing of substances capable of
producing malformation in the developing fetus

Direct Effect
  Drugs
    Thalidomide
    Aminopterin, methotrexate (folic acid antagonists)
    Dilantin, methadone
    Androgens
  Chemicals and environmental substances
    Lead
    Methyl mercury
    PCB (polychlorinated biphenyl)
    Nuclear radiation
    Excessive dosages of diagnostic or therapeutic radiation

Indirect Effect
  Maternal infection (may result in transplacentally acquired infection in
  fetus, with consequent malformation)
    Rubella
    Herpes viruses
    Cytomegalovirus
    Toxoplasmosis
    Syphilis
  Maternal metabolic dysfunction (may produce hostile in utero environment for fetus, with consequent malformation)
    Maternal alcoholism
    Maternal diabetes
    Maternal hyperthermia
    Maternal hyperthyroidism
    Maternal hypothyroidism
    Maternal phenylketonuria

drome. Since the original report of this syndrome in 1973, numerous
reports have documented the association of moderate to heavy maternal alcohol ingestion during pregnancy with a syndrome of malformations in affected offspring. Consistently reported characteristics of the syndrome include mild mental retardation, pre- and
postnatal growth deficiency, craniofacial anomalies, joint anomalies,
and heart murmurs. A recent prospective study of alcoholic women
who continued drinking heavily throughout pregnancy demonstrated that two-thirds of their offspring were adversely affected: one-
third of their offspring had identifiable fetal alcohol syndrome and
one-third had some features of the syndrome (Olegard, 1979). Hanson et al. (1978) found 11% of the offspring of moderate drinkers (1
to 2 ounces of absolute alcohol per day) during the first trimester
had some features of the fetal alcohol syndrome. Although it seems
that the most severe expression of prenatal effects of alcohol occur
when the exposure is during the first trimester and when the dose

is great, the mechanism by which alcohol produces these recognizable malformations in the developing fetus is not yet understood.

Other Abused Substances   Since the initial reports of the fetal alcohol syndrome, suspicion of teratogenic associations of almost all abused substances has been raised by isolated case reports. Although scientific studies have not consistently confirmed initial reports of such associations in all cases, it is prudent for women who are or plan to become pregnant to be alert to the possibility of teratogenic potential in these substances. It may well be that many teratogens can be actuated only by certain environmental or genetic cofactors. Nonetheless, because our knowledge in this area is uncertain, pregnant women would be well-advised to avoid use of such substances. Some of the known teratogens are classified in Table 2.1.

Although no specific teratogenic risk is currently attributed to tobacco, cigarette smoking has been shown to result in decreased birthweight of offspring whose mothers smoke during pregnancy. Additional studies in this area are in progress.

There have been conflicting reports in animal studies of the potential teratogenicity of marijuana and its components. However, there have as yet been no adequate human studies of the potential teratogenic effects of prenatal exposure to marijuana. Human studies (Larsson, 1980; Mulkovich and VandenBerg, 1977) have been designed to assess the risk of maternal amphetamine ingestion and/or addiction during pregnancy, but no statistically significant risk to offspring has been demonstrated. No physical or chromosomal abnormalities were found in infants with prenatal LSD exposure in the studies of Aase et al. (1970) (10 infants) and Cohen and Shiloh (1978) (63 infants). Although there have been reports of increased chromosome damage in nearly 20 children with prenatal LSD exposure, the lack of subsequent confirmation suggests that further studies are indicated to clarify the risk status of LSD as a potential teratogen.

Neither heroin nor methadone has been implicated as a human teratogen. However, infants born to heroin- or methadone-addicted mothers have an increased incidence of low birthweight, intrauterine growth retardation, and prematurity. Increased perinatal morbidity and mortality may also be found in affected offspring due to the effects of drug withdrawal.

Prescriptive Drugs   It should be assumed that no drug can be considered completely safe and risk-free to all unborn infants. Thus, the risk of prescribing versus that of withholding a drug from the pregnant mother must be seriously considered in each situation.

Although never approved by the U.S. Food and Drug Administration, thalidomide was widely used in Europe in the early 1960s for the treatment of nausea during pregnancy. It soon became evident that thalidomide exposure during the first trimester (i.e., first 3 months after conception) carried a greater than 90% risk of terato-genicity, resulting in phocomelia (i.e., flipper-like limb reduction anomalies) and a myriad of other structural defects in affected infants. Scores of infants were tragically affected, as thalidomide had been readily available and presumed both safe and effective for the treatment of morning sickness. Most complaints of morning sickness or nausea associated with pregnancy occur in the first trimester after conception, which is, of course, the most vulnerable time in terms of embryologic development. Professional and lay press coverage of this irrefutable association greatly increased the level of awareness of teratogens in general and of the need for exercising meticulous care to prevent similar occurrences in the future. Among such preventive considerations are extensive animal studies and field trials of all new drugs before they are approved by the Food and Drug Administration for U.S. distribution.

The anticoagulant, Warfarin, interferes with the normal clotting of blood and is often prescribed for individuals who have had prosthetic heart valve surgery. Warfarin is a known teratogen which results in a pattern of malformation known as the fetal warfarin syndrome, which includes dysmorphic physical features, developmental delay, hypotonia, seizures, and optic atrophy (Smith, 1976; Kerber et al., 1968).

Convincing data have established certain anticonvulsant medications (hydantoins and tri- and paramethadione) as human teratogens (Meadow, 1968; Smith, 1976). Affected infants are also generally growth retarded and mentally deficient. With such anticonvulsants, there seems to be no safe dose. In other words, there is increased risk for teratogenicity even with minimal doses of such anticonvulsants taken during pregnancy.

Diazepam (Valium), a frequently used muscle relaxant, during the first trimester of pregnancy may produce a slightly increased risk for cleft lip and/or palate in exposed infants. Studies suggest a four-fold increased risk with such exposure, but the risk is still quite low (.4% in diazepam-exposed versus .1% in non-diazepam–exposed infants) (Safra and Oakley, 1975).

A prospective assessment of the effects of lithium (a drug used to treat manic-depressive psychosis) on prenatally exposed infants has been developed. Data suggest that lithium should be considered a potential teratogen associated with cardiovascular malformations in humans (Weinstein and Goldfield, 1975).

It is yet unclear whether oral contraceptive agents or birth control pills (i.e., progesterone and progesterone/estrogen combinations) carry a teratogenic risk when used during pregnancy. It has been observed that if such risk exists, it is quite small (Chernoff and Jones, 1981). Although not associated with developmental delay, diethyl-stilbestrol (DES) has achieved recent widespread notoriety since its reported association with increased incidence of cervical and vaginal dysplasia and cancer in young women with a history of prenatal exposure to the drug (Herbst et al., 1971).

Other Environmental Factors

Radiation   Radiation exposure of pregnant women is a frequent cause for anxiety regarding the risk of possible birth defects or genetic abnormalities in the developing fetus. When diagnostic or therapeutic radiation procedures are necessary during pregnancy, recommended levels of radiation are sufficiently low so they are unlikely to produce teratogenic effects. If radiological procedures are essential during pregnancy, the limit for maternal exposure to radiation should not exceed 500 millirads total during the entire 40 weeks of pregnancy. For example, a chest x-ray (roentgenogram) of a pregnant woman delivers a 10- to 15-millirad dose to the woman and a 1-millirad dose to her unborn fetus. An x-ray of the pregnant abdomen delivers a 221-millirad dose of radiation to the fetus (U.S. Department of Health, Education, and Welfare, 1976). Studies of fetal effects of exposure to dosages of 1,000 to 3,000 millirads have demonstrated no evidence of malformation or developmental defect. However, it is thought that these levels of exposure may produce an approximate 1.5 times increased risk that the child may develop leukemia or cancer during his/her lifetime. Accidental exposure of the human fetus to large doses of radiation (10,000 to 30,000 millirads) has resulted in central nervous system damage. Therapeutic abortion may be considered when radiation exposure exceeds 10,000 millirads (Swartz and Reichling, 1978).

Another question of concern is whether changes in genetic material (DNA) of the exposed fetus might be produced by exposure to radiation dosages in the sublethal range (i.e., 1,000 to 10,000 millirads). If so, it can be postulated that such damage might be passed on to subsequent generations, resulting in sterility, spontaneous abortions or miscarriages, or offspring with birth defects. Compared with generation time in human terms (about 25 years), our experience with large dose radiation exposure is limited. Pregnant women should be advised to avoid any radiation exposure other than that absolutely essential for their health care.

Ultrasound   In many instances, ultrasound may provide a preferable alternative to diagnostic x-rays during pregnancy. Diagnostic ultrasound, also referred to as sonography, echography, and ultrasonography, is increasingly popular as an important procedure for noninvasive prenatal evaluation. Ultrasound refers to sound waves beyond frequencies audible to the human ear. Unlike ionizing radiation, ultrasound is not cumulative in tissues and has no known biological effects. Ultrasonography is frequently employed for prenatal diagnosis in pregnancies of mothers who have previously borne offspring with structural abnormalities (Dunne and Johnson, 1979).

Hyperthermia   Studies suggest that exposure to temperatures of 38.9°C (102°F) or greater during the first 14 weeks of pregnancy has teratogenic risk. A malformation pattern including central nervous system defects, abnormal development of the mid-face, and growth deficiency has been consistently observed in infants with such exposure. In one study, 25% of the cases reported had heat exposure associated with hot tub or sauna use, and not with any infectious agent (Pleet et al., 1980). Additional studies of a possible association with generalized CNS defects and neural tube defects (Miller et al., 1978) are in progress.

Mercury   Severe mental retardation, intractable seizures, abnormal brain development, and cerebral palsy were common signs of congenital mercury poisoning reported in a small epidemic in the early 1960s in the area around Minamata Bay, Japan. Epidemiological studies of the cause of this sudden epidemic of severe disabilities in infants revealed that local fish had been grossly contaminated by methyl mercury chlorides and sulfides discharged into the bay as effluent from a local industrial plant (Murakami, 1960). Congenital mercury poisoning was reported in the U.S. following exposure of a pregnant mother to agricultural methyl mercury fungicide (Snyder, 1971). Environmental contaminants such as pesticides, fungicides, polychlorinated biphenyls (PCB), and other toxic substances should be treated with caution by everyone, but especially by pregnant women.

Lead   The neurological consequences of brain damage caused by lead have been known since the 1930s, when the association between lead paint ingestion (pica) and a wide spectrum of abnormalities was first recognized. Such abnormalities range from poor performance in school to severe developmental disabilities, coma, and death. Lead poisoning has also been reported in association with the burning of lead storage cell battery casings and with the ingestion of lead contaminated moonshine whiskey, foods prepared or stored in lead-glazed containers, and lead shot or lead jewelry. Less well-known was the use of lead to induce miscarriage in the late 1800s. An increased incidence of malformations as well as stillbirths was noted among the offspring of mothers with a history of high lead exposure. Thus, lead should be considered a teratogen as well as a substance with direct toxic potential.

Prenatal Infections

In utero infection of the fetus with syphilis, rubella, cytomegalovirus, toxoplasmosis, or herpes may result in spontaneous abortion or a variety of manifestations depending upon the severity of infection and the gestational age when infection occurs (Table 2.2). Clinical features such as growth retardation, skin rash, jaundice, and enlargement of the liver and spleen in affected newborns are common in all these prenatal infections, and reliable laboratory tests to confirm the type of infection are essential. A blood test that screens for the presence of antibodies against these infectious agents is provided to infants suspected of having an intrauterine infection. This screening test is the STORCH titre (syphilis, *t*oxoplasmosis, *r*ubella, *c*ytomegalovirus, *h*erpes). Other laboratory tests may be obtained to document serial measurements of quantitative antibody titres and other confirmatory evidence of intrauterine infection. No effective treatment is yet available for rubella, cytomegalovirus, and herpes infections. Treatment of the infected mother with appropriate antibiotics can effectively prevent transplacental infection with syphilis (if treated in time with adequate penicillin) or toxoplasmosis (if treated in time with triple sulfa). Prevention of prenatal rubella has been available since the mid-1960s, by the use of rubella vaccination of susceptible or nonimmune females prior to conception. Prevention is definitely the preferred mode with all these infections, as is noted in the following discussion.

Syphilis   Adequate treatment during the first trimester of pregnancy with penicillin or other appropriate antibiotics of the mother with asymptomatic (latent) syphilis may prevent the occurrence of congenital syphilis in her infant. If the infected mother is untreated, there is a 25% risk for spontaneous abortion and a 75% risk of congenital syphilis in the infant.

It is essential to evaluate fully any infant suspected of having prenatal exposure to syphilis because many prenatally infected infants may not demonstrate clinical abnormalities for weeks or

Table 2.2. Effects of in utero infection as related to gestational time of exposure

	Trimester of pregnancy		
	First	Second	Third
Rubella	Hearing loss Congenital heart disease Mental retardation Cataracts and other eye abnormalities Low birthweight	Hearing loss Mental retardation	Uncommon
Herpes	Possibly low birthweight Possibly skin lesions	Possibly low birthweight Possibly skin lesions Prematurity	Prematurity Perinatal infection leading to systemic herpetic infection
Cytomegalovirus	Low birthweight Microcephaly Hearing loss Chorioretinitis Cerebral calcification	Low birthweight Microcephaly Hearing loss Chorioretinitis Cerebral calcification Anemia	Hearing loss Anemia

Syphilis	Rare cause of miscarriage or
	  spontaneous abortion
		Stillbirth
		Lesions of skin, bone, CNS,
		  eyes
		Enlargement of liver, spleen,
		  lymph nodes
			Same as in second trimester

Toxoplasmosis	Chorioretinitis Hydrocephalus Cerebral calcifications	Chorioretinitis Hydrocephalus Cerebral calcifications Anemia	Anemia

months. Central nervous system (CNS) syphilis associated with congenital syphilis may result in mental retardation, hydrocephalus, convulsions, hemiplegia (partial paralysis), and other neurological disabilities if untreated. More commonly, CNS syphilis causes dull, irritable, or antisocial behavior often associated with some degree of mental retardation.

Syphilis is characterized by periods of prolonged latency interrupted by occasional activity, making lifelong persistence of the organism possible, despite successful treatment of acute phases of the disease. The use of the serological test for syphilis (STS), a simple blood test in premarital and obstetric visits (first and third trimester), and the widespread use of effective antibiotics have greatly reduced the incidence of infectious syphilis in the U.S. However, an increasing incidence of syphilis has been reported among the U.S. adolescent population in recent years. Because latent syphilis seems to be more frequently activated during pregnancy, the importance of detection and treatment of maternal syphilis cannot be overly stressed.

Rubella   Rubella (German measles, 3-day measles) is a relatively innocuous infectious viral illness of preschool children. However, this usually innocent disease of preschoolers can produce a variety of devastating teratogenic effects in the developing fetus. Depending upon the gestational time and severity of infection, prenatal rubella may result in fetal death or any of several predictable patterns of malformation. The most common findings in affected infants are congenital cataract, deafness, microcephaly (head size more than 2 standard deviations below average), mental deficiency, chorioretinitis (inflammation of the choroid plexus and retina of the eye), and cardiovascular defects. In addition to these permanent sequelae, infants born with the congenital rubella syndrome may demonstrate intrauterine growth retardation, jaundice (yellow discoloration of the skin due to obstructive liver disease, resulting in inadequate breakdown of bilirubin), anemia, thrombocytopenia (inadequate numbers of blood platelets, necessary for normal clotting), bone lesions, and pneumonia. An approximate 50% risk is estimated for the likelihood of fetal infection if the mother contracts rubella during the first trimester of pregnancy. Significant risk persists during the second trimester for deafness, mental deficiency, and growth deficiency. It is now known that congenital rubella is a chronic infection and that the virus can be cultured from affected infants during the first 6 months of life and intermittently thereafter for a year or more. Thus, females of childbearing age who care for infants with identified congenital rubella syndrome should obtain rubella vaccination if they do not have serological confirmation of protective levels of immunity to rubella.

With the introduction of effective attenuated rubella vaccine in the mid-1960s, it became possible to prevent the devastating effects of prenatal rubella by assuring that all women of childbearing age could be made immune to the rubella virus. It is now common practice in initial obstetric visits and in employee high-risk situations (newborn nurseries, infant care centers) to obtain rubella titres. Many states require a premarital rubella titre in order to obtain a marriage license. In most laboratories, a rubella titre of 1:8 is evidence of immunity (either on the basis of prior infection or of vaccination) and a prospective mother can be ensured of protection against the rubella virus. If the woman's titre is less than 1:8 and she is not pregnant, she should obtain a rubella vaccination. Such vaccinees should be warned not to become pregnant for at least 2 months following the immunization because it is thought that even attenuated virus (i.e., vaccine virus) might pose some teratogenic risk to the fetus.

The U.S. Public Health Service and American Academy of Pediatrics Committee on Infectious Diseases recommend routine administration of rubella vaccine, in combination with mumps and measles (i.e., rubeola) vaccine, at 15 months of age. If this recommendation were effected with 90% success, the wild rubella virus would be eliminated in the U.S.

Cytomegalovirus Cytomegalovirus (CMV) is one of the four known herpes viruses in humans. CMV seems to be an ubiquitous viral organism which is excreted by approximately 1% of all newborns in the U.S. It is estimated that 10% of these CMV shedding infants (about 3,000 infants per year) have a significant birth defect due to infection with this virus (Melish and Henshaw, 1973). The clinical findings in congenital cytomegalic inclusion disease (CID) include variable central nervous system defects such as microcephaly, chorioretinitis, cerebral calcifications, deafness, and mental retardation. It is now thought that some of the CMV shedding infants with no visible evidence at birth may actually have "silent" CMV infections, resulting in a greater incidence of sensorineural hearing loss, minimal cerebral dysfunction, and mental retardation than in controls (Hanshaw, 1973).

Studies increasingly implicate intimate contact as the necessary means of transmitting CMV. CMV infections have also been shown to follow the transfusion of fresh blood. If an infant sheds CMV in body excretions such as urine and saliva, improved hygiene practices become increasingly important to prevent transmission to vulnerable caregivers (e.g., women of childbearing age) or to other children. However, transmission of CMV from an infected neonate remains an unproven theoretical possibility. The danger of CMV transmission to nursery personnel is clearly not as great as that of rubella. The CMV antibody titre is not as reliable as that for rubella antibody, and it is not generally available. No effective CMV vaccine has yet been developed. Therefore, it is recommended that any at-risk nursery personnel or caregivers for CMV infected infants exercise good judgment about hygiene and conscientious hand washing. From the standpoint of risk of transmission, it has been stated that "the safest CMV infant is the identified one," as caregivers tend to exercise improved hygienic practice with known virus shedding infants.

Toxoplasmosis   Toxoplasmosis is a parasitic infection of mammals which may be transmitted by the ingestion of raw or inadequately cooked meat and possibly by other means. Congenital toxoplasmosis is the result of prenatal fetal infection and appears to inflict most severe damage when maternal infection occurs between the 7th and 26th week of gestation (Couvreur, 1980). The clinical findings most commonly found in toxoplasmosis (in addition to the transient hepatosplenomegaly, jaundice, and rash of infected neonates) are chorioretinitis, intracranial calcification, hydrocephaly or microcephaly, and CNS involvement resulting in psychomotor pathology (Couvreur and Desmonts, 1962). To avoid infection pregnant women should be cautioned to avoid eating raw meat and to be scrupulously hygienic about caring for household pets.

Herpes   Neonatal or congenital herpes infection is still relatively uncommon, despite the epidemic status of venereal herpes in the U.S. Although isolated cases of prenatal fetal infection with herpes simplex virus (HSV) (Florman et al, 1973) and spread of HSV by nursery personnel (Francis et al., 1979) from one infant to another have been reported, the vast majority of congenital HSV infections are acquired during delivery from the infected maternal genital tract. It is estimated that 50% of infants delivered through an infected birth canal will develop HSV infection. However, about 70% of infected mothers are asymptomatic at time of delivery, and manifestations of HSV infection may not be evident for 1 to 4 weeks (incubation period) in the newborn.

More than 50% of pregnancies associated with congenital HSV infection deliver prematurely, usually between 30 and 37 weeks (Whitley et al., 1980). It is thought that HSV is a cause of premature labor, although the mechanism is yet unknown. Prematurity of infected infants, of course, increases the morbidity and mortality with a high incidence of respiratory distress in infected newborns.

Congenital herpes is a fulminant, devastating disease with severe morbidity and high mortality. Even for the few survivors of this disease, the prognosis is usually bleak due to associated morbidity. Prevention is once again the preferred course. Expectant mothers approaching term who have: 1) a history suggestive of genital HSV infection; or 2) a sexual partner with HSV genital lesions should be considered at high risk. Such women should be carefully evaluated for any evidence of HSV infection, so that labor and delivery can be properly managed (e.g., Cesarean section delivery in the presence of active genital infection). It is important to note that recurrent HSV infections in adults are less frequently associated with pain than are the lesions of a primary infection. Thus, individuals may be unaware of recurrent infections. Scrupulous handwashing techniques and close attention to hygiene are necessary for caregivers of HSV-infected infants to prevent virus spread.

Varicella Zoster   Herpes virus varicellae (varicella zoster, or VZ virus) is the common causative agent for both varicella (chickenpox) and herpes zoster (shingles). Although approximately 96% of U.S. adults are immune to varicella, active maternal infection within 21 days prior to delivery can result in congenital varicella, which has a mortality rate of about 20%. Congenital abnormalities (muscular atrophy, skin scarring, small size for gestational age, chorioretinitis, seizures, mental retardation, and decreased resistance to infections) have been reported in offspring of mothers with varicella infection during the first trimester.

Genetic and Chromosomal Abnormalities

Many birth anomalies and syndromes are genetically or chromosomally determined. Birth defects occur in approximately 4% of U.S. live births. More than half of birth defects are of unknown cause, 25% are due to gene disorders, 12% are due to chromosomal disorders, and 7% are due to teratogens (B. Hall, personal communication, 1980). With our increasing knowledge of genetically determined disorders, genetic counseling is recommended for families in which such disorders are suspected or identified.

Genetic counseling is a communication process concerning the occurrence of genetic disorders and the risk for recurrence of such disorders within a family. Such counseling attempts to provide the client(s) with a complete understanding of the genetic disorder and its implications, as well as with a clear perception of available options (e.g., screening or confirmatory laboratory tests and prenatal diagnosis). For example, couples who have had one or more children seriously affected with an autosomal recessive disease have a 25% risk for such disease in each subsequent offspring. However, genetic counseling can clarify the situation (e.g., 75% chance of the subsequent offspring not having this disease). Prenatal diagnosis (i.e., amniocentesis and appropriate analyses) in some cases can confirm whether or not evidence of the disease is present in the fetus, thus helping parents to decide whether to continue the pregnancy.

Couples concerned about prenatal diagnosis should seek genetic counseling for the following indications (Milunsky, 1979):

1. Advanced maternal age (age 35 or more)
2. Previous history of a child with a serious or fatal defect
3. Family history of a known genetic disorder
4. One or both of the couple are known or suspected carriers of a genetic disease (often detected by community screening programs)
5. History of a potentially significant environmental exposure.

Primary health care providers should be aware of these major indications plus the additional category of three or more unexplained consecutive spontaneous abortions or miscarriages and should either provide appropriate genetic counseling or refer the couple to a center where this service is available.

Chromosomal Abnormalities   Chromosomal defects are found in term infants in 1 : 161 live births. Studies of spontaneously aborted first trimester fetuses demonstrate chromosomal abnormalities in nearly two-thirds of the abortuses (Boué et al., 1975). Nature thus effectively reduces the incidence of chromosome defects in term infants.

Examination of an individual's chromosomes is a rather complicated procedure beginning with a simple blood test. Certain blood cells are incubated until the chromosomes become adequate for examination. The incubated cells are then treated with a chemical that stops cell division and causes the cells to expand so the chromosomes can be "harvested." Once the chromosomes are harvested, they are identified according to appearance and number. They are then arranged into groups having similar characteristics, forming a "map" of the individual's chromosome profile. This map is the individual's karyotype (Figure 2.1).

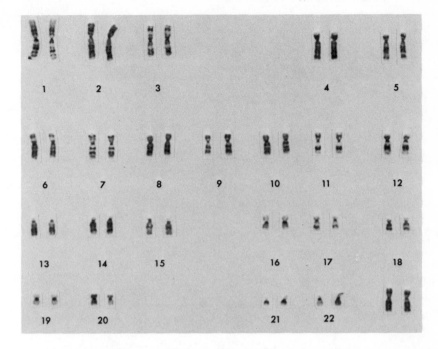

Figure 2.1.   Karotype of normal male (46, XY).

Advanced maternal age is significantly associated with increased risk of certain chromosomal abnormalities. This is especially true for trisomy 21, an abnormal chromosomal rearrangement associated with Down syndrome in which the 21st chromosome consists of three parts instead of the usual two (Figure 2.2). There are some studies suggesting that the frequency of chromosome abnormalities in offspring of mothers under age 20 is similar to that of mothers age 35 to 39. Considering recent observations that there may also be a higher frequency of neural tube defects among offspring of young women under age 20, the current policy of not routinely recommending prenatal genetic studies for young mothers is under serious scrutiny.

A chromosomal translocation results when a portion of one chromosome pair detaches from its normal location and reattaches to another chromosome pair. This may result in a balanced translocation in which the affected individual's outward appearance (phenotype) is entirely normal despite the abnormal chromosomal configuration (genotype). Translocation carriers (balanced structural

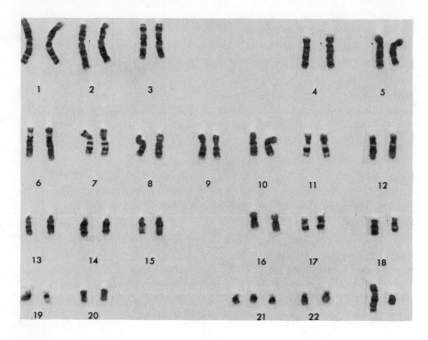

Figure 2.2.   Karotype of female with Down syndrome due to Trisomy 21
(47, XX).

rearrangements of parental chromosomes) generally have higher
risks of bearing chromosomally defective offspring than do chromosomally normal mothers over age 35. About 1:500 individuals
are balanced translocation carriers. Despite this, balanced translocations are a relatively uncommon cause of major phenotypic (outward physical appearance) abnormalities. Depending upon the type
of translocation in the phenotypically normal parent, the risks for
having a child with a chromosomal rearrangement resulting in a
phenotypically abnormal child vary widely.

    Down syndrome is the best known example of a chromosomal
disorder. Recent data suggest that the overall incidence of Down
syndrome in the U.S. has been significantly decreased to a current
1:1000 live births (Adams et al., 1981). It has been postulated that
the decreased incidence is due to halving the proportion of Down
syndrome births to women age 35 and older through the use of prenatal diagnosis and genetic counseling.

    Nearly 95% of individuals with Down syndrome have trisomy
21 (Figure 2.2). Advanced maternal age is significantly associated

with increased incidence of trisomy 21 (Table 2.3) (and other autosomal trisomies as well, e.g., trisomies 13 and 18).

Individuals with Down syndrome usually have a characteristic facial appearance with a small nose and flattened nasal bridge, somewhat flattened skull and small, somewhat underdeveloped ears. They generally demonstrate small stature, hypotonicity, mental retardation of varying degree, and underdevelopment (hypoplasia) of the pelvic bones and of the frontal sinuses. They may also have cardiac anomalies and eye abnormalities.

Investigations have also studied increased paternal age as an additional factor. Recently developed staining techniques now make it possible to determine the origin of the extra chromosome, which has been shown to be of paternal origin in about 25% of cases of Down syndrome. Data from various studies cast doubt on whether or not there may be a correlation between advanced paternal age (age 55 or more) and increased incidence of Down syndrome offspring.

The chromosome defects in 3.5 to 5.0% of individuals with Down syndrome are due to translocations. The relatively increased incidence of Down syndrome observed in very young mothers is largely accounted for by parental translocation carrier status. Although the diagnosis of Down syndrome is usually evident on the basis of physical examination alone, it is important to determine the chromosomal karyotype (the full complement of chromosomes in an individual or a cell line). This is especially true for infants of young mothers who will have subsequent pregnancies because of the recurrence risks of certain types of translocations.

Chromosomal mosaicism is a condition in which varying percentages of an individual's chromosomes are abnormal in some systems (e.g., skin) and normal in other systems. Chromosomally mosaic individuals may look normal, depending upon the proportion and types of cell systems affected.

Table 2.3.   Incidence rates per 1000 births for Down syndrome by maternal age (Adams et al., 1981)

Maternal age (Years)	Incidence
under 15	1.28
15–19	0.66
20–24	0.61
25–29	0.78
30–34	1.54
35–39	2.63
40–44	14.29
45 and over	34.19

Women under age 30 with one Down syndrome child have a 1 to 2% risk for recurrence. Women with their first affected child after age 30 have the same risk as that due to age.

Sex Chromosome and X-Linked Disorders   Sex chromosome disorders are relatively frequent (1:700 female and 1:400 male live births) (Grant and Hamerton, 1976), but they are not commonly associated with severe mental retardation or death. The Klinefelter syndrome (XXY) occurs in approximately 1:600 males and presents with wide variability in clinical phenotype. The degree of mental retardation is usually mild in affected males, who also usually have gynecomastia (breast enlargement at puberty), small testes, infertility, diminished male hair distribution, and psychosocial problems.

About 1:1000 male newborns has the XYY chromosome karyotype. Despite usual phenotypic (outward appearance) normality of such affected individuals, studies suggest that they may have an increased risk of having children with sex chromosome anomalies.

Gonadal dysgenesis in males (Turner syndrome) with a normal 46XY chromosome genotype is associated with a variety of clinical features. About one third of affected individuals have severe mental retardation. Sex chromosome disorders in phenotypic females include the Turner syndrome (45XO) with an incidence of about 1:3000 newborn females. Nearly 75% of such individuals are mosaic. Clinical features include gonadal dysgenesis (poorly developed ovaries), webbed neck, hearing impairment, small stature (100%), mental retardation (only 10%), and other abnormal physical characteristics.

McKusick (1978) listed approximately 200 sex-linked or sex-limited disorders, many of which are fatal. An X-linked disorder is caused by a mutant gene carried on one of the X chromosomes of the mother. The mother may have inherited the mutant gene from her carrier mother (or, less commonly, from her affected father). Each son of the carrier mother has a 50% risk of inheriting the mutant gene and thus expressing the X-linked disorder. Each daughter of the carrier mother also has a 50% chance of inheriting the mutant gene and thus becoming a carrier herself. For the majority of X-linked disorders, prenatal diagnosis is available only through fetal sex determination (and thence, a decision on continuation of the pregnancy). Among the sex-linked or limited disorders are hemophilia, Duchenne muscular dystrophy, Hunter syndrome, and Lesch-Nyhan syndrome.

Genetically Determined Disorders of Metabolism   In the 50 years since the initial description of the association of an abnormal metabolic product of phenylalanine in the urine of mentally retarded patients with phenylketonuria (PKU), vast progress has occurred in identifying biochemical characteristics associated with a variety of genetic disorders. It is now possible to make the prenatal diagnosis of approximately 75 biochemical disorders (Golbus, 1976).

Tay-Sachs Disease   Tay-Sachs disease is one of the most common indications for prenatal biochemical studies. Tay-Sachs disease is a genetic disorder with an autosomal recessive pattern of inheritance. An affected child appears normal until age 3 to 6 months, when mental and physical deterioration begins. Tay-Sachs disease is uniformly fatal within the first 6 years of life. There is no effective treatment. Generalized spasticity, deafness, blindness, seizures, and mental retardation are usually evident by age 18 months, and death usually results from pneumonia associated with progressive neurodegeneration.

It is estimated that about 1:30 Ashkenazi Jews in the U.S. is a carrier of the gene for this disease, compared with 1:300 non-Jewish carriers. About 1:3,600 Jewish infants is affected with Tay-Sachs disease; about 1:360,000 non-Jewish infants is affected (Milunsky, 1979). Carrier detection is accurate and rapidly accomplished. In contrast, prenatal diagnosis may take two to three weeks for determination of results from cultured cells in amniotic fluid.

Mass screening for Tay-Sachs disease has led to the detection of thousands of carriers of the disease. If both potential parents are carriers of the Tay-Sachs gene, their union would result in a 25% risk for bearing affected offspring.

Galactosemia   Galactosemia is a well-known glycogen storage disease with autosomal recessive inheritance. Clinical features include vomiting and diarrhea within days of initiating milk feedings. Jaundice, liver enlargement, failure to thrive, and cataracts become evident within the first few weeks of life. Without appropriate dietary treatment, progressive psychomotor retardation appears within the first few months of life. Although carrier detection and prenatal diagnosis are possible, screening for galactosemia is usually directed toward routine neonatal screening for metabolic diseases (along with screening for PKU and hypothyroidism).

Phenylketonuria (PKU)   Disorders of amino acid metabolism may cause few or no symptoms or may be associated with profound mental retardation and/or serious or fatal disease. Early diagnosis and treatment for many of these disorders may prevent mental retardation and other serious sequelae. PKU is a well known example with an incidence of about 1:11,000 births. Clinical manifestations in individuals who do not receive early dietary treatment (i.e., low phenylalanine diet) include seizures, hyperactivity, psychomotor re-tardation, spasticity, eczema, and microcephaly. The classic type of PKU results from a deficiency of phenylalanine hydroxylase, an en-zyme which normally facilitates the metabolism of the essential amino acid phenylalanine to tyrosine. In the absence of normal amounts of this enzyme, excess phenylalanine accumulates in levels which become toxic to the brain. By about 4 weeks of age, by-prod-ucts of excessive phenylalanine spill over into the urine of affected individuals. The most optimistic prognoses are obtained when PKU is detected by routine newborn screening of blood levels of phen-ylalanine, so that appropriate treatment consisting of a diet low in phenylalanine can begin within the first month of life. Prenatal di-agnosis is not yet feasible and carrier detection of this autosomal recessive disorder is not yet acceptably accurate.

Congenital Hypothyroidism   Congenital hypothyroidism, with an incidence of about 1 : 3,400 live births (Hulse et al., 1980), is the most common preventable known cause of mental retardation. There are several etiologies for congenital hypothyroidism, but the most common are developmental defects of the thyroid gland.

The clinical diagnosis of congenital hypothyroidism is rarely made at birth. However, signs and symptoms of hypothyroidism (e.g., constipation, lethargy, prolonged jaundice, poor feeding, hy-pothermia) may be present in neonates. Affected neonates often have umbilical hernia, hypotonia, large anterior and posterior fontanelles, mottled, dry skin, hoarse cry, and macroglossia (large tongue).

Feeding and respiratory difficulties also are often reported in the first month of life of untreated infants with congenital hypothy-roidism. These difficulties and other clinical findings are often subtle enough to delay diagnosis beyond the critical period, after which mental development is irreversibly affected. By 3 to 6 months of age, untreated children with congenital hypothyroidism usually dem-onstrate more apparent abnormalities of mental and physical de-velopment (e.g., facial puffiness, swollen, protruding tongue, de-layed dentition, dry, scaly skin, coarse hair, constipation, abdominal distention, poor growth in length). Bone age is delayed, as are de-velopmental milestones. Without treatment, affected infants may die of respiratory obstruction or infections, or they may survive to be-come mentally retarded individuals with severely stunted growth.

The prompt diagnosis and initiation of appropriate thyroid hor-mone replacement therapy before 3 months of age has been asso-ciated with normal mental and physical development (Klein et al., 1972). Early intervention to prevent deleterious effects of absent or abnormally low thyroid hormone is essential, and current methodologies should make such intervention possible by 4 weeks of age. Screening for congenital hypothyroidism is a part of routine neonatal screening (along with PKU, galactosemia, and selected other disorders) in an increasing number of states.

Neural Tube Defects

The clinical spectrum of neural tube defects (NTD) varies from the devastating entity of anencephaly (absence of most of the brain and overlying tissues) to the relatively innocuous and often unrecognized spina bifida occulta (normal spinal cord, incomplete vertebral arches with intact overlying skin). Meningomyeloceles (spinal hernias) associated with spinal defects usually are associated with major neurological problems due to abnormal spinal cord tissue and nerve roots protruding through the spinal defect, which may or may not be covered by a sac of intact meninges (e.g., the meningeal covering of the central nervous system). The higher the lesion on the spine, the greater is the severity of neurological deficit. Understandably, major orthopedic and urological disabilities may be associated with such lesions, and affected individuals usually need many specialized services.

Approximately 6,000 to 8,000 infants with NTD are born each year in the U.S. NTDs are thought to be due to multifactorial causes (i.e., the cumulative effects of possible gene aberrations interacting with unknown environmental factors). There is also a recognized correlation with advanced maternal age and open neural tube defects. Other reported environmental associations include poverty, social class, seasons of birth (more common in autumn and winter), parity (number of births), urban setting, maternal health, multiple pregnancies, oral contraceptive use, fetal loss in preceding pregnancy, hyperthermia, and seasonal epidemics or clusters of births with NTD (suggesting an unidentified viral origin). An affected child is the most significant risk factor for recurrence (5 to 6%), and with two affected children, the risk in future pregnancies may approach 25% (Lippman-Hand et al., 1978). However, about 90% of all infants with spina bifida or anencephaly are delivered to mothers with no previously affected child. Thus, effective mass screening of all pregnancies for these defects would be desirable. Unfortunately, this capability is not yet available. Experience with screening maternal serum for alpha-fetoprotein (AFP), though, offers great promise for such a screening instrument if sensitivity and reliability factors can be adequately improved. AFP is a glycoprotein synthesized by the embryonic yolk sac and by the fetal liver and gastrointestinal tract.

AFP is passed via the fetal urine into the amniotic fluid. In the presence of an open (i.e., not skin covered) NTD and, to a lesser extent, in covered NTDs, excess amounts of AFP enter the amniotic fluid, resulting in abnormally elevated levels. The optimal time for maternal serum AFP screening is 16 to 18 weeks gestation. This is a potentially effective screening test with promise for mass application (Milunsky, 1979).

Trauma

Prenatal trauma is rarely a cause of infant developmental problems, as the fetus is generally well protected in the amniotic sac. However, severe direct trauma and penetrating injuries (i.e., gunshot or stab wounds) may inflict serious or fetal damage to the fetus. Motor vehicle accidents are a major cause of direct abdominal trauma, and use of seat belts and other automobile safety precautions are especially sound recommendations during pregnancy. Occasionally, child abuse/wife abuse is acted out against the gravid female, resulting in direct blows or penetrating injuries to the abdomen and/or fetus. Sequelae of such trauma are determined by the extent of injuries.

Birth trauma of extracranial lesions (e.g., scalp swelling or hemorrhage into the scalp) may result from physical trauma to the fetal head. Although these conditions alone are usually benign, they may be associated with serious underlying damage. Fortunately, these lesions have become less common with improved obstetric techniques, as cephalopelvic disproportion has become a major indication for Cesarean delivery. However, marked compression of the fetal head during prolonged labor and complicated vaginal delivery may result in tears and thromboses of the larger cerebral veins and the dural sinuses. Such complications may be minor and clinically unnoticed or they may be major and potentially fatal. Postpartum trauma may result from accidental injuries (e.g., dropping infant onto a hard surface), child abuse, or motor vehicle accidents. Prospective parents should be counseled to obtain and always use an appropriate infant car safety restraint device (e.g., infant care seat) for any transportation of the infant by automobile.

Maternal Status

Maternal Nutrition   Numerous prospective studies have documented the causal relationship between maternal malnutrition and developmental disabilities in offspring. Adequate maternal protein intake is crucial to normal fetal development. In several major studies, approximately 50% of infants born to women on poor diets (under 45 gm protein daily) were of low birth weight (median weight 2500 gm), while infants born to mothers with adequate diets (at least 80 gm protein daily) had a median weight of 3865 gm (Burke, 1943). In addition to birth weight, length and general neonatal health are also strongly correlated with prenatal nutritional status.

Other studies of poor prenatal diets have demonstrated an increased incidence of miscarriages, placenta praevia, abruptio placentae, stillbirths, idiopathic respiratory distress syndrome (IRDS) or Hyaline Membrane Disease, and toxemia of pregnancy. (Toxemia of pregnancy, consisting of maternal hypertension associated with sodium and fluid retention as well as proteinuria, usually results in serious maternal and fetal morbidity and mortality if untreated.)

One can more readily appreciate the physiological effects of malnutrition by noting the remarkable proliferation of brain cells during the development of the fetus and young child. Brain cell division is most active from the 8th gestational month until age 18 months. By age 5 months, the number of brain cells is about 80% of adult capacity. Most brain growth after age 5 months is due to individual cell enlargement (Winick, 1968). Malnutrition during the most rapid period of brain development (last trimester of pregnancy to approximately 2 months of age) can cause permanent underdevelopment of the brain and irreversible neurological damage (Shanklin and Hodin, 1979). Malnutrition does not appreciably reduce the amount of protein or RNA per brain cell, but it dramatically reduces the aggregate number of brain cells. One study reported three infants with birthweights under 2,000 g who died from malnutrition. These infants had only 40% as many brain cells as adequately nourished infants of comparable age (Winick and Rosso, 1969).

Brain development is selectively vulnerable to malnutrition at different stages. From gestational weeks 18 to 28, brain cellular growth is characterized by the rapid multiplication of neurons formed before birth. From gestational week 20 to at least age 24 months, glial multiplication predominates. Glial cells form the myelin sheaths or insulating coverings of nerves, and myelination occurs from age 12 to 48 months. Malnutrition after midpregnancy can reduce the number of glial cells, which are extremely vulnerable to the effects of inadequate nutrition. Malnutrition during infancy can reduce the individual size of glial cells and hence slow the process of myelination (Shanklin and Hodin, 1979).

Data from approximately 40,000 pregnancies studied in the National Institute of Neurologic Disease and Strokes Collaborative

Study of Cerebral Palsy and Other Sensory and Neurologic Disorders of Infancy and Childhood reconfirmed high correlations between nutritionally related complications of pregnancy (e.g., toxemia, abruptio placentae, placenta praevia, and dystocia) and birthweight and neurological damage in offspring (U.S. Department of Health, Education, and Welfare, 1972). General health status, maternal age, parity (i.e., number of previous pregnancies), and intervals between pregnancies are all correlated significantly with birthweight and general status of offspring.

Maternal Diseases

Thyroid Abnormalities   Several reports have noted the association of increased chromosomal abnormalities in offspring of mothers who are either hyperthyroid or hypothyroid. For example, mothers with hyperthyroidism have eight times the risk of having chromosomally abnormal offspring than do mothers with normal thyroid function (Milunsky, 1979).

Diabetes   Maternal diabetes mellitus is associated with both increased birthweight in offspring and about a two-fold increase in all types of birth defects and cardiac anomalies. Pregnancies of diabetic mothers should be considered high risk for both the mother and the infant. Prenatal and perinatal hypoglycemia is a common complication in offspring of diabetic mothers, especially when optimal control of the diabetes has not been achieved or maintained.

Other Maternal Diseases/Conditions   Significant maternal anemia may result in fetal hypoxia (decreased amount of oxygen) and its associated consequences due to the decreased oxygen carrying capacity of abnormally low hemoglobin. Maternal hypertension and other cardiovascular diseases may also produce abnormal placental blood flow and result in fetal hypoxia and/or abnormal development.

SUMMARY

As can be shown, prenatal factors contribute significantly to the causes of atypical infant development. Among those prenatal factors with such a causal association are prenatal malnutrition and certain maternal diseases, abnormalities in structural development (i.e., dysmorphogenesis), prenatal infections, genetic and chromosomal abnormalities, inborn metabolic defects, and trauma. Prevention is the recurrent theme in each of these prenatal factors, as interventions ranging from the establishment of adequate maternal nutrition to avoidance of potentially teratogenic substances and genetic screening and counseling are logical means for decreasing the risk of abnormalities. Early detection and diagnosis of inborn errors of metabolism such as hypothyroidism and phenylketonuria which require specific hormonal or dietary treatment are essential. Prompt therapeutic intervention with such disorders may make the difference between normal and atypical infant development.

Chapter Outline

OVERVIEW: Prenatal causes of atypical infant development are described in terms of incidence, characteristics, and prevention. Factors are clustered according to the following groupings.

I.   TERATOGENS
Teratogens are nongenetic substances which may cause malformations in the developing fetus. Teratogenic factors of importance for this discussion include:

A.   Fetal alcohol syndrome
B.   Other abused substances
C.   Prescriptive drugs

II.   OTHER ENVIRONMENTAL FACTORS
Other factors which are potential teratogens include:

A.   Radiation
B.   Hyperthermia
C.   Mercury
D.   Lead

III.   PRENATAL INFECTIONS
Prenatal infections, a major cause of subsequent developmental disability, are described. Infectious agents include:

A.   Syphilis
B.   Rubella
C.   Cytomegalovirus
D.   Toxoplasmosis
E.   Herpes
F.   Varicella

IV.   GENETIC AND CHROMOSOMAL ABNORMALITIES
The importance of providing genetic counseling to prospective parents believed to be at risk for delivering a developmentally disabled child is discussed. Genetic and chromosomal disorders are described. They include:

A.   Chromosomal abnormalities (e.g., Down syndrome)

B. Sex chromosome and X-linked disorders
C. Inborn errors of metabolism (e.g., Tay-Sachs, gal-
     actosemia, PKU, congenital hypothyroidism)

V. NEURAL TUBE DEFECTS
    Neural tube defects such as spina bifida are described.

VI. TRAUMA
    Both birth trauma and postnatal trauma risks are re-
    viewed.

VII. MATERNAL STATUS
    Maternal factors such as maternal nutrition and maternal
    diseases are discussed in light of their potential impact
    on the developing fetus. The importance of maternal
    protein intake and the relationship of poor prenatal diet
    to fetal morbidity and mortality are considered.

REFERENCES

Aase, J., Laestadius, N., and Smith, D. Children of mothers who took LSD in pregnancy. *Lancet,* 1970, *2,* 100–101.

Adams, M., Erickson, J., Layde, P., and Oakley, G. Down's syndrome: Recent trends in the United States. *Journal of the American Medical Association,* 1981, *246(7),* 758–760.

Boué, J., Boué, A., and Lazar, P. Retrospective and prospective epidemiological studies of 1500 karyotyped spontaneous human abortions. *Teratology,* 1975, *12,* 11–26.

Burke, B. Nutrition studies during pregnancy. IV. Relation of protein content of mother's diet during pregnancy to birth length, birth weight, and condition of infant at birth. *Journal of Pediatrics,* 1943, *23,* 506–515.

Chernoff, G., and Jones, K. Fetal preventive medicine: Teratogens and the unborn baby. *Pediatric Annals,* 1981, *6,* 14–27.

Cohen, M., and Shiloh, Y. Genetic toxicology of lysergic acid diethylamine (LSD-25). *Mutation Research,* 1977–78, *47,* 183–209.

Couvreur, J. Parasitic infections in pregnancy. In *Perinatal Infections,* Ciba Foundation Symposia 77, Amsterdam: Excerpta Medica, 1980.

Couvreur, J., and Desmonts, G. Congenital and maternal toxoplasmosis: A review of 300 congenital cases. *Developmental Medicine and Child Neurology,* 1962, *4,* 519–530.

Dunne, M., and Johnson, M. The ultrasonic demonstration of fetal abnormalities in utero. *Journal of Reproductive Medicine,* 1979, *23,* 195–206.

Florman, A., Gershon, A., Blackett, P., and Nahmias, A. Intrauterine infection with herpes simplex virus: Resultant congenital malformation. *Journal of the American Medical Association,* 1973, *225,* 129.

Francis, D., Hermann, K., MacMahon, J., Chavigny, K., and Sanderlin, K. Nosocomial and maternally acquired herpes virus hominis infections. *American Journal of Diseases of Children,* 1979, *129,* 889.

Golbus, M. The antenatal diagnosis of genetic disorders, In R. Glass (Ed.), *Office Gynecology.* Baltimore: Williams & Wilkins, 1976.

Grant, W., and Hamerton, J. A cytogenetic survey of 14,069 newborn infants. II. Preliminary clinical findings on children with sex chromosome anomalies. *Clinical Genetics,* 1976, *10,* 285.

Hanshaw, J. Congenital cytomegalovirus infections. *New England Journal of Medicine,* 1973, *288,* 1406–1407.

Hanson, J., Streissguth, A., and Smith, D. The effects of moderate alcohol consumption during pregnancy on fetal growth and morphogenesis. *Journal of Pediatrics,* 1978, *92,* 457–460.

Herbst, A., Ulfelder, H., and Poskanzer, D. Adenocarcinoma of the vagina: Association of maternal stilbestrol therapy with tumor appearance in young women. *New England Journal of Medicine,* 1971, *284,* 878–881.

Hulse, J., Grant, D., Clayton, B., et al. Population screening for congenital hypothyroidism. *British Medical Journal,* March 8, 1980, 675–678.

Kerber, I., Warr, O., and Richardson, C. Pregnancy in a patient with a prosthetic mitral valve associated with the fetal anomaly attributed to warfarin sodium. *Journal of the American Medical Association,* 1968, *203,* 223.

Klein, A., Meltzer, S., and Kenny, F. Improved prognosis in congenital hypothyroidism treated before three months. *Journal of Pediatrics,* 1972, *81,* 912.

Larsson, G. The amphetamine addicted mother and her child. *Acta Paediatrica Scandinavica* (Suppl. 278), 1980, pp. 6–24.

Lippman-Hand, A., Fraser, F., and Biddle, C. Indications for prenatal diagnosis in relatives of patients with neural tube defects. *Obstetrics and Gynecology*, 1978, *51*, 72.

McKusick, V. *Mendelian Inheritance in Man. Catalogue of Autosomal Dominant, Autosomal Recessive, and X-linked Phenotypes.* Baltimore: Johns Hopkins Press, 1978.

Meadow, S. Anticonvulsant drugs and congenital abnormalities. *Lancet*, 1968, *2*, 1296.

Melish, M., and Hanshaw, J. Congenital cytomegalovirus infection: Developmental progress of infants detected by routine screening. *American Journal of Diseases of Children*, 1973, *126*, 190–194.

Miller, P., Smith, D., and Shepard, T. Maternal hyperthermia as a possible cause of anencephaly. *Lancet*, 1978, *1*, 519–521.

Milunsky, A. *Genetic Disorders of the Fetus.* New York: Plenum Press, 1979.

Mulkovich, L., and VandenBerg, B. Effects of antenatal exposure to anorectic drugs. *American Journal of Obstetrics and Gynecology*, 1977, *129*, 637–642.

Murakami, U. The effect of organic mercury on intrauterine life. *Advances in Experimental Medicine and Biology*, 1960, *27*, 301.

Olegard, R. Effects on the child of alcohol abuse during pregnancy. Retrospective and prospective studies. *Acta Paediatrica Scandinavica* (Suppl. 275), 1979.

Pleet, H., Graham, J., Harvey, M., and Smith, D. Patterns of malformation resulting from the teratogenic effects of first trimester hyperthermia. *Paediatric Research*, 1980, *14*, 587.

Safra, M., and Oakley, J. Association between cleft lip with or without cleft palate and prenatal exposure to diazepam. *Lancet*, 1975, *2*, 478–480.

Shanklin, D., and Hodin, J. *Maternal Nutrition and Child Health.* Springfield, IL: Charles C Thomas, 1979.

Smith, D. *Recognizable Patterns of Human Malformation.* Philadelphia: W.B. Saunders, 1976.

Smith, D., and Simons, E. Rational diagnostic evaluation of the child with mental deficiency. *American Journal of Diseases of Children*, 1975, *129*, 1285–1290.

Snyder, R. Congenital mercury poisoning. *New England Journal of Medicine*, 1971, *284*, 1014.

Swartz, H., and Reichling, B. Hazards of radiation exposure for pregnant women. *Journal of the American Medical Association*, 1978, *239*, 1907–1980.

U.S. Department of Health, Education, and Welfare. Gonad Doses and Genetically Significant Dose from Diagnostic Radiology. Washington, DC: U.S. Government Printing Office, 1976.

U.S. Department of Health, Education, and Welfare. *The Women and Their Pregnancies.* Philadelphia: W. B. Saunders, 1972.

Weinstein, M., and Goldfield, M. Cardiovascular malformations with lithium use during pregnancy. *Am. J. Psychiatry*, 1975, *132*, 529–531.

Whitley, R., Nahmias, A., Visintine, A., et al. The natural history of herpes simplex virus infection of mother and newborn. *Pediatrics*, 1980, *66*(4), 489–494.

Winick, M. Changes in nucleic acid and protein content of the human brain during growth. *Pediatric Research*, 1968, *2*, 352–355.

Winick, M., and Rosso, P. The effect of severe early malnutrition on cellular growth of human brain. *Pediatric Research*, 1969, *3*, 181–184.

CHAPTER 3

Infants at Risk
Peter A. Gorski

As these chapters develop a conceptual framework toward recommending and designing efforts to optimize the growth and development of atypical infants, let us first consider who are these children thought to be at risk for exceptional development. After identifying populations for concerned attention, we can analyze the advantages and limitations of several of the most widely used screening and assessment tools currently directed at following the progress of these atypical infants.

Although not originally designed for program evaluation, these instruments are increasingly called on to evaluate progress as a result of efforts to intervene positively on behalf of developmental recovery. While intervention research is only beginning to tool up for a vital future, this chapter orients the reader to current examples and trends of medical as well as behavioral models of developmental intervention. The final discussion focuses on motives, opportunities, and concerns for influencing the existence and quality of life for at-risk infants and their families.

DEFINITIONS OF RISK FACTORS

Ultimately, research convinces us that developmental outcome is determined both by inherent biological health and by the caregiving environment's ability to nurture continued physical growth, neurological maturation, and behavioral development (Yarrow, 1979). Whereas damage or stress to the infant brain may seem logically relevant to later risk for normal development, the contribution of caregiver-infant behavioral synchrony may seem less obviously contributory. Healthy, full-term infants can largely cope with and compensate for a disorganized, unsupportive, or depriving environment. Infants born prematurely or neurologically disordered seem less adaptable to suboptimal caregiver responses. This handicap com-

pounds earlier medical problems and is evidenced by a dispropor-
tionately high number of biologically at-risk infants among children
suffering from such diverse conditions as failure to thrive (Rosenn
et al., 1980), kwashiorkor (Brazelton et al., 1976b; Cravioto et al.,
1966), and child abuse (Klein and Stern, 1971; Solomons, 1979).

Significantly, parents who cannot support healthy development
in these children are often successful parents of other children, with
or without apparent physical handicaps (Brazelton et al., 1976a). We
need methods for identifying and predicting which infants might
contribute to failure of the crucial environment-infant interaction.
To accomplish this end, we must learn more about neurological and
behavioral factors in infants that might help or hinder caregiver efforts to support further development. Likewise, we must better assess
stress factors in families and individual caregivers that interfere with
parents' capacities to support the special needs of their atypical infants.

The preceding chapter delineated examples of biological adversity occurring during fetal growth and development. A few
additional causes of risk originating from within the organism are
worthy of extended mention, namely, prematurity, postmaturity, low
birthweight for gestational age and perinatal complications stressing
the newborn's central nervous system.

Prematurity

A few facts are known about infants born at or before 37 weeks'
gestation. Their number approximates 7 to 10% of all live births in
the U.S. (Hobel et al., 1973). Premature births occur from a variety
of structural, physiological, and nutritional problems. The more
common predisposing factors include inability of the cervix to remain tightly closed, insufficient placental circulation to the fetus,
unusual uterine or placental position, maternal hypertension or diabetes, multiple fetuses, and general poor maternal health and nutrition. Whereas 10 years ago upwards of 40% of prematurely born
infants were likely to die or develop moderate to severe developmental disability, current follow-up research places the percentage
of very adversely affected neonates at under 15 to 20% (Drillien,
1975; Kopp and Parmelee, 1979). Extremely immature neonates are
understandably more vulnerable to trauma resulting from difficulties
at or around delivery. However, not all infants born at the same
gestational age are prone to similar vulnerabilities. Some immature
newborns (less than 32 weeks' gestation) recover full health and
behave like full-term infants as early as the first year of postnatal

life (Kopp and Parmelee, 1979). Premature infants of socioeconomically stressed families often recover less optimal neurological and behavioral development than do infants born under similar adversity to economically more advantaged parents (Francis-Williams and Davies, 1974). Perhaps parents who are relatively free from all-consuming demands of sustaining a family's needs for shelter, food, and livelihood enjoy an extra measure of energy and time to attend to the wearying demands of these exceptional children. These infants must rely heavily on their caregivers to stimulate and stabilize the attention and activities these babies themselves only weakly control for the first few postnatal months.

Advances in hospital technique for supporting life and growth in fragile premature infants are largely credited with the decreased mortality and morbidity noted above. At one time these tiny infants had to direct energy away from growth to maintain normal body temperature while suddenly having to breathe and feed themselves. Modern techniques of temperature-stabilized incubators, respiratory assistance devices, feeding catheters, and intravenous alimentation help secure the physiological fragilities of today's premature neonates. Despite masterful early life support, however, not all prematurely born infants are saved from such chronic disabilities as blindness, hearing deficits, movement disorders, expressive and receptive language communication, mental subnormality, school underachievement, and behavior problems. Although infants can overcome these risks, to do so all premature newborns must somehow recover from initial stress to an immaturely developed central nervous system.

Unsolved mysteries about premature infant developmental outcome continue to dominate our interest. Extensive research (Francis-Williams and Davies, 1974; Parmelee and Haber, 1973; Sameroff and Chandler, 1975) demonstrates no single or compound perinatal factors predict consistently neurological behavior after the first postnatal year. Indeed, socioeconomic and parent-infant interactional assessments (Beckwith et al., 1976; Brown and Bakeman, 1979; Field, 1979; Sigman and Parmelee, 1979; Werner et al., 1971) seem to be the strongest indicators of later health or lingering vulnerability. We, therefore, need to discover whether certain prenatal, perinatal, or postnatal influences have lasting effect on the developing organism when they occur at specific intervals in development and/or given certain economic and personal-social variables about the family care environment. Likewise, the role played by such extrauterine environments as an intensive care nursery represents a new area for concerned investigation (Gorski, 1982). Perhaps analagous to animal models of sensory stress causing change in structure and function of the nervous system (Gantt, 1979; Hinsendamp, 1978), infants in modern high-risk nurseries are forced to contend with continuous, noncontingent inputs from the activity, sounds, and movement about them. Investigators are attempting to learn possible associations and relationships between professional caregiving events and perinatal stability or distress. Such signs are assessed via observations of sleep state regulation, activity patterns, and autonomic control over heart rate, respirations, and circulatory perfusion (Gorski et al., 1983).

At the present time, we can identify the neurological and physical immaturities of prematurely born neonates; we realize a range of medical injuries to which they are vulnerable; and we appreciate the parents' emotional stress from unexpected high-risk birth, uncertain hopes, and prolonged separation from their fragile infants. Yet, while anxious to prove which prenatal or perinatal circumstances create long-standing developmental risks in this population, we are left uncertain about the consequences of any early conditions or occurrences.

Small for Gestational Age

Infants born small for gestational age (SGA) deserve special attention when identifying risk groups. Regardless of when they are born, SGA infants are underweight for age as determined by low ponderal index (weight in grams divided by the cube of length in centimeters) (Miller and Hassanein, 1971) below 3rd percentile weight for age (Ounsted and Ounsted, 1973), below 10th percentile (Lubchenko, 1970), or birthweight 2 standard deviations below the mean for gestational age (Ounsted and Ounsted, 1973). The smallness of these neonates indicates intrauterine fetal growth retardation. Such misfortune can occur at any time during gestation and can be due to inadequate maternal-fetal nutrition via placental insufficiency, genetic or chromosomal anomalies, or other causes not yet determined. Known causes of poor oxygen and nutrient transport from placenta to fetus include various maternal conditions such as cyanotic heart disease, toxemia, smoking, drug use, or systemic infection (De Myer, 1975; Gruenwald, 1975; Ounsted and Ounsted, 1973).

Curiously, the brain seems less affected by intrauterine growth retardation than are other body organs (Gruenwald, 1963). This suggests that brain cell size may not critically affect higher neurological functioning as much as do adverse effects of fetal malnutrition upon organization of dendritic branching and synaptic connections, especially during late gestation periods of cortical growth (Dobbing, 1974).

Follow-up studies of full-term but underweight neonates find mild deficits in intellectual functioning when compared to full-weight peers (Fitzhardinge and Steven, 1972b; Parmelee and Schulte, 1970). Similar results were found in a large follow-up of preterm infants (Fitzhardinge and Steven, 1972a, 1972b; Francis-Williams and Davies, 1974). Whether these lasting effects are attributable solely to prenatal growth factors or are compounded by difficulties resulting from deviant behavioral interactions with their caregivers is illuminated by several studies. Michaelis et al. (1970) found decreased reflex behavior, tone, and activity level in term SGA newborns compared to full-weight peers. Als et al. (1976) noted additional weaknesses in alertness and responsiveness of SGA neonates. Although all the SGA infants were functioning normally at 1 year by standard developmental assessment, their parents most often described them as intense, very active, and unrewarding as social partners. This factor raises concern regarding the potential for continued behavioral deviance resulting from unpleasant, strained interactions between these children and their caregivers at home and later at school.

Postmaturity

Pregnancy lasting beyond 41 to 42 weeks' gestation continues at the risk of relying on an old placenta to function beyond the time for which it is naturally programmed. The appearance of infants born postterm is often characterized by thickened peeling skin, a long, thin body, and a wizened facial expression (Clifford, 1954). A recent study (Field et al., 1977) found such neonates prone to suffer an increased number of prenatal complications and difficult deliveries. These babies also performed suboptimally on interactional and motoric measures of neonatal behavior when compared to normal controls. During the first year of life, these postmature infants scored lower on scales of mental development, and their parents reported higher incidence of illnesses, feeding, and sleep disturbances.

Perinatal Complications

Untoward accidents can complicate the early course of infants born at any age or size. Perinatal problems were analyzed during the National Collaborative Perinatal Project (including over 40,000 births) to determine their relative risk for later association with cerebral palsy (Nelson and Ellenberg, 1979). Complications associated with a greater than 20-fold occurrence of cerebral palsy included neonatal seizures, multiple apneic episodes (cessation of breathing for greater than 20 seconds), diminished crying longer than 24 hours, and feeding difficulties requiring tube feedings. Greater than 15 times normal risk for developing cerebral palsy was associated with fluctuation in muscle tone, hypoactivity lasting beyond 24 hours, or marked myoclonus (involuntary sudden jerking of muscle groups).

Another risk factor particularly common to very premature neonates is cerebral hemorrhage. The all-pervasive contemporary concern with intraventricular hemorrhage springs from the new-found capacity to diagnose this complication with computerized tomography and ultrasound. Unfortunately, the predictive ability of these and similar methods remains unsatisfactory. Severe bleeding into ventricles and/or cerebral brain matter does contain major risk for abnormal development as indeed more than 50% of these infants die (Papile et al., 1978; Volpe, 1979). Mild to moderate lesions including subependymal (bleeding limited to an area outside the cerebral ventricles) or small intraventricular bleeding leave uncertain marks on the infant's further developmental course (Volpe, 1979; Krishnamoorthy et al., 1979). Volpe (1979) writes that prognosis depends on the severity of the hypoxic-ischemic insult that preceded the bleeding, on the severity and length of intracranial pressure increase at the time of the bleeding, on the destruction caused by the bleeding in the periventricular white matter and germinal matrix, and on the evolution toward posthemorrhagic hydrocephalus. Perinatal medical factors such as intracranial hemorrhage, seizures, respiratory problems, and aberrant muscle tone threaten normal neurological functioning of infants. Efforts made to assess the neurological status of infants include scores of perinatal and postnatal neurological optimality (Prechtl, 1980) (optimal conditions considered to enjoy the least risk for mortality and morbidity, drawn from social factors, maternal and obstetrical history, pregnancy, delivery, and neonatal adaptation), indexes of neonatal problems (Nelson and Ellenberg, 1981), and postnatal complications (Littman and Parmelee, 1978). Rigorous attempts to apply these scores fail to explain later neurological or developmental outcome sufficiently. The wealth of data accumulating toward an ambiguous relationship between perinatal medical complications and ultimate development thus demands further serious investigation into the real, yet poorly understood, interaction between early condition of the infant and subsequent influences of the social environment. Why do some infants suffer early biological insult and then recover normal function? Why do similarly afflicted neonates exhibit a differing extent and pattern of later development? Are there hidden consequences of perinatal injury that appear for the first time years after apparent complete recovery? Which early insults to the central nervous system are most amenable to behavioral intervention from parents and professionals? How much developmental casualty is contributed by disorganizing, non-individualized care in the name of administering services during the neonatal crisis? All these questions await further solution. Their answers will certainly determine the course of preventive care and appropriate treatment of a plethora of developmental disabilities in young children.

IDENTIFYING THE INFANT AT RISK— SCREENING AND NEONATAL ASSESSMENTS

Two fundamental interests guide attempts to develop assessment instruments for identifying infants at risk for atypical development. First, the wish to determine early on which infants will benefit from special considerations and interventions; and second, professional reliance on available testing instruments for verifying and/or defining the population of children who should receive special attention. With so great an onus of responsibility placed on screening, we need techniques that can be highly sensitive and prognostically accurate.

Many attempts to determine the developmental potential of newborns have been designed and practiced. The most commonly heralded or applied will be outlined below. Each represents a useful, intelligent orientation to that complex organism, the human neonate. However, none can be used independently of each other, of assessments of the home environment, or of family social interaction as a means of identifying the capacities and needs of infants considered at risk during the perinatal period. Furthermore, assessment must be repeated to determine the most current strengths and vulnerabilities of the emerging child.

Undoubtedly, the relative inability of any technique to predict wholly the future course of development reflects the structural and functional changes over time in the infant's central nervous system. Ultimate behavior and intelligence are not determined solely by circumstances at birth. The human brain demonstrates marvelous capacities to adapt to untoward events or conditions (Littman, 1979; Sameroff and Chandler, 1975). Moreover, the caregiver environment seems greatly responsible for enriching, stagnating, or disturbing original neonatal behavior (Beckwith, 1979). The foregoing caveat declared, readers may now arm themselves with identification standards. Above all, their enormous value comes from allowing the examiner to appreciate the fantastic opportunities for learning to support normal patterns of development and early opportunities for learning skills needed to cope with atypical directions.

Medical Risk Scales

Historically, clinicians have been concerned about the lasting effects of contrary occurrences during pregnancy, labor, delivery, and the postnatal periods. Several approaches were designed to assess the relationship between early medical risk factors and later developmental outcome. All commonly used risk factor scales stem from the traditional attempt to locate single factors that might dictate the quality of neurological and behavioral recovery. Some, like the Prenatal Risk Factors Scale of Hobel et al. (1973) and the Parmelee Obstetric Complications Scale (Littman and Parmelee, 1978), assess the numbers of abnormal events during pregnancy, labor, delivery, and previous maternal obstetric history. Examples include third trimester bleeding, inadequate weight gain during pregnancy, maternal hypertension, serious illness or injury during pregnancy, prolonged labor or ruptured membranes, and meconium-stained amniotic fluid. Others, like the Optimality Score of Prechtl (1980) combine prenatal conditions with neonatal adaptation. While the UCLA and Prechtl scales assigned one count to every event, risk scales such as Hobel's predetermine greater or lesser weightings of certain conditions or events. Because we remain unsure of the relative long-term contributions of any factor and because untoward events often cluster (e.g., respiratory distress, acidosis, and infection), assigning equal weight to each event most clearly presents the risks accumulated in the neonatal period.

Parmelee designed additional scales for assessing risks to health and development; that is, they add considerations such as the newborn's breathing, activity, and skin color after birth. The Postnatal Complications Scale (Littman and Parmelee, 1978) records presence or absence of medical problems during the first month of life. The Pediatric Complications Scales (Littman and Parmelee, 1978) review events occurring from age 1 to 4 months and again from 4 to 9 months. These scales assess physical development, health, behavior, congenital anomalies, and neurological and sensory handicaps.

Results from the UCLA Infant Studies Project found that the later Pediatric Complications Scales correlated significantly better with

2-year cognitive and motor development than did assessments of obstetric or neonatal medical complications. This information argues strongly for recognizing the continuing significance of postnatal events upon the developmental course of infants born at risk. Concurrently, one learns of the nervous system's capacity to recover function after initial insult during the perinatal period. Thus, rather than focusing our assessments and interventions on the medical crisis of the high-risk infant, we must learn to measure better the importance of continuing biological and social influences upon the developing organism.

No discussion of medical risk scores and their correlation with later development would be complete without mention of the neonatal Apgar score. The Apgar has long been the most simple and appealing measure of neonatal risk (Apgar, 1960). Originally conceived in 1953, Apgar scores are now routinely integrated into the medical assessment of newborn infants. Scored at 1, 5, and sometimes 10 minutes after delivery, the infant is given 0, 1, or 2 points each for heart rate, respiratory effort, muscle tone, reflex response, and skin color. The composite score portrays the infant's ability to adapt to the immediate postnatal environment.

The usefulness of the Apgar scores for later neurological development remains an unsettled matter. While large scale studies report up to a 4-fold increase in neurological abnormalities at 1 year in infants with 5-minute Apgars below 5, upwards of 95% of infants with low Apgar scores seemed neurologically normal at 1 year of age (Drage et al., 1968). A recent study reported a 7-year follow-up of 49,000 infants whose Apgar scores were recorded at birth (Nelson and Ellenberg, 1981). Although low scores were considered risk factors for cerebral palsy, 55% of children who developed cerebral palsy had Apgar scores of 7 to 10 at 1 minute, and 73% scored 7 to 10 at 5 minutes. Furthermore, of the children who had Apgar scores of 0 to 3 at 10 minutes or later and survived, 80% were free of major handicap at 7 years. The optimality and Apgar scores serve to measure initial obstacles to normal postnatal adaptation and development. They do not directly assess an infant's neurological functioning, nor can they anticipate future circumstances that might enhance or disturb ultimate recovery from early identified crises.

Infant Neurological Examination

Although a history of healthy or problematic events may indicate neurological risk, only direct examination of central nervous system controls and behavior can determine how the brain is functioning at any point in time. Over the past 20 years, several excellent protocols have been tested for tapping central nervous system maturation and function during the first year of life.

Prechtl and Beintema's (1977) neurological examination of the full-term infant includes observation of behavioral states of arousal (five states ranging from deep sleep through sustained crying), motor tone, and reflex behaviors in both supine and prone positions. Relating all of the neonate's responses within the context of state behavior acknowledges how much the performance of motor acts depends upon being optimally alert or asleep. This provides solid evidence for recognizing that higher cortical functioning regulates the quality of all neurological activity.

Although some researchers are currently trying to apply the Prechtl examination to preterm infants (Casaer et al., 1981), the assessment is oriented more directly to the highly organized processes of full-term infants. Saint-Anne Dargassies takes an evolutionary approach to assessing stages of neuromaturation specific to premature infants between the 28th and 41st weeks of gestation (Saint-Anne Dargassies, 1966). She follows the development of motor tone and reflex responses, as well as sensory and autonomic responses over serial examinations. This stage-oriented approach appreciates maturational differences not just in isolated behaviors but in the gradually emerging central organization of the infant's entire nervous system. Moreover, repetitive assessments every few weeks identify the curve of recovery from initially fragile conditions. Because the immature brain is capable of remarkable adaptation to internal and environmental events, the accuracy of prediction increases with repeated examinations.

Regarding the ability of any of these neurological assessments of neonates to foretell ultimate developmental potential, we again face several critical issues. Bierman-Van Eedenburg et al. (1981) reported a recent evaluation of the predictive value of neonatal neurological examination. Using the Prechtl examination on a large cohort of infants tested at term age, the newborn examination correctly identified all but two of the infants who were neurologically abnormal at 18 months. The two who passed the neonatal examination had mild abnormalities at 18 months. However, six times as many infants had abnormal neurological examinations at birth than at 18 months. Therefore, the neonatal neurological assessment fails to differentiate abnormalities that will persist as pathological from those initial weaknesses that later recover normal functioning. This high false positive rate has great importance clinically. Because the caregiver-infant social interaction strongly influences the extent of optimal recovery from perinatal casualty (Beckwith et al., 1976), mislabeling an infant as relatively incompetent, damaged, or weak may reinforce caregiver responses, which fulfill these prophecies through protecting the infant from exercising independent efforts to overcome frustrations. Alternatively, parents of children with a damaged label may feel too discouraged to provide enough ongoing support and stimulation. Both the overprotected and the undersupported child may fail to achieve developmental potential in part due to the mistaken early diagnosis.

The authors offer a plausible hypothesis for the high rate of false positive findings. Citing such disorders as hyperexcitability syndrome and choreiform dyskinesia (a movement disorder characterized by involuntary rhythmic action of limbs), the investigators offer the possibility that at 18 months eventual signs of neurological dysfunction may not be detectable. Neonatal abnormalities may presage later developmental disabilities that are temporarily masked before age 2 years. Answers to this critical puzzle await more longitudinal results from the current prospective approach to data.

With the above qualifications considered, there exists a general consensus as to which neurological signs are alarming when observed during the neonatal period (Amiel-Tison and Grenier, 1980; Prechtl, 1980; Saint-Anne Dargassies, 1977). These pathological signs include persistent fussing, difficult feeding, persistent deviation of head and/or persistent abnormal eye position, persistent asymmetry in posture and movements, imperative opisthotonus (backward arching of neck and back), apathy and immobility, floppiness, hyperexcitability with jittery movements, convulsions, abnormal cry, the combination of setting-sun sign, vomiting, wide sutures and/or abnormal increase in skull circumference, occurrence and especially the reoccurrence of respiratory difficulties and apnea, and the loss of variability in such physiological parameters as respiration, heart rate, and transcutaneous oxygen pressure. Intraventricular hemorrhage in newborns presents concern about neurological recovery. However, especially with mild to moderate lesions, prognoses are as yet unreliable (Volpe, 1979). Although the bleeding is perhaps telling as a sign reflecting some particular insult to the brain (De Courten and Rabinowicz, 1981), we will need to rely on indicators besides extent of bleeding alone. With intraventricular hemorrhage as with all other untoward neonatal events, we have yet to learn which infants will suffer most from early difficulties.

Sensory Assessments

There exist few more amazing neurological functions than the sensory capacities of vision and hearing. Consequently, they represent important areas for testing central nervous system integrity. That infants can hear and see at term age is now accepted fact. Much interest, however, applies to the quality of auditory and visual processes in neonates. Fantz (1965) initially demonstrated the infant's capacity to recognize a variety of complex visual stimuli. Assessments of visual function can record electroencephalographic latencies to evoked responses, alertness, duration of alertness, and smoothness of locating and following stimuli presented (Fantz et al., 1975; Goren et al., 1975). Visual behavior may indicate central nervous system prognosis as well as intactness (Sigman et al., 1973). Future studies can now take advantage of newly sophisticated assessment techniques.

Auditory processes are similarly under investigation as potential indicators of neurological integrity. Sucking paradigms (Lipsitt, 1967), heart rate responses (Schulman, 1973), brainstem-evoked responses (Schulman-Galambos and Galambos, 1979), and alerting behavioral responses (Brazelton, 1973), are all ways of assessing the quality of auditory function. Because adequate vision and hearing greatly facilitate social communication and learning, early identification and intervention for sensory-perception must accompany all efforts to support optimal development.

Neonatal Behavioral Assessment

Brazelton elaborated on earlier assessments of newborn behavior to complement and potentially enrich neurological assessment of motor tone and reflexes. Framed within the matrix of observing and manipulating changes in states of arousal of neonates, the Neonatal Behavioral Assessment Scale (NBAS) (Brazelton, 1973) follows the infant through sleep, drowsiness, bright and active alertness, and crying while the examiner interacts with the newborn. The examination elicits 20 neurological reflex behaviors. It also scores 26 behavorial items that often mimic routine caregiver experiences such as cuddling, consoling, and visual and/or auditory stimulation.

A most important concept of the NBAS lies in assessing the infant's capacities to initiate support from the environment, modulate or terminate his/her response to excess outside stimulation, and rely on self for coping with a rewarding or distressing situation. Reflecting the range of behavorial capacities of the normal neonate, the behavorial items assess the infant's ability to: 1) organize states of consciousness; 2) habituate reactions to disturbing events; 3) attend to and process simple and complex environmental events; 4) control motor tone and activity while attending to these events; and 5) perform integrated motor acts.

Brazelton and associates believe that the examination brings out the most complex and integrated central nervous system functioning in the newborn infant. Therefore, they expect the behavorial assessment to serve as a rich adjunct to a standard neurological examination, which mostly tests isolated reflexive functioning rather than central nervous system integration or adaptability. Hoping to demonstrate the added power of neurological prediction based on neonatal capacities, a prospective investigation compared the accuracies for long-term prediction of the neonatal behavioral and neurological examinations (Tronick and Brazelton, 1975). Fifty-three infants were rated by nursery staff pediatricians to be "abnormal" or "suspect" at 3 days of age. This group was then examined by the behavorial pediatricians and by neurologists who in turn rated the infants neurologically "normal," "suspect," or "abnormal." Follow-up assessments including vision, school, psychometric, and neurological evaluations were continued to 7 years of age at which time the children were also classified as normal, suspect, or abnormal. In comparing the predictive validity of the behavioral and neurological examinations, the investigators found them to be almost equally sensitive in detecting ultimately abnormal children. The neurological assessments correctly diagnosed 13 of the 15 abnormal infants (87%) while the behavorial assessment caught 12 of the eventual 15 (80%). However, the two exams had striking differences in mislabeling normal infants. The neurological examination mislabeled 30 of 50 normal infants as suspect/abnormal, while the behavorial assessment mislabeled only 9 of the 50 normals as suspect/abnormal. This false alarm rate of 80% versus 24% reflects increased risk of mislabeling a child as damaged or vulnerable.

The Brazelton examination is designed and validated to elicit the behavorial capacities of full-term infants. Although attempts have been made to apply this tool to premature infants (Field et al., 1978; Scarr-Salapatek and Williams, 1973; Solkoff and Matuszak, 1975), results are not wholly satisfying or meaningful because the neurological organization of these infants is qualitatively different. As a result, responses to stimuli are often uninterpretable using the full-term scale. Als et al. (1979) are developing a complex set of assessment techniques appropriately packaged to evaluate quality of behavioral organization at various ages prior to term.

Our own research efforts use a somewhat distinct approach to analyze the neurological and behavioral development of preterm infants. Responding to the current search for ways to improve nursery care with respect to later development, we have designed an elaborate computerized system for recording continuous observation of the neonate's physiological and behavioral condition concurrent with observation of the caregiving environment (Gorski et al., 1983). By continuously recording personnel, interventions, sounds, and events that occur during an infant's care in the intensive care nursery, we can correlate infant stability or signs of distress with the timing, intensity, and style of caregiving interventions. Infant parameters recorded include heart rate, respirations, transcutaneous oxygen pressures, behavorial state of arousal, skin color, motor activity, and observed specific behavioral responses (e.g., vomiting, seizures, gaze aversion, frown, smile, opisthotonus, and directed visual gaze) among others.

Some fascinating results have emerged thus far. We record, for example, when a nurse begins and ends an intervention or approaches and leaves an infant's bedside. We were first surprised to find that even during the busy daytime hours, nurses were present within view of their patients only 15 to 20% of the total time. Moreover, nurses tended to leave their infant's area within 2 minutes after completing a caregiving task. Unfortunately, our observation computer often records signs of distress (e.g., cyanosis, precipitous drop in heart rate or respirations, precariously low oxygen levels in the capillary circulation, hyperexcitability states of arousal and activity, and vomiting or gasping) that occur within 5 minutes of a caregiving intervention. Had the nurse stayed to observe these episodes, he/she might connect the infant's responses with the preceding caregiver effort. Over time, it is hoped that the nurse would look for predictable consequences specific to each infant. Many sudden physiological catastrophes could be prevented by the caregiver's appropriate response to early warning signs before the signs escalate unsupported into serious distress. For example, if a caregiver stops handling an infant who insists on averting his/her gaze from the caregiver, the infant could relax his/her guard and thus avoid the apnea or vomiting that commonly result from the infant's persistent effort to limit the amount of sensory input, which may be intolerable if it comes when the infant's nervous system has already been overly taxed.

Contrary to general myth, social interaction can produce as much stress in weak infants as can painful stimuli. We compared the baseline incidence of physiological and/or behavioral distress signs occurring throughout the day with the incidence of distress 5 minutes following each of several caregiver interventions. We found that social interaction (holding, touching, talking, singing, or *en face* positioning) and chest physical therapy were both associated with significantly more physiological and behavioral distress within 5 minutes following intervention than the comparative baseline distress incidence (Gorski et al., 1983). This startling result seems to imply that the timing may be as important as the content of an intervention. Alternatively, immature nervous systems may be unable to tolerate a great amount of any stimulation. We are currently testing these possibilities by analyzing our data for distress incidences following identical interventions begun in each of several states of consciousness.

This work represents an essential investigation of the central nervous system capacities of infants of various gestational ages to cope with, adapt to, or benefit from existing clinical efforts to support their physical and developmental needs. If we can better understand the neonate's limits and capacities for tolerating outside care, we could devise intervention programs based on real knowledge of the organism in the extrauterine environment. To date, intervention programs have sprung from theoretical hypotheses about the preterm's deficiencies and needs. We now outline the nebulous conclusions thus far drawn from research on intervention in the neonatal hospitalization. As we consider this important and exciting work, the reader should realize how much of the methodological and conceptual difficulties indicate still primitive understanding of the individual organism under study.

INTERVENTION RESEARCH

As neonatal care has progressed, enabling greater numbers of premature infants to survive, health care professionals are eagerly considering ways to optimize the quality of survival. With technological advances seemingly at a peak, further improvements are likely to come from molding our caregiving efforts to the needs of the developing nervous system of these infants. Researchers design neonatal interventions in hopes of preventing the potentially harmful handicapping effects of the intensive care nursery environment on the infant at risk.

Early studies in the mid-1960s planned hospital interventions from the hypothesis that infants in high-risk nurseries were deprived of the stimulation usually gained from family interactions in a home environment (Cornell and Gottfried, 1976). Examples of compensatory intervention included provision of extra handling by nurses. Hasselmeyer (1964) found the premature infants who received extra amounts of stroking, rocking, and cuddling cried less and were quieter than were preterm controls. The work of Solkoff et al. (1969)

corroborated some positive effects from extra tactile/kinesthetic stimulation. Preterm infants who received 10 days of extra stroking from nurses cried less, gained weight faster, and were more active than controls. At 8 months, treated infants scored higher on the Bayley Motor Scale. Other important examples of applying early tactile/kinesthetic stimulation are presented in the literature (Freedman et al., 1966; Solkoff and Matuszak, 1975; White and Labarba, 1976).

Korner et al. (1975) examined the utility of providing increased vestibular stimulation to preterm infants. Using a continuously oscillating water bed, experimental infants suffered fewer episodes of apnea (serious breath holding) than did untreated controls. No differences between control and experimental groups, however, appeared with respect to weight gain or to other parameters of physiological stability.

Barnard (1972) examined the effect of repetitive kinesthetic and auditory stimulation on sleep/wake state organization in premature infants. Experimental subjects showed significantly greater increases in proportion of quiet sleep and decrease in active sleep during the 32nd to 35th week of gestation when compared to age-matched controls.

Katz (1971) and Segall (1972) studied the effects of adding patterned auditory stimulation to the routine care of premature infants in the hospital. Repeated playing of a tape recording of mother's voice seemed to improve auditory, visual, and habituation responses at the 36th week of gestation.

These and similar studies, while provocative, must be accepted with extreme caution. None of the research examined the continued effects over a long period of time. Many did not identify possible initial differences between groups as tested by the outcome measures before intervention started. None of the research answered the crucial question as to whether any positive long-term effects stem from the early intervention itself or from the intervention's changing the infant's behavior, which in turn influenced parent-infant interactions in support of developmental gains. Furthermore, no investigators examined the contingent relationship of interventions to the infant's ability to use this type of stimulation. Therefore, potentially positive effects may have been neutralized by offering intervention at inappropriate times.

A second school of thought among intervention researchers is reviewed by Lawson et al. (1977). These investigators hypothesize that rather than suffering from a variety of sensory deprivation, preterm neonates in an intensive care unit may in fact be overstimulated by the 24-hour lights, activity, and environmental noise. These workers design ways to compensate through limiting the amount of stimuli presently offered in nurseries. Our own observational research (Gorski, 1982) certainly verifies hazardous medical events frequently coinciding with episodes of peak caregiver activity. Episodes of apnea, for example, frequently cluster soon after the busy intensity of morning and evening medical team rounds (Gorski, 1979).

In review, then, although behavioral intervention during neonatal hospitalization is tempting and a potentially useful adjunct to present medical regimens, we must give much deeper thought to a few related possibilities:

1. How long do the effects last?
2. How long must each intervention persist to achieve optimal results?
3. What potentially untoward consequences are produced by intervention?
4. What is the relative importance of the content, timing, and style of intervention to ultimate success?
5. Do some infants react adversely while others respond positively to the same intervention?
6. Are some interventions beneficial only within a specifiable stage of neurobehavioral development?
7. Are certain unintended examiner effects (Rosenthal, 1966) influencing the results as much as the intervention itself?

I believe that the next decade will reward the efforts to satisfy our cautious optimism about behaviorally influencing the course of recovery from perinatal risk. Logic alone dictates the sensibility of protecting the bounds while challenging the capacities of the developing nervous system of premature infants. Because the brain indeed regulates functioning of all the vital organ systems including the heart and lungs, directing care to the needs of the maturing nervous system will undoubtedly in turn foster recovery of general health, growth, and development.

Chapter Outline

OVERVIEW: The developmental processes of infants born at biological risk for delay are described. Risk factors of neonatal screening and assessment techniques are identified. Early intervention research with this population is reviewed.

I. DEFINITION OF RISK FACTORS
Factors associated with biological risk are described in terms of causation and developmental effects. They include:

A. Prematurity
B. Small-for-gestational age status
C. Postmaturity
D. Perinatal complications (e.g., birth asphyxia and intracranial hemorrhage)

II. IDENTIFYING THE INFANT AT RISK—SCREENING AND NEONATAL ASSESSMENTS
Perinatal risk assessments although useful and necessary for identifying babies at risk are not sufficiently predictive of later development to be utilized as the sole criterion for identification and diagnosis. Assessments include:

A. Medical risk scales
B. Apgar screening technique
C. Neonatal neurological examinations
D. Sensory assessments
E. Neonatal behavioral assessment
F. Ecological scale describing intensive care nursery interactions

III. INTERVENTION RESEARCH

A. Early hospital interventions in the high-risk nurseries focused on the provison of compensatory stimulation (e.g., handling, rocking, and stroking); reports indicated various degrees of success with these approaches.
B. Gorski argues that the future of high risk newborn care must turn increasingly toward supporting the developing nervous system of at-risk infants. At the

same time, because we still have limited understanding of preterm neuromaturational influences, a careful study of the positive or disturbing effects of our caregiving behavior and environment on the ultimate course of neurological development in high-risk infants is warranted.

REFERENCES

Als, H., Lester, B. M., and Brazelton, T. B. Dynamics of the behavioral organization of the premature infant: A theoretical perspective. In T. Field, A. Sostek, S. Goldberg, and H. Shuman (Eds.), *Infants Born At Risk*. New York, Spectrum, 1979.

Als, H., Tronick, E., Adamson, L., and Brazelton, T. B. The behavior of the full-term yet underweight newborn infant. *Developmental Medicine and Child Neurology*, 1976, *18*, 590–602.

Amiel-Tison, C., and Grenier, A. *Evaluation Neurologique du Nouveau-ne-et-du Nourrisson*. Paris: Masson, 1980.

Apgar, V. Proposal for a new method of evaluation of the newborn infant. *Anesthesia and Analgesia*, 1960, *32*, 260.

Barnard, K. E. *The Effect of Stimulation on the Duration and Amount of Sleep and Wakefulness in the Premature Infant*. Unpublished doctoral dissertation. Seattle: University of Washington, 1972.

Beckwith, C. The influence of caregiver-infant interaction on development. In E. Sell (Ed.), *Follow-up of the High Risk Newborn: A Practical Approach*. Springfield, IL: Charles C Thomas, 1979.

Beckwith, C., Cohen, S. E., Kopp, C. B., et al. Caregiver-infant interaction and early cognitive development in preterm infants. *Child Development*, 1976, *47*, 579–587.

Bierman-Van Eedenburg, M., Jurgens-Van Der Zee, A. D., Olinga, A., et al. Predictive value of neonatal neurological examination: A follow-up study at 18 months. *Developmental Medicine and Child Neurology*, 1981, *23*, 296–305.

Brazelton, T. B. Neonatal Behavioral Assessment Scale. *Clinics in Developmental Medicine* (No. 50). London: Spastics International Medical Publications, William Heinemann Medical Books, 1973.

Brazelton, T. B., Parker, W. B., and Zuckerman, B. Importance of behavioral assessment of the neonate. *Current Problems in Pediatrics*, 1976a, *7*(2).

Brazelton, T. B., Tronick, E., and Koslowski, B. Neonatal behavior among urban Zambians and Americans. *Journal of the Academy of Child Psychology*, 1976b, *15*, 97.

Brown, J. V., and Bakeman, R. Relations of human mothers with their infants during the first year of life: Effects of prematurity. In R. Bell and W. Smotherman (Eds.), *Maternal Influences and Early Behavior*. Holliswood, NY: Spectrum, 1979.

Casaer, P., Eggermont, E., Daniels, H., et al. Neurological assessment in the neonatal special care unit. *Postgraduate Courses in Pediatrics*. Basel, New York: Karger, 1981.

Clifford, S. H. Postmaturity with placental dysfunction. *Journal of Pediatrics*, 1954, *44*, 1–13.

Cornell, E. H., and Gottfried, A. W. Intervention with premature human infants. *Child Development*, 1976, *47*, 32–39.

Cravioto, J., Delcardie, E., and Birch, H. G. Nutrition, growth and neurointegrative development. *Pediatric Supplements*, 1966, *38*, 319.

De Courten, G. M., and Rabinowicz, T. Intraventricular hemorrhage in premature infants: Reappraisal and new hypothesis. *Developmental Medicine and Child Neurology*, 1981, *23*, 389–403.

De Myer, W. Congenital anomalies of the central nervous system. In D. B.

Tower (Ed.), *The Nervous System. The Clinical Neurosciences.* New York: Raven, 1975.

Dobbing, J. Prenatal nutrition and neurological development. In J. Cravioto, L. Hambraeus, and B. Vahlquist (Eds.), *Early Malnutrition and Mental Development.* Symposia of the Swedish Nutrition Foundation (No XII). Stockholm: Almquist & Wiksell, 1974.

Drage, J. S., Kennedy, C., Berendes, H., et al. The 5-minute Apgar scores and 4-year psychological performance. *Developmental Medicine and Child Neurology,* 1968, *8,* 141.

Drillien, C. M. Prevention of handicap in infants of very low birth weight. In Primrose (Ed.), *Proceedings of the Third Congress of the International Association for the Scientific Study of Mental Deficiency.* Warsaw: Polish Medical Publishers, 1975.

Fantz, R. L. Visual perception from birth as shown by pattern selectivity. *Annals of the New York Academy of Science,* 1965, *118,* 793.

Fantz, R. L., Fagan, J. F., and Miranda, S. B. Early visual selectivity. In L. Cohen and P. Salapatek (Eds.), *Infant Perception: From Sensation to Cognition (Vol. I): Basic Visual Processes.* New York: Academic, 1975.

Field, T. M. Interaction patterns of preterm and term infants. In T. Field, A. Sostek, S. Goldberg, and H. Shuman (Eds.), *Infants Born At Risk.* New York: Spectrum, 1979.

Field, T. M., Dabiri, C., Hallock, N., and Shuman, H. H. Developmental effects of prolonged pregnancy and the postmaturity syndrome. *Journal of Pediatrics,* 1977, *90,* 836–839.

Field, T. M., Hallock, N., Ting, G., et al. A first follow-up of high risk infants: Formulating a cumulative risk index. *Child Development,* 1978, *49,* 173–192.

Fitzhardinge, P. M., and Steven, E. M. The small-for-date infant. I. Later growth patterns. *Pediatrics,* 1972a, *49,* 671–681.

Fitzhardinge, P. M., and Steven, E. M. The small-for-date infant. II. Neurological and intellectual sequelae. *Pediatrics,* 1972b, *50,* 50–57.

Francis-Williams, J., and Davies, P. A. Very low birth weight and later intelligence. *Developmental Medicine and Child Neurology,* 1974, *16,* 709–728.

Freedman, D., Boverman, H., and Freedman, N. *Effects of Kinesthetic Stimulation on Weight Gain and on Smiling in Premature Infants.* Paper presented at the American Orthopsychiatric Association, San Francisco, April, 1966.

Gantt, R. Flourescent light-induced DNA crosslinkage and Chromatid breaks in mouse cells in culture. *Proceedings of the National Academy of Science,* 1979, *75,* 3809–3812.

Goren, C. C., Sarty, M., and Wie, P. Y. K. Visual following and pattern discrimination by newborn infants. *Pediatrics,* 1975, *56,* 544.

Gorski, P. A. Observation: The heart of intervention. In *Proceedings of the Fourth Keystone Conference on Parenting.* Keystone, CO: Mead Johnson, 1979.

Gorski, P. A. Premature infant behavioral and physiological responses to caregiving interventions in the intensive care nursery. In J. Call and E. Galenson (Eds.), *Frontiers of Infant Psychiatry.* New York: Basic Books, 1982.

Gorski, P. A., Hole, W. T., Leonard, C. H., and Martin, J. A. Direct computer recording of premature infants and nursery care. *Pediatrics*, 1983, *72*, 198–202.

Gruenwald, P. Chronic fetal distress and placental insufficiency. *Biologia Neonatorum*, 1963, *5*, 215–265.

Gruenwald, P. *The Placenta*. Baltimore: University Park Press, 1975.

Hasselmeyer, E. G. The premature neonate's response to handling. *American Nursing Association*, 1964, *1*, 15–24.

Hinsendamp, M. Cell behavior and DNA modification in pulsing electromagnetic fields. *Acta Orthopedica Belgica*, 1978, *44*, 636–649.

Hobel, C. J., Hyvarinen, M. A., Okada, D., and Oh, W. Prenatal and intrapartum high risk screening. *American Journal of Obstetrics and Gynecology*, 1973, *117*, 1. *Infant Death: An Analysis by Maternal Risk and Health Care: Contrasts in Health Status*. Washington, DC: National Academy of Sciences, 1973.

Katz, V. Auditory stimulation and developmental behavior of the premature infant. *Nursing Research*, 1971, *20*, 196–201.

Klein, M., and Stern, L. Low birthweight and the battered child syndrome. *American Journal of Diseases of Children*, 1971, *15*, 122.

Kopp, C. B., and Parmelee, A. H. Prenatal and perinatal influences on infant behavior. In J. Osofsky (Ed.), *Handbook of Infant Development*. New York: Wiley, 1979, 29–75.

Korner, A. F., Kraemer, H. C., Faffner, M. E., and Cosper, L. M. Effects of waterbed flotation on premature infants: A pilot study. *Pediatrics*, 1975, *56*, 361–367.

Krishnamoorthy, K. S., Shannon, D. C., deLong, G. R., et al. Neurologic sequelae in the survivors of neonatal intraventricular hemorrhage. *Pediatrics*, 1979, *64*, 233–237.

Lawson, K., Daum, C., and Turkewitz, G. Environmental characteristics of a neonatal intensive care unit. *Child Development*, 1977, *48*, 1633–1639.

Lipsitt, L. P. Learning in human infants. In H. Stevenson, E. Hess, and H. Rheingold (Eds.), *Early Behavior: Comparative and Behavioral Approaches*. New York: Wiley, 1967.

Littman, B. The relationship of medical events to infants development. In T. Field, A. Sostek, S. Goldberg, and H. Shuman (Eds.), *Infants Born At Risk*. New York: Spectrum, 1979.

Littman, B., and Parmelee, A. H. Medical correlates of infant development. *Pediatrics*, 1978, *61*, 470.

Lubchenko, L. Assessment of gestational age and development at birth. *Pediatric Clinics of North America*, 1970, *17*, 125–145.

Michaelis, R., Schulte, F. J., and Nolte, R. Motor behavior of small for gestational age newborn infants. *Journal of Pediatrics*, 1970, *76* 208–213.

Miller, H. C., and Hassanein, K. Diagnosis of impaired fetal growth in newborn infants. *Pediatrics*, 1971, *48*, 511–522.

Nelson, K. B., and Ellenberg, J. H. Neonatal signs as predictors of cerebral palsy. *Pediatrics*, 1979, *64*, 225–232.

Nelson, K. B., and Ellenberg, J. H. Apgar scores as predictors of chronic neurologic disability. *Pediatrics*, 1981, *68*, 36–44.

Ounsted, M., and Ounsted, C. On fetal growth rate. In *Clinics in Developmental Medicine (No. 46)*. London: Spastics International Medical Publications, Heinemann Medical Books, 1973.

Papile, L., Burstein, J., Burstein, R., and Koffler, H. Incidence and evolution of subependymal and intraventricular hemorrhage. *Journal of Pediatrics,* 1978, *92,* 529–534.

Parmelee, A. H., and Haber, A. Who is the risk infant? *Clinical Obstetrics and Gynecology,* 1973, *16,* 376–387.

Parmelee, A. H., and Schulte, F. Developmental testing of pre-term and small-for-dates infants. *Pediatrics,* 1970, *45,* 21–28.

Prechtl, H. F. R. The optimality concept. *Early Human Development,* 1980, *4,* 201–206.

Prechtl, H. F. R., and Beintema, D. J. The neurological examination of the full-term newborn infant. In *Clinics in Developmental Medicine (No. 63).* London: Spastics International Medical Publications, William Heinemann Medical Books, 1977.

Rosenn, D. W., Loeb, L. S., and Jura, M. B. Differentiation of organic from nonorganic failure to thrive syndrome in infancy. *Pediatrics,* 1980, *66,* 698.

Rosenthal, R. *Experimenter Effects in Behavioral Research.* New York: Appleton-Century-Crofts, 1966.

Saint-Anne Dargassies, S. Neurological maturation of the premature infant of 28 to 41 weeks' gestational age. In F. Faukner (Ed.), *Human Development.* Philadelphia: W. B. Saunders, 1966.

Saint-Anne Dargassies, S. *Neurological Development in the Full-term and Premature Neonate.* Amsterdam: Elsevier/North Holland. 1977.

Sameroff, A. J., and Chandler, M. J. Reproductive risk and the continuum of caretaking casualty. In F. Horowitz (Ed.), *Review of Child Development Research* (Vol. 4). Chicago: University of Chicago Press, 1975.

Scarr-Salapatek, S., and Williams, M. L. The effects of early stimulation on low-birthweight infants. *Child Development,* 1973, *44,* 94–101.

Schulman, C. A. Heart rate audiometry. Part I. An evaluation of heart rate response to auditory stimuli in newborn hearing screening. *Neuropaediatrie,* 1973, *4,* 362–374.

Schulman-Galambos, C., and Galambos, R. Brainstem evoked response audiometry in newborn hearing screening. *Archives of Otolaryngology,* 1979, *105,* 86–90.

Segall, M. Cardiac responsivity to auditory stimulation in premature infants. *Nursing Research,* 1972, *21,* 15–19.

Sigman, M., Kopp, C. B., Parmelee, A. H., and Jeffrey, W. E. Visual attention and neurological organization in neonates. *Child Development,* 1973, *44,* 461.

Sigman, M., and Parmelee, A. H. Longitudinal follow-up of premature infants. In T. Field, A. Sostek, S. Goldberg, and H. Shuman (Eds.), *Infants Born At Risk.* New York: Spectrum, 1979.

Solkoff, N., and Matuszak, D. Tactile stimulation and behavioral development among low-birthweight infants. *Child Psychiatry and Human Development,* 1975, *6,* 33–37.

Solkoff, N., Yaffe, S., Weintraub, D., and Blase, B. Effects of handling on the subsequent development of premature infants. *Developmental Psychology,* 1969, *1,* 765–768.

Solomons, G. Child abuse and developmental disabilities. *Developmental Medicine Child Neurology,* 1979, *21,* 101–108.

Tronick, E., and Brazelton, T. B. Clinical uses of the Brazelton Neonatal

Scale. In B. Friedlander, B. Sterritt, and G. Kirk (Eds.), *Exceptional Infant* (Vol 3). New York: Brunner/Mazel, 1975.

Volpe, J. J. Intracranial haemorrhage in the newborn: Current understanding and dilemmas. *Neurology*, 1979, *29*, 632–635.

Werner, E. E., Bierman, J. M., and French, F. E. *The Children of Kauai.* Honolulu: University Press of Hawaii, 1971.

White, J., and Labarba, R. The effects of tactile and kinesthetic stimulation on neonatal development in the premature infant. *Developmental Psychobiology*, 1976, *9*, 569–577.

Yarrow, L. J. Historical perspectives and future directions in infant development. In J. Osofsky (Ed.), *Handbook of Infant Development*. New York: Wiley, 1979.

CHAPTER 4

Assessment of Infants
Robert Sheehan and R. J. Gallagher

Infant assessment is a topic either mentioned or implied in any discussion of infant development. The various chapters in this text contain references to infant assessment. Whenever an area of infant development is discussed (e.g., cognitive development, social development, language development), the discussion reflects concerns about and values toward infant assessment. This chapter is written to go beyond these content-specific assessment concerns to address the commonalities found among several areas of infant assessment. It identifies and discusses three commonalities: purposes of infant assessment, a rationale for screening of very young infants, and a classification of infant measures.

Assessment is a term connoting a number of different meanings. At its most basic level, assessment refers to data collection. When defined in this fashion, assessment includes formal and informal observation, direct testing, post hoc reporting by parents, teacher reports, anecdotal records, and so forth. In practice, assessment generally can be separated into two major approaches: structured and unstructured. Structured assessment efforts are those observations, reports, or direct testings that compare an infant's performance to an existing standard such as a behavioral item. Unstructured assessment efforts are those recordings of infants' performances without an existing standard. For example, the use of anecdotal records or general parent surveys asking parents to describe an infant's behavior might be considered assessment efforts. Focus in this chapter is directed toward structured assessment efforts.

Although few intervenors have had formal training in infant assessment, their clinical skills often lead to an acute understanding of the infant state, rapport, temperament, and developmental processes. Intervenors are often the individuals who best articulate the purposes for conducting an assessment. Such a clinical understanding of why and for whom an assessment is necessary is critical to any assessment effort and provides a firm foundation for many of the concepts we discuss in this chapter. A major point made in this chapter is that the purpose for assessment must guide selection and use of assessment measures.

THE PURPOSES OF INFANT ASSESSMENT

Early Views

A complete historical discussion of the history of infant intelligence testing is beyond the scope of the present chapter and is well discussed in Brooks and Weinraub (1976). Limited discussion of the early purposes of infant assessment is, however, necessary to an understanding of current assessment issues.

The first efforts in assessing infant performance were the products of attempts to demonstrate the continuity of intelligence from infancy to adulthood (Honzik, 1976). During the 1920s the search was on among psychologists to isolate the "g" intelligence constant, that stable aspect of intelligence that was assumed to be unchanged from birth to death. Such efforts met with consistent failure, resulting in extremely small and unstable correlations between performance in infancy and later performance in childhood and adolescence.

During the ensuing decades a shift occurred in the field of infant assessment—a shift away from assessment for the purpose of isolating a stable intelligence factor. This shift was toward assessment of infant behavior to describe the course of development during the early years and for clinical usage in working with infants. Such efforts ultimately yielded a number of important measures including the Bayley Scales of Infant Development (Bayley, 1969) and the Gesell Developmental Schedules (Gesell and Amatruda, 1941).

Once the general course of development in infancy was charted, professionals returned to the topic of stability and continuity in development and began to use the developmental measures for research purposes in labs and preschools throughout the country. Numerous research studies were conducted during the 1940s and 1950s, largely with normal populations of infants and often for the purpose of exploring the stability of developmental age scores and constructs across the infancy period into later years.

Description and long-term prediction as purposes for infant assessment dominated the activities of professionals in early childhood until the last two decades. Recently, McCall (1979) discussed the assumptions underlying this research effort as well as the reasons why the effort met with so little success. He maintained that an attempt to establish predictive relationships between an infant's test results and an adult's measured intelligence is an examination of the stability-instability of individual differences and ignores the continuity-discontinuity of development as described in Piaget.

The distinction made by McCall (1979) and others (Dunst and Rheingrover, 1981; Scarr-Salapatek, 1976) between stability-instability of individual differences and continuity-discontinuity of development is critical to an understanding of current thinking in infant assessment. Correlational studies examining the predictive value of infant measures are actually examining the stability of an ordered group of infants from one time period to another. Such studies assume that development is a continuous, quantitative process that occurs additively. For example, one might assume that 24-month-old infant performance differs from 12-month-old infant performance only in the addition of 12 months of skills. An infant performing in the 80th percentile is assumed to be functioning in a similar rank at both time periods.

McCall (1979), Scarr-Salapatek (1976), Dunst and Rheingrover (1981), and others point out that the assumption of continuous, additive development is not consistent with current developmental theory or research (McCall et al., 1977). Rather, development in infancy is now viewed as a series of qualitative transformations.

Research efforts that have concentrated on prediction of later intelligence from infant test results may have failed to distinguish between variables that control sequence in an infant's sensorimotor intelligence and variables that control the rate at which an infant passes from stage to stage. Sequence variables are likely to differ from rate variables and are also more likely to be fixed than rate variables. The developmental function may in fact be highly influenced by genetic maturational control while the rate of progression through stages that results in measured individual differences may be controlled by another set of variables. Unfortunately, most infant measures are constructed by intertwining sequence and rate constructs. This results in a limited ability to differentiate reliably among individuals in a systematic fashion across time.

Attempts to improve the low predictive ability of infant tests have been instructive, if somewhat futile. In 1979 McCall examined variables that might affect the predictive validity of later IQ from infant tests. Modest gains in prediction were obtained when sexes were separated, when infant test results were combined with an estimate of socioeconomic class, and when clusters of test items were examined apart from the total test results (e.g., verbal items). However, the overriding conclusion was that:

> *. . . infant tests do not typically reveal highly stable individual dif-*
> *ferences within the first 18 months or from infancy to later IQ . . .*
> *(p. 715).*

Continuing, McCall states:

> It would appear that the study of mental development is considerably
> more complex than observing stability in a single concept called "in-
> telligence." Rather, infancy is a period of enormous metamorphoses
> in the predominant character of mental behavior and fluctuations in
> the stability of individual differences in mental performance (p. 731).

As we have indicated, infant assessment measures have not been successful in demonstrating the continuity of development of normal individuals from infancy to later age periods. Brooks and Weinraub (1976) suggested the following reasons for this lack of success. Many of their suggestions are supportive of McCall's (1979) concerns regarding the stability-instability of individual differences and the continuity-discontinuity of development:

1. Early development does not proceed at a uniform rate; therefore, there is little measured stability in the first 2 years of life.
2. The quality of intelligence at one age may be different from another age in the first 2 years of life, and the ways of measuring intelligence may not be appropriate from one age to another.
3. Environmental effects and changes/adaptations an individual makes to the environment are not accounted for in standard developmental instruments.
4. Child variables such as state, motivation, temperament, and a limited repertoire of behavior, as well as factors influencing test conditions, are likely to increase test unreliability.

In reviewing the ability of infant tests to predict reliably later intellectual or developmental status, three conclusions can be made:

1. The shorter the time between testing periods, the higher the correlations between tests.
2. A linear trend is associated with the testing age, that is, the correlations between infant tests and IQ measures up to age 18 years increase the later in infancy the test results are obtained (McCall et al., 1977).
3. Infant measures generally are not able to predict reliably future performance of infants' functioning; predictive capability only holds true for infants exhibiting below average performance (Lewis, 1975; Meier, 1975, 1976). Said differently: Infant tests are reliable predictors for infants' functioning at the extreme low end of the development continuum. Of course, as Brooks-Gunn

and Lewis (1981) point out, such low functioning performance is usually self-evident and likely to remain relatively low, even with immediate intervention.

Although infant measures have not proved useful in demonstrating the stability of individual differences in normal infants, such measures are still widely used for a number of purposes. These current purposes are applied in focus and are largely directed toward populations of atypical infants and young children.

Current Views Regarding the Purpose of Infant Assessment

Concern for the development of typical and atypical infants has rapidly increased over the past decade, causing a significant change in the purpose(s) of infant assessment. Expansion of intervention programs for atypically developing and high-risk infants has aided in expanding the emphases of infant assessment by creating a demand for data to aid intervention activities. The expanded emphases of infant assessment have occurred in several directions. First, the purpose for infant assessment has become more immediate. Whereas early purposes for infant assessment were for long-term prediction, current assessment purposes are directed at the generation of assessment data to meet current needs. Additionally, whereas early assessment efforts were directed at using a single source of information (i.e., infant performance on test items) to yield a single score (a developmental age score), many current assessment purposes require an array of prenatal, perinatal, and postnatal information to yield a more comprehensive view of infant functioning.

Increased interest in infant intervention has led to the addition of a number of specific purposes for infant assessment. Three such purposes are as follows:

1. To provide a cost-efficient method of reliably *screening* infants in need of further diagnostic assessment (Frankenburg, 1975).
2. To provide information regarding infants' strengths and weaknesses with the results used as a basis for *planning intervention strategies* (Bricker and Littman, 1982).
3. To provide an information base for *evaluating intervention program effectiveness* (Sheehan and Keogh, 1981).

To date, little information is available regarding the ability of specific infant measures to accomplish these expanded purposes of infant assessment. Cross and Johnston (1977) provided an initial source of this information by reviewing 98 early childhood assessment instruments, many of which related to infants, and indicating whether the instruments were primarily useful for screening, diagnosis, or educational programming. Although Cross and Johnston did discuss the use of instruments for evaluation purposes (sometimes called documentation of progress), they did not attempt to classify instruments according to that use. One limitation of the Cross and Johnston classification is that it seems to be based upon comments provided by test publishers or, in the absence of such comments, by the authors' knowledge of the measures. Empirical support for such classification is absent.

Screening   As discussed earlier in this chapter, current assessment efforts are directed at more immediate outcomes than the assessment efforts of previous decades. These current assessment activities are based on an attempt to provide data indicating which infants might benefit from early intervention and also to guide intervention and evaluation efforts.

Neonatal Screening   If long-term prediction were maintained as a primary purpose for neonatal assessment (or assessment of the very young infant), it likely would receive little emphasis among educators. The long-term predictive ability *of any single measure* is marginal when used with almost all but the most profoundly involved neonates.

Despite the obvious shift in emphasis away from long-term prediction as a primary assessment purpose, at least some assumptions of developmental continuity must be at the basis of intervention and assessment; otherwise assessment and intervention would be a totally random process. The answer to this paradox is to be found in the slow but steady expansion of the data base upon which neonatal assessment rests. *No single neonatal index successfully predicts long-term development. A number of neonatal indices, taken in concert, can provide sufficiently reliable prediction to justify and make a strong argument for neonatal assessment and subsequent intervention and/or monitoring.*

Self and Horowitz (1979) delineated reasons for performing neonatal assessments. First, assessments are performed to appraise the clinician of the current developmental status of the child. This information can then form the basis for decisions regarding appropriate treatment for the neonate. Furthermore, results of the assessment may signal professionals that more extensive tests should be performed to answer more specific questions. In addition, neonatal assessment can reflect the environment's effects on the child and in turn supply extensive information to the caregiver about the infant.

This knowledge may be important in promoting interaction between the parent and the child. Finally, neonatal assessment can be used to identify how the child is behaviorally affected by the birth events and how the child makes the necessary adaptation to a new environment.

Traditional neonatal assessments have suffered from two limitations. First, they have yielded rather simple dichotomies as outcomes, indicating whether newborns are typical or atypical. The second limitation of traditional neonatal assessments is that they have yielded such dichotomies based upon single sources of information. The limitations found in several neonatal assessment efforts are typified by using indices such as birthweight (2,000 or 1,500 grams), gestational age (37 weeks), or presence or absence of a particular problem (e.g., respiratory distress syndrome) to categorize infants as high risk or normal (O'Donnell and Gallagher, 1981).

Several methodologies that go beyond yielding dichotomous variables based upon single indices have been used with varying degrees of success as neonatal screening tools. One of the most widely applied screening techniques is the Apgar scoring system (Apgar, 1953). This simple technique involves rating the condition of the newborn at specified time intervals after birth (e.g., most often 1 minute, 5 minutes, and/or 10 minutes) on five signs: heart rate, respiration, reflex irritability, muscle tone, and skin color. Scoring is on a basis of 0, 1, or 2, with 10 the maximum score for the five factors. For example, a child whose heart rate is between 100 and 140 beats per minute is given a score of 2; one whose rate is less than 100 is given a score of 1; and if no heart beat is discerned the child scores 0. For respiration, effortless, regular breathing and lusty crying rate a 2; if the child is apneic a 0 is scored, and anything else is scored 1. This procedure continues for the other three signs, with skin color being the most questionable of the five signs to score. Few infants are entirely pink at 1 minute and, therefore, seldom score a 2 on the initial 1-minute Apgar but do show improvement with the repeated exam. Also, non-white children are difficult to rate (Self and Horowitz, 1979).

The Apgar has predicted infant outcome with some degree of accuracy; low scores are associated with higher mortality rates (Apgar and James, 1962; Apgar et al., 1958). However, the ability of the Apgar to correlate highly with later intellectual measures is mixed. Lower Apgar scores have been found to correlate with lower Bayley Mental and Motor Scale performance at 8 months (Serunian and Broman, 1975); similar results were reported when correlating Apgar scores with Stanford-Binet performance at 4 years of age, with decreasing Apgar scores being associated with lower IQ (Edwards, 1968). However, two similar studies that attempted to relate Apgar scores with later IQ found no significant relationships (Broman et al., 1975; Shipe et al., 1975).

The Apgar as a screening instrument combines a few easy-to-administer factors and is designed to identify quickly children who may require special attention on a 10-point scale. These factors provide information on the state of the child. Because the examination is repeated, a process of change is observed which in a limited way provides a view of the child's adaptive ability.

Another approach to neonatal screening is the use of multiple factors comprised of many prenatal, intrapartum, and postnatal variables (e.g., Problem Oriented Perinatal Risk Assessment [POPRAS]). This screening method is predicated on identifying a high-risk pregnancy by prospective, multifactoral analysis of occurrences during the prenatal and intrapartum periods. It provides the caregiving physician extensive information from which to plan proper intervention if deemed necessary. "By properly utilizing risk assessment we need to rely less on the often erroneous and increasingly outmoded method of clinical impressions based on adjectives and adverbs" (Hobel, 1978, p. 287).

Using a pregnancy screening system as a data organizer, Hobel et al. (1973) followed 738 pregnancies to establish the relationship among infant morbidity, mortality, prenatal, intrapartum, and neonatal factors. Four groups were established on the basis of scoring the multiple variables that discriminate risk pregnancies from normal pregnancies. Of the total group, 46% were low risk for both prenatal and intrapartum factors, and the incidence of high-risk neonates and perinatal mortality was low. For the 18% who were identified as high risk prenatally and low risk during the intrapartum period there was no increase in mortality or incidence of high-risk infants. However, the two remaining groups, the 20% who were identified as high risk for only the intrapartum period and the 20% who were considered high risk in both the prenatal and intrapartum periods, perinatal mortality increased as did the number of high-risk infants. Using a multiple regression model researchers found that the intrapartum score was the best predictor of neonatal risk. The research demonstrated the existence of a continuum of reproductive causality as first postulated by Lilienfeld and Pasamanick (1955).

This method of screening using multiple factors shows promise for identification of high-risk newborns. Furthermore, it demonstrates that prenatal and perinatal events do not occur in isolation and that an accumulation of and/or the interaction of several events influences developmental outcome.

One assessment instrument that is currently receiving wide acceptance as a research and clinical tool is the Neonatal Behavioral Assessment Scale (NBAS) (Brazelton, 1973). The NBAS scores a child's available responses to the environment and, therefore, his/her ability to affect his/her environment. It is more complete than the neurological examinations that account for an infant's reflexes, responsiveness to stimulation, muscle tone, physical condition, and general state (e.g., The Neurological Examination of the Full-Term Infant, Prechtl and Beintema, 1964) in that it examines both neurological responses and general behaviors in 46 items. This more comprehensive view of the infant provides greater information about the child because it samples several aspects of neonatal behavior including interactive processes, motor development, and state control as well as reflex activity.

The NBAS was effective in discriminating behavioral differences in neonates that resulted from maternal medication (Aleksandrowicz and Aleksandrowicz, 1974) as well as in identifying other at-risk infants (Brazelton and Robey, 1965; Tronick and Brazelton, 1975). Presently, the NBAS is used primarily as a research tool. However, given its value in describing behaviors of neonates and the course of their early environmental adaptation, it may be fruitful in providing clinical information to parents and interventionists.

Neonatal assessments, thus, have evolved to include variables that provide a more complete view of the child. Furthermore, in the process of developing infant assessment techniques, we have learned more about infant development in general and the relationships that exist among an infant's behavior, the environment in which he/she functions, and the people with whom he/she interacts.

Infant Screening   One instrument that has received empirical support for its ability to screen older subjects is the Denver Developmental Screening Test. The reliability of the Denver Developmental Screening Test for screening purposes has been demonstrated by Frankenburg et al. (1971b):

> Tester-observer agreement and test-retest stability of the Denver Developmental Screening Test (DDST) were evaluated with 76 and 186 subjects, respectively. The correlation coefficients for mental ages obtained at a 1-week interval were calculated for 13 age groups between .66 and .93 with no age trend displayed (p. 1315).

The validity of the DDST was demonstrated by comparing the performance of 236 children on the DDST with performances on the

Stanford-Binet, Revised Yale Developmental Schedule, Cattell, and the Revised Bayley Infant Scale. Correlations between the DDST and the other tests ranged from .86 to .97. Furthermore, there was agreement between the traditional assessment instruments and the DDST when scoring the DDST using the clinical categories of normal, questionable, or abnormal (Frankenburg et al., 1971a). The DDST can be administered by a variety of assessors including pediatricians, psychologists, educational specialists, and parents. Although not useful as a predictor of later intelligence or behavior (Erikson, 1976), the DDST has support as a screening test for *identifying children who may be developmentally delayed.*

One issue of critical interest to those employing the results of infant screening tools is the use of parent reports in the screening process. Several studies have been conducted during recent years confirming the ability of parents to provide reliable screening information (Blacher-Dixon and Simeonsson, 1981; Gradel et al., 1981). These studies suggest, however, that when parents and diagnosticians disagree about an infant's developmental status, the disagreement is almost always in the direction of parental overestimation (or diagnostician underestimation).

Planning Intervention Strategies   Most of the current interest in assessment exhibited by intervenors is directed toward the purpose of planning intervention strategies. Kaiser and Hayden (1977) indicated this need when they argued that:

> While the environment is important for the normal baby, it becomes critical for the handicapped baby. It will no longer be the case that one of a multitude of reasonably good environments will provide a fertile learning ground. A baby with a handicap is a baby with highly specialized needs. A handicapped baby will likely be far more dependent upon his environment than a normal infant. Some handicapped infants may be totally dependent on their environment to give them the input that they are unable to seek out for themselves. A baby with learning problems may not be able to make much sense out of the world in which so much seems to happen so fast; he may not be able to see the relationships between things that are so important in figuring out how to predict the behaviors of persons and objects. A handicapped baby may need very special teaching (p. 9).

Much of the teaching that goes on with handicapped infants is drawn directly from developmental measures. As Kaiser and Hayden (1977) note, "Special educators try to facilitate the progression of handicapped infants through normal learning sequences that most babies go though naturally" (p. 9).

Few existing infant measures were designed for the purpose of planning educational interventions (Sheehan, 1982). This limitation suggests a number of cautions that must be considered before infant intervenors select a developmental measure for educational planning: Does the measure have enough items to design a comprehensive intervention? Are the items contained within a measure educationally relevant? Do items suitably reflect an intervenor's theoretical rationale or view of child development? Unfortunately, the answers to these questions are not immediately forthcoming.

One infant measure that has great potential for use in planning educational intervention is the Adaptive Performance Inventory (CAPE, 1977). This instrument contains over 400 items, many of which are considered educationally relevant and teachable. Field testing of this instrument is still occurring although initial analyses of the Adaptive Performance Inventory are quite positive.

Bricker and Littman (1982) have recently discussed strategies for the use of assessment data for instructional planning purposes. As they indicated, individual educational plans are developed and revised in response to daily, weekly, and quarterly assessment of children and infants. Furthermore, Bagnato (1981) commented on the use of developmental scales in curricular planning. As the result of a study with 48 early childhood special education teachers, he framed the following guidelines:

1. Select scales that match the curriculum employed within the early intervention program, that is, those that are developmentally sequenced, cover multiple functional domains, and sample congruent tasks and processes.
2. Choose a diagnostic battery composed of a variety of measures reflecting both *qualitative* and *quantitative* child performance data. The use of adaptive process measures enhances this aspect.
3. Organize developmental diagnostic reports by multiple behavioral domains rather than by the individual measures given to facilitate the synthesis of child data, comprehensive coverage, and a balanced curriculum-area goal planning.
4. Report developmental ages (DA) for *each* functional area rather than a global developmental quotient (DQ) to portray general child functioning. Research indicates that no unitary factor of infant intelligence ("g") exists.
5. Provide a behavioral narrative that discusses in detail the strengths, weaknesses, needed management, strategies, and modes of operation that characterize the child's developmental functioning within each area.
6. Use "advance" or "summary" organizers for highlighting critical child performance data to guide assessment-curriculum link-

ages, that is lists of developmental ceilings, functional levels, skills sequences, and instructional needs (p. 7).

Evaluating Intervention Program Effectiveness We are not aware of any assessment measures that have been developed for the specific purpose of evaluating the effect of intervention or of any measure that has been empirically determined to be reliable and valid for evaluation purposes with an atypical infant population. Keogh and Sheehan (1981) specifically discuss limitations of developmental data for evaluation purposes, as do Sheehan and Gallagher (1982). The consensus among those authors is that developmental data are necessary but insufficient indices of the effects of early intervention. Keogh and Sheehan (1981) emphasize that critical issues related to assessment for evaluation purposes may have more to do with the evaluation perspectives of intervenors than the actual measures available to them. They note:

> We conclude by arguing that both psychometric and alternative assessment techniques are useful in documenting handicapped children's progress and in demonstrating program impact. In our view, the continuing debate as to the "validity" of developmental tests is specious. More important questions have to do with the appropriateness of exclusive reliance on specific techniques, with the inferences drawn from the data, and with the purposes for which the data are used. Whatever the techniques, the documentation of child progress is difficult. It requires sensitivity yet objectivity, and it is a demanding and time-consuming process. It seems possible that the problems relate less to the actual tests or techniques used and more to the frame of mind the intervenor beings to the documentation task. Effective intervention programs may well require real commitment and a belief that the practices will be effective. While important as a clinical influence, this attitude or "set" makes objective evaluations particularly difficult (p. 46).

Summary of Concerns about the Purposes of Infant Assessment

We suggest a number of cautions that must be applied to the use of infant measures. Cautions are necessary as most infant measures were not designed to provide guidance to intervenors and evaluators. Also, test items of many standard measures are often "high frequency" items that have little or no teachability value and are not sensitive to intervention efforts. The following is a summary of our cautions:

1. The original purposes guiding the development of infant measures, the description and long-term prediction of typical infant performance, are quite different from many current uses of in-

fant measures and may not effectively support those current uses (Brooks-Gunn and Lewis, 1981; Keogh and Sheehan, 1981; Sheehan, 1982). Infant intervenors must carefully consider the content and procedures of any measure to ensure its relevance to their current assessment purpose.

2. Most infant measures historically have used a similar sequence of arranging test items in a presumed or verified developmental sequence and assessed infants' performance relative to that sequence (Johnson and Kopp, 1979). The use of presumed developmental continuum, although appropriate for most children, obscures the possibility of differing profiles or patterns for some children. Such profiles or patterns may be observable through preservation of data in item form and consideration of factors such as infant range and density of performance (see Keogh and Sheehan, 1981).

3. Factors specific to the testing situation (e.g., home versus lab testing or training of examiners) may have as much of an effect on infant test performance as the effects of intervention (Durham and Black, 1978; Gradel et al., 1981; Simeonsson et al., 1980). Such factors must be considered in any assessment effort, particularly a data collection effort involving repeated assessments across intervention.

4. The information needs of infant intervenors (i.e., extensive information regarding infant performance under a variety of conditions) may at times conflict with the outcome of standard developmental assessment. Such assessment typically is conducted yielding a single score which holds environmental factors constant. This approach provides minimal information to intervenors. By attending to item performance, selecting measures with reliable subscores and engaging in repeated assessments under differing contexts, intervenors can partially compensate for this conflict.

Despite our identification of these cautions, we are not entirely pessimistic about the usefulness of existing infant measures for accomplishing the expanded objectives of infant assessment. Our experiences with many infant intervenors have left us impressed with their clinical skills and confident in their ability to successfully design infant intervention programs. Many assessors are successfully confronting problems in infant measurement and arriving at resolutions, albeit partial solutions, to ensure useful assessment of infants.

Additionally, new instruments are continually being developed.

We estimate that as many as 300 infant assessment measures currently exist with many new measures being proposed each year. Although the psychometric characteristics of most of these measures are suspect, we are optimistic that continued effort in this regard will result in infant measures designed to accommodate the variety of purposes of infant assessment.

CLASSIFICATION OF INFANT MEASURES

Several reviews of infant assessment instruments have appeared in recent years. These include the annotated bibliographies of Cross and Johnston (1977), Johnson and Kopp (1979), and Walls et al. (1977). They also include the summarization of developmental items across assessment measures reported by Cohen and Gross (1979) and Sheehan's (1982) identification of emergent trends in infant assessment. Such reviews provide useful sources of information about the range, content, and psychometric characteristics of specific infant measures.

The field of early education currently is lacking a clear empirically validated taxonomy of assessment instruments. Such a taxonomy would indicate categories and subcategories of measures yielding an orderly classification of assessment tools. In attempting to develop classifications of measures, we considered and rejected a number of alternatives. We rejected the approach chosen by Cross and Johnston (1977) to categorize measures by purpose as so little data exist supporting the argument that particular instruments are useful for one purpose but not another (e.g., the Denver Development Screening Test is used as a screening measure but has also been used to successfully demonstrate child change). We also rejected the approach common in the field of psychology to classify measures by characteristics of examiners, as many instruments used in the early education area are administered by all types of examiners (e.g., the Developmental Profile is used by parents, aides, teachers, evaluators, and others).

We wanted to suggest a classification of measures in a fashion relevant to intervenors yet defensible on the basis of actual characteristics of the measures (rather than their type of usage or user). We are suggesting one method of classifying measures while recognizing that at this point our choice is somewhat arbitrary. We hope that additional classification schemes will be developed, eventually resulting in a validated taxonomy of instruments. The first classification scheme we suggest differentiates between domain-referenced, criterion-referenced, and norm-referenced measures used in infant assessment.

Domain-Referenced Measures

Domain-referenced measures consist of a collection of test items that assess performance of an individual *relative to a well-defined behavioral domain*. The defining characteristic of a domain-referenced measure is the inclusion as test items of an entire domain of functioning. If the content area being measured by a domain-referenced test is fine motor performance, then a domain-referenced test should have *all* items relevant to find motor performance for the age group of the tested individual.

A domain-referenced measure is useful because it provides a clear indication of what an infant can and cannot do. To accomplish this, the test must be more than a random set of items and more than a random sample of items from a larger domain. Rather, the domain-referenced measure must accurately reflect an entire domain of functioning. In most cases, items contained within a domain-referenced measure are educationally relevant, although this requirement is not part of the defining characteristic of a domain-referenced measure (Sheehan, 1982).

The requirement that domain-referenced measures totally represent a domain of functioning is more an ideal than a fact for most of the domain-referenced infant measures in early childhood special education. Very few measures do (or can) accurately represent an entire domain of functioning as infant development is so complex and reflects a range of developmental processes including maturation, learning, and environmental interactions. For example, no infant measures totally represent the area of cognitive development, although several measures represent it more extensively than others. The recently developed Adaptive Performance Inventory (CAPE, 1977) and the Infant Learning Accomplishment Profile (Griffin and Sanford, 1975) are two measures that have an unusually large number of items for assessing infant performance.

A well-developed domain-referenced measure is clearly useful for instructional planning purposes. Intervenors must recognize that several domain-referenced measures (e.g., the Uniform Performance Assessment System) do also provide rather general norms in the form of developmental age scores, although such scores are not nearly as important for the measure as is item performance and curricular planning. The rapid expansion that we have seen in the area of infant assessment is largely due to an increase in these domain-referenced measures (Sheehan, 1982).

Criterion-Referenced Measures

Criterion-referenced measures are similar to domain-referenced measures with the exception that they have an additional defining characteristic. In addition to assessing performance of an individual *relative to a well-defined behavioral domain, they also indicate mastery/nonmastery for the individual.* Said differently, they provide an overall indication of pass/fail performance on a well-defined behavioral domain.

Criterion-referenced measures were developed during the rapid expansion of competency-based educational programs, programs in which all content of instruction was specified along with measurable objectives and an a priori criterion of pass or fail. Public schools became very involved in this type of education during the early 1970s.

Glaser and Klaus (1962) were among the first to apply the term *criterion-referenced measures* to tests designed to assess individuals' proficiency on an entire domain of behavioral items. The purpose of these tests was to determine whether the individuals had mastered those domains, thus categorizing the individuals as either proficient or nonproficient. For example, mastery of 85% of the items might be considered sufficient for success. All students taking a test could achieve such mastery or no students might achieve such mastery; the criterion score (85%) would stay constant. Reliability and validity concerns of criterion-referenced tests refer to the items within the domain of the measure as well as the mastery/nonmastery cutoff score. Since the conception of criterion-referenced measures, a number of authors, including Popham and Husek (1969), Millman (1974), and Popham (1978), have discussed salient characteristics of the measures.

As indicated earlier, domain-referenced measures differ from criterion-referenced measures in that they represent an entire domain of desired behavioral items, although no claim is made as to a mastery/nonmastery criterion. Recently Popham (1978) concluded that although important distinctions could be made between domain- and criterion-referenced measures, it would be unfortunate to do so as the public would likely only be confused by such a distinction.

Although we are sympathetic to Popham's comments regarding public confusion, we hesitate to overlook differences between criterion-referenced and domain-referenced measures because in early childhood such testing rarely involves an a priori criterion of mastery/nonmastery. Overall statements of success and failure are uncommon in early childhood. Rather, infants and children are assessed continually and then taught individual items or clusters of items that have been failed. These assessment strategies often labeled criterion-referenced in early childhood simply reflect performance of individual children relative to a well-defined behavioral domain and, as such, should appropriately be called domain-referenced measures. Accordingly, we do not have examples to cite of criterion-referenced measures.

Norm-Referenced Measures

Norm-referenced measures are different in construction and purpose from criterion-referenced and domain-referenced measures. They also have two defining characteristics: They provide an assessment of an individual's performance *relative to a norming population of other individuals* on a *sampling of items from a larger behavioral domain*. Tests such as these were among the first formal tests to be developed and they have been used in psychology and education to yield a relative ordering of individuals. Norm-referenced measures provide a prediction of success or failure (relative to a norming population) provided that the rank performance of individuals stays constant across time. In contrast, criterion-referenced measures provide an indication of success or failure relative to item content.

Norm-referenced measures are primarily useful in screening and diagnosis. Most classification schemes for disabilities are based on a normative model, which identifies disabled individuals as individuals whose developmental performance differs significantly from the general population. Screening and diagnosis are integral parts of these classification schemes. Examples of norm-referenced infant measures include the Bayley Scales of Infant Development (Bayley, 1969) and the Gesell Developmental Schedules (Gesell and Amatruda, 1941).

The distinction between criterion-referenced and norm-referenced measures becomes clear when one realizes that a developer of a norm-referenced test would despair if all students passed 85% of the test, as the purpose of the test is to space individuals out in a relative ordering on sampled items. Generalizations are made as to the relative ability levels of the individuals on the larger domain of items (most of which are never actually tested with students).

The actual content of a measure is an important point of difference between norm-referenced and either criterion-referenced or
domain-referenced measures. To accomplish its purpose (yielding a
relative ordering of individuals), a norm-referenced measure is developed by sampling items from a larger behavioral domain, with
items chosen because they effectively discriminate among individuals at the time of testing (thereby allowing infant A to be viewed
as superior to infant B, or superior to 85% of infants in the norming
population). The index of success for a norm-referenced measure is
that the relative ordering of infants be stable across time.

The distinctions between criterion- or domain-referenced measures and norm-referenced instruments point to important differences
in their usefulness. These differences depend on the purpose of assessment. A norm-referenced measure might have few teachable
items and, therefore, provide little guidance for instructional planning other than a sense that an infant needs intervention (i.e., the
infant is functioning very low compared to the norm), or that one
infant needs intervention more than another infant. A domain- or
criterion-referenced measure is likely to be longer than a norm-
referenced measure, have far more items at a given age range, and
therefore, be unwieldy for a diagnostic or screening assessment.

Just as criticism could be leveled at domain- and criterion-
referenced measures, so also could fault be found with norm-referenced measures. How representative a sample are items on standard
norm-referenced measures? We suspect that some sampling may
have occurred long ago in the development of infant measures, but
that many current norm-referenced measures have chosen items because they were found on earlier measures. The claim is heard all
too often that a measure is reliable and valid because it contains
items drawn from previously validated measures.

The approach taken in reviewing infant measures is to view
norm-referenced and domain- or criterion-referenced as two points
along a continuum with many instruments being more domain-
referenced than norm-referenced and vice versa. An ultimate selection of a measure should be based upon a careful review of its
contents and procedures rather than its position at either end of this
continuum.

SUMMARY AND CONCLUSIONS

Now is an exciting time to be working in the area of infant assessment. We have seen dramatic changes occurring in the purposes of
infant assessment—changes that have broadened the applications of

assessment data. Although current instrumentation does not yet adequately support the broadened purposes of infant assessment, we are confident that the needs of intervenors and others concerned with infant assessment will provide the necessary motivation to ensure that adequate instrumentation is developed during the next decade.

We conclude with the concern that infant intervenors must become more discriminating in their selection of infant measures and in their requests for such measures from test developers. A large number of "instruments" exist that are infant measures in name only. In fact they represent a collection of items with little regard for sequencing, integration, and working of items or of the overall reliability and validity of measures. We are optimistic that these "instruments" will become more psychometrically sophisticated as intervenors insist on being provided sound measurement tools.

Chapter Outline

OVERVIEW: The purposes of assessing infants are listed and a classification system for measures is provided.

I.   THE PURPOSE OF INFANT ASSESSMENT

   A.   Early views regarding infant assessment focused on attempts to demonstrate the continuity of intelligence from infancy to adulthood and later, on the use of assessment to chart the course of development. The capability of infant assessments to predict future child performance was found to be low.

   B.   Current views regarding the purpose of infant assessment include the following three purposes:

      1.   Screening

      2.   Planning intervention strategies

      3.   Evaluating intervention program effectiveness

II.   CLASSIFICATION OF INFANT MEASURES

Infant assessment measures are catalogued and described according to the following classification system:

   A.   Domain-referenced measures

   B.   Criterion-referenced measures

   C.   Norm-referenced measures

REFERENCES

Aleksandrowicz, M. K., and Aleksandrowicz, D. R. Obstetrical pain-relieving drugs as predictors of infant behavior variability. *Child Development*, 1974, 45, 935–945.

Apgar, V. A proposal for a new method of resolution of the newborn infant. *Current Researchers in Anesthesia and Analgesia*, 1953, 32, 260–267.

Apgar, V., Holaday, D. A., James, L. S., et al. Evaluation of the newborn infant—second report. *Journal of the American Medical Association*, 1958, 168, 1985–1988.

Apgar, V., and James, L. S. Further observations on the newborn scoring system. *American Journal of Diseases of Children*, 1962, 104, 419–428.

Bagnato, S. Developmental scales and developmental curricula: Forging a linkage for early intervention. *Topics in Early Childhood Special Education*, 1981, 1(2), 1–8.

Bayley, N. *Manual for the Bayley Scales of Infant Development.* New York: Psychological Corp., 1969.

Blacher-Dixon, J., and Simeonsson, R. Consistency and correspondence of mothers' and teachers' assessments of young handicapped children. *Journal of the Division of Early Childhood*, 1981, 3, 64–71.

Brazelton, T. B. *Neonatal Behavioral Assessment Scale.* National Spastics Society Monograph. Philadelphia: Lippincott, 1973.

Brazelton, T. B., and Roby, J. S. Observations of neonatal behavior. *Journal of the American Academy of Child Psychiatry*, 1965, 4, 613.

Bricker, D., and Littman, D. Intervention and evaluation: The inseparable mix. *Topics in Early Childhood Special Education*, 1982, 2(4), 23–34.

Broman, S., Nichols, P., and Kennedy, W. A. *Preschool IQ: Prenatal and Early Development Correlates.* Hillsdale, NJ: Erlbaum, 1975.

Brooks-Gunn, J., and Lewis, M. Assessing young handicapped children: Issues and solutions. *Journal of the Division for Early Childhood*, 1981, 2, 84–95.

Brooks, J., and Weinraub, M. A history of infant intelligence testing. In M. Lewis (Ed.), *Origins of Intelligence.* New York: Plenum Press, 1976.

CAPE (Consortium on Adaptive Performance Evaluation). *Adaptive Assessment for Evaluating the Progress of Severely/Profoundly Handicapped Children Functioning between Birth and 2 Years.* The annual reports of a field-initiated research project funded by the Bureau of Education for the Handicapped, Grant No. GD07702139, 1977.

Cohen, M., and Gross, P. *The Developmental Resource: Behavioral Sequences for Assessment and Program Planning* (Vol. 1). New York: Grune & Stratton, 1979.

Cross, L., and Johnston, S. A bibliography of instruments. In L. Cross and K. Roin (Eds.), *Identifying Handicapped Children: A Guide to Case-Finding, Screening, Diagnosis, Assessment, and Evaluation.* New York: Walker Publishing, 1977.

Dunst, C., and Rheingrover, R. Discontinuity and instability in early development: Implications for assessment. *Topics in Early Childhood Special Education*, 1981, 1(2), 49–60.

Durham, M., and Black, K. The test performance of 16- to 21-month-olds in home and laboratory settings. *Infant Behavior and Development*, 1978, 1, 216–223.

Edwards, N. The relationship between physical condition immediately after birth and mental and motor performance at age four. *Genetic Psychology Monographs*, 1968, *78*, 27–289.

Erikson, M. L. *Assessment and Management of Development Changes in Children*. St. Louis: Mosby, 1976.

Frankenburg, W. K. Criteria in screening test selection. In W. K. Frankenburg and B. W. Camp (Eds.), *Pediatric Screening Tests*. Springfield, IL: Charles C Thomas, 1975.

Frankenburg, W. K., Camp, B. W., and Van Natta, P. A. Validity of the Denver Developmental Screening Test. *Child Development*, 1971a, *42*, 475–485.

Frankenburg, W. K., Camp, B. S., Van Natta, P. A., and Demersseman, J. A. Reliability and stability of the Denver Developmental Screening Test. *Child Development*, 1971b, *42*, 1315–1325.

Gesell, A., and Amatruda, C. S. *Developmental Diagnosis*. New York: Hoeber, 1941.

Glaser, R., and Klaus, D. Proficiency measurement: Assessing human performance. In R. M. Gagne (Ed.), *Psychological Principles in Systems Development*. New York: Holt, Rinehart, and Winston, 419–474.

Gradel, K., Thompson, M., and Sheehan, R. Parental and professional agreement in early childhood assessment. *Topics in Early Childhood Special Education*, 1981, *1*(2), 31–40.

Griffin, P., and Sanford, A. *Learning Accomplishment Profile*. Winston-Salem, NC: Kaplan Press, 1975.

Hambleton, R., Swaminathan, H., Algina, J., and Coulson, D. Criterion-referenced testing and measurement: A review of technical issues and developments. *Review of Educational Research*, 1978, *48*, 147.

Hobel, C. J. Risk assessment in perinatal medicine. *Clinical Obstetrics and Gynecology*, 1978, *21*, 287–295.

Hobel, C. J., Hyvarineu, M. A., Okada, D. M., and Oh, W. Prenatal and ultrapartum high-risk screening. *American Journal of Obstetrics and Gynecology*, 1973, *117*, 1–9.

Honzik, M. P. Value and limitations of infant tests: An overview. In M. Lewis (Ed.), *Origins of Intelligence*. New York: Plenum Press, 1976.

Johnson, K., and Kopp, C. *A Bibliography of Screening and Assessment Measures for Infants*. Unpublished manuscript, 1979.

Kaiser, C., and Hayden, A. The education of the very, very young or but what can you teach an infant? *Educational Horizons*, 1977, *56*(1), 4–15.

Keogh, B., and Sheehan, R. The uses and limitations of developmental data in documenting early intervention. *Journal of Division for Early Childhood*, 1981, *3*, 42–47.

Lewis, M. The development of attention and perception in the infant and young child. In W. M. Cruickshank and D. P. Hallahan (Eds.), *Perceptual and Learning Disabilities in Children* (Vol. 2). Syracuse, NY: Syracuse University Press, 1975.

Lilienfeld, A. M., and Pasamanick, B. The association of maternal and fetal factors with the development of mental deficiency. *American Journal of Obstetrics and Gynecology*, 1955, *60*, 557–569.

McCall, R. B. The development of intellectual functioning in infancy and the prediction of later I.Q. In J. Osofsky (Ed.), *Handbook of Infant Development*. New York: Wiley, 1979.

McCall, R. B., Hogarty, P. S., and Hurlburt, N. Transitions in infant sensorimotor development. *Monographs of the Society for Research in Child Development*, 1977, 42(171).

Meier, J. H. Screening, assessment and intervention for young children at developmental risk. In N. Hobbs (Ed.), *Issues in the Classification of Children* (Vol. 2). San Francisco: Jossey-Bass, 1975.

Meier, J. H. Screening, assessment and intervention for young children at developmental risk. In T. D. Tjossem (Ed.), *Intervention Strategies for High-Risk Infants and Young Children*. Baltimore: University Park Press, 1976.

Millman, J. Criterion-referenced measurement. In W. J. Popham (Ed.), *Evaluation in Education: Current Applications*. Berkeley, CA: McCutcheon, 1974.

O'Donnell, K. E., and Gallagher, R. J. *Psychoeducational Intervention with the High-Risk Infant: Methods and Issues*. Paper presented at the Southeast Psychological Association, Atlanta, 1981.

Popham, W. *Criterion-Referenced Measurement*. Englewood Cliffs, NJ: Prentice-Hall, 1978.

Popham, W., and Husek, T. Implications of criterion-referenced measurement. *Journal of Educational Measurement*, 1969, 6, 1–9.

Prechtl, H. F. R., and Beintema, D. The neurological examination of the full-term newborn infant. In *Clinics in Developmental Medicine* (No. 12). London: Spastics International Medical Publications, William Heimemann Medical Books, 1964.

Scarr-Salapatek, S. An evolutionary perspective on infant intelligence: Species patterns and individual variations. In M. Lewis (Ed.), *Origins of Intelligence*. New York: Plenum Press, 1976.

Self, P. A., and Horowitz, F. D. The behavioral assessment of the neonate: An overview. In J. Osofsky (Ed.), *The Handbook of Infant Development*. New York: Wiley, 1979.

Serunian, S. A., and Broman, S. H. Relationship of Apgar scores and Bayley mental and motor scores. *Child Development*, 1975, 46, 696–700.

Sheehan, R. Infant assessment: A review and identification of emergent trends. In D. Bricker (Ed.), *Application of Research Findings to Intervention with At-Risk and Handicapped Infants*. Baltimore: University Park Press, 1982.

Sheehan, R., and Gallagher, R. J. Conducting evaluations of infant intervention programs. In S. G. Garwood and R. Fewell (Eds.), *Educating Handicapped Infants*. Rockville, MD: Aspen Systems, 1983.

Sheehan, R., and Keogh, B. Design and analysis in the evaluation of early childhood special education programs. *Topics in Early Childhood Special Education*, 1981, 1(4), 81–88.

Shipe, D., Vandenberg, S., and Williams, R. D. P. Neonatal Apgar scores and Bayley mental and motor scores. *Child Development*, 1975, 46, 696–700.

Simeonsson, R. J., Huntington, G. S., and Parse, S. A. Assessment of children with severe handicaps: Multiple problems—multipariate goals. *TASA*, 1980, 6, 55–72.

Tronick, E., and Brazelton, T. B. Clinical uses of the Brazelton Neonatal Behavioral Assessment. In B. Z. Friedlander, G. M. Sterritt, and G. E. Kirk (Eds.), *Exceptional Infant* (Vol. III). New York: Bruner/Mazel, 1975.

Walls, R., Werner, T., Bacon, A., and Zane, T. Behavior checklists. In J. Cone and R. Hawkins (Eds.), *Behavioral Assessment: New Directions in Clinical Psychology*. New York: Brunner/Mazel, 1977.

Appendix

BIBLIOGRAPHY OF SELECTED INFANT MEASURES

As indicated earlier in this chapter, a number of reviews of infant intelligence measures have appeared in recent years. Readers are referred to those reviews for extensive listings of infant measures. The following are the characteristics of 13 of the infant measures that seem to be most frequently used throughout the country. Each of the instruments below is supported by at least some reliability and validity data. We caution readers interested in any specific measure to carefully review the reliability and validity data for that measure to determine whether the measure will be appropriate for its desired use.

Alpern-Boll Developmental Profile
    Type of Measure: norm-referenced
    Age Range: birth to 60 months
    Content Areas: language, gross motor, fine motor, self-help, academic
    Available from: Psychological Development Publications
        7150 Lakeside Drive
        Indianapolis, IN 46278

Bayley Scales of Infant Development
    Type of Measure: norm-referenced
    Age Range: birth to 36 months
    Content Areas: mental, motor, behavior
    Available from: The Psychological Corporation
        1372 Peachtree Street, N.E.
        Atlanta, GA 30309

Brigance Diagnostic Inventory of Early Development
    Type of Measure: domain-referenced
    Age Range: birth to 72 months
    Content Areas: psychomotor, self-help, speech and language, general knowledge and comprehension, early academic skills
    Available from: Curriculum Associates, Inc.
        Woburn, MA 01801

Callier-Azusa Scales
    Type of Measure: domain-referenced
    Age Range: birth to adult
    Content Areas: motor, perceptual, daily living, language, socialization
    Available from: Callier Center for Communication Disorders
        University of Texas/Dallas
        1966 Inwood Road
        Dallas, TX 75235

Cattell Infant Intelligence Scale
    Type of Measure: norm-referenced
    Age: 2 months to 30 months
    Content Area: cognitive
    Available from: The Psychological Corporation
        1327 Peachtree Street, N.E.
        Atlanta, GA 30309

Denver Developmental Screening Test
    Type of Measure: norm-referenced
    Age Range: birth to 72 months
    Content Areas: gross motor, fine motor, receptive and expressive language, personal-social
    Available from: Ladoca Project and Publishing Foundation
                     East 51st Street and Lincoln
                     Denver, CO 80216
Gesell Developmental Schedules
    Type of Measure: norm-referenced
    Age Range: birth to 36 months
    Content Areas: gross motor, fine motor, receptive and expressive language, cognitive, self-help, personal-social
    Available from: The Psychological Corporation
                     1327 Peachtree Street, N.E.
                     Atlanta, Georgia 30309
Griffith's Mental Developmental Scale
    Type of Measure: norm-referenced
    Age Range: birth to 24 months
    Content Areas: gross motor, fine motor, receptive and expressive language, cognitive, self-help, personal-social
    Available from: Western Psychological Services
                     12031 Wilshire Boulevard
                     Los Angeles, CA 90025
Learning Accomplishment Profile for Infants
    Type of Measure: domain-referenced
    Age Range: birth to 36 months
    Content Areas: gross motor, fine motor, social, self-help, cognitive, language
    Available from: Kaplan School Supply Corporation
                     600 Jonestown Rd.
                     Winston Salem, NC 27103
Memphis Comprehensive Developmental Scale
    Type of Measure: domain-referenced
    Age Range: birth to 60 months
    Content Areas: gross motor, fine motor, receptive and expressive language, cognitive, self-help, personal social
    Available from: Fearon Publishers
                     6 Davis Drive
                     Belmont, CA 94002
Milani-Comparetti Motor Development Screening Test
    Type of Measure: norm-referenced
    Age Range: birth to 24 months
    Content Area: gross motor
    Available from: Meyer Children's Rehabilitation Institute
                     University of Nebraska Medical Center
                     Omaha, NB 69131
Portage Behavior Checklist
    Type of Measure: domain-referenced
    Age Range: birth to 60 months

Content Areas: infant stimulation, socialization, language, self-help,
    cognitive, motor
Available from: Portage Project
                412 East Slifer St.
                Portage, WI 53901
Vineland Social Maturity Scale
    Type of Measure: norm-referenced
    Age Range: birth to adult
    Content Area: self-help
    Available from: American Guidance Service Inc.
                Publishers Building
                Circle Pines, MN 55014

SECTION III
DEVELOPMENTAL ISSUES

The potential effects of disability cannot be fully understood without a knowledge of the normal course of development. This section, thus, presents descriptions of developmental trends and markers in various behavioral domains and relates how conditions posing developmental risk to the infant may alter the developmental course. In each developmental area implications for assessment and intervention efforts are considered.

Hanson and Hanline (Chapter 5) introduce this section with an outline of the typical infant's sensory-perceptual development and information processing skills, and a review of sensorimotor development. They follow with descriptive information on the developmental effects of specific disabilities and a consideration of developmental outcomes for disabled children.

In Chapter 6 Hanson discusses one of the most crucial factors in the young child's development—the parent-infant interactional system. The challenges faced by parents of atypical infants are explored and implications for intervention are derived.

The remaining chapters in this section are devoted to issues within specific developmental areas. Rothbart (Chapter 7) discusses the course of normal social development and the importance of the social/affective system in determining the atypical infant's ability to adapt to the environment. Ramey, Breitmayer, and Goldman in Chapter 8 review learning and cognition during infancy from four theoretical approaches—psychometric, constructivist, behavioral, and information processing—and analyze assessment and intervention practices. The interrelationships between cognitive and language development are described further by Bricker, Levin, and Macke in Chapter 9. They review prelinguistic and early language developmental goals and draw implications for devising speech and language intervention strategies. Finally, developmental issues in the area of motor development are discussed by Fetters in Chapter 10. She reviews normal motor developmental sequences and defines guidelines for assessment and intervention in this area.

CHAPTER 5

Behavioral Competencies and Outcomes
The Effects of Disorders

Marci J. Hanson and Mary Frances Hanline

Scientists have begun to verify what parents, grandparents, and other astute observers of infant bvehavior have long acknowledged: the active, organized behavior of the infant. Although expectations before experience with an infant may reflect James' (1890) view of the infant's world as a buzzing confusion, careful observation of even the newborn infant reveals a human being who is capable of active responding and initiation.

As a result of a surge in infancy research, contemporary articles typically extol the abilities of the infant. The phrase "the competent infant" has become commonplace in this literature, with "competent" used to describe the active, perceiving, learning, information organizing infant who is capable of modifying and being modified by the immediate environment. The normal infant, thus, enters the world with a developing set of perceptual and behavioral competencies that allow the infant to interact with and control the world around him/her. However, when development fails to proceed according to the normative course due to either sensory deficits, information processing disorders, or general developmental delays, the ensuing limitations to the infant's behavioral repertoire may require extraordinary efforts or interventions to achieve an optimal developmental outcome.

Lest the developmental prognosis for babies who are at risk for delay or disabled be seen as severely limited and unidirectional, the discussion in this chapter describes both the similarities and the differences in the development of atypical infants as compared with normal babies. This analysis of the behavior of the at-risk and disabled infant reveals that although the mode of response or means of acquiring information may differ, similar behavioral outcomes may be accomplished. Understanding these developmental similarities and differences allows for the design of more effective and desirable interventions—interventions that highlight the dynamic, interactional qualities of the child's development.

The chapter is divided into four sections. The first section presents a review of the sensory and perceptual competencies of the normal infant and discussions of sensorimotor development and information gathering and processing mechanisms. The impact of disabling conditions (e.g., sensory impairment, motor disability, and cognitive delay) is discussed in the second section. The third and fourth sections relate this descriptive evidence to issues of determining developmental outcomes for at-risk and disabled infants and implications for intervention design and implementation.

THE NORMAL INFANT

One cannot fully understand the potential effects of a disability without a thorough knowledge of what constitutes the normal course of development. Therefore, we have chosen to provide a brief account of the "normal" perceptual and sensory capabilities of the young infant and a descriptive outline of sensorimotor developmental milestones and information processing abilities. More thorough reviews of the capabilities of the young infant are found in several major review papers (Appleton et al., 1975; Kessen et al., 1970; McCluskey, 1981; Reese and Lipsitt, 1970). Furthermore, a list of normal developmental milestones or pinpoints (Cohen et al., 1976) is supplied for reference in the Appendix to this chapter. The brief description of the infant's sensory-perceptual development in the first year immediately follows.

Sensory-Perceptual Development

Visual Development   The development of an infant's visual system begins during the first month of gestation. At birth, the system is immature in that the optic nerve is incompletely mylenated, and the structure of the newborn's eye differs from that of an adult in a number of ways. Retinal cellular structures are not completely differentiated; the diameter of the infant's eye is smaller than that of the adult; the pupillary opening is smaller than that of the adult; and the macular area is not fully pigmented (Reese and Lipsitt, 1970). In addition, the refractive index of the cornea produces a tendency toward hyperopia or farsightedness (Mann, 1964; Spears and Hohle, 1967). However, at birth the infant is able to respond differentially to various aspects of visual stimuli and during the first 4 months of life, the fovea undergoes cellular changes (Mann, 1964) and the infant's ability to focus comes to approximate adult performance (Haynes et al., 1965; White, 1971).

At birth, an infant has a focal distance of approximately 19 centimeters (Haynes et al., 1965); the visual acuity range has been reported from 20/800 (Fantz et al., 1962) to 20/150 (Dayton et al., 1964a). Neonates are able to follow a moving stimulus (Dayton et al., 1964b), but convergence occurs irregularly at this age (Hershenson, 1964; Wickelgren, 1967). By 1 month of age an infant spends approximately 5 to 10% of the time scanning the visual field and by 2½ months this increases to approximately 35% (White, 1971). At this age, an infant tends to scan external elements of the stimuli (Milewski, 1976) with more horizontal than vertical scans (Salapatek and Kessen, 1966).

Neonates also are capable of responding differentially to various aspects of visual stimuli. A newborn infant responds to changes in light intensity and is attracted to bright light, but prefers a light of moderate brightness (Blanton, 1917; Hershenson, 1964; Sherman et al., 1936). This sensitivity to brightness increases during the first 4 months of life and allows the infant to respond to weaker intensities of light (Doris and Cooper, 1966). Neonates also are able to discriminate colors (Barnet et al., 1965; Jones-Molfese, 1977; Werner and Wooten, 1979) and actually show preferences for certain colors with gray being preferred the least (Staples, 1932). In addition, newborns show a preference for moving stimuli (Ames and Silfen, 1965), a preference for patterned over nonpatterned stimuli (Brennan et al., 1966; Fantz, 1958, 1963), and a preference for three-dimensional over two-dimensional stimuli (Fantz, 1961; Fantz and Nevis, 1967). One-month-old infants respond to a live face by fixating or showing arousal (Stechler and Latz, 1966) and respond in the same manner to a schematic drawing of a face (Fantz, 1963). Scanning at 3 and 7 weeks tends to be focused on the eye region of the face (Bergman et al., 1971; Wolff, 1963).

By the age of 3 months, convergence is well-developed in infants (Coakes et al., 1979). They anticipate regular movements of light (Nelson, 1968), visually pursue objects as they are brought near and taken farther away, follow a visual arc of 180 degrees (Gesell et al., 1949; Ling, 1942), and perceive figures as being the same across rotational transformations (Caron et al., 1979). Infants of this age prefer regular faces over distorted faces and abstract stimuli (McCall and Kagan, 1967), discriminate faces at 0-degree, 90-degree, and 180-degree angles (Watson, 1966), discriminate eyes as a separate facial feature (Fantz, 1967; Spitz, 1965), and tend to respond along a continuum of "faceness" rather than complexity (Haaf and Bell, 1967; McCall and Kagan, 1967).

By the age of 4 months, an infant's ability to focus approximates adult performance (White, 1971; Haynes et al., 1965), an infant focuses on both internal and external elements of stimuli (Milewski, 1976; Salapatek, 1972), and an infant is able to recognize familiar visual stimuli (Pancratz and Cohen, 1970). At 5 months, the infant is able to recognize stimuli even after a 2-hour interval (Fagan, 1970) and discriminates the mouth as a separate facial feature (Fantz, 1967; Spitz, 1965). An infant is capable of discriminating faces of different ages and sexes by 5½ months (Fagan and Shephard, 1979; Fagan and Singer, 1979) and facial expressions by 7 months (Fantz, 1967; Spitz, 1965). An infant of 7 months also is able to recognize a picture of a face as being the same when presented as a profile and a three-quarter view (Fagan, 1978). Thus, before the first birthday the infant displays a wide range of visual capabilities which allow for exploration of the environment, particularly the social aspects.

Auditory Development   The anatomy of the auditory system is completely developed before birth, and by 6 months gestational age the ear is totally differentiated (Arey, 1965). The auditory nerve is completely myelinated at birth, enabling auditory information to be transmitted along the nerve at this time (Peiper, 1963). However, the occipital cortex is immature at birth and the integration of sounds from both ears may be limited (Conel, 1952; Dreyfus-Brisac, 1966). Sound conduction and auditory acuity also may be limited because of the presence of vernix caseosa (a waxy substance covering the skin of the fetus) and mucus which fills the inner ear, but these obstructions disappear shortly after birth (Spears and Hohle, 1967).

Various thresholds for response to sound in the newborn have been reported ranging from 40 decibels (Steinschneider, 1967) to 105 decibels (Wedenberg, 1956). Between the ages of 3 and 8 months, there is a sharp reduction in the response threshold (Hoversten and Moncur, 1969).

Infants respond to sound within the first hours after birth (Graham et al., 1968; Richman et al., 1953) and can be alerted by sound to visually attend at the age of 2 months (Culp, 1971; Self, 1971). Neonates exhibit a startle response to sounds with a sudden onset (Graham et al., 1968; Graham and Jackson, 1970), but are soothed by rhythmic sounds and by sounds of low frequencies (Birns et al., 1965; Brackbill et al., 1966; Salk, 1962; Weiss, 1934). Neonates habituate to tones with the habituation carrying over from one day to the next (Keen et al., 1965).

Neonates also are able to discriminate various speech sounds, including taped voices (Boyd, 1972). An infant 4 to 14 weeks of age is capable of differentiating voiced and unvoiced consonants (Trehub and Rabinovitch, 1972) and discriminating the speech sounds of "ba" and "pa" (Eimas et al., 1971). Cardiac responses to changes in speech syllables and tone frequencies have been observed in infants as young as 6 weeks (Leavitt et al., 1976). Additionally, babies are able to discriminate rising and falling intonations (Kaplan, 1969; Morse, 1972).

By the age of 4 to 6 months, infants localize (turn) to the sound of a bell or rattle (Bayley, 1969; Cattell, 1940). They also respond to a change in the tempo of auditory stimuli (Brooks and Berg, 1979). At this age, infants show differential smiling to the voice of their mother (LaRoche and Tcheng, 1963), are distressed if they hear their mother's voice but cannot see her (Turnure, 1971), and are more soothed by a female voice than a male voice (Kagan and Lewis, 1965). Infants of this age are also capable of making even more discriminations of speech sounds. They discriminate "bah-gah" (Moffitt, 1971), "we-ue" (Hillenbrand et al., 1979), and p, t, k, s, and n (McCaffrey, 1972). From birth the infant, thus, is able to actively process auditory stimuli. Infants seem particularly attuned to and able to benefit from social auditory stimuli, such as the human voice.

Gustation and Olfaction   At birth, an infant's oral mucosa is filled with taste buds. It would seem therefore that infants would be sensitive to taste stimulation although few studies have explored this area of sensory processing. Two reasons for this lack of research are apparent. First, in order to carry out studies of taste perception, a researcher must interfere with the infant's feeding routine. Second, an infant's state would be affected and measures of response therefore would also be modified (Reese and Lipsitt, 1970). The few studies in this area indicate that neonates prefer sugar over water solutions (Desor et al., 1973) and prefer sugar solutions with higher concentrations of sugar (Engen et al., 1974).

Like gustation, studies assessing infant olfactory capabilities are rare. The limited number of studies in this area indicate that infants are capable of responding differentially to various odors (Engen et al., 1968). Self et al. (1972) found that infants 72 hours old showed consistent, but individual, preference patterns for lavender, asafetida, and valerian odors. Although the research is limited in these areas, the available information does indicate that the newborn is capable of responding to gustatory and olfactory stimuli.

Tactile Development   Infants are born with the ability to respond to tactile stimulation. A light stroking of the cheek or lips will elicit the rooting reflex, a response in which the infant turns his/her head in the direction of the stimulus (Turkewitz et al., 1966). The Babkin reflex, produced by squeezing the infant's palm, will result in the infant opening his/her mouth without a cry (Kaye, 1965; Parmelee, 1963). Furthermore, certain parts of the infant's body seem to be more sensitive to tactile stimulation than other parts. A neonate's hands are more sensitive than the calf (Dockeray and Rice, 1934) and the Babinski (dorsiflexion of the big toe on stimulation of the sole of the foot) and cross-extensor reflexes are dependent on the different locations of tactile stimulation (Peiper, 1963).

A variety of responses have been elicited in the newborn with tactile stimulation. Infants respond to warm or cold stimuli on the forehead by snapping the head back (Jensen, 1932). Strong pressure to the cheek or forehead results in the head "locking" in place (Turkewitz et al., 1966). Infants 6 and 20 weeks old increase muscle tone during both quiet and paradoxal sleep when tactually stimulated (Paul and Dittrichova, 1974). Although an infant's thermal regulation is not stable until approximately 1½ weeks (Adamson and Towell, 1965; Bruck, 1961), an increase in environmental temperature also tends to change body activity and facilitate sleep (Bruck et al., 1962).

The infant's sensitivity to tactile stimuli increases during the first 4 to 5 days after birth (Graham, 1956; Kaye, 1964; Kaye and Lipsitt, 1964; Lipsitt and Levy, 1959). For example, Sherman and Sherman (1925) found that as an infant ages from 1 to 5 days, the number of pinpricks required to elicit a response decreases. Decreases in response thresholds during the first 4 days of life also have been found with stimulation presented on the foot (Kaye and Karp, 1963; Lipsitt, 1963).

Response to tactile stimulation is further demonstrated by studies that showed that infants habituate to noxious tactile stimuli (Gullickson and Crowell, 1964) and babies as young as 3 days old are conditioned to tactile stimulation (Lipsitt et al., 1966). Infants as young as 10 and 12 months tactually discriminate novel and familiar objects and manipulate the novel objects more often (Gottfried and Rose, 1980; Soroka et al., 1979). Thus, a review of literature in this area indicates that infants even several days old are responsive to tactile stimuli.

This description of the sensory and perceptual development of the normal infant establishes the infant as an organism capable of gathering and actively processing meaningful information in the environment. The manner in which this information is utilized by the developing child is described, albeit briefly, in the following sections on information processing and sensorimotor development.

Information Processing

One of the earliest indicators of information assimilation in the very young infant has been termed the orienting response. This response may include turning (e.g., visually) toward an environmental stimulus and a change or cessation in infant's activity. The repeated presentation of the same stimulus typically results in response decrement, a process referred to as habituation. This process is believed related to a central process rather than to infant or receptor fatigue. One theoretical explanation of this central process is presented by Sokolov (1963), who suggested the repeated presentation of the stimulus allows the infant to establish a neuronal model or internal representation of the stimulus. When, through repetition, the stimulus becomes familiar, a "match" occurs with the internal model and the orienting response decreases. The orienting response is reactivated upon the presentation of a novel stimulus for which an internal model has not been formed.

The theoretical explanation of habituation suggests a relationship between the infant's ability to process and store the information and the rapidity of response decrement. That response decrement is a measure of a central or "cognitive" process is further supported by a number of studies linking "predictors" of cognitive status with response decrement. For example, studies reviewed by Lewis and Goldberg (1969) reported a relationship between response decrement and age variables (older infants showed a more rapid response decrement) and a relationship to IQ scores at 3½ (the greater the response decrement at 1 year, the higher the preschool IQ). Furthermore, findings from another investigation indicated a positive correlation between maternal response to infant behavior (e.g., vocalizing, and crying) and response decrement (Lewis and Goldberg, 1969). Birth conditions also have been linked to response decrement outcomes. Eisenberg et al. (1966) reported high-risk neonates failed or required a larger number of trials to habituation than did normal newborns. A positive relationship between rapid habituation and high scores on a neurological exam were noted also by Sigman et al. (1973). Thus, links between rate of response decrement and factors such as age, preschool IQ, and birth condition have been documented. These results suggest the potential utilization of the habituation paradigm as a diagnostic tool for measuring cognitive functioning. However, practical applications await further research on the reliability and predictive capabilities of such measures.

Other indicators of the young infant's ability to process environmental information include the infant's visual attention to and preference for various patterns. Before the second month of age, investigations indicate the infant shows little selective interest and memory for patterns and visually attends only to particular portions of figures (e.g., outermost contours). The infant's discrimination capabilities are largely "quantitative" at this point; "selection" is made for the greater size or number of elements rather than among different patterns (when brightness and contour density are held constant across target stimuli). After 1 to 2 months, however, the infant seems capable of storing visual information and attending to distinct patterns (Salapatek, 1975).

The study of infant recognition memory, the ability to store information about a stimulus such that the infant recognizes the stimulus as familiar at a later point in time, is a useful indicator of infant information processing skills. Recognition memory is tested by the infant's selective attention to novel over familiar stimuli (stimuli to which the infant was previously given exposure). Fantz et al. (1975), utilizing this procedure to compare normal infants and infants with Down syndrome (infants with probable mental retardation), found that infants with Down syndrome were retarded in their development of responses to novel over familiar target stimuli. These results suggested that the developmental sequences of the groups of infants were the same although the rate was slower for the infants with Down syndrome. Studies such as these lend evidence that these processes are related to cognition. As such these methods may hold future promise as a means for measuring sensory and cognitive abilities. Our limited knowledge to date, however suggestive, is insufficient to provide predictive or diagnostic tools. This evidence, though, does provide a beginning understanding of the young infant's information processing abilities and relationships between sensory, perceptual, and cognitive abilities in the early months of life.

Sensorimotor Development

Sensorimotor functioning involves the coordination of both the sensory and motor systems. Three trends are evident in the development of sensorimotor functioning. The first is that of cephalocaudal progression which means that development of voluntary control proceeds from head to foot. For instance, infants develop control of the head first, then the arms, then the legs. Proximal progression is the second trend. This refers to development of control in a proximal to distal manner, with control beginning at body midline and moving in an outward and downward direction. The third general trend is for control of large muscles to precede control of small muscles (Appleton et al., 1975; Cohen and Gross, 1979; Cratty, 1970).

At birth, an infant is capable of large muscle movements, but these movements are uncoordinated. A neonate engages in hand-mouth activity, but success at this activity is only by chance (Piaget, 1952). Tonic neck and grasp reflexes are also present at birth (Andre-Thomas et al., 1960; Prechtl and Beintema, 1964). A neonate makes jerky attempts to follow a visual stimulus (Dayton and Jones, 1964) and also makes head adjustments in response to visual stimuli (Kessen et al., 1970). By the age of about 4 months, however, an infant is capable of smooth visual tracking (White, 1971), moves his/her head to follow a dangling ring (Bayley, 1969), and visually follows an object that disappears behind a screen (Bower et al., 1971). The tonic neck reflex has disappeared (White et al., 1964) and the infant actively engages in hand-watching (Bayley, 1969). By this age, the head and arms act independently (White et al., 1964) and unilateral hand raising is present (White and Held, 1967). The 4-month-old neonate may swipe at objects (Bruner, 1969; Bayley, 1969), reach for objects that touch his/her hand (Piaget, 1952), hold objects in the hand (Griffiths, 1954), and occasionally bring the held objects to the mouth (Piaget, 1952). An infant of this age also can hold his/her hands at midline when viewing grasped objects (Gesell and Thompson, 1938).

During the period of 4 to 7 months of age, infants develop control of the arms and head (Gesell, 1954). At this age, they are capable of bilateral responses with the arms (White and Held, 1967) and utilize a two-handed reach with accuracy (Bower, 1974). Infants open their hands in anticipation of contact with an object (White and Held, 1967), reach for objects out of range, and utilize a palmar grasp (Cruikshank, 1941; Halverson, 1931). At this time infants also explore objects by banging them together (Bayley, 1969) and shaking them (Uzgiris and Hunt, 1975). An infant of this age also holds an object in one hand while touching it with the fingers of the other hand (Bruner, 1973). The concept of object permanence is beginning to develop at this stage; the infant anticipates the trajectory of visual stimuli (Bower et al., 1971) and looks for fallen objects (Gesell and Thompson, 1938). Although infants do not yet search for a covered object, they will show surprise if an object changes when it is behind a screen (Bower et al., 1971) and will find an object if it is covered by an opaque cloth after reaching begins (Uzgiris and Hunt, 1975). Additionally the infant is able to successfully retrieve a partially covered object (Gratch and Landers, 1971).

By around 7 to 10 months, the infant develops control of trunk and hands and is able to sit (Gesell, 1954). At this stage of development, the infant maintains a grasp on one object while attempting to grasp another (Bruner, 1971), develops partial thumb opposition

(Bayley, 1969; Halverson, 1931), and likes to repeatedly drop or throw objects (Uzgiris and Hunt, 1975). An infant will finger the holes of a pegboard, place a cube in a cup (Bayley, 1969; Cattell, 1940), and begin to demonstrate the social use of objects (i.e., pretending to drink from a cup) (Uzgiris and Hunt, 1975). Object permanence continues to develop so that at the end of this period, an infant will search for an object that is hidden if the hiding is observed (Buhler and Hetzer, 1935), will search under two screens for a hidden object (Uzgiris and Hunt, 1975), and will act surprised if an object different from the one hidden is revealed (LeCompte and Gratch, 1972). Infants of this age also begin to exploit the relationship between two objects (e.g., pulling a pillow to retrieve an object placed on it or pulling a string tied to an object) (Uzgiris and Hunt, 1975).

By the end of the first year, the infant typically is able to place pegs in a pegboard, remove a round shape from a form board, take a cube out of a cup, and open and close boxes (Bayley, 1969; Cattell, 1940). The infant also combines objects together with functional relationships (i.e., places a cup on a saucer) (Lowe, 1975) and searches longer for a hidden object if the infant has handled (as well as seen) the object (Harris, 1971).

Infants typically demonstrate the ability to build cube towers, successfully use form boards, and remove pegs from pegboards by the end of 2 years (Bayley, 1969; Cattell, 1940). They also are able to hold a crayon and accurately use a spoon (Frankenburg and Dodds, 1967). Object permanence skills have advanced to the point where infants systematically search for hidden objects behind three screens by either searching from the first to the last screen (Miller et al., 1970) or by searching along the path the object was observed to take (Uzgiris and Hunt, 1975).

The sensorimotor development of the infant thus proceeds from reflexive responding to the immediate world to an understanding of the properties of the world around her/him. Sensory and motor experiences lead to an awareness of spatial relationships and the development of the concept of permanence of objects. In this fashion the early activities in sensing and manipulating objects in the environment allow the infant to gain increased knowledge of and organization of the environment.

Summary

This brief account of normal developmental processes is provided for reference and as the groundwork for a discussion of atypical development. Although the processes and sequences of development examined may be universal, the ages for attainment of milestones and the behavioral characteristics may indicate tremendous developmental variability. This rich variation from infant to infant—even infants who are biologically intact and share common environmental circumstances—underscores an important point. This variation often blurs the differences between those infants we classify as developing normally and those who may be at risk for delay or who are diagnosed as being developmentally deviant. The succeeding discussion of the atypical infant examines the nature of the developmental similarities of these children and also ways in which the behavioral outcomes achieved may actually be the same or similar to that of the normal infant.

THE ATYPICAL INFANT

The child with a disability or developmental disorder by definition enters the world with a limited repertoire for initiating and responding to the environment—limited "equipment" for processing information in that environment. Furthermore, the characteristics of newborns may affect their caregiver's behavior and also may not enable them to become full or typical partners in interactions. In short, the at-risk or disabled infant may have fewer ways to signal or impact the environment,

The difficulty in describing the development of the atypical infant begins with the inability to define "atypical." This literature has included babies who range from those born prematurely to those with multiple and severe disorders incurred pre- and perinatally. As becomes apparent from Gorski's discussion in Chapter 3 of the infant at risk, prediction as to the persistence and severity of early trauma or disorders remains elusive,

The purpose of this section is to cluster the descriptive information on specific disorders into a patchwork allowing us to map out what is known and not known and how similar or different the development of children with specific disabilities is from that of normal children. Only those disabilities for which documented, descriptive information on infant development is available are reviewed. These disabilities include visual impairment, hearing impairment, motor impairment, and Down syndrome.

The paucity of the empirical and descriptive information on the atypical infant can most likely be attributed to several factors. First, the fragile status and medical complications typically associated with the births of these children make them unsuitable candidates for studies of developmental processes. Furthermore, those babies who are diagnosed at birth or shortly thereafter are typically severely involved with multiple disorders. Mild disorders may not even be identified during the infancy period. Third, given the low incidence of children born with many of these disabilities it is difficult to draw conclusions about their development. Furthermore, many children are born with more than one condition that establishes them as "at risk." There are few children, for example, who are born only with a visual impairment or only with hearing disorders. Most children have multiple handicaps, and these handicaps encompass the entire range of degrees of severity. As such, "atypical" children represent an extremely heterogeneous group, one from which clustering for the purposes of testing and analysis becomes difficult at best. Finally, most of the infant development measures (e.g., Bayley Scales and Cattell) are not appropriate for use with children with sensory and motor impairments. The results of such tests may only indicate that children are not normal rather than identify how developmental processes differ. Given the scarcity of descriptive information, conclusions as to developmental sequences and patterns for atypical infants remain incomplete. Nevertheless general trends can be charted and examined for treatment implications.

Developmental Disorders

Visual Impairment   Few investigations have examined the effects of blindness or severe visual impairment on the development of the young infant. However, more information exists in this area than for most other disabilities. Given the difficulty in utilizing developmental tests on babies who are unable to respond visually to test items, the majority of studies are of a clinical, observational, or case study nature. These studies, although scarce, have allowed us to make some general assertions about the motor, language, cognitive, and social development of infants with visual impairments.

Motorically, blind infants seem to develop similarly to sighted infants in terms of amount, type, and sequence of motor activities (Adelson and Fraiberg, 1974; Norris et al., 1957; Warren, 1977). However, several investigators (Adelson and Fraiberg, 1974; Fraiberg, 1968) found marked delays in those areas requiring self-initiated mobility and locomotion. Fraiberg (1968) reported that crawling did not occur with these babies until well into the first year, often after the children acquired the ability to reach to a sound object. Delays in elevating self on arms in prone, raising self to sitting and standing, and walking were noted when the development of blind infants was compared with norms for sighted children (Adelson and Fraiberg, 1974). As the remarkable observations of blind infants made by Fraiberg and colleagues suggest, blindness does not uniformly affect gross motor development. Vision seems to be a powerful incentive for mobility. Consequently only after experience with sounds does the blind child master activities that require reaching out and exploring the world.

These findings raise questions regarding the development of the blind infant's response to sound. Studies have shown smiling in the first few months to parents' and others' voices (Freedman, 1964), attention to sounds created by actions of the hands at about 7 months (Burlingham, 1964), beginning coordination of auditory and tactile modes at 9 to 11 months, and reaching for objects on the basis of a sound cue at around 11 months (Fraiberg et al., 1966). Given the delay in the development of reaching, the auditory cue alone does not seem to be a sufficient substitute for the visual cues available to sighted infants (Fraiberg and Freedman, 1964; Wills, 1970).

Although it would seem that lack of visual stimuli may not be as critical for language development as for other developmental areas, unfolding literature in this area paints a different picture. Blind babies apparently babble the same as do sighted babies (Burlingham, 1961; Haspiel, 1965), but reports on early vocabulary development range from those indicating that development is similar to that for sighted infants (Haspiel, 1965; Wilson and Halverson, 1947) to studies that reported delays (Keeler, 1958; Burlingham, 1961, 1965). Fraiberg's (1977) studies indicated essentially normal attainment by blind infants of the following developmental milestones measured on the Bayley Scales: listens selectively to familiar words, responds to verbal requests, jabbers expressively, imitates words. Delays were found for the blind infants, however, on "says two words," "uses words to make wants known," and "sentence of two words." Fraiberg suggested that the "experiential poverty" of the blind child might be an impediment to concept formation. However, it is important to note, as she does, that the blind child "does get there," albeit at a later age.

Other recent work in linguistics (Andersen et al., 1982) involving detailed microanalyses of the language development of young blind children revealed that the use of words and linguistic structures may differ with these children as compared to sighted children. These differences include misuse of pronouns (e.g., substitution of "you" for "I"), less generalization about the properties of objects and more attention only to a specific property, imitation of larger "chunks" of speech in an almost echolalic fashion, and more focus on self as a topic (e.g., "I want"). These investigators also found some differences in the linguistic conversational input for blind infants. Parents of blind infants centered conversations on labeling and on more child-related topics than other environment-related topics. The researchers suggested that it may be easier to converse by talking about the child; whereas with a sighted child one can more easily identify other things to which the child may be attending and expand the conversational topic to include those items or activities (Kekelis and Andersen, 1982).

On cognitive dimensions similar findings have been noted. Fraiberg (1977) discussed the delays of the blind in self-representation in play as well as in language. Delays in the development of object concept possibly due to limitations in search behavior also were observed (Fraiberg, 1968). The developmental processes of blind and sighted subjects, however, were found to be similar on measures of haptic perception (Gottesman, 1971) and tasks of conservation (Gottesman, 1973), although delays were found for blind children in the latter.

Finally, again similarities and differences are observed in the social behavior of blind infants as compared to sighted peers. Freedman (1964) suggested the blind infant's smile appeared to be more reflexive than "normal." Fraiberg's (1970) observations indicated that blind babies smile and smile selectively (e.g., to mothers' voices) and that blind infants come to rely on manual-tactile recognition behavior just as the sighted baby uses visual recognition behavior to explore the social environment and form attachments (Fraiberg, 1977).

This brief review of the literature on the development of blind infants indicates that the development generally follows a normal course or sequence. However, selective delays were noted and attributed to the lack of normal visual stimulation feedback.

Auditory Impairment   As limited as the literature is on visual impairments, so too has there been little empirical investigation of the developmental effects of auditory impairments. We can probably attribute this lack of information to the low incidence of occurrence, to the variability in amount and onset of hearing loss and its subsequent effects, and to the fact that diagnosis is often not made until after the first year of age (Meadow, 1980).

The obvious and most studied area of development for deaf and hearing-impaired infants is that of language development. Studies of deaf babies have documented the apparently normal language development in the first months (i.e., babbling and vocalizations) (Downs, 1968; Lenneberg, 1967; Lenneberg, Rebelsky, and Nichols,

1965). However, in the absence of corrective hearing aids, a disruption in the normal language acquisition process occurs by around 9 months (Schlesinger and Meadow, 1972). An extensive study by Lach et al. (1970) of deaf infants from 11 to 32 months indicated speech and language differences in these children in terms of voice quality and vocabulary development with some differences persisting even after a 1-year training program. Although little systematic study of the language development of deaf children between 9 months and 6 to 7 years has been conducted, clinical evidence discloses a cumulative language deficit (Schlesinger and Meadow, 1972).

With respect to cognitive development, the bulk of the literature on deaf children pertains to those preschool age or older. This evidence suggests that these children learn concepts in the same sequence and manner as hearing children although delays may occur (Meadow, 1980). Research on the social development of deaf children also "begins" with the preschool child and suggests a relationship between social maturity and communicative competence (Schlesinger and Meadow, 1972).

Motor Impairment   The overall development of the child with motor impairment has received almost no attention outside of an examination of the motor domain itself. The heterogeneity of this "group" makes a systematic investigatory effort close to impossible; even within the category of cerebral palsy, children's motor problems range from spastic or high muscle tonus to fluctuating tone. Only a few research efforts have attempted to document the cognitive development of young children with motor problems. A major investigation in this area is Gouin-Decarie's (1969) study of the mental development of "the thalidomide child." The mental development of children born with severe congenital malformations (deformed limbs) was studied using the Griffiths Mental Development Scale (Griffiths, 1954) and an object-concept and object-relations scale. Testing indicated that one-third of the 22 children studied scored below average in the mental development test. The area most affected was that of language. Interpretation is somewhat difficult, however, due to the confounding variable of environmental placement (home reared versus institutionalized). On the object-concept scale, surprisingly, marked delays were not apparent. Despite severe limitations in the functional use of hands and other limbs, the children seemed to have compensated by the use of substitute channels.

Data from a study by Young (1978) comparing young cerebral palsied children with nonhandicapped children found differences for 13 to 26 month olds using instruments that assessed sensorimotor intelligence and object permanence. When motor differences between groups were statistically controlled, however, differences between groups of children were not evident. Fetters' (1981) investigation of the effects of motor handicaps on the development of object permanence produced similar findings. Her study indicated that physically handicapped infants (ages 13 to 29 months) developed object permanence at expected ages when tested using nontraditional assessments (e.g., heart rate and visual tracking). These studies suggest that although children with physical disabilities may face severe limitations in their ability to motorically explore the world and manipulate objects, they nevertheless develop object concepts.

Down Syndrome   The most studied group of children with a known congenital disability or developmental delay is that with Down syndrome. The development of these children has undoubtedly been of scientific interest for several reasons: 1) Down syndrome accounts for the largest cause of congenital mental retardation; and 2) Down syndrome can be positively identified at birth making early diagnosis and follow-up feasible.

Documentation of the development of infants with Down syndrome is extensive in the areas of motor, language, and mental development; limited investigations of social development have been conducted as well. The descriptive research universally notes delays in their mental, language, and motor development. Although these children were found to achieve developmental milestones in the same sequence as did normal children, developmental delays in the attainment of these milestones occurred (Carr, 1970; Dameron, 1963; Dicks-Mireaux, 1972; Share et al., 1964; Share and French, 1974). Similar findings were reported by Miranda and Fantz (1974) in their study of the recognition memory of infants with Down syndrome. Children in that study followed the same course of stimulus preference development as did normal children but exhibited developmental lags.

Children with Down syndrome have been regarded stereotypically as lovable, happy, and affectionate (Benda, 1969; Smith and Wilson, 1973). However, few investigations systematically examined their social development, and those studies that did do not necessarily uphold these stereotypes. Emde et al. (1978) observed that the social smiles of infants with Down syndrome were somewhat delayed in onset and were of "dampened intensity." Furthermore, Cicchetti and Sroufe's (1976) longitudinal investigation of the affective development of infants with Down syndrome found that babies laughed at stimulus items in the same developmental order as normal infants but that onset of laughter was delayed. In another study (Serafica and Cicchetti, 1976) differences in attachment and exploration behavior were noted only with regard to one behavior—crying. Mother's absence was found to provoke more crying with normal infants than with the children with Down syndrome. Finally, comparative investigations of the temperamental characteristics of infants with Down syndrome and normal infants revealed few differences (Bridges and Cicchetti, 1982; Rothbart and Hanson, 1983). Differences between the two groups were found primarily on amount of vocal activity and on smiling and laughter, with Down syndrome infants scoring lower (Rothbart and Hanson, 1983). Additionally, at 6 and 9 months the infants with Down syndrome showed greater distress and/or latency to approach intense or novel stimuli and longer periods of orienting to stimuli than the normal infants. It is important to note, however, that no group differences were noted on other temperamental dimensions: activity level, distress to limitations, and ability to be soothed. Likewise, Bridges and Cicchetti (1982) observed that the infants with Down syndrome, contrary to typical stereotypes, were not more placid than normal babies. Further, they found that infants with Down syndrome scored lower than the comparison group on persistence, approach, and threshold for stimulation. A more comprehensive review and discussion of the development of infants with Down syndrome is provided in Hanson (1981).

The descriptive literature on the development of infants with Down syndrome indicates, as does the literature reviewed on other specific disabilities, that the sequence and structure of development seems to be the same as that for normal infants. (This may not be the case, though, for children with severe and multiple handicapping conditions.) However, developmental lags or delays typically are noted for disabled children. The implications of this research for determining developmental outcomes for these children and identifying implications for intervention practices are examined in the remainder of this chapter.

DEVELOPMENTAL OUTCOMES

In a recent discussion of the transactional approach to studying development, Sameroff (1981) highlighted three points: the divergence of development, the convergence of development, and the inseparability of the organism from the environment. The first tenet, that development is divergent in nature, contradicts the notion that biology is necessarily destiny. Rather, as Sameroff suggests, the same beginnings may eventuate vastly different endings or outcomes in different individuals. The powerful effects of caregiving styles and socioeconomic status variables can be seen by reviews of research linking developmental outcomes to the interactional effects of these environmental factors with early biological trauma (Sameroff and Chandler, 1975). In the final analysis, what an individual achieves or how an individual develops is the product of the dynamic, shifting interaction between biological factors and environmental ones. The inseparability of the organism from its environment, thus, is apparent and is a central theme of this volume on atypical infant development.

The notion of convergent development (i.e., the notion that the same developmental outcome can be reached in many different ways) provides a hopeful approach to our work with high-risk and developmentally disordered infants. Monitoring of today's television programs and news articles and careful observations of other persons in our environment provide convincing evidence of developmental convergence. Almost on a daily basis we see an example of this phenomenon: the amputee who is skiing, the person with Down syndrome working in a restaurant and commuting to and from work independently, the quadriplegic who although unable to communicate orally is finishing a graduate degree in business, a congenitally deaf man teaching at a university. All are testimony to the human organism's resilience in adjusting to sensory impairment or brain damage through utilization of intact systems to become a functioning member of society.

Although developmental convergence is evident in the examples provided, the way in which disabled individuals acquire and process information essential for developmental advancement is not fully understood. One question, for instance, focuses on the issue of sensory substitution. The resilience of many sensorially impaired persons (e.g., blind) has led to a generally accepted notion that they are able to compensate almost totally for their impairment by developing their other senses (e.g., touch and auditory). In other words, there is a belief that one sense can be substituted for another. Although persons with sensory impairments can become fully integrated into society, the fact remains that we often see the blind infant who does not walk and the deaf child with delayed speech and language skills and poor school performance. A close examination of this substitution notion is warranted for it may have important implications for early intervention.

The starting point is an examination of intersensory coordination. At some point, the blind child and deaf child acquire knowledge of object concept, although both face experiential deprivation with respect to exploration of the environment. Research with young normal infants sheds the most light on this phenomenon. Is there an intermodal perception of objects, for instance? A brief review of this literature offers a far from definitive and rather equivocal response, but highlights the complex nature of the question.

Some support for *early* intersensory integration is provided by the research on auditory-visual integration in neonates and young infants. Sound stimuli were found to affect infants' visual scanning behavior (Mendelson and Haith, 1976). Likewise, evidence that neonates turn toward sound was provided (Wertheimer, 1961), although the characteristics of the sound stimulus (continuous rather than short duration) were critical for producing reliable responding (Muir and Field, 1979). Observation that infants searched for a voice that was discordant with the visual presentation also lends support to early auditory-visual coordination (Aronson and Rosenbloom, 1971; Spelke and Owsley, 1979). However, this early coordination does not necessarily imply that the auditory and visual modes provide the same or redundant information to the infant or that early intersensory coordination continues.

Intersensory integration between the visual-tactual modes and tactual-auditory modes also has been investigated in young infants. Studies reported avoidance responses by infants presented with a visual stimulus that appeared to be on an approaching collision course with the child (Ball and Tronick, 1971; Bower et al., 1970b) and coordinated early reaching when an object was visually and tactilely evident. Bower et al. (1970a) and Gratch (1972) found that tactual feedback (grasping toy) was insufficient to overcome a visual occlusion (opaque cloth) in a task to find a toy hidden under a cloth. Any early tactual-visual integration seems to be dominated by the role of vision; apparently touch does not teach vision and infant visual responses are more advanced than tactile ones. This finding is further supported by the work of Rose et al. (1978), who showed that providing infants with the opportunity to manipulate objects actually interfered with recognition memory. These researchers also examined cross-modal transfer of information with 1-year-old infants. Infants were familiarized with an object in the oral or tactile mode and later visually presented with the familiar and a novel stimulus. Full-term, middle-class infants demonstrated cross-modal transfer of knowledge from the oral or tactile mode to the visual mode; however, preterm infants did not, which suggested possible differences in information processing or intersensory integration between these groups.

Given the training needs of sensory impaired and physically disabled youngsters, intersensory coordination (particularly auditory-visual integration) early in life is of primary interest. Work with blind children has suggested that sound is not an effective substitute for vision until around 9 to 11 months when developmentally the coordination of auditory and visual modalities is expected to occur (Fraiberg et al., 1966). Gross motor delays in the mobility of blind infants as reported in these studies showed that sound apparently provides no substitute for visual information (Adelson and Fraiberg, 1974). Bower, however, has indicated that many of the limitations of sound as an index of spatial information might be circumvented were one to use echoes as a source of information about position and relative change of position (Bower, 1977). He further proposed that sensory surrogates, such as the ultrasonic echolocation device described in his studies, would be best incorporated early in the developmental history of the organism. His initial studies on the use of the surrogate (the Sonicguide) by blind infants were followed by a more controlled series of studies investigating longitudinal and cross-sectional use of the Sonicguide aid by both blind subjects and subjects in whom blindness was simulated (Aitken, 1981; Aitken and Bower, 1982a, 1982b). These studies have provided tentative evidence for more rapid and effective use by younger subjects. It was reported that exposure to the aid from early infancy allowed for development to approximate more closely that of sighted infants.

These studies leave us with a general impression of early sensory coordination in the first months. However, they also show that the senses do not necessarily process redundant information—one sense does not always substitute for the other. As discussed, this phenomenon is seen in the development of blind children. Although blind babies demonstrate early ear-hand coordination by about 4 to 5 months of age, this coordination "drops out" and is not displayed again until the last part of the first year. Only after this coordination at 9 to 11 months occurs does sound become a "lure," as Fraiberg (1977) suggests, for reaching out into the environment. The inability of sound cues to substitute for visual information may be due to physical limitations as to what sound can provide. Sound does not give, for example, accurate information on distance, height, or locations in front of or behind another object. Capitalizing on the early coordination, which does typically exist, and providing substitute information for vision when possible (e.g., utilizing an echolocation device) may overcome in part the early sensory deprivation imposed by congenital blindness. The importance of providing this intervention early during the first months of age must be underscored.

Although this discussion of intersensory coordination and sensory substitution focuses on blind children, the implications are the same for other sensory impairments. Furthermore, sensory substitution is discussed in depth as only one issue essential to understanding the developmental process of disabled individuals. Another key issue relates to the young child's establishment of control over the environment. Sensory, physical, or cognitive impairments may impose severe limitations on the child's ability to explore the world and glean new information essential for further development. Some disabled children gain control over the environment using intact systems; others become increasingly withdrawn and inactive. A critical developmental task faced by young children is learning to recognize relationships between their actions and environmental events, and consequently learning to initiate and exert control over both social and nonsocial elements in the environment. The processes whereby disabled children learn cause-effect relationships and procedures for facilitating learning is further discussed in Chapters 6 and 11.

In summary, although clinical observations support the notion of developmental convergence—the attainment of the same behavioral level through different routes—as can be seen from the review of literature, this is a complex process. It does not necessarily follow, for instance, that one sense "takes over" for another or that the process of development is the same for developmentally disabled individuals. One cannot simply suggest that the same information can be supplied through another channel or modality or that the young child will learn to engage the environment. Where does this leave us in making decisions on how best to intervene in facilitating the development of the young child with developmental disabilities?

IMPLICATIONS FOR INTERVENTION

When intervention is viewed as a comprehensive dynamic delivery of services constructed around the individual needs of the child and her/his family, our work becomes clearer. The fact remains that children with motor impairments, sensory impairments, and brain damage do acquire concepts, develop communication skills, develop attachments, and learn to function in society. Evidence suggests that the sequence of development is generally the same. However, the process may or may not differ and the behavior of the individual topographically may differ even radically from that of the normal child.

Nevertheless, as is reviewed more extensively in Chapter 12, it seems that systematic, comprehensive intervention efforts do make a difference. As Adelson and Fraiberg (1974) pointed out, the blind infants in their study were unable to substitute information from other modalities in lieu of the missing visual information and were developmentally delayed. Early intervention procedures did positively affect their development, however. When these youngsters were compared with another group of blind children not receiving comparable assistance, their gross motor development was found to be less delayed. It appeared that the intervention that focused on *early* auditory-tactile experiences and parent-child interactions served to motivate the children to become more involved with the world and, thus, derive benefits and information from those sources that were available to them.

The consequences of early trauma are varied and far-reaching, making it difficult to determine developmental outcomes. Developmental processes or patterns may actually differ in disabled youngsters. Intervention efforts must focus both on curriculum content—individualized, systematic attempts to provide information to these children—and on the process of learning—assisting children to gain control over the environment by learning relationships between their actions and external events. Major goals include maximizing and building on the skills the children do have and preventing passivity or withdrawal due to the experiental deprivation produced by handicapping conditions. The key to this process is assisting parents to become careful observers of their children in order to read and understand the child's signals. The research suggests that it is crucial that the provision of these intervention services begins as *early* as possible (in the first months). Through these attempts we may assist disabled children in gaining information in unique ways and overcoming potential biological effects.

Chapter Outline

OVERVIEW: The development of atypical infants is compared with that of normal infants both in terms of similarities and differences: Though the response modes or means of acquiring information may differ for infants at risk, in many cases optimal developmental outcomes may be achieved.

I. THE NORMAL INFANT
A review of the sensory-perceptual capabilities of the normal infant reveals that infants are capable of actively gathering and processing information in their environment early in life. Additionally, brief descriptions of sensorimotor developmental milestones and the information processing abilities of the young infant underscore this viewpoint. This overview of normal development provides a background for the discussion of the effects of disability.

II. THE ATYPICAL INFANT
Disabilities may differentially affect the infant's motor, communication, cognitive and social developmental course. Disabilities for which descriptive developmental information is available include:

    A. Visual impairment
    B. Auditory impairment
    C. Motor impairment
    D. Down syndrome

III. DEVELOPMENTAL OUTCOMES

    A. Developmental outcomes are examined in light of three tenets:
        1. The divergence of development
        2. The convergence of development
        3. The inseparability of the organism from the environment

    B. Developmental convergence, the notion that the same developmental outcome can be reached in many different ways, is discussed; disabled children may utilize different response and information acquisition modes to acquire information.

IV.   IMPLICATIONS FOR INTERVENTION

Early family intervention services are advocated. Services which emphasize building on skills in the child's repertoire and individualized, systematic educational efforts aimed at giving the child control over the environment are recommended.

REFERENCES

Adamson, K., and Towell, M. E. Thermal homeostasis in the fetus and new-born. *Anesthesiology*, 1965, *26*, 531–548.

Adelson, E., and Fraiberg, S. Gross motor development in infants blind from birth. *Child Development*, 1974, *45*, 114–126.

Aitken, S. *Differentation Theory: Intersensory Substitution and the Use of the Sonicguide.* Unpublished doctoral dissertation, University of Edinburgh, 1981.

Aitken, S., and Bower, T. G. R. The use of the Sonicguide in infancy. *Journal of Visual Impairment and Blindness*, 1982a, *76*(3), 91–100.

Aitken, S., and Bower, T. G. R. Intersensory substitution in the blind. *Journal of Experimental Child Psychology*, 1982b, *33*, 309–323.

Ames, E., and Silfen, C. *Methodological Issues in the Study of Age Differences in Infant's Attention to Stimuli Varying in Movement and Complexity.* Paper presented at meeting of Society for Research in Child Development, Minneapolis, 1965.

Andersen, E., Dunlea, A., and Kekelis, L. Blind children's language: Resolving some differences. In *Papers and Reports on Child Language Development* (No. 21), Stanford University, 1982.

Andre-Thomas, C. Y., and Saint-Anne Dargassies, S. *The Neurological Examination of the Infant.* London: Medical Advisory Committee of the National Spastic Society, 1960.

Appleton, T., Clifton, R., and Goldberg, S. The development of behavioral competence in infancy. In F. D. Horowitz (Ed.), *Review of Child Development Research* (Vol. 4). Chicago: University of Chicago Press, 1975.

Arey, L. B. *Developmental Anatomy* (7th ed.). Philadelphia: Saunders, 1965.

Aronson, E., and Rosenbloom, S. Space perception in early infancy: Perception within a common auditory-visual space. *Science*, 1971, *172*, 1161–1163.

Ball, W., and Tronick, E. Infant responses to impending collision: Optical and real. *Science*, 1971, *171*, 818–820.

Barnet, A. B., Lodge, A., and Armington, J. C. Electroretinogram in newborn human infants. *Science*, 1965, *148*, 651–654.

Bayley, N. *Bayley Scales of Infant Development.* New York: Psychological Corp., 1969.

Benda, C. E. *Down's Syndrome: Mongolism and Its Management.* New York: Grune & Stratton, 1969.

Bergman, T., Haith, M., and Mann, L. *Development of Eye Contact and Facial Scanning in Infants.* Paper presented at meeting of Society of Research in Child Development, Minneapolis, 1971.

Birns, B., Blank, M., Bridger, W. H., and Escalona, S. K. Behavioral inhibition in neonates produced by auditory stimuli. *Child Development*, 1965, *36*, 639–645.

Blanton, M. G. The behavior of the human infant during the first 30 days of life. *Psychological Review*, 1917, *24*, 456–483.

Bower, T. G. R. *Development in Infancy.* San Francisco: W.H. Freeman, 1974.

Bower, T. G. R. Blind babies see with their ears. *New Scientist*, February 3, 1977, 255–257.

Bower, T. G. R. Visual development in the blind child. In V. Smith and J. Keen (Eds.), *Visual Handicap in Children, Clinics in Developmental Med-*

icine (No. 73). London: Spastics International Medical Publications, William Heineman Medical Books, 1979.

Bower, T. G. R., Broughton, J. M., and Moore, M. K. The coordination of visual and tactual input in infants. *Perception and Psychophysics*, 1970a, *8*(1), 51–53.

Bower, T. G. R., Broughton, J. M., and Moore, M. K. Infant responses to approaching objects: An indicator of response to distal variables. *Perception and Psychophysics*, 1970b, *9*, 193–196.

Bower, T. G. R., Broughton, J., and Moore, M. K. Development of the object concept as manifested in changes in the tracking behavior of infants between 7 and 20 weeks of age. *Journal of Experimental Child Psychology*, 1971, *11*, 182–193.

Bower, T. G. R., Watson, J. S., and Umansky, R. *Auditory surrogates for vision in sensorimotor development.* Unpublished manuscript, 1976.

Boyd, E. *Voice Responsibility and Discrimination in Two-month-old Infants.* Unpublished doctoral dissertation. Lawrence: University of Kansas, 1972.

Brackbill, Y., Adams, G., Crowell, D. H., and Gray, M. L. Arousal level in neonates and preschool children under continuous auditory stimulation. *Journal of Experimental Child Psychology*, 1966, *4*, 178–188.

Brennan, W. M., Ames, E. W., and Moore, B. W. Age differences in infants' attention to patterns of different complexities. *Science*, 1966, *151*, 1354–1356.

Bridges, F. A., and Cicchetti, D. Mothers' ratings of the temperament characteristics of Down syndrome infants. *Developmental Psychology*, 1982, *18*, 238–244.

Brooks, P. R., and Berg, W. K. Do 16-week-old infants anticipate stimulus offsets? *Developmental Psychobiology*, 1979, *12*(4), 329–334.

Bruck, K. Temperature regulation in the newborn infant. *Biologia Neonatorum*, 1961, *3*, 65–119.

Bruck, K., Parmelee, A. H., and Bruck, M. Neutral temperature range and range of "thermal comfort" in premature infants. *Biologia Neonatorum*, 1962, *4*, 32–51.

Bruner, J. S. Eye, hand, and mind. In D. Elkind and J. H. Flavell (Eds.), *Studies in Cognitive Development: Essays in Honor of Jean Piaget.* New York: Oxford University Press, 1969.

Bruner, J. S. The growth and structure of skill. In K. J. Connolly (Ed.), *Motor Skills in Infancy.* New York: Academic Press, 1971.

Bruner, J. S. The organization of early skilled action. *Child Development*, 1973, *44*, 1–11.

Buhler, C., and Hetzer, H. *Testing Children's Development from Birth to School Age.* New York: Fannar Rinehart, 1935.

Burlingham, D. Some notes on the development of the blind. *Psychoanalytic Study of the Child*, 1961, *16*, 121–145.

Burlingham, D. Hearing and its role in the development of the blind. *Psychoanalytic Study of the Child*, 1964, *19*, 95–112.

Burlingham, D. Some problems of ego development in blind children. *Psychoanalytic Study of the Child*, 1965, *20*, 194–208.

Caron, A. J., Caron, R. F., and Carlson, V. R. Infant perception of invariant shape of objects varying in slant. *Child Development*, 1979, *50*(3), 716–721.

Carr, J. Mental and motor development in young mongoloid children. *Journal of Mental Deficiency Research*, 1970, *14*, 205–220.

Cattell, P. *The Measurement of Intelligence of Infants and Young Children.* New York: Psychological Corp., 1940.

Cicchetti, D., and Sroufe, L. The relationship between affective and cognitive development in Down's syndrome infants. *Child Development,* 1976, 47, 920–929.

Coakes, R. L., Clothier, C., and Wilson, A. Binocular reflexes in the first six months of life: Preliminary results of a study of normal infants. *Child Care, Health, and Development,* 1979, 5(6), 405–408.

Cohen, M. A., and Gross, P J. *The Developmental Resource: Behavioral Sequences for Assessment and Program Planning,* (Vol. I). New York: Grune & Stratton, 1979.

Cohen, H., Gross, P., and Haring, N. G. Developmental pinpoints. In N. G. Haring and L. Brown (Eds.), *Teaching the Severely Handicapped* (Vol. I). New York: Grune & Stratton, 1976.

Conel, J. L. Histologic development of the cerebral cortex. In *The Biology of Mental Health and Disease.* New York: P. B. Hoeber, 1952.

Cratty, B. J. *Perceptual and Motor Development in Infants and Children.* New York: Macmillan, 1970.

Cruikshank, R. M. The development of visual size constancy in early infancy. *Journal of Genetic Psychology,* 1941, 58, 327–351.

Culp, R. *Looking Response, Decrement and Recovery, of Eight to Fourteen-week-old Infants in Relation to Presentation of the Infants' Mothers' Voice.* Unpublished master's thesis. Lawrence: University of Kansas, 1971.

Dameron, L. E. Development of intelligence of infants with mongolism. *Child Development,* 1963, 34, 733–738.

Dayton, G. O., Jr., and Jones, M. H. Analysis of characteristics of fixation reflexes in infants by use of direct current electroculography. *Neurology,* 1964, 14, 1152–1156.

Dayton, G. O., Jones, M. H., Aiu, P., Rawson, R. A., Steele, B., and Rose, M. Developmental study of coordinated eye movement in the human infant. I. Visual acuity in the newborn human: A study based on induced optokinetic nystagmus recorded by electro-oculography. *Archives of Opthalmology,* 1964a, 71, 865–870.

Dayton, G. O., Jones, M. H., Steele, B., and Rose, M. Developmental study of conditioned eye movements in the newborn infant. II. An electro-eulographic study of the fixation reflex in the newborn. *Archives of Opthalmology,* 1964b, 71, 871–875.

Desor, J. A., Maller, O., and Turner, R. E. Task acceptance of sugars by human infants. *Journal of Comparative and Physiological Psychology,* 1973, 84, 496–501.

Dicks-Mireaux, M. J. Mental development of infants with Down's syndrome. *American Journal of Mental Deficiency,* 1972, 77(1), 26–32.

Dockeray, F. C., and Rice, C. Responses of newborn infants to pain stimulation. *Ohio State University Studies,* 1934, 12, 82–93.

Doris, J., and Cooper, L. Brightness discrimination in infancy. *Journal of Experimental Child Psychology,* 1966, 3, 31–39.

Downs, M. P. Identification and training of the deaf child—Birth to one year. *Volta Review,* 1968, 70, 154–158.

Dreyfus-Brisac, C. The bioelectric development of the central nervous system during early life. In F. Faulkner (Ed.), *Human Development.* Philadelphia: W. B. Saunders, 1966.

Eimas, P. D., Siqueland, E. R., Jusczyk, P., and Vigorito, J. Speech perception in early infants. *Science,* 1971, 171, 303–306.

Eisenberg, R. G., Cousin, D. B., and Rupp, N. R. Habituation to an acoustic pattern as an index of differences among human neonates. *Journal of Auditory Research*, 1966, 6, 239–248.

Emde, R. N., Katz, E. L., and Thorpe, J. K. Emotional expression in infancy: II. Early deviations in Down's syndrome. In M. Lewis and L. Rosenblum (Eds.), *The Development of Affect: Genesis of Behavior* (Vol. I). New York: Plenum Press, 1978.

Engen, T., Lipsitt, L. P., and Kaye, H. Olfactory responses and adaptation in the human neonate. *Journal of Comparative and Physiological Psychology*, 1968, 56, 73–77.

Engen, T., Lipsitt, L. P., and Peck, M. B. Ability of newborn infants to discriminate sapid substances. *Developmental Psychology*, 1974, 10, 741–744.

Fagan, J. F. Memory in the infant. *Journal of Experimental Child Psychology*, 1970, 9, 217–226.

Fagan, J. F. Facilitation of infants recognition memory. *Child Development*, 1978, 49, 1066–1075.

Fagan, J. F., and Shephard, P. A. Infants perception of face orientation. *Infant Behavior and Development*, 1979, 2(3), 227–233.

Fagan, J. F., and Singer, L. T. The role of simple feature differences in infants' recognition of faces. *Infant Behavior and Development*, 1979, 2(1), 39–45.

Fantz, R. L. Pattern vision in young infants. *Psychological Record*, 1958, 8, 43–47.

Fantz, R. L. A method for studying depth perception in infants under 6 months of age. *Psychological Record*, 1961, 11, 27–32.

Fantz, R. L. Pattern vision in newborn infants. *Science*, 1963, 140, 296–297.

Fantz, R. L. Visual perception and experience in early infancy: A look at the hidden side of behavior development. In H. W. Stevenson, E. H. Hess, and H. L. Rheingold (Eds.), *Early Behavior: Comparative and Developmental Approaches*. New York: Wiley, 1967.

Fantz, R. L., Fagan, J. F., and Miranda, S. B. Early visual selectivity. In L. B. Cohen and P. Salapatek (Eds.), *Infant Perception: From Sensation to Cognition* (Vol. 1) *Basic Visual Processes*. New York: Academic Press, 1975.

Fantz, R. L., and Nevis, S. The predictive value of changes in visual preferences in early infancy. In J. Hellmuth (Ed.), *Exceptional Infant* (Vol. 1): *The Normal Infant*. Seattle: Special Child Publications, 1967.

Fantz, R. L., Ordy, J. M., and Udelf, M. S. Maturation of pattern vision in infants during the first 6 months. *Journal of Comparative and Physiological Psychology*, 1962, 55, 907–917.

Fetters, L. Object permanence development in infants with motor handicaps, *Physical Therapy*, 1981, 61(3), 327–333.

Fraiberg, S. Parallel and divergent patterns in blind and sighted infants. *Psychoanalytical Study of the Child*, 1968, 23, 264–300.

Fraiberg, S. Smiling and stranger reaction in blind infants. In J. Hellmuth (Ed.), *Exceptional Infant* (Vol. 1): *The Normal Infant*. New York: Brunner-Mazel, 1970.

Fraiberg, S. *Insights from the Blind*. New York: Basic Books, 1977.

Fraiberg, S., and Freedman, D. A. Studies in the ego development of the congenitally blind child. *Psychoanalytic Study of the Child*, 1964, 19, 113–169.

Fraiberg, S., Siegel, B., and Gibson, R. The role of sound in the search behavior of a blind infant. *Psychoanalytic Study of the Child*, 1966, *21*, 327–357.

Frankenburg, W. K., and Dodds, J. B. The Denver Developmental Screening Test. *Journal of Pediatrics*, 1967, *71*, 181–191.

Freedman, D. G. Smiling in blind infants and the issue of innate vs. acquired. *Journal of Child Psychology and Psychiatry*, 1964, *5*, 171–184.

Gesell, A. L. The ontogenesis of infant behavior. In L. Carmichael (Ed.), *Manual of Child Psychology* (2nd ed.). New York: Wiley, 1954.

Gesell, A. L., Ilg, F. L., and Bullis, G. O. *Vision: Its Development in Infant and Child*. New York: Paul Hoeber, 1949.

Gesell, A., and Thompson, H. *The Psychology of Early Growth*. New York: Macmillan, 1938.

Gottesman, M. A comparative study of Piaget's developmental schema of sighted children with that of a group of blind children. *Child Development*, 1971, *42*, 573–580.

Gottesman, M. Conservation development in blind children. *Child Development*, 1973, *44*, 824–827.

Gottfried, A. W., and Rose, S. A. Tactile recognition memory in infants. *Child Development*, 1980, *5*, 69–74.

Gouin-Decarie, T. A study of the mental and emotional development of the thalidomide child. In B. M. Foss (Ed.), *Determinants of Infant Behavior* (Vol. 4). London: Methuen, 1969.

Graham, F. K. Behavioral differences between normal and traumatized newborns. I. The test procedures. *Psychological Monographs*, 1956, *70*, (20, Whole No. 427).

Graham, F. K., Clifton, R. K., and Hatton, H. Habituation of heart rate responses to repeated auditory stimulation during the first five days of life. *Child Development*, 1968, *39*, 35–52.

Graham, F. K., and Jackson, J. C. Arousal systems and infant heart rate responses. In H. W. Reese and L. P. Lipsitt (Eds.), *Advances in Child Development and Behavior* (Vol. 5). New York: Academic Press, 1970.

Gratch, G. A study of the relative dominance of vision and touch in six month old infants. *Child Development*, 1972, *43*, 615–623.

Gratch, G., and Landers, W. F. Stage IV of Piaget's theory of infant object concepts: A longitudinal study. *Child Development*, 1971, *42*, 359–372.

Griffiths, R. *The Abilities of Babies: A Study in Mental Measurement*. New York: McGraw-Hill, 1954.

Gullickson, G. R., and Crowell, D. H. Neonatal habituation to electro-tactual stimulation. *Journal of Experimental Child Psychology*, 1964, *1*, 388–396.

Haaf, R. A., and Bell, R. Q. A facial dimension in visual discrimination by human infants. *Human Development*, 1967, *38*, 895–899.

Halverson, H. M. An experimental study of prehension in infants by means of systematic cinema records. *Genetic Psychology Monographs*, 1931, *101*, 107–284.

Hanson, M. Down's syndrome children: Characteristics and intervention research. In M. Lewis and L. Rosenblum (Eds.), *Genesis of Behavior* (Vol. 3): *The Uncommon Child*. New York: Plenum Press, 1981.

Harris, P. L. Examination and search in infants. *British Journal of Psychology*, 1971, *62*, 469–473.

Haspiel, G. S. Communication breakdown in the blind emotionally disturbed child. *New Outlook for the Blind*, 1965, *59*, 98–99.

Haynes, H., White, B. L., and Held, R. Visual accommodation in human infants. *Science*, 1965, *148*, 528–530.

Hershenson, M. Visual discrimination in the human newborn. *Journal of Comparative Physiological Psychology*, 1964, *58*, 270–276.

Hillenbrand, J., Minifie, F. D., and Edwards, T. J. Tempo of spectrum change as a cue in speech-sound discrimination by infants. *Journal of Speech and Hearing Research*, 1979, *22*(1), 147–165.

Hoversten, G. H., and Moncur, J. P. Stimuli and intensity factors in testing infants. *Journal of Speech and Hearing Research*, 1969, *12*, 687–702.

James, W. *The Principles of Psychology* (Vol. 2). New York: Holt, 1890.

Jensen, K. Differential reactions to taste and temperature stimuli in newborn infants. *Psychological Monographs*, 1932, *12*, 363–479.

Jones-Molfese, V. J. Responses of neonates to colored stimuli. *Child Development*, 1977, *48*, 1092–1095.

Kagan, J., and Lewis, M. Studies of attention in the human infant. *Merrill-Palmer Quarterly*, 1965, *11*, 95–127.

Kaplan, E. L. *The Role of Intonation in the Acquisition of Language*. Unpublished doctoral dissertation. Ithaca, NY: Cornell University, 1969.

Kaye, H. Skin conductance in the human neonate. *Child Development*, 1964, *35*, 1297–1305.

Kaye, H. The conditioned Babkin reflex in human newborns. *Psychonomic Science*, 1965, *2*, 287–288.

Kaye, H., and Karp, E. *Tactile Threshold in the Human Neonate*. Unpublished manuscript. Atlanta: Emory University, 1963.

Kaye, H., and Lipsitt, L. P. Relation of electrotactual threshold to basal skin conductance. *Child Development*, 1964, *35*, 1307–1312.

Keeler, W. R. Autistic patterns and defective communication in blind children with retrolental fibroplasia. In P. H. Hoch and J. Zubin (Eds.), *Psychopathology of Communication*. New York: Grune & Stratton, 1958.

Keen, R. E., Chase, H. H., and Graham, F. K. Twenty four hour retention by neonates of a habituated heart response. *Psychonomic Science*, 1965, *2*, 265–266.

Kekelis, L., and Andersen, E. *Blind Children's Early Input: Mother Accommodations*. Unpublished manuscript. Los Angeles: University of Southern California, 1982.

Kessen, W., Haith, M., and Salapatek, P. H. Human infancy: A bibliography and guide. In P. H. Mussen (Ed.), *Carmichael's Manual of Child Psychology* (Vol. 1, 3rd ed.). New York: Wiley, 1970.

Lach, R. D., Ling, D., Ling, A. H., and Ship, N. Early speech development in deaf infants. *American Annals of the Deaf*, 1970, *115*, 522–526.

La Roche, J. L., and Tcheng, F. C. Y. *Le Sourire du Nourrison*. Lowain: Publications Universitaries, 1963.

Leavitt, L. A., Brown, J. W., Morse, P. A., and Graham, F. K. Cardiac orienting and auditory discrimination in 6 week old infants. *Developmental Psychology*, 1976, *12*(6), 514–523.

LeCompte, G. K., and Gratch, G. Violations of a rule as a method of diagnosing infant's level of object concept. *Child Development*, 1972, *43*, 385–396.

Lenneberg, E. H., Rebelsky, F. G., and Nichols, I. A. The vocalizations of infants born to deaf and to hearing parents. *Human Development*, 1965, *8*, 23–37.

Lenneberg, E. H. *Biological Foundations of Language*. New York: Wiley, 1967.

Lewis, M., and Goldberg, S. Perceptual-cognitive development in infancy: A generalized expectancy model as a function of the mother-infant interaction. *Merrill-Palmer Quarterly*, 1969, *15*, 81–100.

Ling, B. C. A genetic study of sustained visual fixation and associated behavior in the human infant from birth to 6 months. *Journal of Genetic Psychology*, 1942, *6*, 227–277.

Lipsitt, L. P. Learning in the first year of life. In L. P. Lipsitt and C. C. Spiker (Eds.), *Advances in Child Development and Behavior* (Vol. 1). New York: Academic Press, 1963.

Lipsitt, L. P., Kaye, H., and Bosack, T. N. Enhancement of neonate sucking through reinforcement. *Journal of Experimental Child Psychology*, 1966, *4*, 163–168.

Lipsitt, L. P., and Levy, N. Electrotactual threshold in the neonate. *Child Development*, 1959, *30*, 547–554.

Lowe, M. Trends in the development of representational play in infants from one to three years: An observational study. *Journal of Experimental Child Psychology*, 1975, *16*, 33–48.

Mann, I. *The Development of the Human Eye*. New York: Grune & Stratton, 1964.

McCaffrey, A. *Speech Perception in Infancy*. Unpublished doctoral dissertation. Ithaca, NY: Cornell University, 1972.

McCall, R. B., and Kagan, J. Attention in the infant: Effects of complexity, contour, perimeter, and familiarity. *Child Development*, 1967, *38*, 939–952.

McCluskey, K. A. The infant as organizer: Future directions in perceptual development. In K. Bloom (Ed.), *Prospective issues in infancy research*. Hilldale, NJ: Erlbaum, 1981.

Meadow, K. P. *Deafness and Child Development*. Berkeley: University of California Press, 1980.

Mendelson, M. J., and Haith, M. M. The relation between audition and vision in the newborn. *Monographs of the Society for Research in Child Development*, 1976, *41*(4), 72.

Milewski, A. E. Infants' discrimination of internal and external pattern elements. *Journal of Experimental Child Psychology*, 1976, *22*(2), 229–246.

Miller, D. J., Cohen, L. B., and Hill, K. T. A methodological investigation of Piaget's theory of object concept development in the sensory-motor period. *Journal of Experimental Child Psychology*, 1970, *9*, 59–85.

Miranda, S. B., and Fantz, R. L. Recognition memory in Down's syndrome and normal infants. *Child Development*, 1974, *45*, 651–660.

Moffitt, A. R. Consonant cue perception by twenty to twenty-four week old infants. *Child Development*, 1971, *42*, 717–731.

Morse, P. A. Speech perception in six-week-old infants. *Journal of Experimental Child Psychology*, 1972, *14*, 477–492.

Muir, D., and Field, J. Newborn infants orient to sounds. *Child Development*, 1979, *50*, 431–436.

Nelson, K. Organization of visual tracking responses in human infants. *Journal of Experimental Child Psychology*, 1968, *6*, 194–201.

Norris, M., Spaulding, P. J., and Brodie, F. H. *Blindness in Children*. Chicago: University of Illinois, 1957.

Pancratz, C. N., and Cohen, L. B. Recovery of habituation in infants. *Journal of Experimental Child Psychology*, 1970, 9, 208–216.

Parmelee, A. H. The hand-mouth reflex of Babkin in premature infants. *Pediatrics*, 1963, 31, 734–740.

Paul, K., and Dittrichova, J. Responsivity in sucklings during sleep. *Activas Resnosa Superior*, 1974, 16(2), 111.

Peiper, A. *Cerebral Function in Infancy and Childhood*. New York: Consultant Bureau, 1963.

Piaget, J. *The Origins of Intelligence in Children*. New York: International Universities Press, 1952.

Prechtl, H. F. R., and Beintema, D. J. The neurological examination of the full-term newborn infant. In *Clinics in Developmental Medicine* (No. 12). London: Spastics International Medical Publishers, William Heinemann Medical Books, 1964.

Reese, H. W., and Lipsitt, L. P. *Experimental Child Psychology*. New York: Academic Press, 1970.

Richman, J. B., Grossman, H. J., and Lustman, S. L. A hearing test for newborn infants. *Pediatrics*, 1953, 11, 634–638.

Rose, S. A., Gottfried, A. W., and Bridger, W. H. Cross-modal transfer in infants: Relationship to prematurity and socioeconomic background. *Developmental Psychology*, 1978, 14(4), 643–652.

Rothbart, M. K., and Hanson, M. J. A comparison of temperamental characteristics of Down's syndrome and normal infants. *Developmental Psychology*, 1983, 19, 766–769.

Salapatek, P. The visual investigation of geometric patterns by the one- and two-month old infant. In C. S. Lavatelli and F. Stendler (Eds.), *Readings in Child Behavior and Development*. New York: Harcourt Brace, 1972.

Salapatek, P. Pattern perception in early infancy. In L. B. Cohen and P. Salapatek (Eds.), *Infant Perception: From Sensation to Cognition (Vol. 1) Basic Visual Processes*. New York: Academic Press, 1975.

Salapatek, P., and Kessen, W. Visual scanning of triangles by the human newborn. *Journal of Experimental Child Psychology*, 1966, 3, 155–167.

Salk, L. Mother's heart beat as an imprinting stimulus. *Transactions of the New York Academy of Sciences*, 1962, 24, 753–763.

Sameroff, A. *Research on Transactions in Early Development*. Paper presented at Clinical and Applied Issues in Infant Development, University of California–Los Angeles, October, 1981.

Sameroff, A., and Chandler, M. Reproductive risk and the continuum of caretaking casuality. In F. Horowitz (Ed.), *Review of Child Development Research* (Vol. 4). Chicago: University of Chicago Press, 1975.

Schlesinger, H. S., and Meadow, K. P. *Sound and Sign: Childhood Deafness and Mental Health*. Berkeley: University of California Press, 1972.

Self, P. A. *Individual Differences in Auditory and Visual Responsiveness in Infants from 3 Days to 6 Weeks of Age*. Unpublished doctoral dissertation. Lawrence: University of Kansas, 1971.

Self, P. A., Horowitz, F. D., and Paden, L. Y. Olfaction in newborn infants. *Developmental Psychology*, 1972, 7, 349–363.

Serafica, F. C., and Cicchetti, H. Down's syndrome children in a strange situation: Attachment and exploration behaviors. *Merrill-Palmer Quarterly*, 1976, 22, 137–150.

Share, J. B., and French, R. W. Early motor development in Down's syndrome children. *Mental Retardation*, 1974, 12(6), 23.

Share, J., Koch, R., Webb, A., and Graliker, B. The longitudinal development of infants and young children with Down's syndrome (mongolism). *American Journal of Mental Deficiency*, 1964, *68*, 685–692.

Sherman, M., and Sherman, I. C. Sensorimotor responses in infants. *Journal of Comparative Psychology*, 1925, *5*, 53–68.

Sherman, M., Sherman, I., and Flory, C. D. Infant behavior. *Comparative Psychology Monographs*, 1936, *12*, 1–107.

Sigman, M., Kopp, C. B., Parmelee, A. H., and Jeffrey, W. E. Visual attention and neurological organization in neonates. *Child Development*, 1973, *44*, 461–466.

Smith, D. W., and Wilson, A. A. *The Child with Down's Syndrome (Mongolism): Causes, Characteristics, and Acceptance*. Philadelphia: W. B. Saunders, 1973.

Sokolov, Y. N. *Perception and the Conditioned Reflex*. New York: Macmillan (S. W. Waydenfeld, translator), 1963.

Soroka, S. M., Corter, C. M., and Abramovitch, R. Infants' tactile discrimination of novel and familiar tactual stimuli. *Child Development*, 1979, *50*, 1251–1253.

Spears, W. C., and Hohle, R. H. Sensory and perceptual processes in infants. In Y. Brackbill (Ed.), *Infancy and Early Childhood*. New York: Free Press, 1967.

Spelke, W. S., and Owsley, C. J. Intermodal exploration and development in infancy. *Infant Behavior and Development*, 1979, *2*, 13–27.

Spitz, R. A. *The First Year of Life*. New York: International Universities Press, 1965.

Staples, R. The responses of infants to color. *Journal of Experimental Psychology*, 1932, *15*, 119–141.

Stechler, G., and Latz, E. Some observations on attention and arousal in the human infant. *Journal of American Academy of Child Psychiatry*, 1966, *5*, 517–525.

Steinschneider, A. Developmental psychophysiology. In Y. Brackbill (Ed.), *Infancy and Early Childhood*. New York: Free Press, 1967.

Trehub, S. E., and Rabinovitch, M. S. Auditory-linguistic sensitivity. *Developmental Psychology*, 1972, *6*, 74–77.

Turkewitz, G., Moreau, T., and Birch, H. G. Head position and receptor organization in the human neonate. *Journal of Experimental Child Psychology*, 1966, *4*, 169–177.

Turnure, C. Response to voice of mother and stranger by babies in the first year. *Developmental Psychology*, 1971, *4*, 182–190.

Uzgiris, J., and Hunt, J. *Assessment in Infancy: Ordinal Scales of Psychological Development*. Urbana: University of Illinois Press, 1975.

Warren, D. H. *Blindness and Early Childhood Development*. New York: American Foundation for the Blind, 1977.

Watson, J. S. Perception of object orientation in infants. *Merrill-Palmer Quarterly*, 1966, *12*, 73–94.

Wedenberg, E. Determinants of the hearing acuity in the newborn. *Nordisk Medicine*, 1956, *50*, 1022–1024.

Weiss, L. P. Differential variations in the amount of activity in newborn infants under continuous light and sound stimulation. *University of Iowa Studies of Child Welfare*, 1934, *9*, 9–74.

Werner, J. S., and Wooten, B. R. Human infants color vision and color perception. *Infant Behavior and Development*, 1979, *2*(3), 241–273.

Wertheimer, M. Psychomotor coordination of auditory and visual space at birth. *Science*, 1961, *134*, 1692.

White, B. L. *Human Infants: Experience and Psychological Development*. Englewood Cliffs, NJ: Prentice-Hall, 1971.

White, B. L., Castle, P., and Held, R. Observations in the development of visually directed reaching. *Child Development*, 1964, *35*, 349–364.

White, B. L., and Held, R. Experience in early human development: Part 2, Plasticity of sensorimotor development in the human infant. In J. Hellmuth (Ed.), *Exceptional Infant (Vol. 1): The Normal Infant*. Seattle: Special Child Publications, 1967.

Wickelgren, L. Convergence in the human newborn. *Journal of Experimental Child Psychology*, 1967, *5*, 74–85.

Wills, D. M. Vulnerable periods in the early development of blind children. *Psychoanalytic Study of the Child*, 1970, *25*, 461–480.

Wilson, J., and Halverson, H. M. Development of a young blind child. *Journal of Genetic Psychology*, 1947, *71*, 155–175.

Wolff, P. A. Observations on the early development of smiling. In B. M. Foss (Ed.), *Determinants of Infant Behavior* (Vol. II). New York: Wiley, 1963.

Young, M. H. Cognitive development in cerebral palsy children. (Doctoral dissertation, State University of New York at Albany, 1977). *Dissertation Abstracts International*, 1978, *38*, 6630A–6631A.

Appendix

FINE MOTOR PINPOINTS

Eye Readiness

I. Moves eyes toward stationary objects, light

    A.   Moves eyes toward stationary objects

Moves eye toward ring	0.1	mo	Bay
	1	mo	Sher
	1	mo	Ges
	2.5	mo	Slos
	3	mo	C
Moves eye toward ring and holds eye on it	0.4	mo	Bay
	1.3	mo	Den
	2	mo	Ges
Turns eyes to ring (at least 30°, Bay; past midline, Den)	1.3	mo	Den
	1.6	mo	Bay
	2	mo	Ges
Moves eye toward cup or cube and holds eye there	2.5	mo	Bay
	3	mo	Ges
	3	mo	C
	3.3	mo	Den
Moves gaze from one object to another	2.6	mo	Bay
Moves gaze to rattle in hand	3	mo	Ges
Moves eyes to stationary objects	3	mo	Sher
within 6–10 in for more than a sec or 2, seldom fixates continuously	3.3	mo	Den
Moves eyes toward ring for sustained length of time (a few sec)	5.4	mo	Bay
Moves eyes in unison; (squint now abnormal)	6	mo	Sher
Moves eyes toward third cube immediately	6	mo	Ges
Moves eyes to inspect details of bell	8	mo	C
Moves eyes to inspect contents of box	9.5	mo	Bay
	11	mo	C

    B.   Moves eyes toward light source

Fixes gaze on brightness of window or blank wall	1	mo	Sher
Turns eyes and head towards light	1	mo	Sher
	1.6	mo	Bay

Reprinted by permission of Grune & Stratton and M. A. Cohen, P. J. Gross, and N. G. Haring. Developmental pinpoints. In N. G. Haring and L. J. Brown (Eds.), *Teaching the Severely Handicapped* (Vol. 1). New York: Grune & Stratton, 1976.

II. Moves eyes to follow moving objects

Moves eyes following ring (in horizontal direction)	0.5 mo 2 mo	Bay C
Moves eyes following vertical light	0.7 mo	Bay
Moves eyes following ring in vertical direction	1 mo 2 mo	Bay C
Moves eyes, following circular path of light	1.2 mo	Bay
Moves eyes following ring in circular path (rattle for 10 sec—Slos; 180°—Den, Ges, Sher)	1.2 mo 2.4 mo 3 mo 3.5 mo	Bay Den Sher/Ges/C Slos
Follows pencil flashlamp briefly with eyes, flashlight at one ft	2 mo	C
Converges eyes as dangling toy is moved toward face	3 mo	Sher
Moves eyes following movement of own hands (fingers—C)	3 mo 3.8 mo 4 mo	Sher/LAP/ Ges Bay LAP
Moves eyes to follow ball across table	3.1 mo 4 mo	Bay C
Moves eyes toward rattle in hand	4 mo	Ges/Slos
Moves eyes toward rolling balls of 2, 1, and ½ in diameter at 10 ft	6 mo	Sher
Moves eyes toward adult movement across room, follows movement	6 mo	Sher
Manipulates bell, moving eyes to inspect detail	6.5 mo	Bay
Moves eyes to correct place where toys dropped within reach of hands	9 mo	Sher
Moves eyes after toys falling over edge of surface (carriage or table)	9 mo	Sher
Moves eyes to correct place for toys that fall out of sight	12 mo	Sher/LAP
Moves eyes to follow small toy pulled across floor up to 12 ft	15 mo	Sher
Moves eyes to follow path of small toy swept vigorously from table	15 mo	Sher
Fixes eye on small dangling toy at 10 ft	18–23 mo	Sher

III. Closes eyes in response to movement of lights and objects

Closes lids tightly when pencil light shone directly into them at 1–2 in	1 mo	Sher
Blinks at shadow of hand, delayed midline regard; blinks at ring	2 mo	Ges
Blinks at toy moved toward face	3 mo	Sher

IV. Fixes gaze on object and reaches

Moves eyes toward raisin; reaches for raisin	4	mo	Ges
	4.4–5.5	mo	Bay
	5	mo	C
Fixes gaze on small objects and reaches for them	4.4	mo	Bay
	6	mo	Ges/Sher
Fixes eyes on and retrieves rolling ball 2½ in, at 10 ft	18–23	mo	Sher

Movement Involving Hands

I. General hand and wrist movements

A. Hand movement

Holds hands open	3	mo	Ges/C

B. Finger movement

Clasps and unclasps hands in finger play	3	mo	Sher/C
	3.2	mo	Bay
Manipulates fingers	4	mo	C
Closes fist and moves thumb	34.5	mo	MPS

C. Wrists

Rotates wrist	5.7	mo	Bay

II. General hand movements in relation to objects

A. Holds, grasps, and/or manipulates objects

Grasps

Grasps handle of spoon, rattle, or like object when fingers are pried open, but may quickly let go	0.7	mo	Bay
	1	mo	Sher
Grasps rattle briefly	2	mo	Ges
	3	mo	LAP
Grasps rattle actively	3	mo	C
	3.3	mo	Den
Grasps with near hand only for rattle, ring	5	mo	Ges
Grasps one cube on contact	5	mo	Ges
Uses whole hand in palmar grasp (cube—Ges)	6	mo	Sher
Grasps with thumb and finger	7.8	mo	Vin
	8.3	mo	Den
Grasps at pellet with unsuccessful inferior scissor grasp	8	mo	Ges
Grasps between finger and thumb in scissor fashion	9	mo	Sher/Ges
Grasps third cube	9	mo	Ges
	10	mo	C

Grasps pellet or raisin in neat pincer grasp	10	mo	Ges/LAP
	10.7	mo	Den
	11	mo	C
Grasps object by handle	10	mo	Ges
Grasps object by top of handle	11	mo	Ges
Grasps and holds 2 small objects in 1 hand	14	mo	Slos
Grasps and holds third cube	14	mo	C
	15	mo	Sher

Holds

Holds ring when placed in hand	1	mo	LAP
Holds cube with ulnar–palmar prehension	3.7	mo	C
Holds 2 cubes in hand	4.7	mo	Bay
Holds 1 cube in hand, approaches another	6	mo	Ges
Holds 2 of 3 cubes offered	6.1	mo	Den
	6.3	mo	Bay
Holds cube with radial palmar grasp	7	mo	Ges
Holds 1 cube, grasps another	7	mo	Ges
Holds 2 cubes more than momentarily	7	mo	Ges
Holds rattle for at least 3-min period	7	mo	Slos
Holds second and third cube presented	7.6	mo	Bay
Holds 2 cubes	8	mo	Ges
	8	mo	Ges
Holds pellet in neat pincer (thumb and forefinger)	8.9	mo	Bay
Holds cube with radial digital grasp	9	mo	Ges
Holds pellet in inferior pincer grasp	10	mo	Ges

Manipulates

Manipulates ring	2.6	mo	Bay
Manipulates rattle in simple way	2.8	mo	Bay
	4	mo	Ges
Moves ring to mouth with hand	3.8	mo	Bay
	4	mo	Ges
Manipulates string (objects—Sher)	8	mo	C
	9	mo	Sher
Manipulates string on ring	9	mo	Ges
Manipulates string with plucking movement	10	mo	Ges
Dangles ring by string	12.4	mo	Bay
	13	mo	Ges

B. Releases objects

Drops rattle immediately when placed in hand	1	mo	Ges
Releases toy by pressing against firm surface but cannot yet put down voluntarily	9	mo	Sher
	10	mo	Ges

C.   Picks up objects
     Takes rattle placed on chest   4   mo   LAP/C
                                                         4.9 mo   Bay
     Picks up cube   4.6 mo   Bay
                                                         6   mo   LAP
     Takes rattle from shoulder   5   mo   C
     Picks up inverted cup   5.2 mo   Bay
     Picks up cup, grasping handle   6   mo   LAP
     Picks up cube from cup in imitation   10.5 mo   Slos
                                                         11   mo   LAP/Ges
     Picks up cube concealed by cup   12   mo   LAP
     Picks up small objects with precise   12   mo   Sher/Ges
       pincer grasp
     Picks up objects one by one, drops,   12   mo   Ges
       picks up again
     Picks up and holds 2 small objects   14   mo   LAP
       in 1 hand
     Picks up string, small objects, neatly   15   mo   Sher
       between thumb and finger
     Picks up small beads, threads, etc.,   18–23   mo   Sher
       immediately on sight with
       delicate pincer grasp
     Picks up pins and thread neatly   24–29   mo   Sher
       and quickly

D.   Uses hands with banging motion
     Bangs objects together in play   5   mo   LAP
                                                         5.4 mo   Bay
     Bangs bell   7   mo   Ges
     Bangs spoon   8   mo   LAP/C
                                                         8.6 mo   Bay
     Hits 2 objects together spontaneously   9   mo   Slos
     Hits cup with spoon   10   mo   C/LAP
     Rattles spoon in cup   12   mo   C/Sher
     Beats 2 spoons together   12   mo   C

E.   Pulls objects
     Pulls down suspended ring   5   mo   C
                                                         5.6 mo   Den
                                                         5.7 mo   Bay
     Pulls string and secures ring   7.1 mo   Bay
                                                         8   mo   C

F.   Transfers objects from hand to hand
     Transfers object from hand to hand   5   mo   C/Slos
                                                         5.5 mo   Bay
     Transfers cube from hand to hand   6   mo   LAP
     Shifts brush from one hand to   18–23   mo   Ges
       another in painting

G.   Uses hands with raking motion
     Rakes and obtains small objects   5.6 mo   Den
       (raisins, beads)   5.8 mo   Bay
                                                         6   mo   LAP

	Attempts to pick up small objects (rakes, contacts—Ges, Bay)	6.8 mo 7 mo	Bay C/Ges
	Rakes small object radially and holds	8 mo	Ges
H.	Shakes objects		
	Shakes bell	7 mo	LAP/Ges
I.	Pokes objects		
	Pokes at holes in pegboard	8.9 mo	Bay
	Pokes at small object with index finger	9 mo	Sher
J.	Pushes objects		
	Pushes cube with cube	9 mo	Ges
K.	Retrieves objects		
	Removes round block easily from formboard	12 mo	Ges
	Retrieves rolling ball with hand	18–24 mo	Ges
L.	Dumps objects		
	Dumps raisins, beads from bottle spontaneously	13.3 mo	Den
	Dumps raisins from bottle (in imitation)	14.8 mo	Den
	Dumps raisins from bottle (spontaneously)	18 mo	LAP
	Fills and dumps containers with sand	24–29 mo	LAP
M.	Closes boxes		
	Closes round box	14.6 mo 16 mo	Bay C
	Closes oblong box	20 mo	C
N.	Uses implements to obtain toys		
	Obtains toy with implement (i.e., stick)	17 mo 20 mo	Bay/LAP C
	Uses string to draw toy closer	27.6 mo	MPS

III. Specific hand movements in relation to objects; often used as part of a preacademic program

    A. Places objects

       Cubes in Containers

Places cube in cup	9 mo 10 mo	Bay C
Places cube in cup on command	9.4 mo 11 mo	Bay C
Puts 3 or more cubes in cup	11.8 mo 12 mo	Bay LAP
Places 1 cube in cup and takes it out (on command—Ges)	12 mo 13 mo	C/Sher Ges

Places 9 cubes in cup	14.3 mo	Bay
Places 6 cubes in and out of cup with demonstration	15 mo	Ges
Places 10 cubes in cup	18 mo	C
Places 13 of 16 cubes in box	21.6 mo	MPS
Places 12 cubes in box (12 of 12)	24 mo	C
Places 16 cubes in box in 125 sec	26.3 mo	MPS
Nests four cubes in 250 sec	27.6 mo	MPS
Places 16 cubes in box in 100 sec	32.3 mo	MPS
Nests 4 cubes in 30 sec	33 mo	MPS

Pegs in Holes

Touches holes in pegboard	8.9 mo	Bay
	10 mo	C
Places 1 peg repeatedly	13 mo	Bay
Pulls out and replaces peg in Wallin Peg Board A	14 mo	C
Puts all pegs in Wallin Peg Board (6 pegs in holes) when used—C; in 70 sec—Bay)	16 mo	C
	16.4 mo	Bay
Puts pegs (6) in holes in 70 sec	16.4 mo	Bay
Puts pegs (6) in holes in 42 sec	17.6 mo	Bay
Puts 6 round pegs in holes in 30 sec (in 38 sec—MPS)	18 mo	C
	20 mo	Bay
	21 mo	MPS
Place 6 square pegs in square holes	20 mo	C
Puts 6 round pegs in pegboard in 25 sec	26.5 mo	MPS
Places 6 round pegs in holes in pegboard in 22 sec	26.6 mo	MPS
Puts 6 square pegs in square holes in 41 sec	27 mo	MPS
Places 6 square pegs in square holes in pegboard in 27 sec	32.6 mo	MPS
Places 6 round pegs in round holes (in 20 sec—MPS)	33–38.4 mo	MPS
	36–48 mo	LAP

Pellets in Containers

Points at pellet released into bottle	11 mo	Ges
Tries to put pellet in bottle; fails	13 mo	Ges
Takes pellet out of bottle	13.4 mo	Bay
Takes pellet out of bottle in imitation	14 mo	C
Puts pellet in and takes it out to solve pellet and bottle problem	16 mo	C

Blocks in Structures
Vertical Structures

Builds tower of 2 blocks	13 mo	LAP
	13.4 mo	Bay
	15 mo	Ges/Sher
	15.5 mo	Slos

Places blocks or spools to make tower of 3 small blocks or spools	16	mo Slos
	16.7	mo Bay
Places blocks or spools to make tower of 4 small blocks or spools	17	mo Slos
	18–24	mo Den
	30–36	mo Bay/C/Ges/ MPS/Minn/ Sher
Places blocks to make tower of 3 blocks	20	mo Sher/Ges/C
	21	mo MPS
Places blocks to make tower of 5–6 blocks	21	mo LAP
	23	mo Slos/Bay
Places blocks to form bridge or tower (in imitation)	30	mo C
	32	mo Den
	36–38	mo LAP
Places blocks to form tower of 7 blocks (8—Ges, Bay)	30 +	mo Sher/Ges
Makes tower with 9 blocks	36–48	mo Sher/Ges LAP

Horizontal Structures

Makes train of blocks, in imitation (places blocks horizontally)	26.1	mo Bay
	27	mo C
Lines up blocks to form "train" (spontaneously)	30–35	mo Sher

Combination, Vertical-Horizontal

Moves blocks to build vertically and horizontally with beginning of symmetry	30–35		mo Ges
Puts chimney on train	30–35	mo	Ges
Places blocks to make bridge (spontaneously)	30–36	mo	Den/MPS
	36–42	mo	Bay/C/Ges H/Sher
Makes bridge of 3 blocks from model	32	mo	Den/C/H/ MPS

Forms in Formboards

Places 1 round block in formboard (2 each, 3 geometric shapes)	13.6	mo	Bay
Places 1 round block in formboard (1 each, 3 geometric shapes)	15	mo	Ges
	16	mo	C
Places circle in rotated formboard	18	mo	C
Places 2 round and 2 square blocks on formboard	19.3	mo	Bay
Places square in 3-hole formboard	20	mo	C
Places 3 blocks correctly on formboard (triangle, square, circle)	21.2	mo	Bay
	22	mo	C
	24–29	mo	H/Ges
Places 6 blocks correctly on formboard (circle, square, triangle)	22.4	mo	Bay
Places blocks correctly after 4 trials	24	mo	LAP

Places 3 blocks (square, circle, triangle) on rotated formboard	25.4 mo	Bay
	30 mo	C
Puts 6 blocks on formboard in 150 sec	30 mo	Bay
Places 6 round and square blocks in formboard in 90 sec	30 mo	Bay
Places 6 round and square blocks on formboard in 60 sec	30 + mo	Bay
Places 2 of three color forms, all 1 color	30–35 mo	Ges
Places forms correctly and repeatedly when formboard is rotated or reversed	30–35 mo	Bay
Places 2 of 10 blocks in correct place on formboard (Séguin)	31.5 mo	MPS
Places 10 shapes on formboard in 222 sec (Séguin)	33 mo	MPS

B. Takes objects apart; puts objects together

Takes things apart and puts them together	24–29 mo	Ges

C. Strings beads

Strings four beads—two sec	36–48 mo	C/H/LAP

GROSS-MOTOR PINPOINTS

I. Static balance

    A. Supports head
        1. Moves head

Makes lateral head movements	0.1 mo	Bay
	1 mo	LAP
Moves head following dangling ring	3.2 mo	Bay
	5 mo	Ges
Moves head and eyes in every direction	6 mo	Sher
Lifts head for 5-sec interval when supine	7.5 mo	Slos

        2. Lifts head

Lifts head when held at shoulder	0.1 mo	Bay
	1 mo	LAP
Lifts head momentarily when prone	1 mo	LAP
	1 mo	Ges
Lifts head from dorsal suspension	1.7 mo	Bay
Lifts head up when prone (90°— Den; for several sec—C)	2 mo	C
	2.2 mo	Ges/Den
	2.5 mo	Sher

Lifts head and upper chest well up in midline using forearms as support, legs straight out, buttocks flat when prone (for 10 sec—Slos)	2.1 mo	Bay
	2.5 mo	Slos
	3 mo	C/Den/Sher
	4 mo	Ges
Lifts head and chest well up supporting himself on extended arms, when prone	6 mo	Sher
Raises head from pillow when supine	6 mo	Sher
	7 mo	Ges

3. Holds head

Holds head erect when held at shoulder for 3 sec	0.8 mo	Bay
	1 mo	Sher
Turns head immediately to sides when prone; arms and legs flexed under body, buttocks humped up	1 mo	Sher/Ges
Lets head fall forward, with back in one complete curve when held sitting (marked head lay—Ges)		
Holds head to one side when supine; with arms and legs on same side outstretched, or both arms flexed, knees apart, soles of feet turned inward, lifted head falls loosely	1 mo	Sher/Ges
Holds head predominately erect when held sitting	2 mo	Ges
	3 mo	Vin
Holds head in midposition when prone	2 mo	Ges
	3 mo	Sher
Holds head steady, set forward when held sitting	2.3 mo	Bay
	2.9 mo	Den
	3 mo	Vin/C
	4 mo	Ges
Holds head in midposition when supine	3 mo	Sher/Ges
Balances head when body is tilted	4.2 mo	Bay
Holds head firmly erect, back straight when sitting	6 mo	Sher/Ges

B. Thrusts, waves arms

Thrusts arm in play when supine	0.8 mo	Bay
	1 mo	Sher
Waves arm symmetrically	3 mo	Sher
Moves arms briskly and holds them up to be lifted	6 mo	Sher
Moves arms very actively in carriage, bath, and crib	9 mo	Sher

C.   Thrusts legs

Thrusts legs in play when supine	0.8	mo	Bay
	1	mo	Sher
Lifts legs into vertical position and grasps foot	6	mo	Sher/Ges
Brings feet to mouth when supine	7	mo	Slos

D.   Sits

Holds back straight, except in	3	mo	Sher/C
lumbar region, with head erect and	4	mo	Ges
steady for several sec, when held sitting	4.5	mo	Slos
Pulls to sit, with no head lag	4.2	mo	Den
	4.8	mo	Bay
	5	mo	Ges
Sits without support (head erect,	5	mo	Ges/LAP
steady—Ges)	5.3	mo	Bay
	5.4	mo	Vin
	5.5	mo	Den
Sits and turns from side-to-side to look around	6	mo	Sher
Sits propped 30 min	6	mo	Ges
Sits briefly, leans forward on hands	7	mo	Ges
Sits erect without support momentarily	7	mo	Ges
Pulls self up to sitting position	7.6	mo	Den
	8.3	mo	Bay
Sits by self, 1 min erect, unsteady	8	mo	Ges
Sits erect without support for 10 min	8.5	mo	Slos
	9	mo	Ges
Sits, leans forward, erect	9	mo	Ges
Sits steady and indefinitely	9.6	mo	Bay
	9.5	mo	Slos
	10	mo	Ges
Sits, goes over to prone	10	mo	Ges
Attains sitting position unaided	12	mo	Ges/LAP/ Sher
Rises to sitting position from lying down	12	mo	Sher
Sits well and for indefinite time	12	mo	Sher
Lets self down from standing or sitting by collapsing backwards with bump, or occasionally by falling forward on hands and then back to sitting	15	mo	Sher/LAP

E.   Stands

On Broad Surface

Sags at knees when held standing with feet on hard surface	3	mo	Sher

Bears some weight on legs when held standing	3	mo	Ges
	4.2	mo	Den
Lifts one foot when held standing	4	mo	Ges
Stands while holding on	5.8	mo	Den
	6	mo	LAP
Pulls self upright	6.6	mo	Vin
Stands, maintaining large fraction of weight	7	mo	Ges
Pulls self to stand	7.6	mo	Den
	8.1	mo	Bay
	8	mo	LAP
Stands, maintains briefly, when hands held	8	mo	Ges
Stands holding on to support self, but cannot lower self	9	mo	Ges/Sher/Slos
Stands momentarily	9.8	mo	Den
	10.2	mo	Vin
Stands alone well	11	mo	LAP/Bay
	11.5	mo	Den
Pulls self to standing and lets self down again holding onto furniture (with support, cruises at rail—Ges)	12	mo	Sher/Ges
May stand alone for a few moments (seconds—Slos)	12	mo	Sher
	13	mo	Slos
Stands (from supine)	12.6	mo	Bay
Stands on right foot with help	16.1	mo	Bay/LAP
Stands on request; turns to side first	21.9	mo	Bay
Stands on left foot alone	22	mo	LAP
	22.7	mo	Bay
	23.2	mo	MPS
Stands with abdomen protruding less than at 18 mo	24–29	mo	Ges
Stands on request; pulls self to sitting position first	30+	mo	Bay
Stands on tiptoe if shown	30–35	mo	Sher
Attempts to stand on one foot	30–35	mo	Ges
Stands on one foot for 1 sec	30	mo	Den

On Walking Board

Tries to stand on walking board	17	mo	LAP
	17.5	mo	Slos
	17.8	mo	Bay
Stands with both feet on walking board	24.5	mo	Bay
	24–30	mo	Bay

F.　Bends from waist

Stoops and recovers	11.5	mo	Den
Stoops to pick up toys from floor	15	mo	Sher/LAP
Picks up toy from floor without falling	18–23	mo	Sher
	18–24	mo	LAP
Bends at waist to pick up something from floor	24–29	mo	Ges

G. Squats

Squats to rest or to play with object on ground and rises to feet without using hands	24–29	mo	Sher

II. Maintains dynamic balance, using basic movement patterns

A. Creeps and crawls

Makes crawling movements when prone	0.1	mo	Bay
Moves body more smoothly and continuously, with more pliable limbs	3	mo	Sher
Attempts to crawl on all fours	9	mo	Sher
Moves about on floor	10	mo	Slos/Ges
Crawls rapidly on all fours	12	mo	Sher/LAP
Crawls upstairs (creeps up—Ges)	15	mo	Sher/Ges
Creeps backward downstairs. Bumps	18–23	mo	Sher
down a few steps on buttocks, facing forward occasionally	18–24	mo	LAP

B. Takes steps

On Level Ground

Presses down feet, straightens body, and often makes reflex stepping movements when held standing on hard surface	1	mo	Sher
Lifts foot when held standing	3	mo	Ges/LAP
Steps on alternate feet when held standing	9	mo	Sher
Takes steps while holding onto furniture	9.2	mo	Den
Takes steps but needs both hands held (with help—Bay)	9.6	mo	Ges
	11	mo	Slos
Takes steps with assistance	11	mo	LAP
Takes steps with one or both hands held (five steps—Slos)	12	mo	Sher/Slos
	13	mo	Ges
Takes steps alone	12	mo	LAP
	17	mo	Den
Takes steps around furniture, stepping sideways	12	mo	Sher
Walks well (without help, may fall— Slos) (unsteadily, with feet wide apart, arms flexed and held slightly above head or at shoulder level to balance—Sher; few steps, falls by collapsing; creeping discarded—Ges)	12.1	mo	Den
	13	mo	Ges
	15	mo	Slos/Sher/ Ges
Takes steps sideways	14.1	mo	Bay
Takes steps backward	14.3	mo	Den
	14.6	mo	Bay

Starts and stops walking without falling	18–23	mo	Sher
Walks well, takes steps with feet only slightly apart	18	mo	Sher/Ges/ Slos
Walks with knees and elbows slightly bent, shoulders hunched, holds arms out and backward	24–29	mo	Ges
Walks, taking steps on tiptoe	25.7	mo	Bay
	30	mo	Sher/H/ Ges/LAP
Walks; takes steps heel-to-toe	43	mo	Den
Walks backward; takes steps heel-to-toe	56	mo	Den/Lap

Upstairs, Downstairs

Takes steps upstairs with help	16.1	mo	Bay
	18–23	mo	Sher
Takes steps downstairs with help	16.4	mo	Bay
Takes steps upstairs unassisted	21	mo	Vin
Takes steps downstairs when one hand is held	21	mo	LAP
	21.5	mo	Slos
Takes steps up and down stairs, without assistance	21	mo	LAP
Takes steps upstairs and down holding on to rail or wall, two feet to a step	24–29	mo	Ges/Sher
Takes steps upstairs alone, with both feet on each step	25.1	mo	Bay
Takes steps downstairs alone, with both feet on each step	25.8	mo	Bay
Takes steps downstairs with alternating forward foot	30 +	mo	Bay
Takes steps upstairs with alternating forward foot	30 +	mo	Bay
Takes steps upstairs alone, but downstairs holding rail, two feet to a step	30–35	mo	Sher

On Walking Board, Line

Takes steps with one foot on walking board	20	mo	LAP
	20.6	mo	Bay
Takes steps on a line, general direction	23	mo	LAP
	23.9	mo	Bay
Attempts step on walking board	24–30	mo	Bay
Attempts step on walking board	27.6	mo	Bay
Takes steps backward for 10 ft	27.8	mo	Bay
Alternates steps part way on walking board	30 +	mo	Bay
Takes steps with feet on line for 10 ft	30 +	mo	Bay
	30–36	mo	Bay
Takes steps part way on walking board	30–36	mo	Bay

| | Takes steps between two parallel lines, 8 in apart on floor, without stepping on the lines for 8–10 ft | 30–36 | mo | H |

C. Rolls body

Rolls partway to side when supine	1	mo	Ges
	1.5	mo	Slos
Turns to same side when cheek touched; turns away when ear rubbed	1	mo	Sher
Turns from side to back	1.8	mo	Bay
	2	mo	LAP
Rolls over	2.8	mo	Den
	3.8	mo	Vin
	3	mo	LAP
Turns from back to side	4	mo	LAP
	4.4	mo	Bay
Verges on rolling when prone	5	mo	Ges
Rolls over front to back	6	mo	Sher
Rolls from back to stomach	6	mo	Slos/Ges
	6.4	mo	Bay
Pivots 180° in order to obtain toy kept just out of reach	6.5	mo	Slos
Pivots body when prone	8	mo	Ges
Turns body to look sideways while stretching out to grasp toy	9	mo	Sher
Progresses on floor by rolling or squirming	9	mo	Sher

D. Runs

Runs stiffly upright, with eyes fixed on ground 1–2 yd ahead, but cannot continue around obstacles	18	mo	Sher/Slos
Runs on whole foot, stopping and starting with ease and avoiding obstacles	24–29	mo	Ges
Runs leaning forward	24–29	mo	Sher
Runs well straight forward	30–35	mo	Sher

E. Climbs

Climbs forward into adult chair then turns around and sits	18–23	mo	Sher
Climbs down from adult chair without assistance	21	mo	LAP
Climbs on furniture to look out of window, and climbs down again without assistance	24–29	mo	Ges/Sher
Climbs easy nursery apparatus	30–35	mo	Sher

F. Jumps

| Jumps (general activities requiring jumping skills) | 18–24 | mo | Bay/Den |
| | 30–36 | mo | Sher/Ges |

Vertically

Jumps in place	23.5	mo	Bay
	24	mo	LAP
Jumps from bottom step	24.8	mo	Bay
Jumps from second step	28.1	mo	Bay
Jumps distance of 4–14 inches	29.1	mo	Bay
Jumps with two feet together	30–35	mo	Sher/Ges
Jumps over string 2 in high	30+	mo	Bay
Jumps over string 8 in high	30+	mo	Bay

III. Maintains other general coordinated movement patterns

    A.   Reaches with arm

Reaches for dangling ring	3	mo	LAP
	3.1	mo	Bay
	3.6	mo	Den
	4.2	mo	Vin
Reaches for cube	4.1	mo	Bay
Holds arms extended when prone	5	mo	Ges
Reaches with two hands to approach rattle, bell	5	mo	Ges
Reaches unilaterally	5.4	mo	Bay
	6.0	mo	C
Reaches for second cube	5.4	mo	Bay
Reaches for rattle held in front with one hand, grabs, and shakes it	6.5	mo	Slos
Reaches for and holds 2 cubes	7	mo	C
Reaches for toy out of reach on table	8	mo	Slos
	9	mo	Sher
Reaches around object for toy	14	mo	C

    B.   Kicks

Kicks vigorously, legs alternating or occasionally together	3	mo	Sher
Kicks strongly, legs alternating	6	mo	Sher
Kicks ball forward	20–22.3	mo	Den
	23.4	mo	Bay
Kicks large ball	21	mo	LAP
	24–29	mo	Ges
	30–35	mo	Sher

    C.   Bounces

Bears weight on feet and bounces up and down actively when held standing with feet touching hard surface	6	mo	Sher
	7	mo	Ges

    D.   Pushes objects: pulls objects

Pushes small toy (pulls car)	11	mo	LAP
	11.3	mo	Bay

Pushes large wheeled toy with handle on level ground	15	mo	Sher
Pushes and pulls large toys, boxes, etc., around floor	18–23	mo	Sher/Ges
Pushes and pulls large toys, boxes, etc., around floor without falling	18–24	mo	LAP
Pulls wheeled toy by cord	24–29	mo	Sher
Pushes and pulls large toys skillfully, but has difficulty steering them around obstacles	30–35	mo	Sher/Ges

E.   Throws objects

Throws ball with examiner	11.6	mo	Den
	13	mo	LAP
Throws ball, releasing with slight cast forward (Ges)	13.6	mo	Bay
	14	mo	Ges
Casts objects in play	15	mo	Ges
Throws small rubber ball	20	mo	LAP/Slos
	21	mo	MPS
Throws ball overhand	18–24	mo	Den
Throws ball overhead	19	mo	LAP
Throws small ball without falling	24–29	mo	Sher

F.   Rolls objects

Rolls ball back and forth in game	12	mo	Ges

G.   Kneels

Kneels unaided or with slight support on floor and in carriage, crib, and bath	15	mo	Sher/LAP

H.   Carries objects

Carries large objects while walking	18–24	mo	LAP
	18–23	mo	Sher

I.   Pedals tricycle

	23.9	mo	Sher/Ges/ H/Den
	24	mo	LAP

RECEPTIVE LANGUAGE PINPOINTS

I.   Responds to sounds

A.   Stops movement in response to sounds

Stops movement at sound of bell	0.1	mo	Bay
	1	mo	Sher
	2	mo	LAP
Stops movement at sound of rattle	0.1	mo	Bay
	1	mo	LAP
Stops movement in response to sharp sound	0.1	mo	Bay

		Stops movement in response to voice	0.7	mo	Bay
			1	mo	LAP
			2	mo	C
		Stops movement or lessens it at the sound from a piece of paper when it is crumpled up close to ear, or two blocks gently knocked together	1	mo	Slos
B.		Stops whimpering in response to sounds			
		Stops whimpering in response to sound of nearby soothing human voice, but not when infant is screaming for feeding	1	mo	Sher
		Stops whimpering or smiles to sound of mother's voice before she touches him, except when infant is screaming	3	mo	Sher
		Quiets to rattle of spoon or sound of bell rung out of sight for 3–5 sec at 6–12 in from ear	3	mo	Sher
C.		Makes "startle" movement in response to sounds			
		Stiffens, quivers, blinks, screws eyes up, extends limbs, fans out fingers and toes, and may cry when startled by sudden loud noises	1–3	mo	Sher
D.		Turns toward source of sound			
	1.	Random sounds			
		Moves eyes toward sound source	2.2	mo	Bay
			3	mo	Sher
		Turns head to sound of bell	3.8	mo	Bay
			5	mo	C
			6	mo	Ges
		Turns head to sound of rattle (crumpling of paper—Slos)	3.9	mo	Bay
			5.5	mo	Slos
		Turns head after fallen spoon	5.2	mo	Bay
		Turns head to sounds such as bell, whistle, clock	18–23	mo	Ges
	2.	Human voice			
		Turns head to voice	3	mo	C
			4	mo	LAP
			5.6	mo	Den
		Stops movement, turns head to familiar words	7.9	mo	Bay
		Responds by turning head, stopping movement to name, "no-no"	9	mo	Ges
			10.1	mo	Bay
			9–12	mo	LAP
		Turns immediately to own name	12	mo	Sher

II. Responds to verbal requests

    A. Makes directional body movements
        in response to requests

Moves body to follow simple	9	mo	C
directions, adjust to gestures (pat-	9.1	mo	Bay
a-cake, bye-bye)	9.5	mo	Slos
	10	mo	Ges
	11–16	mo	Vin
Unwraps block upon question,	10.5	mo	Bay
"Where's the block?"			
Moves body appropriately to show	12	mo	Sher/LAP
that he understands several words			
in usual context (e.g., own and			
family names, bye-bye, walk,			
dinner, kitty, cup, spoon, ball, car)			
Moves body in response to two of	28.2	mo	Bay
the following prepositions; on, in,			
under, behind, in front of			

    B. Gives objects upon request

Gives several common objects on	12	mo	Sher
request	15	mo	LAP
	15.3	mo	Bay
Follows command to give pencil,	26–27	mo	Slos
paper to examiner; choice of			
pencil, paper, book			

    C. Points to objects, body parts, and
        pictures on request

        1. Objects

Points to familiar persons,	15	mo	Sher
animals, toys, etc., when			
requested			
Points to objects showing	22	mo	LAP
discrimination of two—cup,			
plate, box			
Points to 2 of 6 objects (kitty,	22	mo	LAP
button, thimble, cup, engine,			
spoon)			
Points to 4 of 6 of the following	24–29	mo	C
objects: kitty, button, thimble,			
cup, spoon, engine			
Points to 3—cup, plate, box	25.6	mo	Bay
(third—C)			
Points upon request to floor,	31	mo	Slos
window, door			

        2. Body parts

Points to one named body part	17	mo	LAP/Den/
			Sher
	19.1	mo	Bay

Points to 3 body parts of self or doll (hair, eyes, nose—Sher)	18	mo	LAP
	18–23	mo	C
	20	mo	C
Points to 5 body parts of self or doll	22	mo	C/LAP
Points to fingers, shoes	30	mo	Slos
Points to 6 body parts of self or doll	30–35	mo	LAP/C
Points to teeth and chin on request	34	mo	LAP

3. Pictures

Points to 3 pictures upon request	19.7	mo	Bay
Points to 5 of 6 pictures of	21.6	mo	Bay/Vin
common objects (2 of 6—	22	mo	C
clock, basket, book, flag, leaf, star—C)			
Points to 7 of 10 pictures of	24.7	mo	Bay
common objects	30	mo	C
Points to 6 of 10 pictures by	27	mo	C
name			

4. Other (size, part-whole)

Can indicate correctly when asked to point to chair and leg of chair	25	mo	Slos

D. Places objects in response to request
One-step directions

Follows direction to put doll in chair	17.8	mo	Bay
Follows 1-step direction	18	mo	LAP
Follows 2 of 3 directions, i.e., "put	19.8	mo	Den
the doll in the chair," "put the	20	mo	C
spoon in the cup," etc.	24	mo	LAP

Complex directions

Carries out 2-step directions with ball	18	mo	LAP
Follows 3 directions with object	21	mo	LAP
Follows a 2-stage command	30–36	mo	LAP

E. Matches objects, pictures, and colors
in response to requests
Objects, Pictures

Matches familiar objects	24	mo	LAP

Colors

Matches colored blocks	30–35	mo	LAP
Matches blocks of 4 colors (red, green, yellow, blue)	30.8	mo	MPS

EXPRESSIVE LANGUAGE PINPOINTS

I. Nonverbal

    A.   Makes eye contact

Turns eyes to fix vision on person temporarily	0.1	mo	Bay
Fixes eye on examiner's face; ceases activity	1	mo	Ges
Fixes eyes directly on examiner's face	3	mo	LAP

    B.   Makes gestures

Smiles as examiner talks and smiles	1.5	mo	Bay
Smiles (spontaneously—Den)	1.9	mo	Den
	2	mo	Ges
	2.1	mo	Bay
Waves "bye-bye"	6–12	mo	LAP
Offers object, such as small toy, to another person	12	mo	Sher
Gestures to make wants known	14.6	mo	Bay
Combines gestures and utterances to make wants known	18–23	mo	LAP

    C.   Imitates motor activities

Plays peek-a-boo	6	mo	LAP
Plays pat-a-cake	9	mo	LAP
Seizes bell in hand, imitates ringing action	9	mo	C Sher
	10	mo	Ges
Imitates putting beads in box	12.9	mo	Bay

II. Verbal

    A.   Makes early sounds

        1.   Emits sounds with a potential relationship to specific situations

Vocalizes once or twice (small throaty voices other than crying—Slos, Ges; babbles—C)	0.9	mo	Bay
	1	mo	Slos/Ges/Sher/LAP
	2	mo	C
Vocalizes at least 4 times	1.6	mo	Bay
Vocalizes—not crying	2	mo	LAP
Squeals	2.2	mo	Den
	5	mo	Ges
Laughs	2	mo	Den
	3	mo	Vin
Coos	3	mo	Slos
Chuckles	3	mo	Slos/Ges/LAP
Laughs aloud	4	mo	Ges
Cries (m-m-m-sound)	7	mo	Ges

    2.   Vocalizes in relation to specific
        primary needs

Cries when hungry or uncomfortable	1	mo	Sher
Vocalizes—babbles or coos in play when alone or when talked to	2	mo	LAP
Cries when uncomfortable or annoyed	3	mo	Sher
Vocalizes when spoken to or pleased	3	mo	Sher/Ges
Grunts, growls spontaneous vocal sounds (social)	6	mo	Ges
Vocalizes deliberately as means of interpersonal relationship	9	mo	Sher
Shouts to attract attention, listens, then shouts again	9	mo	Sher
Indicates wants by gesture and vocalization	12	mo	LAP

B.   Establishes control of potential
       speech sounds
     1.   Phonological development

Differentiated Speech Sounds

Makes single vowel sounds—ah, eh, uh	2	mo	Ges/LAP
Vocalizes 2 different sounds	2.3	mo	Bay
Babbles, using series of syllables	4	mo	LAP
Vocalizes 4 different syllables	7	mo	Bay
Makes polysyllabic vowel sounds	7	mo	Ges
	7.8	mo	Bay
Says "da-da" or equivalent	7.9	mo	Bay
	8	mo	Slos/C
	9	mo	Ges
	10	mo	Den
Vocalizes single syllable as da, ba, ka	8	mo	Ges
Babbles tunefully, repeating syllables in string (mam-mam)	9	mo	Sher
Jabbers loudly using wide range of inflections and phonetic units	12	mo	LAP
	15	mo	Sher
Uses jargon	15	mo	Sher
On 1 word responses, often uses initial consonant with a vowel, but seldom the final consonant	18	mo	LAP

Expanded Control of Intonation, Pitch, Stress

Jabbers tunefully to self at play	18–23	mo	Sher
2. Imitates sounds	6.6	mo	Vin
Imitates speech sounds	7	mo	LAP

Imitates sounds such as cough, tongue click, smacking lips, brrr, etc.	9	mo	Sher/Ges

3. "Masters" consonants

The information below represents the average age at which correct consonant production first occurs and the upper age limit of customary production. At the upper age limit, according to sources consulted (Sanders, 1972), 90% of the population tested could produce the required consonants in two out of three positions in words.

p, m, h, w, b	18–36	mo
k, g, d	24–48	mo
t, ng	24–72	mo
f, y	30–48	mo
r, l, s	36–72	mo
ch, sh, z	42–84	mo
j	48–84	mo
v	48–96	mo
th (think)	52–84	mo
th (then)	60–96	mo
zh	72–96 + mo	

C. Says words

1. Says words in response to environmental cues; expands vocabulary (although not specifically stated by sources consulted, one suspects that imitation plays an important part)

Says 1 word other than mama or dada, this 1 word can be short syllable child uses consistently to designate an object	10	mo	Slos/Ges
	11	mo	C
Uses 2 words in speaking vocabulary besides "ma-ma" or "da-da" (including "da-da"—Bay; says "ta-ta" or equivalent—Ges)	12	mo	C
	12.5	mo	Slos
	13–15	mo	Ges
	14.2	mo	Bay
Says 3 words other than ma-ma and da-da	12.3	mo	Den
	12.5	mo	Slos
	14	mo	Ges/LAP/C
Says 4 or 5 words including names	15	mo	LAP
Says vocabulary of 4–6 words (including names—Ges; 5 words—C, Slos)	15	mo	Ges
	16	mo	C/Slos

Says 6 words (besides mama and dada)	17	mo	LAP/Slos
Uses 6–20 recognizable words and understands many more	18–23	mo	Sher
Uses expressive vocabulary of at least 15 words (25—Vin)	20.5	mo	Vin/Slos
Says 20 words	21	mo	LAP
	24–29	mo	Sher/Slos
Uses expressive vocabulary of 50 or more words (average vocabulary—272 words—H)	24–29	mo	LAP
Uses 200 or more recognizable words (speech shows numerous "infantilisms")	30–35	mo	LAP/Sher

2. Says words in imitation

Imitates words	12	mo	Sher
	12.5	mo	Bay
Echoes prominent or last words addressed to him	18–23	mo	Sher
Says words; echolalia almost constant, with 1 or more stressed words repeated	24–29	mo	Sher

3. Says words, labeling objects, pictures, colors

Objects

Labels 1 object (When asked "What is this?")	17.8	mo	Bay
Labels 2 of 5 objects (ball, watch, pencil, scissors, cup)	21.4	mo	Bay
Labels 3 of 4 objects of following: ball, watch, pencil, scissors, cup	24	mo	Bay
Labels 3 of the following objects: chair, automobile, box, key, fork (4 at 27 mo—C)	24	mo	C
Names special miniature toys at distance of 10 ft	24–29	mo	Sher
Names 4 of 5 common objects: chair, auto, box, key, fork	27	mo	C/LAP
Labels own mud and clay products as pies, cakes	30–35	mo	Ges/LAP
Names 6 of 6 common objects: flag, chair, car, box, key, fork	30–35	mo	LAP
Names block structure as a bridge, bed, track	30–35	mo	Ges
Names agent of 6 of 20 actions (What cuts?—knife)	34.4	mo	MPS

Pictures

Names 1 of 5 pictures of common objects (cat, bird, dog, horse, man)	19.3	mo	Bay
	20.3	mo	Den

Names 3 of 4 pictures of common objects	22	mo LAP
	22.1	mo Bay
Names 3 of 18 pictures of common objects	24	mo C
Names familiar picture cards	24	mo LAP
Names 5 of 10 pictures	25	mo Bay
Identifies 6 of 10 pictures of common objects	27	mo C
Names 8 of 18 pictures of common objects (most of *Golden ABC* pictures—Vin)	30–35	mo C/Vin

Colors

Names 1 color	30–35	mo Vin

4. Says words imitatively in response to verbal cue (i.e., "say 'kitty'")

Imitates 2 of 4 words (ball, kitty, bird, dinner)	22.4	mo MPS
	24	mo LAP
Imitates 4 of 4 words (ball, kitty, bird, dinner)	24.4	mo MPS
Imitates names for hair, hands, feet, nose, eyes, mouth, shoes	24–29	mo LAP
Shows correctly and imitates on request words for hair, hands, feet, nose, eyes, mouth, shoes	24–29	mo Sher

D. Uses words in sentences—words categorized according to "parts of speech." While the generative linguistics model attempts to avoid using this type of categorization, it may yet be of interest to note when these "parts of speech" are first used according to adult rules, and which constructions seem to present more problems.

Nouns and Verbs
Nouns and verbs appear to be among the first words acquired and are still used most frequently even between the third and fourth year.

Uses nouns and verbs most frequently	36–48	mo LAP

Pronouns

Uses "me," "you," and refers to self by name	23.5	mo Slos
Uses "I," "me," "you," etc., in speech, not always correctly	24–29	mo Vin
	24	mo LAP
	30–35	mo Sher/Ges

Plural and Tense Inflections

Uses plural inflections	28	mo	Vin/C/Den/ Ges/Sher
	36–48	mo	LAP

Adjectives and Adverbs

Says words, verbalizing opposites	30	mo	LAP

E. Says phrases
1. Makes statements

Combines 2 different words in speech	18	mo	LAP
	20.6	mo	Bay
	21	mo	Slos
Demands desired objects by pointing, accompanied by loud, urgent vocalization or single words (uses words to make wants known—C, Bay, Ges)	18	mo	C
	19	mo	Slos
Asks for water when thirsty	23	mo	LAP
Asks for food when hungry	23	mo	LAP
Talks to self continually during play	24–29	mo	Sher
Combines 2 or more words to form simple sentences (3— Slos)	24–29	mo	Sher/Slos/ LAP
Says 10 words in a group	30.5	mo	MPS
Utters negative statement	30–36	mo	LAP
Talks intelligibly to self at play concerning events happening here-and-now	30–35	mo	Sher/Ges
Says 13 words in a group	34.0	mo	MPS

2. Asks questions

Constantly asking names of objects	24–29	mo	Sher
Asks for "another"	24–29	mo	Vin
Forms a verbal unsolicited question	30–36	mo	LAP

3. Gives description, definition, or information about functions of objects, pictures, words

Answers 1 of 10 questions (e.g., "What is this?" "Chair.")	21	mo	MPS
Answers 6 of 10 questions	28.5	mo	MPS
Answers correctly "What do you hear with?" (pointing or saying "Ear.")	29	mo	Slos/LAP
Identifies 3 of following 6 objects by use: cup, shoe, penny, knife, auto, iron	30	mo	C

Identifies 6 objects by use. Points to cup, shoe, penny, knife, auto, iron. When asked a question such as "What do you drink out of?"	30 mo	C/LAP
Says phrase giving use of test object	30–35 mo	Ges/LAP

SELF-HELP SKILLS PINPOINTS

I. Eating

    A. Establishes general feeding schedule, habits

Requires 2 night-feedings	1–2 mo	Ges
Requires only 1 night-feeding		
Takes solids well	7 mo	Ges
Feeds self for at least first half of meal; insists on being independent	30–35 mo	Ges

    B.

Makes body movements anticipating feeding	3 mo 4 mo	C Ges
Licks lips in response to sounds of preparations for feeding	3 mo	Sher
Discriminates edible substances (say, do)	12–24 mo	LAP
Asks for food when hungry	22.5 mo	Slos
Asks for drink when thristy	22.5 mo	Slos
Asks for food and drink	24–29 mo	Sher

    C. Takes liquids

        1. Establishes sucking behavior

Sucks well with inner mouth parts and lips	1 mo	Sher
Closes mouth without drooling	10.8 mo 11 mo	Vin LAP

        2. Uses bottle

Takes fluid from a dropper or bottle	No norms	
Pats bottle during feeding	5 mo	Ges
Puts hands around bottle or cup when feeding	9 mo	Sher
Holds bottle to feed self	9 mo	Ges
Discards bottle in feeding	15 mo	Ges

        3. Uses cup

Opens mouth for cup with some prodding	No norms	
Opens mouth when sees cup approaching	No norms	
Reaches for cup	No norms	

Lifts inverted cup	5.2 mo	Bay
Lifts cup with handle	5.8 mo	Bay
	6 mo	LAP/C
Drinks from cup when cup is held (some spilling)	10.5 mo	Slos
	11 mo	LAP/Ges
	11.7 mo	Den
Drinks from cup with little assistance	12 mo	Sher/Ges
Holds cup when adult gives and takes	15 mo	Sher
Drinks from cup or glass unassisted	16.6 mo	Vin
	17 mo	LAP
Drinks without much spilling	18–23 mo	Sher/Ges
Lifts and holds cup between both hands	18–23 mo	LAP
	20.5 mo	Sher/Ges/Slos
Hands cup back to adult	18–23 mo	Sher/Ges
Lifts and drinks from cup and replaces on table	24–29 mo	LAP/Sher Ges/H
Gets drink unassisted	24–29 mo	LAP
	29 mo	Vin

D. Takes solids
  1. Establishes chewing behavior

Chews and swallows without spilling	12–24 mo	LAP/Sher
	13.2 mo	Slos
Chews well	18–23 mo	Sher/Ges
Chews competently	24–29 mo	Sher/Ges

  2. Takes finger food

Feeds self cracker	5.3 mo	Den
Holds, bites, and chews cracker	9 mo	LAP/Sher/Ges
Reaches for food	No norms	
Grasps finger food and brings toward mouth	No norms	
Puts finger food into mouth	12 mo	Ges/LAP

  3. Uses implements

Spoon

Fixes gaze on spoon during feeding	3 mo	C
Picks up spoon	5 mo	C/LAP
Looks for fallen spoon, moves eyes toward fallen spoon	6 mo	Bay
Reaches for spoon when being fed	9 mo	Bay
Stirs with spoon in imitation	9.7 mo	Ges
Holds spoon but cannot use it alone	12 mo	Ges/Sher
Dips spoon in cup, releases it	12 mo	Ges

Holds spoon, brings it to mouth	14	mo	LAP
and licks it but cannot prevent	14.4	mo	Den
it turning over (uses spoon,	15	mo	Sher
spilling little—Den)	16	mo	LAP
	20	mo	Slos
Spoon-feeds without spilling	24–29	mo	Sher/H/ LAP
Takes bites from spoon (low error rate)	30–35	mo	Sher

Fork

Puts fork in mouth, eats	28	mo	LAP/Vin

II. Dressing

A. Establishes general dressing behavior
1. Dressing

Mother supports at shoulders when dressing	3	mo	Sher
Mother supports at lower spine when dressing	9	mo	Sher
Helps more constructively with dressing	15	mo	Sher
Pulls on simple garment	24	mo	LAP
Has to be helped during whole process of dressing, can sometimes put on socks	30–35	mo	Ges
Dresses with supervision	32	mo	Den/LAP

2. Undressing

Removes garment	15.8	mo	Den
Undresses completely	21	mo	Ges

B. Puts on, removes clothing
1. Coat, dress, shirt

Cooperates by putting arm into armhole	12–13	mo	Kep
Puts on coat or dress unassisted	34	mo	LAP/Vin

2. Pants and shirts

Cooperates in dressing by	12	mo	Sher
putting arm in armhole or	13	mo	Ges
extending leg to have pants put on			

3. Socks

Enjoys having socks removed (smiles, giggles)	12–13	mo	LAP
Pulls off socks	12–24	mo	LAP
Takes off socks	18–23	mo	LAP
Puts on socks, some errors still	30–35	mo	Kep

4. Shoes

Enjoys having shoes removed	12	mo	LAP
	12–13	mo	Kep

Pulls shoes off	18–23 mo	Kep
	24–29 mo	LAP
Attempts to pull shoes on	22.3 mo	Den/Ges
Pulls shoes on	22.3 mo	Den/Ges
	24–29 mo	Kep

5. Hats, mittens

Enjoys taking off hat, shoes, and pants (socks—Slos)	12 mo	Ges/LAP
	13–56 mo	Slos
Takes off shoes, socks, hat (mittens—Ges)	18–23 mo	Sher/Ges
	24–29 mo	LAP
Puts on shoes, hat (mittens—Ges)	24–29 mo	Sher/Ges

C. Manipulates zippers, buttons
  1. Zippers

Can unzip zipper	18–29 mo	LAP
	18–23 mo	Ges

  2. Buttons

Buttons 1 button	30.5 mo	MPS
	31 mo	LAP
Buttons 2 buttons (170 sec 2-button strip) (30 sec—49.5 mo) (23 sec—54.7 mo)	33 mo	LAP/MPS

III. Toileting

  A. Establishes general toileting schedule, habits

Usually dry after nap	12 mo	LAP/Ges
Fusses to be changed after having bowel movement	12 mo	Ges/LAP
Indicates wet pants	15 mo	LAP/Sher/Ges
Has bowel control	15 mo	LAP/Ges
Bowel control usually attained	18–23 mo	Sher
Bladder control in transitional stage (usually wet after naps)	18–23 mo	Ges
Indicates toilet needs by restlessness and vocalization (or fetches the pot—Ges)	22.5 mo	Sher/Ges/Slos
Verbalizes toilet needs fairly consistently	24 mo	LAP/Sher/Vin
Dry at night if taken up	24 mo	LAP
	24–29 mo	Ges
	30–35 mo	Sher
Wakes wet but tolerates condition	24–29 mo	Ges
Dry during day; muscles of bladder coming under control	24–29 mo	Sher/Ges

  B. Carries out toileting routine

Pulls down pants at toilet, but seldom able to replace	24–29 mo	LAP
	30–35 mo	Sher

C. Dries self
     Dries face, hands (with supervision)   23   mo   Sher/Den
                                                  31   mo   Vin
                                                  42   mo   Ges/LAP
     Dries hands   24–36   mo   LAP
                                                  31   mo   Vin

IV. Keeping house in order

A. Imitates activities
     Imitates housework   13.8 mo   Den
     Follows mother around house and   24–29   mo   Sher
         copies domestic activities in
         simultaneous play

B. Performs activities independently
     Picks up toys and puts them away   18–23   mo   LAP/Den
     Helps put things away   30–48   mo   LAP/Ges

V. Manipulates household fixtures

A. Turns handles
     Turns door handles   24–29   mo   LAP/Sher/
                                                                 Ges
     Manipulates egg beater (1 of 3 trials)   28   mo   C/LAP

B. Turns knobs
     Turns knob (radio)   18–23   mo   LAP/Ges

VI. Giving general information about self
      Refers to self by name   24–29   mo   Sher
      Gives full name on request   30–35   mo   Sher/Ges
                                                  30   mo   LAP
                                                  31–32   mo   Vin/Den

SOCIAL INTERACTION PINPOINTS

I. Establishes self–other discrimination

A. Identifies self
     Reacts to paper on face   1.7 mo   Bay
     Fingers mirror image   4.4 mo   Bay
                                                  6   mo   C
     Smiles at mirror image   5   mo   Ges
                                                  5.4 mo   Bay
     Smiles and vocalizes at image in   6   mo   Ges/LAP
         mirror   6.2 mo   Bay
     Pats and smiles at reflection in   7   mo   C
         mirror
     Reaches for image of ball in hand,   11   mo   Ges
         reflected in mirror

Plays with or reaches for mirror image	12 mo	Ges
Refers to self by name	18–24 mo	LAP
Identifies self in mirror	24.4 mo	MPS
Recognizes self in photographs when shown once	30–35 mo	Sher/LAP

B. Identifies others

Visually recognizes mother	2 mo	Bay
Reaches for familiar persons	3.6 mo	Vin
	4 mo	LAP
Discriminates strangers	4.8 mo	Bay
	5 mo	LAP
	6 mo	Ges
Clearly distinguishes strangers from familiars; requires assurance before accepting their advances; clings to known adult and hides face	9 mo 9.5 mo	Sher Den
Recognizes familiars approaching from 20 ft or more away	12 mo	Sher
Names possessions of others and tells to whom they belong	24–29 mo	Ges

II. Establishes dependence, independence

A. Maintains dependence

Reaches for familiar persons	12–24 mo	LAP
Demands personal attention	12–24 mo	LAP
Demands proximity of familiar adult	18–23 mo	Sher
Alternates between clinging and resistance to familiar adult	18–23 mo	Sher
Plays contentedly alone, but likes to be near adult	18–23 mo	Sher
Clings tightly in affection, fatigue, or fear	24–29 mo	Sher
Constantly demands mother's attention	24–29 mo	Sher
Cries, pouts when attention shown to other children	24–29 mo	Sher

B. Establishes independence

Walks about room unattended	12–36 mo	Vin
Constantly explores and exploits environment	15 mo	Sher
Gives up baby carriage	16–17 mo	Vin
Plays contentedly alone if near adults	18–23 mo	LAP
Explores environment energetically	18–23 mo	Sher/Ges
Goes about house, yard, causing little concern	19 mo	Vin

III. Establishes play routines

    A. Establishes manner and type of
        activity

        1. Manner of playing

*Potentially Positive Aspects of
Play*

Plays, sits propped in play area 10–15 min	4	mo	Ges
Plays by pulling dress over face	4	mo	Ges
Plays actively with small toy, such as rattle—shakes rattle	4	mo	C
Works for toy out of reach	5.8	mo	Den
	8	mo	Ges
Cooperates in games with adult	7.6	mo	Bay
Handles everything within reach	15	mo	Sher
Fills pots and dishes with sand, dumps, throws	24–29	mo	Ges
Initiates own play activities	24	mo	Vin

*Negative Behaviors Exhibited
While Playing*

Throws self to floor in tantrum	18–23	mo	Ges
Casts objects to floor in play or anger, but less often	18–23	mo	LAP
Does opposite of what is asked	21	mo	Ges
Throws violent tantrums when thwarted or is unable to express urgent needs and less easily distracted	24–29	mo	Ges/Sher
Brings favorite toy to school to show but refuses to share it	24–29	mo	Ges
Snatches and grabs toys	30–35	mo	Ges
Clings to favorite possession when insecure	30–35	mo	Ges
Has interest in acquiring possessions of others, but seldom plays with them	30–35	mo	Ges
Demands independence and complete help (on things he/she can do) alternately	30–35	mo	Ges
Has more disputes with others than at any other age	30–35	mo	Ges

        2. Type of play activity

Bites, chews toys	8	mo	Ges
Still takes everything into mouth	9	mo	Sher
Takes objects to mouth less often	12	mo	Sher
Seldom takes toys to mouth	15	mo	Sher
No longer takes toys to mouth	18–25	mo	Sher
Engages in simple make-believe activities	24–29	mo	Sher

Engages in prolonged domestic make-believe play (putting dolls to bed, washing clothes, driving cars) but with frequent references to friendly adult	30–35	mo	Sher

B. Establishes interaction pattern
   1. Isolate play

Initiates own play activities	24	mo	LAP
Prefers solitary play	24–29	mo	Ges

   2. Parallel play

Parallel play predominates	24	mo	LAP
Does little sharing of toys (has difficulty sharing—Ges)	24–29	mo	Sher/Ges
Plays near other children but not with them	24–29	mo	Sher
Enjoys using identical equipment as child next to him (clay, paints, beads)	30–35	mo	Ges
Enjoys going to park to see other children or to play with equipment	30–35	mo	Ges

   3. Cooperative play

Plays with other children	18	mo	Vin/LAP
Plays interactive games, e.g., tag	24	mo	Den
Has little notion of sharing	30–35	mo	Sher
Domestic make-believe play	30–35	mo	LAP
Plays simple group games as "Ring Around the Rosy"	30–35	mo	Sher
Observes other children at play and joins in for a few minutes	30–35	mo	LAP/Sher

SOURCE KEY

Bay	Bayley N: Bayley Infant Scales of Development. New York, Psychological Corp., 1969
C	Cattell P: The Measurement of Intelligence of Infants and Young Children. New York, Psychological Corp., 1940
Vin	Doll E: The Measurement of Social Competence: A Manual for the Vinland Social Maturity Scale. Circle Pines, Minn., American Guidance Service, 1966
Den	Frankenburg W, Dodds J: Denver Developmental Screening Test. Denver, Colo., Ladoca Project and Publishing Foundation, 1966
Minn	Goodenough F, Maurer K, Van Wagen M: Minnesota Preschool Scale. Circle Pines, Minn.: American Guidance Service, 1940
Ges	Gesell A: The First Five Years of Life: a Guide to the Study of the Preschool Child. New York, Harper, 1940
	Gesell A, Armatruda C: Developmental Diagnosis: Normal and Ab-

normal Child Development, Clinical Methods and Applications. New York, Hoeber, 1962

H   Hurlock E: Child Growth and Development. St. Louis, McGraw-Hill, Webster Division, 1968

Kep   Kephart N: The Slow Learner in the Classroom. Columbus, Ohio, Merrill, 1971

LAP   Sanford A: Learning Accomplishment Profile. Chapel Hill, N.C.: University of North Carolina at Chapel Hill, Chapel Hill Training–Outreach Project.

Sher   Sheridan M: The Developmental Progress of Infants and Young Children. London, Her Majesty's Stationery Office, 1968

Slos   Slosson R: Slosson Intelligence Test. New York, Slosson Education, 1964

MPS   Stutsman R: Mental Measurement of Preschool Children, with a Guide for the Administration of the Merrill–Palmer Scale of Mental Tests. Yonkers-on-Hudson, World, 1931

CHAPTER 6

Parent-Infant Interaction
Marci J. Hanson

Like every expectant parent I had a mental image of what our child would look like and who he or she would resemble most. "He" (I had already decided it was a boy!) would be a chubby, healthy baby and the envy of all the new parents on the maternity ward. As it happened, I couldn't have been farther from the truth.

When Miles made his appearance nearly three months premature and weighing only two pounds, I cried at my first glimpse of him. He was so incredibly tiny and so pathetic. I was reminded of the detailed pictures of a developing fetus in Nilsson's famous book A Child is Born [New York: Delacorte Press]. His head was the size of an orange and his skin was transparent. He was covered with a downy hair, "lanugo," which usually disappears in the last few weeks of pregnancy. His movements were jerky and disjointed, and he seemed confused and upset by his new surroundings.

I was filled with emotion. One moment I'd want to gather him up in my arms and reassure him that everything would be fine, and the next moment I was afraid to touch him or get too close to him for fear he'd die and I wouldn't be able to cope.

When I left the hospital a few days later, I was no longer pregnant yet I had no baby to carry home with me. At times it seemed like I had imagined Miles' birth. I felt empty and sad. Each day that I visited Miles I never knew what to expect. I often wondered if he'd still be there when I arrived.

Since Miles' lungs were not fully developed at birth, he needed a respirator to help him breathe. With the respirator and a multitude of other paraphernalia attached to his fragile body, I was unable to hold him. I tried to compensate for this by stroking his thin little body and talking to him. I remember distinctly asking a nurse, "Do you think he hears me talking to him?" And over and over again I would ask, "Do you think he knows who I am?"

As the chances of Miles' survival increased with each passing day, so did my confidence in mothering him. I would stand for hours at the side of his incubator reaching through the portholes and massaging him. I would always begin by rubbing his temples and saying, "Miles, it's your Ma Ma here." I became convinced that he would come to know me through my touch.

To help ensure a healthy weight gain for Miles I rented an electric breast pump and faithfully used it every few hours. My milk was given to Miles through a tube inserted in his mouth and leading directly to *his stomach. It gave me a deep sense of satisfaction to see him grow and thrive on my breast milk. I knew it was something I alone could give him and it helped reassure me that I was important to Miles.*

Three weeks after his birth, when Miles was no longer on the respirator, I held him for the first time. He was bundled up tightly and wore a stocking cap. I kissed his tiny face and put my cheek against his. I wanted so much to take him home.

Seven weeks later when Miles finally did go home I was both extremely happy and frightened. I had come to rely on the hospital for Miles' care and now, suddenly, I would be his primary caregiver. To my relief, the transition from part-time mom to full-time mom was much smoother than I had envisioned, and Miles and I couldn't have been happier.

Kathy Reed
Parent

When I observe Kathy and Miles today I see an enthusiastic and responsive mother with a smiling, active toddler. Even the most casual observer would have no doubt about the attachment between these two people. How after such a fragile beginning—a traumatic birth, prolonged hospitalization and the pronouncement that Miles might have cerebral palsy—did Kathy and Miles establish this relationship? What factors have contributed to this positive outcome? Kathy answers these questions in part in her story. In her determination to build a relationship with her premature baby she developed a special signal to Miles; a stroking of his temples came to mean "I am your Ma-Ma and I am here with you." The giving of breast milk to Miles despite the artificial and difficult circumstances ensured a role for Kathy in his survival and development, a role often denied parents by the very nature of the life supporting necessities of the intensive care nursery.

Miles' family and many others like them continue to teach us about human development. What is more academically considered throughout this volume and labeled for instructional purposes as a transactional model of development is reflected in the story of Kathy and Miles. Although a child may experience a "bad" beginning—physiological damage, an isolated early environment for life support—a positive developmental outcome may be achieved. One of the most crucial variables in this process—the parent-infant interaction—is considered in this chapter. Discussion focuses on the ranges of parental reactions to the birth of an at-risk or disabled child and the parent and child variables that may influence the interactional process. In addition, the empirical information on caregiver-infant interaction when the infant is at risk or disabled is examined, and implications for early intervention services are identified.

REACTION TO THE BIRTH OF A HANDICAPPED CHILD

Anticipation of a child's birth includes formulating expectations for that child—expectations about the child's appearance, his/her personality, and notions of the type of adult the child will become. The recent popularity in the U.S. of childbirth preparation and coaching training also has focused increased attention on the birth event. As such, many parents today are extremely knowledgeable and expectant about their child's birth. However, when a discrepancy occurs between those expectations and the characteristics of the child born, a trauma may be produced (Solnit and Stark, 1961). These expectations may be violated by differences between the parents' wishes for the expected baby and the actual child, by an extremely traumatic birthing event, or by the birth of an at-risk or disabled child.

A number of clinicians and theorists have studied parents' reactions to the birth of a child with a congenital syndrome or abnormality. Such studies document the potential problems faced by families undergoing this stressful experience and also discuss the adaptation of families to such an event. A hypothetical model for understanding parental adaptation is presented by Drotar et al. (1975). This model, constructed from an analysis of family interviews, outlines five stages of parental reactions. These stages are shock, denial or disbelief, sadness and anger, adaptation, and reorganization. Solnit and Stark (1961) discuss similar feelings parents may experience and liken parents' reactions to the mourning process in that the parent mourns the loss of the expected normal child.

These discussions of parental reactions provide useful guides to educators, mental health specialists, and health care providers in understanding and assisting parents to cope with the birth of a child with developmental problems. Models can be useful, however, only if viewed as a general guide. Parents may not pass through these stages or they may go through the stages but at vastly different rates. Individual personalities and histories, of course, dictate reactions at a given point in time. Clinical investigations and documentations merely assist us to appreciate the range of reactions parents may experience and also the changeability and progression of those responses.

The distress and trauma experienced around the birth of a child with developmental problems is magnified further today by the significance attached to early parent-child interactions. This process of early contact and the formation of attachment during the neonatal period is typically referred to as "bonding." Klaus and Kennell

(1976) outlined the factors they believe to be crucial to the early attachment process. Two of these factors are:

> There is a sensitive period in the first minutes and hours of life during which it is necessary that the mother and father have close contact with their neonate for later development to be optimal (p. 14).

> Some early events have long-lasting effects. Anxieties about the well-being of a baby with a temporary disorder in the first day may result in long-lasting concern. That may cast long shadows and adversely shape the development of the child (p. 14).

Thus, events during this early "sensitive period" are seen as critical to the achievement of an optimal developmental outcome. This notion coupled with the thesis that "the original mother-infant bond is the wellspring for all the infant's subsequent attachments" (Klaus and Kennell, 1976, p. 1) places great emphasis on the birth experience and subsequent few hours. Parents who deliver a child who is at risk or disabled most likely will be denied these early opportunities for relating to their infant. Our insistence on the importance and irreversibility of the effects of these interactions shortly after birth further exacerbates the anxieties and negative emotions already associated with the prospects of parenting a "damaged" child.

As Chess and Thomas (1982) aptly relate, the studies and writings of Klaus and Kennell have made important positive contributions to restructuring the experiences of parents and families in nurseries. However, Chess and Thomas question several tenets of the bonding concept and review literature to support their position. Their critique focuses primarily on the tenet that the mother's contact or relationship to the infant is unique and, secondly, that there is a critical period for this relationship beyond which optimal attachment cannot occur. They conclude:

> We know a great deal about the importance of a positive parent-child relationship. We know a great deal about many of the specific factors that promote or deter such a relationship, and how these factors in the child and in the parent interact in a mutually influential developmental sequence. But just as the child's nutritional requirements can be met successfully with a wide range of individual variation, so can his psychological requirements. Once mothers can appreciate this, that the neonate separated from his mother is not permanently damaged by this experience as such, that the child whose signals are not always easy to understand is not doomed to an unhealthy parent attachment, that the infant who appears "insecure" with strangers is not necessarily suffering from poor mothering, they can perhaps relax and actually become better mothers (p. 221).

The increase in early intervention services for high-risk infants and their families provides us with the opportunity to support parents in this early adjustment process. Support can be provided through a range of service formats: individual or group counseling, parent training, and parent-to-parent discussion. We must be vigilant to ensure that parents receive support appropriate to individual needs while avoiding the attempt to "pigeonhole" or categorize parents' responses into rigid stages.

FACTORS AFFECTING INTERACTION PATTERNS

Since the parent and infant represent the actors in this drama, the primary factors to be considered are the individual characteristics that each brings to the interactional situation. Other factors, such as cultural expectations, environmental forces, and restraints, likewise influence the way the script is written. These variables as well as the other members of the cast—the peers, family members, and significant others in the life of the parent and child—determine the final outcome or performance. The relationship between the parent and infant, thus, is seen as a dynamic interaction constantly being modified as the variables impinge on the players and the players' behavior influences one another. This interactional or transactional model provides us with a positive perspective for viewing developmental outcomes.

Parent Characteristics

The term *parent* in this subheading represents an attempt to focus attention on the child's primary caregiver whether that be the natural mother or father or another person responsible for parenting activities. However, the power and mystique surrounding the mother's influence on the young child has produced a body of literature almost solely focused on mother-infant, rather than parent-infant, relationships. Mothering behavior has been credited as the critical variable for positive child development on one hand, and on the other hand, has been blamed for child psychopathology ranging from retardation to autism. This section, thus, considers the maternal variables associated with child behavior as reflected by the available body of literature.

The overwhelming conclusion from studies of mother-infant interaction is that a positive relationship exists between maternal competency and infant competency. Links between early maternal actions and later child behavior (several months to 1 to 2 years) have been noted. Data from a longitudinal investigation by Clarke-Stewart

(1973), for instance, showed a positive relationship between the quality of early mother-infant interaction and child cognitive development. Similar results were noted by Tulkin and Covitz (1975) in their study relating early interaction patterns to the intellectual functioning of children 6 years of age. Furthermore, Lewis and Goldberg (1969) found a positive correlation between maternal responsiveness to infant behavior (e.g., vocalizations and cries) and infant cognitive development as measured by response decrement. Investigations also have linked maternal responsiveness or stimulation to infant exploratory behavior (Rubenstein, 1967; Yarrow et al., 1972) and to advanced communication development (Bell and Ainsworth, 1972). Other maternal factors that may influence infant development, such as maternal attitudes and perceptions and social class differences, are reviewed by Osofsky and Connors (1979).

The notion that maternal behavior poses a powerful force in infant development prompts little debate. The empirical investigation of these relationships between mother and infant behavior is not a simple issue, however. The central problem remains determining directionality. Do more responsive mothers produce more active, exploring babies, for example? Or do more active babies in fact elicit more attention and feedback from their mothers? Based on a contemporary view of infant development, the obvious conclusion is that both partners—the parent and the infant—may exert an influence over the other's behavior. A discussion of infant characteristics that affect interaction patterns follows.

Infant Characteristics

The review by Bell (1968) shifted the emphasis away from a view of parent-child interaction as determined by the parent to an acknowledgment of the great contributions of the infant to developing human relationships. Most of us can honestly admit to having been controlled by infants' gazes, coos, and cries at some time in our adult lives. In fact, most of us would be able to describe in detail the characteristics of infants that we most favor.

It is not surprising then that our behavior toward various infants may differ and that we all differ in our interpretations of the ideal child based on a number of factors. These factors include our relationship to the child, the attractiveness of the child, and the child's means of engaging our attention.

Studies with "normal" infant populations have provided evidence that adults do differentially respond to infants on the basis of many infant characteristics. These characteristics include age and developmental status (Beckwith, 1972; Green et al., 1980; Jones and Moss, 1971; Moss, 1967), sex (Brown et al., 1975; Jones and Moss, 1971; Korner, 1974; Lewis, 1972; Moss, 1967; Parke and O'Leary, 1975), state (Brazelton, 1961; Jones and Moss, 1971; Korner, 1973; Lewis, 1972; Moss, 1967), birth order (Parke and O'Leary, 1975; Thoman et al., 1970, 1971), responsiveness to stimuli (Brazelton et al., 1974; Osofsky and Danzger, 1974; Wolff, 1971, 1976), and temperament (Thomas and Chess, 1977). A thorough review of these infant characteristics and their relationship to mother-infant interactions is provided in Osofsky and Connors (1979).

Given the highly probable impact of these "normal" variations in infants on caregiver behavior, it is not surprising that characteristics that identify infants as at risk or disabled may likewise exert a powerful influence on the dynamics of caregiver-infant interaction. The literature provides ample documentation that at-risk and disabled infants may differ behaviorally from "normal" babies. Studies have indicated, for example, that pre- and perinatal complications[1] may produce differences in infant responsivity, irritability, motor, feeding, and visual responses. As is reviewed in Chapter 5, the few investigations in which behavioral observations of disabled infants were made noted marked differences in these babies. Studies showed that the development of infants with Down syndrome, for example, is characterized by delays in affective, cognitive, and motor behavioral domains (Cicchetti and Sroufe, 1976, 1978; Emde et al., 1978; Hanson, 1981; Serafica and Cicchetti, 1976). Observations of blind infants similarly documented deviations from normal development in the motor and signaling behavior of these infants (Fraiberg, 1974, 1977). As Fraiberg's work aptly points out, these behavioral deviations may produce and/or necessitate concomitant adjustments in caregiver behavior.

INTERACTION RESEARCH

The study of individual differences among infants and the effects of these characteristics on caregiver behavior has captured the attention of a number of researchers (Carey, 1972; Escalona, 1963; Korner,

---

[1] Complications include pre- and perinatal complications (Beckwith and Cohen, 1978; Honzik et al., 1965), prematurity and/or low birthweight (Brown and Bakeman, 1979; DiVitto and Goldberg, 1979; Field, 1977a; Harper and Weiner, 1965; Honzik et al., 1965; Lester and Zeskind, 1978; Zeskind and Lester, 1978), anoxia (Graham et al., 1957), and cesarean section (Als et al., 1980).

1969; Rothbart, 1981; Thomas and Chess, 1977). Studies have shown, for instance, that infant's physical characteristics (e.g., muscle tone and posture) may affect the mother's handling techniques and feelings about her relationship with the child (Wolff, 1971). An examination of interaction and attachment between parent and child is of particular interest when the infant is disabled or at risk for delay. A potential disruption of the interactional process exists because one partner, the baby, enters the interaction with an atypical or limited behavioral repertoire. Surprisingly, few empirical investigations of caregiver-infant interactive behavior in which the infants are at risk or disabled have been conducted. Given the inclusions of *both* parents and infants as targets for early intervention services and clinical concerns regarding the effect of the birth of an atypical child on the parent, systematic study of this early interaction is needed.

Investigations that examined the interaction patterns of parent-infant pairs at risk are reviewed in this section. These studies highlight the important similarities and differences when these pairs are compared with groups of nondisabled children and their caregivers.

Infants Born Prematurely

Medical technology has guaranteed the survival of many infants born prematurely. Research attention to these babies has veered from a focus solely on medical and physical concerns to examinations of the preterm infant's capabilities to interact with the animate and inanimate environment. These studies have shown that indeed the premature infant does behave differently from the full-term baby, thus creating special problems for its caregivers. Als et al. (1979) described the "task" faced by the baby born prematurely.

> The first consideration must be that the surviving human premature is an artifact of modern medicine, therefore, there is no single model from which to glean what behavior is appropriate for adaptation of the preterm infant. The 32-week-old organism, for instance, is adapted to an intrauterine environment of a regulated temperature, contained movement pattern, suspension of gravity, limited and regular sensory inputs and physiological restraints which have evolved to ensure normal intrauterine development for a large percentage of fetuses. Should a premature delivery ensue, most fetuses would die since their organismic adaptations do not fit the environment they find themselves in. Modern technology and medicine has changed this, but is still at a loss as to how best provide for such organism, given the incongruence of the situation. Artificial re-creation of the intrauterine environment for the preterm infant is inappropriate since the transition from the intrauterine environment to the extrauterine environment automatically triggers independent functioning of organ systems necessary

for extrauterine survival, such as the respiratory, cardiac, and the digestive systems. Not only is the preterm infant an organism in an environment he has not yet evolved for, but he is an organism whose biological program is called upon prematurely so that the normal sequence of subsystem differentiation and integration generally found by term has not yet been executed (p. 179).

Descriptive studies of the behavior of preterm infants as compared to full-term infants indicate preterms have poorer motoric processes and state modulation (Sostek et al., 1979) and demonstrate less frequent and acoustically different crying (Lester and Zeskind, 1979). Additionally, infants born prematurely appear less alert and responsive to stimulation. As such, they require more stimulation to become attentive and socially responsive but show a lower threshold for stimulation (Field, 1977a, 1979). Preterm infants, thus, in their fragile state are less capable or competent than full-term infants at responding/adjusting to environmental demands. This presents special problems to parents in caregiving and social interactions.

Parents, too, enter the interactional situation with an at-risk status having had parenting responsibilities thrust upon them prematurely. While denied the anticipated preparation time they also are faced with an infant who is behaviorally different than the expected full-term baby. The anxiety associated with delivering an infant prematurely is reflected by the finding that mothers evidenced increased autonomic arousal when the label of "preterm" was applied to a normal infant (Frodi et al., 1978).

Empirical investigations of parent-preterm infant interactions verifies that differences are observed when these dyads are compared with full-term infants and their parents (Field, 1977b; Goldberg, 1978). Investigations of early feeding interactions found that mothers of preterm infants more actively stimulated their infants during feedings, thus showing less sensitivity to the individual infant's rhythms and signals. Brown and Bakeman (1979) also reported that lower class mothers of preterm infants were more active during feedings in order to interact with their less active and responsive infants. Similar results were noted by DiVitto and Goldberg (1979). The preterm infants, judged to be less responsive, received more auditory and tactile stimulation including functional stimulation (e.g., nipple movement) during feeding. Other group differences indicated relationships between medical status and maternal behavior. Mothers of sicker babies were more likely to hold the babies at arm's length and less likely to nestle the baby closely in the arms. Full-term infants were cuddled, touched, and talked to more than preterm infants when observed in feedings during the first 10 days. These differences were statistically significant in early feedings, and although the same pattern was evident for feedings observed at 4 months of age those differences were not significant. Studies, thus, suggest that parents of prematurely born infants "work harder" to elicit social and feeding behavior from their less responsive infants during feeding interactions.

Documentation of early face-to-face interactions between preterm infants and their parents reveals similar trends. These interactions were characterized by more maternal activity (mothers of preterms) during attention getting and spontaneous play situations even during periods of infant gaze aversion. Analysis revealed that the mothers' increased activity particularly during attention getting episodes may have overloaded the infant's information processing mechanisms, thus creating aversion behavior or pauses in the interactions. During periods when mothers imitated their infants' behavior, the interactions seemed more closely modulated and the infants demonstrated less gaze aversion (Field, 1977a). Face-to-face interactions of game playing between parents and 4-month-old infants were studied also (Field, 1979). Results indicated fewer game playing (e.g., pat-a-cake and peekaboo) episodes for preterm and postterm groups when compared to term groups. Goldberg et al. (1980) also compared groups (full-term, healthy preterm, sick preterm, and infants of diabetic mothers) during floor playing interactions at 8 months. They found that sick preterms spent the least amount of time playing and smiling and the most time fretting; their parents spent more time being close, touching, and demonstrating toys. Parents of full-term infants by contrast were least active and had infants who smiled, played most, and fretted least. The healthy preterms, although playing less than the full-term group, were not more distressed and their parents did not differ from full-term parents. Differences apparent at 8 months were not significant at 12 months.

A review of the parent-infant interaction literature suggests that the problematic behavior of the preterm infant affects interactions with others. In the neonatal period, the social interaction between preterm infant-parent dyads may be different (e.g., less cuddling) than that for full-term dyads. In the early weeks and months, parents of preterm infants apparently come to invest more active effort in interactions with their babies even though they may experience less success in arousing and alerting their less responsive babies. Some of these differences appear to persist through the first year of age as evidenced by the study of play interactions at 8 months. The parent of the preterm infant, thus, faces the task of learning to provide an optimal amount of stimulation to the baby—enough to alert the infant but not too much to overstimulate.

As reviewed previously, early caregiver-infant interactions are linked to child developmental outcomes. Our examination of these early patterns may be particularly crucial for studying the development of preterm infants. Relationships between early caregiver-preterm infant interactions and cognitive development of infants was investigated by Beckwith et al. (1976). These researchers found that mutual mother-infant gazing at 1 month, smiling interchanges during gazing and responses to distress at 3 months, and maternal attentiveness and contingent responding to nondistress vocalizations at 8 months were related to higher infant sensorimotor scores at 9 months. This study highlights the importance of early interactions and their effects on subsequent child behavior.

Developmentally Delayed Infants

The presence of a disabling condition in a young infant also poses a potential hazard to the interactional patterns between parent and child. The challenge parents face in coping and interacting with a baby that is developmentally and behaviorally deviant has received little research attention. The few empirical investigations available are reviewed in this section and descriptions of mother-delayed infant interactions are provided.

In a study aimed at describing early (first 5 weeks) mother-infant interactions, Thoman et al. (1978) discovered three pairs from their sample for which there were indications of infant developmental delay. These pairs were compared to the rest of the group of healthy, full-term infants and their mothers. Several interactional differences were noted: the pairs with delayed infants demonstrated less social interaction (looking, noncaregiving, and stimulation activities) and more caregiving during holding or carrying. Groups of infants did not differ in amount of time in various states. One of these pairs was selected for more detailed analysis. The infant presented mixed cues and rapid behavioral state changes from sleep to wakefulness, thus making his/her behavior difficult for the mother to interpret. The mother verbally expressed her uncertainty and behaviorally showed more frequent and brief episodes of feeding and holding than did the rest of the mothers in the group.

Vietze et al. (1978) also compared families with delayed children to those with nondelayed children. Subjects were compared as to contingencies operating between parents and children. Results suggested that at 1 year the mothers and their delayed children were

markedly similar to the nondelayed sample pairs. Evidence of reciprocal vocal interactions was found, and dyads with both high and
low functioning developmentally delayed children did not differ
significantly with respect to maternal vocal interactional behavior.
Differences were noted between the higher and lower functioning
children, however, in that the lower group showed less contingent
responding to maternal vocalizations. The authors suggested that
infant failure to contingently respond may influence the mother's
responses at a later point.

The attachment behavior of handicapped infants and their parents has received limited attention in the research literature. Stone
and Chesney (1978) studied behavior related to attachment patterns
in 15 mother-infant dyads who were participants in an early intervention program for developmentally delayed children. The children's handicaps included Down syndrome, brain injury, blindness,
and congenital, multiple handicaps. The investigators questioned
the mothers of these handicapped infants as to the occurrence of
infant behavior disturbances (e.g., delayed or infrequent smiling and
vocalizing, tenseness when handled, limpness or unresponsiveness
when handled, and not demanding of attention). All of the 15 children studied demonstrated some disturbances in these infant behaviors typically associated with attachment patterns. This study
presented suggestive data regarding the potential for attachment
problems, but did not attempt to document other factors that may
contribute to the disturbances found (i.e., environmental factors) nor
did it document parent-infant attachment patterns in this group. Systematic observations of parent-infant attachment behavior in dyads
where the infant is developmentally delayed are needed before conclusions or clinical assumptions can be drawn.

Infants with Cognitive Disorders   The most attention to parent-
disabled child interaction patterns has been given to young children
with mental retardation and their mothers. Several studies have examined these interaction variables with preschool-age children.
Kogan et al. (1969), for example, analyzed verbal and nonverbal interactions in a comparative study of mentally retarded and nonretarded children and their parents. Mothers of the retarded children
differed from the comparison group on only two variables: 1) these
mothers displayed low status (e.g., accepted control, acknowledged
others' leadership, and were deferential) in relation to their children
significantly less often; and 2) they were more extreme in their
expression of warmth and friendliness to their children. The two
groups of children, on the other hand, were comparable on measures

of affect, but the children diagnosed as mentally retarded exhibited less assertiveness and more submissiveness. In terms of interactional styles, the retarded children and their mothers "did nothing together" more often, whereas the comparison groups took turns during interactions. An investigation of mother-retarded child verbal interactions with preschool-aged children determined that few differences existed between these pairs and a comparison group of mother-nondisabled child pairs (Marshall et al., 1973). The children differed qualitatively with regard to verbal responses, but the mother groups varied significantly only in terms of mand (command) usage; mothers of retarded children used mands at a higher rate. A similar study of verbal interaction between young children with Down syndrome and their mothers and nonretarded child-mother pairs was conducted by Gutmann and Rondal (1979). They found that as the mean length of child utterance increased, the verbal response classes used increased for both mothers and children in the two groups. Group comparisons indicated, however, that nonretarded children and their mothers displayed more echoics (repetition of sound patterns) whereas children with Down syndrome and their mothers used more intraverbals.[2] Furthermore, the mothers of Down syndrome children did not differ in mand usage; they did not show more directive behavior than the mothers of nonretarded children. These investigations of preschool child-mother interactions revealed few differences between groups of mentally retarded and nonretarded preschool children and parents. Additionally, the differences that have been noted are not consistent or replicated from study to study.

Mother-child interactions between groups of children with different levels of intellectual performance were studied by Terdal et al. (1976). Mentally retarded preschool-age children were divided into three groups on the basis of severity of retardation; nonretarded children of the same chronological age were observed also. Findings indicated links between interactional patterns and degree of mental retardation. Mothers of mentally retarded children in all groups showed equivalent levels of interactive behavior even though the groups of children differed as to their responses to interactions (the low group responded 48.7% of the time, middle group 81.6%, and high group 80%). Thus, although children varied as to responsiveness, mothers demonstrated the same likelihood of responding to

---

[2] Intraverbals are defined as "verbal operants that are made in the presence of a stimulus and do not show any point-to-point correspondence to that stimulus" (Gutmann and Rondal, 1979); for example, "How are you?" "Fine, and you?"

their children's behavior. Other analyses, however, indicated that mothers of the lower functioning group were more directive to their children and showed a higher "no response" rate in a play session than were the mothers in the other groups of retarded children. Additionally, mothers of the retarded children were not as consistent as the comparison group of mothers of nonretarded children in providing positive feedback for compliant behavior and negative consequences for noncompliant behavior. The authors attributed this finding to the possible "blurred input" retarded children may provide their parents.

Only a few descriptive investigations have been conducted on interaction patterns with mothers and very young cognitively disabled children. Mothers of 2-year-old children with Down syndrome were compared with mothers of nondisabled children on verbal interaction dimensions (Buium et al., 1974). Results indicated that these mothers used more but shorter and less complex utterances than did the comparison group mothers of nondisabled children. Jones (1977, 1980) also examined mother-child communication patterns between infants with Down syndrome and their mothers. His detailed analyses of videotaped interactions contrasting the Down syndrome group with a normal comparison group revealed that both groups showed approximately equal numbers and equal lengths of interactions. However, the interactions involving the infants with Down syndrome tended to be more "mother-directed" and those with the normal group were more "child-dependent" (mother supporting child's initiative). In terms of eye-to-eye interaction patterns, the rates of eye contact, although greater for normal children, did not differ significantly between the two groups. However, referential eye contacts (transfer of attention from play object or activity to mother's face and then back) occurred a greater proportion of the time with the normal infants. Finally, the children with Down syndrome were involved in more vocal "clashes" or occasions where mothers and children vocalized at the same time than were the normal children. Thus, they seemed to exhibit less interactive turn-taking. Although differences between groups were identified in this study, the results also clearly indicated that infants with Down syndrome can be capable prelinguistic communicative partners with their mothers.

A descriptive investigation of the developmental and interactional behavior of infants with Down syndrome and their parents also was conducted by Hanson (1979, 1981). When infants with Down syndrome (all participants in an intensive early intervention program) were compared with a group of same-age peers, they demonstrated lower rates of vocal behavior and qualitative differences in movement. However, few differences were discovered between the groups of mothers of these infants. The frequency of praise and smiling was slightly greater for mothers of infants with Down syndrome and mothers of normal infants provided slightly more explanations to their babies. On physical behavior dimensions, the mothers of the normal infants exhibited more restraining behavior (probably due to the fact their babies were more active and likely to move away from the setting), and mothers of the infants with Down syndrome used more physical primes (perhaps because of their involvement in the intervention program). No differences were found between groups of mothers in terms of attention to infants.

Attachment behavior, another dimension of parent-child interaction, has been empirically investigated in toddlers with Down syndrome and their mothers (Serafica and Cicchetti, 1976). Observations of these mothers and babies using "the strange situation" task showed few differences in the attachment and exploration behavior of infants with Down syndrome as contrasted with a normal comparison group. Differences were noted primarily on the use of a signaling behavior, crying, with Down syndrome children showing less crying when their mothers left the room. The researcher's explanation for this finding was that the groups of infants attached different meanings to being left alone, not that children with Down syndrome were less attached to their mothers. All studies reviewed regarding early mother-child interaction with pairs that included a baby with cognitive delays revealed markedly few differences between these dyads and mother-nondisabled infant pairs.

Infants with Physical Disabilities   The interpersonal adaptation of mothers of young children (1 to 4 years of age) with cerebral palsy was studied by Kogan et al. (1974). Their observations over several years indicated a decrease in mothers' affection and positive acceptance over time. This was particularly evident for those mothers whose children were not walking. Similarly, Shere and Kastenbaum (1966) observed that parents of children with cerebral palsy tended to focus on the physical disability and failed to express much concern in other areas such as psychological development.

Systematic observations of the verbal and nonverbal behavior of young physically handicapped children and their mothers were investigated by Kogan and Tyler (1973). Mother-child interaction patterns of this group were compared to groups with nondisabled children and with mentally retarded children. Results indicated that the physically handicapped children exhibited lower levels of involvement than the nondisabled children and showed a greater number of assertive and controlling behaviors than the retarded children. The mothers of the physically disabled children displayed more assertive control and warm behavior than the comparison nondisabled group mothers; they showed no differences from the mothers of the mentally retarded children. This brief literature review also indicates that few systematic studies have been conducted on parent-infant interaction with a physically disabled infant. The scant evidence available discloses few differences between these parent-infant pairs and groups of nondisabled infant-parent pairs.

Deaf Infants   Investigations of mother-infant interaction involving a deaf or hearing-impaired infant are not available in the research literature. However, several empirical examinations of interactions with preschool-aged deaf children have been conducted. Schlesinger and Meadow (1972) compared groups of mothers of deaf and hearing children from videotaped mother-child interaction scenarios. Mothers of hearing children received significantly higher ratings on the variables of permissiveness, nonintrusiveness, nondidactic behavior, creativity, flexibility, and approval of the child. No group differences were noted on enjoyment of the child, degree to which mothers were relaxed in the observation situation, or effectiveness in gaining the child's cooperation. Differences between groups of children (deaf versus hearing) were found favoring the hearing children on the dimensions of compliance versus resistance, creativity versus lack of imagination, enjoyment of interaction with mother versus absence of enjoyment, happiness versus unhappiness, and pride in mastery versus absence of pride. The child's enjoyment of the interaction with the mother was found also to be significantly related to the mother's enjoyment of the interaction.

The attachment patterns of deaf preschool children with their hearing mothers was investigated by Greenberg and Marvin (1979). Two groups of deaf child dyads were observed: those using an oral communication approach and those using a total communication approach (oral plus manual). Mother-child pairs were observed in a laboratory situation, and results indicated that the deaf children showed little distress when separated from their mothers, possibly because of their mothers' means of preparing them for departure. When oral and total communication groups were compared, total communicators were found to be more sociable and displayed more relaxed behavior when mothers returned. Additionally, when grouped by level of communicative competence, findings indicated that high communicators displayed more goal-corrected partnership attachment patterns (i.e.: 1) approved of mother's departure; 2) displayed no distress during separation; and 3) greeted mother sociably upon return). It is noteworthy that the attachment and separation patterns studied were similar to those reported in other studies for preschool hearing children.

Greenberg (1980) also examined the interactional patterns of mothers and deaf preschool children during free play. Children were divided by mode of communication (oral versus oral and manual, or total) and level of communicative competence. Results revealed that high communicators asked more questions and discussed their own actions, declared information, and discussed absent persons and events more than did low communicators. They also had a longer total interaction time. Additionally, total communicator children showed more spontaneous communication and showed longer and more complex interactions than did the oral-only pairs.

Blind Infants   As Fraiberg recounted, blind children often "appear to have no significant human ties" (Fraiberg, 1975). Because vision functions as such a critical factor in smile elicitation and discrimination of familiar and nonfamiliar persons, blind babies' development of attachments and interaction with caregivers may be disrupted. Fraiberg's (1977) extensive observations of young blind children have determined that blind children do develop attachments to their parents and that the same developmental milestones— smiling, discrimination of familiar persons, stranger avoidance, person permanence, and separation protest—are evident for blind infants albeit at later ages than for sighted children. Fraiberg (1975) described the communicative interactions of normal infants and their parents as governed by visual cues, and as such it is largely a "visual vocabulary." The sighted baby's differential smile upon seeing the mother conveys "I know you," "I love you." The parents of blind infants, however, must be assisted in reading and interpreting their infants affectional responses and initiations. The intervention program developed by Fraiberg and colleagues (1975, 1977) was aimed primarily at this role of becoming the baby's interpreter and teaching parents to discern their infant's interactional patterns through watching the infants hand signals. Given the lack of early coordination between ear and hand and the consequent delay blind infants demonstrate in reaching for sound cues—either from an object or person—the infant's lack of initiation is often interpreted as unaffectionate. Careful observations led these investigators to discover that specific behavior associated with mother-infant attachment may be delayed or somewhat different (e.g., reaching with hand rather than eye contact and smile), but that healthy, normal attachments and interactions could be achieved.

Empirical investigations of the linguistic competence of blind babies including their communication patterns with parents also have been studied by Kekelis and Andersen (1982) utilizing microanalytic analyses of taped parent-infant interactions. Their data revealed differences in the early language development of blind children (described in Chapter 5) and also in the communicative interactions between parents and infants. Parents of these children differed in the nature of their language input (form, function, and focus of language). They generally demonstrated a more restrictive use of kinds of sentences (possibly because they were provided with fewer or different cues from their children), tended to emphasize labeling and function of objects rather than expansions and descriptions, and focused on child-centered rather than environment-related and abstract topics. These studies offer a detailed analysis and view of early interactional patterns between blind infants and their parents.

Infants with Affective Disorders   Although early mother-infant interaction patterns are often implicated as causal factors in the development of early affective disorders, the catalyst for and directionality of these effects is difficult to determine. Are disturbed interactional patterns caused by the infant's behavior, the parent's behavior, or both?

Theories on infantile autism often have attributed causation to these early relationship disturbances, and as such, studies on autism have placed more attention (theoretical although not empirical) on early mother-infant interaction than have studies of other disabilities. Massie's (1982) creative approach to the study of early affective development utilizing analyses of home movies links early maternal patterns to later infant psychopathology. However, causative agents whether physiological or behavioral have not been positively determined for early autism; establishing linkage between early behavioral patterns and later disability remains elusive.

The examination of early caregiver-infant interactional patterns is perhaps of most interest for this group from an interventionist's perspective. Regardless of whether the mother's or the child's behavior promotes dysfunction, identification of the crucial issues in the formation of early personal relationships and early support for parents may allow for facilitation of more modulated and mutually responsive and reinforcing interchanges between parent and child.

IMPLICATIONS FOR INTERVENTION

This discussion and review of the literature on early parent-infant interaction establishes that the central focus of early intervention approaches must be both the parent(s) and the infant. Each brings special needs and challenges to the intervention setting. The infant needs preventive or remedial training and therapy to overcome aspects of the disability or potentially disabling condition; the parent needs aid in understanding the atypical characteristics of the child and support in coping with the ramifications of the disability. Beyond these factors, the parent and the infant must be assisted in communicating with each other and in establishing positive relationships both with one another and with other persons in their environment.

Ramey et al. (1980) suggest four principles or guidelines for facilitating the development of at-risk and handicapped infants. These principles are:

1. Recognizing the infant's active role
2. Using the infant's repertoire
3. Using natural reinforcers
4. Using daily routines as educational settings.

A major thrust of this text is identifying the active nature of the infant's role in interactions with the environment. Because infants with atypical characteristics bring a behavioral repertoire to an interaction that may produce limited or deviant responses from normative expectations, examining infants' contributions is of central concern to infant intervenors. Intervention strategies are typically of most use when, as these authors suggest, they capitalize on the infant's repertoire (principle 2). By assisting parents in observing the child and modifying tasks or environmental demands such that the child can use existing skills to achieve an outcome, the intervenor ensures more successful responses and interactions for both parent and child. The third principle, the use of natural reinforcers, follows from the previous point. Parents are typically the most effective source of reinforcement to their children. Likewise, they are best able to identify natural consequences to the child's actions and utilize these situations to encourage the child to function more effectively in the environment. Additionally, parents as the primary persons in the child's life are faced with the task of incorporating educational/treatment activities into the daily routine. Support in integrating these activities with a family's schedule can be provided by educational personnel.

To these principles I would add the following goals for intervention with at-risk and handicapped infants:

1. Assessing the strengths and resources and needs of the family
2. Identifying the infant's unique signaling system
3. Assisting parents to read and understand their infant's cues

4. Recognizing that early learning is largely social in nature
5. Providing contingent responding to infant's behavior
6. Furnishing continuous follow-up and support to parents in their interactions with their infants as the developmental and interactional needs change over time.

Taken point by point, these recommendations begin with an assessment of family strengths and needs. The intensity and type of parental response to the demands of a disabled infant will vary from day to day and will depend on the resources that the parent brings to the interactions. Interactional or transactional models of development (Sameroff and Chandler, 1975) underscore the importance of environmental circumstances including parent-child interactions in determining the child's developmental outcome. Realistically, families who are experiencing a variety of stresses (e.g., financial, marital, and health concerns) cannot be expected to respond fully and adequately to the needs of the disabled child. Until these family needs are met, specific interventions or services related to the child may not be implementable. Likewise, capitalizing on the strengths or resources of a particular family facilitates the entire intervention process. The contributions of other family members or friends, the organizations that provide advocacy, social services, and respite support services, the insurance options, and the services supplied by medical clinics are but a few examples of resources that may be available to families that could alleviate stressful aspects of raising a child with developmental problems.

The second, third, and fourth goals (identifying individual infant's signaling systems, assisting parents to read these cues, and recognizing that learning is largely social in nature) are integrally related. As Robson and Moss (1970) reported, mothers indicated their first recognition of positive feelings toward their infants were elicited primarily by their babies' eye contact, visual fixation, and smiling behavior. For the parent of a disabled infant whose behavioral repertoire may differ—the blind child who shows no visual regard, the infant with Down syndrome whose smile may be less intense than the smile of a normal baby—interactions with the baby may be frustrating and perplexing. The work of Fraiberg and colleagues beautifully demonstrates the interventions that are possible. In lieu of "reading" an infant's smile or eye contact, the parents of blind babies were taught to interpret their infants' hand signals and utilize stimuli other than visual feedback (e.g., kinesthetic) to alert and communicate with the infants (Fraiberg, 1974). These creative interventions resulted in less delayed development than could have been expected and also the establishment of healthy attachments between parents and children despite the fact that the presence of the visual disability precluded many typical interaction patterns.

The previous discussion concerning the contributions of maternal characteristics to interactional and infant developmental outcomes establishes the importance of contingent parental responsivity to infant behavior. The work of Lewis and Goldberg (1969), for example, determined a positive relationship between maternal response to infant behavior and the cognitive development of the infant. Contingent responsivity also has been identified as a crucial variable in promoting infants' feelings of competence and control over their environment (Lewis and Goldberg, 1969; Watson, 1967; White, 1959). Likewise, Field (1979) viewed contingent responsivity as a critical variable for sustaining caregiver-infant interactions.

The final goal submitted is that of continuous provision of follow-up services for parents to support the adult-infant relationship. Each new transition or phase of the infant's development—entering an infant program, talking, becoming ambulatory, needing prostheses, graduating to a public preschool—brings new needs and concerns as well as the joys of mastering another "milestone." As such, the type, duration, and frequency of interventions with a given child and family must constantly be adjusted.

It is apparent that early intervention procedures must be multifaceted and flexible. This challenge demands that early intervenors envision themselves as advocates willing to construct a comprehensive plan to meet the constantly shifting needs of individual infants and their families. When professionals in education, the social sciences, and the health care sciences work together jointly to promote and support beneficial and satisfying relationships between parents and their children, we can hope to achieve the prevention and remediation of long-term emotional and developmental difficulties.

Chapter Outline

OVERVIEW: Discussion focuses on the range of parental reactions to the birth of an at-risk or disabled child and the parent and child variables that may influence the interactional process. The empirical information on caregiver-infant interaction when the infant is at risk or disabled is examined and implications for early intervention services are identified.

I.   REACTION TO THE BIRTH OF A HANDICAPPED CHILD
Models describing reactions to this traumatic event are useful for understanding parents' responses. However, appreciation for individual differences in response is crucial.

II.   FACTORS AFFECTING INTERACTION PATTERNS

A.   *Parent characteristics*
Maternal competence and responsiveness are integrally linked to infant competence.
B.   *Infant characteristics*
Infant characteristics such as age, sex, state, birth order, responsiveness, and temperament affect the interactional process.

III.   INTERACTION RESEARCH
The presence of an at-risk or disabling condition in the infant may exert a profound effect on parent-infant interaction.

A.   Infants born prematurely
Differences between the interactions of groups of full-term and preterm infants and their parents are identified. Parents of preterm babies may exert more active effort in attempting to arouse their less responsive babies.
B.   Developmentally delayed infants
Although the presence of an infant's disabling condition poses a threat to the interactional patterns between parent and child, the limited research on parent-disabled child interaction reveals few disruptions. Children's characteristics may deviate from normal but few effects on attachment and interactional behavior have been detected. Disabil-

ities for which limited information is available include cognitive disorders, physical disabilities, hearing impairment, visual impairment, and affective disorders.

C. Implications for intervention

Principles or guidelines for educating at-risk and handicapped infants and facilitating optimal parent-infant interactions are presented. Guidelines focus predominantly on supporting parents and assisting them to read, understand, and respond contingently to their infants' unique cues.

REFERENCES

Als, H., Brazelton, T. B., Lester, B. M., and Landers, C. *Caesarean Section: Differential Impact on Newborn Behavior.* Paper presented at the International Conference on Infant Studies, New Haven, CT, April, 1980.

Als, H., Lester, B. M., and Brazelton, T. B. Dynamics of the behavioral organization of the premature infant: A theoretical perspective. In T. M. Field, A. M. Sostek, S. Goldberg, and H. H. Shuman (Eds.), *Infants Born At Risk: Behavior and Development.* New York: Spectrum, 1979.

Beckwith, L. Relationships between infants' social behavior and their mothers' behavior. *Child Development,* 1972, *43,* 397–411.

Beckwith, L., and Cohen, S. Preterm birth: Hazardous obstetrical and postnatal events as related to caregiver-infant behavior. *Infant Behavior and Development,* 1978, *1,* 403–411.

Beckwith, L., Cohen, S. E., Kopp, C. B., et al Caregiver-infant interaction and early cognitive development in preterm infants. *Child Development,* 1976, *47,* 579–587.

Bell, R. Q. A reinterpretation of the direct effects of studies of socialization. *Psychological Review,* 1968, *75,* 81–95.

Bell, S. M., and Ainsworth, M. D. S. Infant crying and maternal responsiveness. *Child Development,* 1972, *43,* 1171–1190.

Brazelton, T. B. Psychophysiological reactions to the neonate. I. The value of observation of the neonate. *The Journal of Pediatrics,* 1961, *58,* 508–512.

Brazelton, T. B., Koslowski, B., and Main, M. The origins of reciprocity: The early mother-infant interactions. In M. Lewis and L. A. Rosenblum (Eds.), *The Effect of the Infant on Its Caregiver.* New York: Wiley, 1974.

Brown, J. V., and Bakeman, R. Relationships of human mothers with their infants during the first year of life. In R. W. Bell and W. P. Smotherman (Eds.), *Maternal Influences and Early Behavior.* New York: Spectrum, 1979.

Brown, J., Bakeman, R., Snyder, R., et al. Interactions of black inner-city mothers with their newborn infants. *Child Development,* 1975, *46,* 677–686.

Buium, N., Rynders, J., and Turnure, J. Early maternal linguistic environments of normal and Down's syndrome language-learning children. *American Journal of Mental Deficiency,* 1974, *79,* 52–58.

Carey, W. B. Clinical applications of infant temperament. *Journal of Pediatrics,* 1972, *82,* 823–828.

Chess, S., and Thomas, A. Infant bonding: Mystique and reality. *American Journal of Orthopsychiatry,* 1982, *52*(2), 213–222.

Cicchetti, D., and Sroufe, L. A. The relationship between affective and cognitive development in Down's syndrome infants. *Child Development,* 1976, *47,* 920–929.

Cicchetti, D., and Sroufe, L. A. An organizational view of affect: Illustration from the study of Down's syndrome infants. In M. Lewis and L. Rosenblum (Eds.), *The Development of Affect: Genesis of Behavior* (Vol. 1). New York: Plenum Press, 1978.

Clarke-Stewart, K. A. Interactions between mothers and their young children: Characteristics and consequences. *Monographs of the Society for Research in Child Development,* 1973, *38,* (6–7, Serial No. 153), 1–109.

DiVitto, B., and Goldberg, S. The effects of newborn medical status on early parent-infant interaction. In T. M. Field, A. M. Sostek, S. Goldberg, and H. H. Shuman (Eds.), *Infants Born At Risk: Behavior and Development.* New York: Spectrum, 1979.

Drotar, D., Baskiewicz, A., Irvin, N., et al. The adaptation of parents to the birth of an infant with a congenital malformation: A hypothetical model. *Pediatrics*, 1975, *56*, 710–716.

Emde, R. N., Katz, E. L., and Thorpe, J. K. Emotional expression in infancy: II. Early deviations in Down's syndrome. In M. Lewis and L. Rosenblum (Eds.), *The Development of Affect: Genesis of Behavior* (Vol. I). New York: Plenum Press, 1978.

Escalona, S. Patterns of infantile experience in the developmental process. *Psychoanalytic Study of the Child*, 1963, *18*, 197–244.

Field, T. M. Effects of early separation, interactive deficits, and experimental manipulations on infant-mother face-to-face interaction. *Child Development*, 1977a, *48*, 763–771.

Field, T. M. Maternal stimulation during infant feeding. *Developmental Psychology*, 1977b, *13*, 539–540.

Field, T. M. Interaction patterns of high-risk and normal infants. In T. M. Field, A. M. Sostek, S. Goldberg, and H. H. Shuman (Eds.), *Infants Born At Risk: Behavior and. Development.* New York: Spectrum, 1979.

Fraiberg, S. Blind infants and their mothers: An examination of the sign system. In M. Lewis and L. A. Rosenblum (Eds.), *The Effect of the Infant on Its Caregiver.* New York: Wiley, 1974.

Fraiberg, S. Intervention in infancy: A program for blind infants. In B. Z. Friedlander, G. M. Sterritt, and G. E. Kirk (Eds.), *Exceptional Infant* (Vol. 3): *Assessment and Intervention.* New York: Brunner/Mazel, 1975.

Fraiberg, S. *Insights from the Blind.* New York: Basic Books, 1977.

Frodi, A. M., Lamb, M. E., Leavitt, L. A., and Donovan, W. L. Fathers' and mothers' responses to infant smiles and cries. *Infant Behavior and Development*, 1978, *1*, 187–198.

Goldberg, S. Prematurity: Effects on parent-infant interaction. *Journal of Pediatric Psychology*, 1978, *3*, 137–144.

Goldberg, S., Brachfield, S., and DiVitto, B. Feeding, fussing, and play: Parent-infant interaction in the first year as a function of prematurity and perinatal medical problems. In T. M. Field, S. Goldberg, D. Stern, and A. M. Sostek (Eds.), *High Risk Infants and Children: Adult and Peer Interactions.* New York: Academic Press, 1980.

Graham, F. K., Pennoyer, M. M., Caldwell, B. M., Greenman, M., and Hartman, A. F. Relationship between clinical status and behavior test performance in a newborn group with histories suggesting anoxia. *Journal of Pediatrics*, 1957, *50*, 177–189.

Green, J. A., Gustafson, G. E., and West, M. J. Effects of infant development on mother-infant interaction. *Child Development*, 1980, *51*, 199–207.

Greenberg, M. T. Social interaction between deaf preschoolers and their mothers: The effects of communication method and communication competence. *Developmental Psychology*, 1980, *16*, 465–474.

Greenberg, M. T., and Marvin, R. S. Attachment patterns of profoundly deaf preschool children. *Merrill-Palmer Quarterly*, 1979, *25*(4), 265–279.

Gutmann, A. J., and Rondal, J. A. Verbal operants in mothers' speech to nonretarded and Down's syndrome children matched for linguistic level. *American Journal of Mental Deficiency*, 1979, *83*, 446–452.

Hanson, M. J. *A Longitudinal, Descriptive Study of the Behaviors of Down's Syndrome Infants in an Early Intervention Program.* Eugene, OR: Monographs from the Center on Human Development, 1979.

Hanson, M. Down's syndrome children: Characteristics and intervention research. In M. Lewis and L. Rosenblum (Eds.), *The Uncommon Child: Genesis of Behavior* (Vol. 2). New York: Plenum, 1981.

Harper, P. A., and Weiner, G. Sequelae of low birthweight. *Annual Review of Medicine*, 1965, *16*, 405–520.

Honzik, M. P., Hutchings, J. J., and Burnip, S. R. Birth record assessments and test performance at eight months. *American Journal of Disorders in Children*, 1965, *109*, 416–426.

Jones, O. H. M. Mother-child communication with pre-linguistic Down's syndrome and normal infants. In H. R. Schaffer (Ed.), *Studies in Mother-Infant Interaction*. London: Academic Press, 1977.

Jones, O. H. M. Prelinguistic communication skills in Down's syndrome and normal infants. In T. M. Field, S. Goldberg, D. Stern, and A. M. Sostek (Eds.), *High-Risk Infants and Children: Adult and Peer Interactions*. New York: Academic Press, 1980.

Jones, S. J., and Moss, H. A. Age, state, and maternal behavior associated with infant vocalizations. *Child Development*, 1971, *42*, 1039–1051.

Kekelis, L., and Andersen, E. *Blind Children's Early Input: Mother Accommodations*. Unpublished manuscript. Los Angeles: University of Southern California, 1982.

Klaus, M. H., and Kennell, J. H. (Eds.). *Maternal-Infant Bonding*. St. Louis: Mosby, 1976.

Kogan, K. L., and Tyler, N. Mother-child interaction in young physically handicapped children. *American Journal of Mental Deficiency*, 1973, *77*, 492–497.

Kogan, K. L., Tyler, N., and Turner, P. The process of interpersonal adaptation between mothers and their cerebral palsied children. *Developmental Medicine and Child Neurology*, 1974, *16*, 518–527.

Kogan, K. L., Wimberger, H. C., and Bobbitt, R. A. Analysis of mother-child interaction in young mental retardates. *Child Development*, 1969, *40*, 799–812.

Korner, A. F. Neonate startles, smiles, erections, and reflex sucks as related to state, sex, and individually. *Child Development*, 1969, *40*, 1039–1053.

Korner, A. F. State as variable, as obstacle, and as mediator of stimulation in infant research. *Merrill-Palmer Quarterly*, 1973, *18*, 77–94.

Korner, A. F. The effect of the infant's state, level of arousal, sex, and ontogenetic stage on the caregiver. In M. Lewis and L. A. Rosenblum (Eds.), *The Effect of the Infant on Its Caregiver*. New York: Wiley, 1974.

Lester, B. M., and Zeskind, P. S. Brazelton scale and physical size correlates of neonatal cry features. *Infant Behavior and Development*, 1978, *1*(4), 393–402.

Lester, B. M., and Zeskind, P. S. The organization and assessment of crying in the infant at risk. In T. M. Field, A. M. Sostek, S. Goldberg, and H. H. Shuman (Eds.), *Infants Born At Risk: Behavior and Development*. New York: Spectrum, 1979.

Lewis, M. State as an infant-environment interaction: An analysis of mother-infant interaction as a function of sex. *Merrill-Palmer Quarterly*, 1972, *18*, 95–121.

Lewis, M., and Goldberg, S. Perceptual-cognitive development in infancy: A generalized expectancy model as a function of the mother-infant interaction. *Merrill-Palmer Quarterly of Behavior and Development*, 1969, *15*, 81–100.

Marshall, N. R., Hegrenes, J. R., and Goldstein, S. Verbal interactions: Mothers and their retarded children vs. mothers and their nonretarded children. *American Journal of Mental Deficiency*, 1973, *77*, 415–419.

Massie, H. N. Affective development and the organization of mother-infant behavior from the perspective of psychopathology. In E. Z. Tronick (Ed.), *Social Interchange in Infancy: Affect, Cognition, and Communication*. Baltimore: University Park Press, 1982.

Moss, H. A. Sex, age, and state as determinants of mother-infant interaction. *Merrill-Palmer Quarterly*, 1967, *13*, 19–36.

Osofsky, J. D., and Connors, K. Mother-infant interaction: An integrative view of a complex system. In J. D. Osofsky (Ed.), *Handbook of Infant Development*. New York: Wiley, 1979.

Osofsky, J. D., and Danzger, B. Relationships between neonatal characteristics and mother-infant interaction. *Developmental Psychology*, 1974, *10*, 124–130.

Parke, R. D., and O'Leary, S. Father-mother-infant interaction in the newborn period: Some findings, some observations, and some unresolved issue. In K. Riegal and J. Meacham (Eds.), *The Developing Individual in a Changing World* (*Vol. 2*): *Social and Environmental Issues*. The Hague: Mouton, 1975.

Ramey, C. T., Beckman-Bell, P., and Gowan, J. W. Infant characteristics and infant-caregiver interactions. In J. J. Gallagher (Ed.), *New Directions for Exceptional Children: Parents and Families of Handicapped Children*. San Francisco: Jossey-Bass, 1980 (No. 4).

Robson, K. S., and Moss, H. A. Patterns and determinants of maternal attachment. *Journal of Pediatrics*, 1970, *77*, 976–985.

Rothbart, M. K. Measurement of temperament in infancy. *Child Development*, 1981, *52*, 569–578.

Rubenstein, J. Maternal attentiveness and subsequent exploratory behavior in the infant. *Child Development*, 1967, *38*, 1089–1100.

Sameroff, A., and Chandler, M. Reproductive risk and the continuum of caretaking casuality. In F. Horowitz (Ed.), *Review of Child Development Research* (Vol. 4). Chicago: University of Chicago Press, 1975.

Schlesinger, H. S., and Meadow, K. P. *Sound and Sign: Childhood Deafness and Mental Health*. Berkeley: University of California Press, 1972.

Serafica, F. C., and Cicchetti, D. Down's syndrome children in a strange situation: Attachment and exploration behaviors. *Merrill-Palmer Quarterly*, 1976, *22*, 137–150.

Shere, E., and Kastenbaum, R. Mother-child interaction in cerebral palsy: Environmental and psychosocial obstacles to cognitive development. *Genetic Psychology Monographs*, 1966, *73*, 255–335.

Solnit, A. J., and Stark, M. H. Mourning and the birth of a defective child. *Psychoanalytic Study of the Child*, 1961, *16*, 523–537.

Sostek, A. M., Quinn, P. O., and Davitt, M. K. Behavior, development, and the neurologic status of premature and full-term infants with varying medical complications. In T. M. Field, A. M. Sostek, S. Goldberg, and H. H. Shuman (Eds.), *Infants Born At Risk: Behavior and Development*. New York: Spectrum, 1979.

Stone, N. W., and Chesney, B. H. Attachment behaviors in handicapped infants. *Mental Retardation,* 1978, *61* (1), 8–12.

Terdal, L., Jackson, R. H., and Garner, A. M. Mother-child interactions: A comparison between normal and developmentally delayed groups. In E. J. Mash, L. A. Hamerlynck, and L. C. Handy (Eds.), *Behavior Modification and Families.* New York: Brunner/Mazel, 1976.

Thoman, E. B., Barnett, C. R., and Leiderman, P. H. Feeding behaviors of newborn infants as a function of parity of the mother. *Child Development,* 1971, *42,* 1471–1483.

Thoman, E. B., Becker, P. T., and Freese, M. P. Individual patterns in mother-infant interactions. In G. P. Sackett (Ed.), *Observing Behavior (Vol. 1): Theory and Applications in Mental Retardation.* Baltimore: University Park Press, 1978.

Thoman, E. B., Turner, A. M., Leiderman, P. H., and Barnett, C. R. Neonate-mother interaction: Effects of parity on feeding behavior. *Child Development,* 1970, *40,* 1103–1111.

Thomas, A., and Chess, S. *Temperament and Development.* New York: Brunner/Mazel, 1977.

Tulkin, S. R., and Covitz, F. E. *Mother-infant Interaction and Intellectual Functioning at Age Six.* Paper presented at the biennial meeting of the Society for Research in Child Development, Denver, April 1975.

Vietze, P. M., Abernathy, S. R., Ashe, M. L., and Faulstich, G. Contingent interaction between mothers and their developmentally delayed infants. In G. P. Sackett (Ed.), *Observing Behavior (Vol. 1): Theory and Applications in Mental Retardation.* Baltimore: University Park Press, 1978.

Watson, J. S. Memory and "contingency analysis" in infant learning. *Merrill-Palmer Quarterly,* 1967, *13,* 55.

White, R. W. Motivation reconsidered: the concept of competence. *Psychological Review,* 1959, *66,* 297–333.

Wolff, P. H. Mother-infant interactions at birth. In J. G. Howells (Ed.), *Modern Perspectives in International Child Psychiatry.* New York: Brunner/Mazel, 1971.

Wolff, P. H. Mother-infant interaction in the first year. *New England Journal of Medicine,* 1976, *295,* 999–1001.

Yarrow, L. J., Rubenstein, J. L., Pedersen, F. A. and Jankowski, J. J. Dimensions of early stimulation and their different effect on infant development. *Merrill-Palmer Quarterly,* 1972, 18, 205–218.

Zeskind, P. S., and Lester, B. M. Acoustic features and auditory perceptions of the cries of newborns with prenatal and perinatal complications. *Child Development,* 1978, *49,* 580–589.

CHAPTER 7

Social Development

Mary K. Rothbart

A recurring issue for students of social development involves the major locus for change in the child. Does it reside in the behavior of the caregiver as controller of social reinforcement for the child, in the previously existing characteristics of the child, or in some combination of the two? Mid-century social learning views placed their emphasis on the caregiver's contributions, whereas more recent sources have emphasized the transactional nature of caregiver-infant interaction. These recent approaches take the characteristics of the developing child into account, and therefore are especially helpful in providing a model for thinking about the social development of atypical infants. In turn, consideration of atypical children's social development illuminates our understanding of children's contributions to their own social experience.

This chapter begins with a brief review of social learning approaches to understanding social development. More recent approaches to social development that take the characteristics of the individual child more fully into account are described and discussed in connection with individual differences in temperament. Special emphasis is given to research on atypical infants, but the general organization of the framework presented is also applicable to non-handicapped infants.

LEARNING APPROACHES TO INFANT SOCIAL DEVELOPMENT

Drive reduction theories of infant social development (Dollard and Miller, 1950, Sears, 1963; Sears et al., 1953) have stressed the importance of the caregiver's satisfaction of the infant's primary needs (i.e., hunger and thirst). As the caregiver repeatedly satisfies the infant's hunger drive, the caregiver comes to take on secondary reinforcing characteristics in his or her own right. In time, a secondary drive is established whose aim for the infant is to maintain the presence of the caregiver. This secondary drive is called dependency, and it was expected by early learning theorists that this social drive would continue to influence child behavior well beyond the period of infancy and to influence future learning and social development (Maccoby and Masters, 1970).

Problems for the drive reduction point of view were created by the results of Harlow's (1958) research with infant rhesus monkeys. Harlow's research demonstrated that infant monkeys' physical contact with a caregiver was more important than satisfaction of their hunger drive in maintaining proximity to the caregiver. Thus, maintenance of physical closeness could not be seen as derivative of satisfaction of the primary drive.

A second learning theory developed by Skinner (1953) called operant learning theory offered a more descriptive view of learning phenomena. This position was not at all threatened by Harlow's findings because drive reduction was not an element of the theory. In the operant view, a reinforcer is defined as any environmental event which increases the probability that a given behavior will be performed in the future. Operant behaviors may thus be thought of as operating upon the environment in order to obtain reinforcement. Operant theory does not concern itself with the existence or nonexistence of primary drives or other processes occurring within the organism, but designates input-output relations only. Operant ideas were adapted to the period of infancy by Gewirtz (1961) and by Bijou and Baer (1965). In infancy, reinforcers could be seen to include the caregiver's giving of food, hugging, providing warmth, smiling, and providing interesting spectacles for the infant. For the older child, reinforcers could include verbal events such as the caregiver saying "That's good" or "You did it right."

Because the caregiver is so frequently the source of reinforcement for the infant, the caregiver's presence frequently becomes the cue for behavior that will be reinforced. In Gewirtz's (1961) view any behavior a child performs that is elicited by the caregiver's presence is an instance of the child's "dependency" on the caregiver. Smiling and laughter in the presence of the caregiver thus have been seen as dependent behaviors, and the expectation of an operant theorist is that the performance of smiling and laughter is dependent upon some social reinforcer or reinforcers. Recent research indicates that caregivers clearly *elicit* smiling and laughter through their exaggerated and exciting behavior toward the infant; however, there seem to be only weak and short-lived reinforcing effects of this stimulation upon smiling (Zelazo, 1971).

It should be clear that operant principles of reinforcement also may be applied to an analysis of a caregiver's behavior. We may say that the parent is reinforced for certain kinds of play and other caregiving by the positive reactions of the child. This analysis allows us to think about a highly reciprocal relationship between child and caregiver in early social interaction. Nevertheless, the major applied contributions of the operant point of view have viewed the caregiver as a shaper and molder of infant learning through the application of social and material reinforcers. This approach has proved useful in the development of intervention programs (e.g., Hanson, 1977), but its usefulness in applied settings need not imply that its principles accurately describe the course of social development.

The third major social learning position was originally developed by Bandura and Walters (1963) and later elaborated by Bandura (1977). This view stresses children's imitative learning or modeling of behavior observed in others, with children's continuing performance of modeled behavior seen as the result of reinforcement. Reinforcement would include both direct consequences to the child for the behavior or observation by the child of others' reinforcements. Bandura's theory has not been explicitly directed toward the period of infancy, but we might expect its principles to apply to infant imitation. These principles also weight the social development balance on the side of the caregiver and social environment, with other individuals seen as the source of behavior patterns to be modeled and frequently as the source of reinforcement for their enactment by the child. This modeling theory is not very useful when applied to the origin of important behavior patterns in infancy, for example, emotional expressions. These expressions are present in deaf-blind infants (Goodenough, 1932) and do not seem to require modeling for their initial appearance. Readers who would like to explore social learning theory positions in more detail are referred to Maccoby and Masters' (1970) extensive review on their contributions to issues involving dependency and attachment.

THE CHILD'S CONTRIBUTIONS TO SOCIAL DEVELOPMENT

At least four major influences have resulted in a shift in the balance from a stress on social reinforcing effects to an investigation of those characteristics of the child that may affect social development. The first of these is Piaget's studies of the cognitive development of children, demonstrating how children may be seen to individually "construct" their worlds from their experiences with it. The second is the work of psychoanalytically oriented investigators such as

Escalona (1968), Sander (1962, 1969), and Spitz (1965), who have noted the influence of infant biology upon social and emotional development. The third is Bowlby's (1969, 1973) writings on attachment, influenced by both psychoanalysis and ethology, emphasizing the importance of the child's contributions to the development of caregiver-infant attachment, and illustrating how the child's changing maturational status can change the nature of the child's relation with the caregiver. The fourth influence is infancy research itself (Osofsky, 1979; Stone et al., 1973), which has provided evidence of competencies in the young infant that had previously not been appreciated. In addition, infancy research has demonstrated in detail the intricate and exciting social interactions between infant and caregiver that may be observed when videotapes of parent-infant interactions are analyzed in great detail (Brazelton et al., 1974; Stern, 1971, 1974).

This review considers this new perspective, and to it adds the importance of considering individual differences in temperament as important contributors to infant social development (Thomas and Chess, 1977). Although most of the research on individual differences to date concerns temperamental differences among nonhandicapped infants, infant temperament provides us with a place to start in thinking about the important challenges facing the caregiver of an atypical child.

INFANT TEMPERAMENT

Temperament in our view (Rothbart and Derryberry, 1982) includes the infant's constitutionally based patterns of reacting to stimulation (reactivity) and the infant's capacities for self-regulation. Reactivity refers to the infant's levels of excitability or responsiveness as reflected in motor activity, vocal activity, direction of attention, facial expressions, and emotional activity in response to stimulation. In our laboratory work (Rothbart and Derryberry, 1981), we have proposed that each of these reactions may be described in terms of its time course (i.e., how quickly an infant shows a reaction in a given channel, the time to the infant's peak intensity of reaction, and the recovery time after stimulation has been removed) and its intensive characteristics (threshold and intensity of reactions).

As an example of infant reactivity, we may consider a 3 month old's reaction to presentation of a novel three-dimensional stimulus, such as a small rubber squeeze toy, over a period of 30 seconds or longer. A child typically shows a general activation pattern, frequently including reactivity in the motor channel (movement of the limbs), the vocal channel (cooing), and facial expression (smiling). The child's responses also may be seen as involving an integration of all these channels in reactions identified as emotion (Derryberry and Rothbart, in press). In the situation described above, the emotional reaction most often would be a positive one, involving smiling and positive vocalization. Observing normal infants in this situation, we note that they vary in their latency to a reaction, in the channels involved in the reaction, in the time it takes between when the reaction begins and when it reaches its peak intensity, and in the time before the infant again returns to a quieter state (or moves to a more agitated emotional state of distress).

Another example of reactivity may be observed in the infant's distress reaction. Infants differ in the intensity of stimulation they can experience before they demonstrate distress. Once a distress threshold is reached, they also differ in the peak to which the distress reaction will rise, ranging in normal infants from moderate fussing to hard wailing, and in the time they take to reach this peak. Infants also differ in their time course of recovery or ability to be soothed, but in discussing the time course of distress we must go beyond ideas of infant reactivity to consider also the self-regulative functions of temperament. Infants influence the levels of stimulation they experience. Older infants may approach or avoid a source of intense stimulation either through motor response or through their direction of attention. They may be more or less distracted by peripheral stimuli, having the effect of soothing, yet they may also soothe themselves or create higher levels of excitement through their own activity. Infants not only *react* to stimulation, to a great extent they act in order to *select* the level of stimulation they will experience and, at least for some infants, to modulate their level of excitement through self-soothing and self-stimulation.

We have argued (Rothbart and Derryberry, 1982) that maturational development may be seen as involving the child's development of progressive inhibitory control over already existing excitatory or reactive processes. At the same time, the infant's developing sensory systems and memory capacities allow for increasing sources of reactivity on which the child's regulatory activities will act. At the beginning, however, and for an extended period in the development of the infant, the caregiver will serve as the major source of external regulation of the child, through caring for the infant's needs for food, warmth, and dryness, and through helping to modulate the infant's state through the use of soothing procedures and through stimulating excitement and games. During this period, the role of the caregiver in the system will also depend on the temperamental characteristics of the child, however. It will rely upon the clarity of the infant's signals and how they are seen and interpreted by the caregiver.

DEVELOPMENTAL ISSUES OF INFANCY

Let us now consider individual differences among infants as they may operate within child-caregiver interaction during the period of infancy. Sander (1962, 1969) has gathered longitudinal data describing the interaction of 22 mother-child pairs over the first 20 months of life. On the basis of these observations, he has identified a sequence of issues or adaptations typically faced by the mother-child "couple" during the period of infancy. The issues he describes are summarized in Table 7.1.

Sander indicates the observations that prompted his development of this set of issues:

> After following ten or fifteen of the (infant-mother) pairs we could begin to anticipate the time of appearance of some of the important concerns the mother would express, or, on the other hand, feel relieved about. This gave the impression that we were watching a sequence of adaptations common to all the different mother-infant pairs, although acted out somewhat differently by each. Each advancing level of activity which the child became capable of manifesting demanded a new adjustment in the mother-child relationship. A new equilibrium had to be reached. The problem was that there appeared to be a certain time scale on which these changes could be placed. If a pair had difficulty getting coordinated on one particular level, they presently were already struggling with the next before they had comfortably adjusted to the first. One could begin to appreciate, too, the difficulties this imposed in reaching the second adaptation (1969, p. 191).

Sander's stages stress mutual adaptation rather than only infant learning. Both infant and caregiver are involved in any given adjustment and the temperamental characteristics of the infant will be very important in determining the extent of disequilibrium and the course of adjustment in each new phase. Thus, the special characteristics brought to the interaction by the atypical infant in combination with the infant's capacities for the regulation of self and others will strongly influence the course of any given adjustment.

Although Sander's position suggests that early problems in adaptation may create lasting difficulties, a second position suggests that early difficulties may be later overcome. If caregivers and their children are better at handling some developmental issues than oth-

Table 7.1. Developmental issues identified by Sander (1969, p. 192)

Issue	Title	Span of months	Prominent infant behaviors that became coordinated with maternal activities
1	Initial regulation	1–2–3	Basic infant activities concerned with biological processes related to feeding, sleeping, elimination, postural maintenance, etc. including stimulus needs for quieting and arousal
2	Reciprocal exchange	4–5–6	Smiling behavior that extends to full motor and vocal involvement in sequences of affectively spontaneous back and forth exchanges. Activities of spoon feeding, dressing, etc. become reciprocally coordinated
3	Initiative	7–8–9	Activities initiated by infant to secure a reciprocal social exchange with mother or to manipulate environment on his/her own selection
4	Focalization	10–11–12–13	Activities by which infant determines the availability of mother on his/her specific initiative; tends to focalize need meeting demands on the mother
5	Self-assertion	14–20	Activities in which infant widens the determination of his/her own behavior often in the face of maternal opposition

ers, earlier issues not adequately dealt with at the time they appeared may be somewhat outweighed by more favorable outcomes of later developmental issues, including those of middle childhood and beyond (R. Harmon, personal communication, 1981).

We may now consider Sander's developmental issues as they might interact with individual characteristics of the child. It should be emphasized that these issues are derived from the study of normal infants. For given populations of atypical infants, there may be special issues that are not discussed here, for example, the blind infant's construction of space (Bigelow, 1980; Fraiberg, 1968) or the deaf infant's acquisition of language (Meadow, 1975; Schlesinger and Meadow, 1972).

Initial Regulation

Sander (1962, 1969) suggests that the first issue faced by the newborn and caregiver involves regulation of the biological processes involved in eating, sleeping, and the modulation of states of excitement in the infant. Although Sander speaks of an issue being "settled," we would also expect the recurrence of some issues, for example, sleeping problems recurring in the latter half of the first year of life. Perhaps another way of thinking about the issues or adaptations Sander describes is to consider each new issue as being added to the previous ones, with previous issues sometimes recurring as the child reaches more differentiated and integrated levels of functioning.

Initial regulation involves initial periodicities or rhythms of children's states and behavior, ranging from approximately 24-hour sleep-wake rhythms (circadian) through 4- to 6-hour rhythms of alertness (ultraradian) to rhythms of scanning, sucking, body movement, and respiration. Sander et al. (1970) report that by the seventh day, an ordering emerges in the infant's sleep-wake patterns for a 24-hour period. It is likely that these patterns have been influenced by both inborn infant periodicities and by caregiver attempts to lengthen periods of sleep and locate them during the night hours. Enough mutual regulation has been established between newborn and caregiver by the tenth day that shifts in foster caregivers for an infant will result in disruption of both infant state and feeding (Sander, 1977).

Additional studies of state and social interaction have been carried out by Thoman et al. (1978) who made home observations of infants and mothers during the first 5 weeks of life. Of 20 pairs of infants and mothers, the interactions of three pairs were studied in detail because the infants later showed evidence of developmental delays on the Bayley tests of infant development. When compared with the group of subjects as a whole, these infant-mother pairs showed much less non-caregiving social interaction. Thoman et al. recounted the mother-infant interactions of one of these pairs, concluding that the mother had difficulty understanding her infant's mixed signals about whether he was awake or asleep. This observation of mother-infant interaction at 4 weeks illustrates the difficulty:

> The episode began with the infant asleep in the crib. During the 3 mins. prior to the mother's intervention, there were six epochs (10-second periods) during which open-eyed rapid eye movements occurred. The mother picked the baby up, undressed him, and gave him an immersion bath which lasted for 5 mins. Throughout the bath the infant's eyes did not open. As she talked to him, one of the mother's comments was that she did not understand why the infant kept his eyes closed. As she dressed her infant after the bath, he began to waken. She put him to her breast and after several efforts to get him to feed, she put him back into the crib and left the room. While in the crib alone, the infant remained awake and primarily alert for 15 mins. (Thoman et al., 1978, p. 108–109).

The observers also noted that this infant changed more rapidly from sleep to wakefulness and from one sleep state to another when compared with the mean of all infants. Adjustments in sleeping and eating routines that might have been easy for some interactive mother-infant pairs were thus highly problematic for this mother-infant pair.

Als et al. (1980) have also discussed state modulation in connection with their observations of handicapped and normal infants in a laboratory situation. In their laboratory, the infant is placed in an infant seat in front of the parent, and the parent is instructed to play with the baby without picking the baby up. One video camera is focused on the mother and a second on the baby, with the two pictures displayed on a split-screen monitor. Als et al. (1980) suggest that the first developmental requirement for a satisfying interchange in this situation is that the infant's basic physiological responses become organized, including heart rate, respiration, color change, and the availability of an alert state over a long enough period for social exchange to occur. The second stage of organization involves the maintenance of mutual orientation between infant and parent and, still later, play dialogues between parent and infant become possible.

Als et al. (1980) illustrate the achievement of these goals by both a sighted and a blind infant and their mothers. In physiological and state organization:

> the parent envelops the infant with arms, hands, and voice, containing the physiological balance and particularly the motoric arousal engendered as the infant attempts to come to midline and simultaneously look at the mother. For the blind infant, containment is more difficult. The visual focus is missing. Closer tactile contact, nuzzling, and more continuous enveloping with the mother's voice make up for it . . . It becomes apparent that the successive goal realization is the same for both pairs, yet the process of implementation is much more conscious for the mother of the blind infant (pp. 198–201).

Als et al. found that allowing parents to observe their videotaped interactions with their infants makes it possible for parents both to see the competencies of the infant and to develop realizable goals for parent and infant in the interaction. In this setting, the parent is encouraged to acknowledge the difficulties the child's handicap presents to the energy of the parent and of the infant in the interaction.

This kind of clinical support and information is important because parents of newborn handicapped children frequently undergo a period of shock and panic and later feelings of helplessness, anger, and guilt (Als et al., 1980; Cohen, 1962; Emde and Brown, 1978; Solnit and Stark, 1961) in dealing with the birth of an atypical infant. This is an issue present during the early days of an atypical infant's life that is not present for normal infants. Jones (1980), for example, interviewed mothers of infants with Down syndrome who expressed their strong desires to understand their babies and to be able to develop expectations about their children's future. One of the mothers in his study reported:

> Mongolism to me meant the child had no hope of ever doing a thing. That was the feeling I had; that this child is never going to know right from wrong, never going to walk or talk. Something I heard said mongolism is something like monsters, they've got this terrible strength and there's nothing you can do with them (Jones, 1980, p. 219).

A second mother reported:

> The first few days I didn't know anything about it and I kept asking the nurses. They were dead cagey; they had good excuses like, "Oh well, you will be seeing Dr. such-and-such in a few days" or "Somebody will be round to see you." Well, nobody ever came . . . It was the first few days I wanted to know what I could. I wanted to know what I could expect from that child; whether he would be a thickie all his life; whether he would ever walk or what (Jones, 1980, p. 210).

Jones concludes that in some cases, the parent of an atypical infant may doubt even the humanity of their child, wondering what future would be possible for the infant, not having the usual expectations of parents of a newborn infant.

In summary, questions of state regulation and maintenance are early and recurring issues for both normal and atypical infants. Knowledge about state variability and patterns of alerting to and withdrawing from stimulation via state change thus is important for the caregiver. Landesman-Dwyer and Sackett (1978) have used rating scales ranging from sleep to activity in describing profoundly retarded children who are nonambulatory, and Simeonsson et al. (1980a) suggested that the assessment of state characteristics should be part of the basic assessment of multihandicapped children.

Reciprocal Exchange

The second set of adaptations described by Sander involves the period of reciprocal exchange, including infants aged 4 through 6 months. This period has probably been the most studied using videotapes and methods of microanalysis (Stern, 1971, 1974; Brazelton et al., 1974). The issues of the period are focused upon the reciprocal coordination of caregiving activities and, especially, social play. Here the affectively toned exchanges between mother and infant have been the source of both research and of poetry:

> During the first six months, the baby has the rudiments of love language available to him. There is the language of the embrace, the language of the eyes, the language of the smile, vocal communications of pleasure and distress. It is the essential vocabulary of love before we can speak of love. Eighteen years later, when this baby is full-grown and "falls in love" for the first time, he will woo his partner through the language of the eyes, the language of the smile, through the utterance of endearments, and the joy of the embrace. In his declarations of love he will use such phrases as "When I first looked into your eyes," "When you smiled at me," "When I held you in my arms." And naturally, in his exalted state, he will believe that he invented this love song (Fraiberg, 1977a, p. 29).

This beautiful description by Fraiberg captures a moment in one of the most positive interactions of a caregiver and a 4-month-old infant, in this case, an infant whose attentional, motor, vocal, and emotional systems are functioning in expectable ways. Others have described positive interaction during this period as an intricate dance, in which each partner knows and anticipates the moves of the other. What the infant knows and whether the infant is capable of anticipation in this interaction is still at issue, however. Studies investigating which member of the couple, the young infant or the caregiver, is more sensitive to the changes in the behavior of the other suggest that most of the behavioral flexibility in the interaction resides in the caregiver (Gottman and Ringland, 1981). Although mothers frequently act "as if" their infants understood them, the dialogues between mother and the infant are frequently highly one-sided (Kaye, 1979).

The caregiver's relation to the infant is, as Spitz (1965) has pointed out, asymmetric. The adult's understanding of the meaning of the infant's signals influences his/her behavior, while the infant is functioning either directly in response to physical stimulus change or possibly on the basis of temporal expectations. Intention and the concept of the self acting upon other selves are not available to the young infant; caregivers' knowledge of infants and their attributions of the meaning of the infants' actions are thus very important. To the extent that research may inform us about the meanings of these infant actions, parent education may be extremely useful during this period as well as during the initial period for parents of atypical infants.

This point returns us again to the importance of the quality of the infant's signals and how they are seen and interpreted by the caregiver. Although the infant's temperamental characteristics may be seen during this period as being primarily reactive, at the same time they serve an extremely important socially *regulative* function—they signal to the parent the affective state of the infant, indicating whether external soothing or excitement is appropriate, and they allow the caregiver to monitor their child's reactions to their attempts to modify the infant's condition. A smile or laugh may be read by the caregiver as "I like it" (although the smile also may indicate "I'm excited by it and I may soon be showing distress"), a distress vocalization, distress face, or extended looking away as "something's wrong," and signs of soothing as "that's better." In social play, the child's own regulatory gaze aversions and turning away may be read as "things are getting too exciting for me." Finally, the infant's overall pattern of positive reactivity, including eye contact, smiling, and positive vocalizations may be read as "you make me very happy" or "I love you." An infant who gives love to the caregiver through these patterns of reaction can be a very easy baby to love in return.

Given effective reading of the infant's signals, the caregiver may provide regulation the infant cannot provide for himself/herself and, of course, the child's affective reactions are also *emotionally* important to the caregiver. Robson and Moss (1970) interviewed mothers about the point at which they felt that their child recognized them as a special person, their own recognition of their child as an individual, and their own feelings of love for their infant. The majority of mothers reported that the child's smiling, eye contact, and vocal responsiveness were instrumental in their development of these feelings. Robson and Moss also reported that the one brain-damaged infant in their sample, who did not smile or look at her mother, elicited from the mother reactions of anger and conscious wishes of abandonment.

Fraiberg's (1974) work with parents of blind children is important in connection with the reading of children's reactive signals. Fraiberg points out that the high levels of stimulation parents of blind infants use with their babies may be more closely related to eliciting positive affect in the infant than to providing extra stimulation to compensate for the missing visual modality. She and her associates have identified alternative infant signals for the caregiver to read, asking them to look at the infant's hands rather than the face for signs of interest, and have developed methods for demonstrating to parents that the special feelings their infant has for them may be demonstrated in response channels other than eye contact and frequent smiling.

Let us now consider another dimension of reactivity—distress. As described above, the time course, peak, and recovery of this reaction differ widely among children, with the time to peak intensity ranging from 2 to 3 minutes to over 30 minutes in our informal observations of infants in the home. Infants also differ widely in their use of self-soothing techniques, such as thumb and finger sucking, body and hair rubbing, and deployment of visual attention. We (Rothbart and Derryberry, 1981) have hypothesized that infants whose distress builds slowly and are easily soothed may be better able to develop techniques for soothing themselves than children who move much more rapidly to a high peak of distress. Thus, some infants need less regulation of distress from their caregivers either because they are less easily distressed or because they have developed their own techniques for self-soothing. At the same time, depending upon how quickly they can be soothed, infants differ in the extent to which the caregiver may be able to act as a source of comfort (Escalona, 1968). Infants who are relatively inconsolable may spend long periods in close contact with others while they are feeling distress; infants who are easily soothed may frequently experience feelings of relief in connection with others and come to appreciate others as sources of security. We suspect that these differences in experience are important to the child's construction of the caregiver as a source of security, with the child's social cognitions thus being influenced by the pattern of *effective* experience (Escalona, 1968; Rothbart and Derryberry, 1981) resulting from the interaction between a child's temperamental characteristics and the stimulation to which the child is exposed.

Another important temperamental dimension is the flexibility of the child's attentional systems in orienting to stimulus change and in maintaining contact with objects long enough to learn about them (Posner and Rothbart, 1981). Some infants seem able to sustain orienting into an ongoing act, producing extended interaction with environmental objects; sometimes this involvement seems *too* extended when the caregiver would wish to divert the infant to another activity. Other infants seem dominated by the tendency of reorienting to each new event in the external and internal world. Others show low thresholds for distress, which frequently result in termination of contact with the unfamiliar or exciting stimulus object. We have much to learn about what these patterns of attention mean in the infant's cognitive and affective growth.

Studies exploring temperamental characteristics of atypical infants are important in the development of programs involving the caregiver-infant system. Infants with Down syndrome, for example, were described in our research (Rothbart and Hanson, 1983) as showing less reactivity in the vocal channel and less smiling than normal infants; for such infants the caregiver may be required to be a more important source of stimulation and excitement then the caregiver of a normal infant. On the other hand, highly irritable or impulsive infants may require more caregiver *regulation* along with careful programs of increasing stimulation within the child's tolerable limits. Safford et al. (1976), for example, have developed a program for working with highly irritable multihandicapped infants that includes use of relaxation techniques such as rocking and warm water baths, progressive desensitization of sensitive body parts such as the mouth and palms of the hands, and presentation of highly simple, graded stimuli for the child's exploration.

We may view the atypical infant and caregiver as achieving patterns of interaction that will allow for growth in the child, but note that the caregiver of an atypical infant is likely to be required to make a greater contribution to achievement of balance in the system than the caregiver of a normal infant, with this contribution involving either additional stimulation or additional modulation, or both. Studies involving infants with Down syndrome (Jones, 1980) and premature infants (Field, 1980) do in fact suggest that their mothers are more active in interaction with their infants than mothers of normal infants.

The emotional side of the caregiver's interaction with infants with Down syndrome during this period has been explored by Emde and Brown (1978). They report that parents of infants with Down syndrome tend to grieve about their infants' disability twice: first, when their child's condition is diagnosed, and again at about 4 months of age when reciprocal play results in less intense reactions from the infants with Down syndrome than from normal babies. Emde and Brown describe the reaction of the researchers to one infant with Down syndrome:

> As we approached, Dawn would smile—but it was different. There was bilateral upturning of the corners of the mouth, but the cheeks and eyes did not crinkle or participate in it; there was no brightening of the eyes, and there was no "activation" or bicycling of the arms and legs as we

are used to in the normal 3- to 4-month-old. Furthermore, eye-to-eye contact was poor and there was no crescendo of sparkling eyes tracking our approach. Each of us experiencing this sequence felt a sense of being let down (1978, p. 305).

Emde et al. (1978) picked the "best smile" from 20 photographs of six infants with Down syndrome and six nonhandicapped infants $3\frac{1}{2}$ months old. In each case the Down syndrome infants' smiles were judged as less intense. They also report that social smiles of infants with Down syndrome tend to lag in their appearance approximately 3 to 4 weeks after the normal infants' first social smiles.

Assessment of infant temperament may be of special use during this period of reciprocal exchange. We are still in the early stages of developing measures for the assessment of temperament, with the most frequently used method for assessment being the parent report questionnaire (Bates et al. 1979; Buss and Plomin, 1975; Carey and McDevitt, 1978; Rothbart, 1980, 1981). We must continue to be cautious about possible contributions of response bias to the parents' reports about temperamental characteristics of their children (described by Bates, 1980), although we expect that our use of concrete behavioral items in these instruments will circumvent this problem to some extent. Aside from this problem, however, the most important caution to bear in mind about using both parent reports and home observation measures for assessing infant temperament is that they measure the infant's functioning within a stimulating and regulating system that involves caregivers, siblings, and other sources of stimulation and regulation. Thus, home-based measures do not give us an independent measure of what the *infant* brings to the caregiver-infant interaction; they give us instead an assessment of the child's behavior in an interactive system where parents and others may be exerting a strong influence.

Nevertheless, parent report measures may be used to describe usual emotional and motor behavior displayed in the home by atypical infants in comparison with nonhandicapped infants. Eventually, these assessments may also serve to point up areas of concern about the atypical infant's production of social signals and possible difficulties in considering the infant a source of emotional satisfaction to the parent. By training parents of atypical infants to observe their children's patterns of reaction to stimulation, parents will become more aware of their children's very human capacities for social interaction, better able to read their children's signals and less likely to be distressed by social expectations that are not met by their children.

Initiative and Focalization

The third issue Sander has identified focuses upon the infant's development of initiative during months 7 through 9. During this period infants become more active agents in getting what they want, both from the general environment and from the caregiver. The important psychological development instigating the issue of initiative is the development of intentionality in the infant. As the child increasingly engages in activities in order to get anticipated results, the child's understanding of means-ends relationships develops, and the caregiver may come to be seen as a means to the child's ends. This creates a new social situation relating to the child's increasing social awareness and thus ushers in a new set of problems for the caregiver. Parents who greatly enjoyed interaction with young infants when it was guided by their own desires and goals may come to see interactions in which the infant attempts to control the direction of interaction as the beginning of a battle of wills. In this battle, parents may come to take a position illustrated by a parent who stated, "Ned has to learn that *he* doesn't win, that *we* win" (Sander, 1969, p. 208).

Sander's third issue is very closely joined to the fourth—the issue of *focalization*—which Sander identifies as becoming important when the infant is 10 to 13 months of age. This is the period during which children are able, through their developing locomotory skills, to establish and maintain proximity with the caregiver on their own initiative. It is a period when security needs may be very much at issue for the child, and the demands the infant places on the caregiver may lead to ambivalent feelings in the caregiver. In turn, the ambivalence of the caregiver may lead to still more heightened proximity seeking by the child (Sander, 1969).

In examining the issue of initiative and focalization, the importance of infant-caregiver attachment must be considered. John Bowlby (1969) has developed an evolutionary view of infant-caregiver attachment. He argues that it has been evolutionarily adaptive for the young of our species to remain close to older, larger, and more experienced figures, thereby avoiding harm from predators and other dangers. Bowlby maintains that behavior that will help the infant maintain proximity to the mother is genetically programmed in the infant and appears at appropriate times in the infant's development for attachment to continue. During the first 2 to 3 months the infant engages in behavior promoting its proximity to others and leading adult caregivers to want to maintain proximity to the infant. The infant's attachment behavior is initially indiscriminately directed toward others, and there is no focusing on a particular attachment figure. Early responses to potential caregivers include orientation of the eyes and body, head-turning, rooting and sucking, grasping, clinging, and reaching. The behavior of crying and later smiling serves a signal function for the caregiver, with crying signifying something is wrong and smiling signifying the child's feelings of satisfaction. Both of these signals promote close interaction between caregiver and infant. Bowlby calls the first phase of attachment the period of "orientation and signals without discrimination of figure." Its culmination coincides with Sander's second developmental issue, that of reciprocity, when the infant gives "the full social response in all its spontaneity, vivacity and delight" (Rheingold, 1961). This social response is initially directed indiscriminately.

During the second phase of the development of attachment, between about 3 to 6 months, Bowlby (1969) notes the presence of "orientation and signals directed toward one (or more) discriminated figures." During this period, children show increasingly differentiated responses in greeting (e.g., smiling, vocalizing, body excitement, and lifting of the arms), exploring and climbing, using the caregiver as a secure base so as to be able to explore, flight to the caregiver when alarmed, and differential clinging. Bowlby sees this differentiation as occurring in connection with exposure learning. With increased familiarity, the infant discriminates the caregiver from others by engaging in approach to the familiar. This genetically programmed response is seen as developing as soon as the infant has developed the motor responses permitting it.

Phase three of attachment as described by Bowlby may be seen to correspond to Sander's phases of initiative and especially focalization. Bowlby calls this period the "maintenance of proximity to a discriminated figure by means of locomotion as well as signals." Now locomotion is possible for the infant, and infants become increasingly differentiating in their behavior toward attachment figures, including the tendency to follow after a departing caregiver. Actively maintaining proximity to attachment figures may now be seen as a goal of the infant, while a special sensitivity develops to unfamiliar others (stranger anxiety) and disruption due to separation from the usual caregiver occurs (separation anxiety). Bowlby illustrates this phenomenon with a study by Yarrow (1967) on the effects of age of shifting infants from a foster home to an adoptive home. In this study, infants placed in adoptive homes between the ages of 6 to 12 weeks showed no emotional upset and at 3 months only a few showed disruption. With increasing age (up to 12 months, the oldest infants placed) increasing proportions of infants showing upset and increasing severity and generality of upset was demonstrated. At 6 months, 86% showed some disturbance, and from 7 to 12 months all showed marked disturbance, with increased distress, decreased smiling and vocalization, sleeping and eating disturbances, and loss of previous abilities. Bowlby suggests that this period of strong and active attachment continues through the second year and into the third.

Finally, Bowlby describes the fourth phase of attachment as the "formation of a goal-corrected partnership." During this period the child is thought to come to see the attachment figure as an independent object, with his/her own goals, feelings, and motivations. Increasing coordination of the infants' and mothers' activities become possible. Bowlby says only a little about this final phase of the development of attachment, suggesting more research is needed on it.

The process of attachment has been identified as being of special importance to social development, with the attachment relation seen as constituting a secure base for later exploration and achievement (Ainsworth, 1973; Sroufe and Waters,1977). Taking a strong position on the importance of the early mother-child relationship for later exploration, Ainsworth (1973) has developed a laboratory assessment of infants' "security of attachment."

Ainsworth (1973) argues that whether a child will become attached to a caregiver depends on the quantity of time the two have spent together, and that most infants therefore will develop an attachment relation. However, the quality of the attachment will depend upon how sensitive the caregiver has been in responding to the infant's signals and the extent of separation experienced by mother and child. Ainsworth suggests that either caregiver insensitivity or separation will lead to insecurity of attachment and proposes that this insecurity may be assessed in an approximately 20-minute episode called the "strange situation." The strange situation involves a series of separations and reunions of caregiver and child in a laboratory setting with a strange experimenter present during part of the procedure. Evidence of insecurity of attachment is taken when infants show little greeting of or involvement with the caregiver or when infants show evidence of insecurity with the caregiver during a preseparation period and mixed anger and approach during reunion. Securely attached infants are identified as showing interest in the caregiver during preseparation, positive greeting upon the parent's return, and not too much emotional disruption during reunion.

Ainsworth suggests that early secure attachment, grounded in the primary caregiver's sensitivity to the child and nonseparation from the infant, forms the basis for later exploration and nondependency in the child. This argument, like that of the early social learning theorists, places the balance of later social development on the early activities of the caregiver and neglects consideration of characteristics of the individual child. The role of the caregiver as a source of security for the infant depends on the caregiver's own sensitivity, but we would expect that it also depends on the infant's requirements for security. A child who rarely uses the caregiver as a secure base may do so because the caregiver is not an effective source of security, but it is also possible that the child is not fearful enough in a given situation to require the parent for security (Rothbart and Derryberry, 1981).

Some infants with low reactivity or quickly recovering emotional reactions thus may not require much comfort from the caregiver. Other infants may be sensitive to distress but have evolved means for soothing themselves that do not require the aid of the caregiver. Other children may require security and satisfy themselves through maintaining caregiver proximity, as is required for the "secure attachment" designation, but still other infants may become so distressed in situations such as the strange situation that even the caregiver's presence is not enough to calm them.

The importance of constitutional differences in the attachment situation may become highlighted if we consider atypical infants. How are we to define sensitivity in the behavior of a caregiver toward an atypical infant? If, as Serafica and Cicchetti (1976) have found, infants with Down syndrome become less distressed in the strange situation than nonhandicapped infants, is it appropriate to attribute this finding to their mothers' insensitivity to them? If the caregiver of a delayed infant attempts to avoid intrusive insensitivity by waiting for the infant's signals in order to know how to act in a given situation, when will the caregiver be able to act? Interactions of mothers with special populations of infants may result in caregiver's seeming intrusiveness (Jones, 1980), but they also may result in developmental gains that would not be possible if the caregiver waited for signals from the child in order to act. I am not suggesting that Ainsworth (1973) has developed particular prescriptions for the caregiver of an atypical infant, but only that we should consider the implications of the security of attachment concept for the existence of individual differences among children before applying it to atypical infants.

In summarizing the important events for infant social development between 7 and approximately 13 months of age, major changes occur in connection with the development of intentionality, locomotion, and the use of the caregiver as a source of security for exploration. For atypical infants who do not develop locomotion, intentionality, use of means-ends relations, and/or fearfulness, we would expect major differences in social behavior and in the ways they would come to construe and to value other human beings. For a child who becomes afraid easily, a soothing caregiver may become an important source of support. For a child who seeks excitement, a caregiver may become an important source of fun. For a child who is easily frustrated, a cooperative caregiver may become the means to innumerable ends. For most children, the caregiver is likely to serve all of these functions. One of the conflicts facing all caregivers is how much comfort and assistance to provide for the infant and how much autonomy to permit or encourage in the child, and these conflicts are heightened when working with atypical children (Jones, 1980). One reason for the heightened conflict is the difficulty of knowing what course of development to expect from the atypical child. A second reason involves the necessity for encouraging feelings of mastery and effectiveness in the child, and we would expect these to be especially likely to follow when the *child* is able to initiate sequences of interaction rather than having responses chiefly elicited by others.

An additional problem involves the interpretation of specific social behaviors in atypical infants. It is very important to determine the extent to which an infant's socially reactive signals are *necessary* accompaniments to infant cognitive development. Intervention-minded practitioners have suggested to me that if we could only get particular groups of infants to smile, we would be thereby enhancing their cognitive development, or that if we could only get extended eye contact, we will have thereby facilitated information processing in the infant. Results with infants with Down syndrome (Miranda and Fantz, 1974; Rothbart and Hanson, 1983) suggest that these children show longer periods of orienting at 6 and 9 months than non-handicapped infants. Does this mean the infants with Down syndrome are processing more information than normal infants as a result of their extended orienting? If we get a child to smile, does this mean the child has developed some new assimilative capacity, or just that we have provided the right modulation of physiological tension in the child to lead to a smile? What are the best predictors of interest and growth for given atypical children? To what extent can the use of prosthetic devices influence affective reactions as well as cognitive growth in atypical infants? We have many important questions to pursue in this area and little to take for granted.

Self-Assertion

The final developmental issue identified by Sander involves infants 14 to 20 months old. During this period children are developing a sense of themselves as separate, effective (or ineffective) individuals. Sander calls the issue in this period one of self-assertion, and at this age the child's assertiveness may also run in directions counter to those desired by the caregiver. Moreover, infants at this time may promote feelings of competence and self-control by disagreeing with and negating the desires of the parent (Spitz, 1957). Again, the caregiver must deal with a set of developing characteristics in the child that create new problems and possibilities. For caregivers whose own needs for control are very strong or who would prefer not to deal with questions of control, new problems may arise during this period. For caregivers whose desire is to allow their children complete self-expression, this period may lead to levels of self-assertion in the child that the caregiver may not be entirely ready to tolerate (Baumrind, 1971).

Development of a sense of self is an extremely important landmark in a child's life. The knowledge of the self as a separate figure which may be set in relation to material objects and other selves allows for levels of functioning that were not present in the younger child. Research on development of a sense of self (Lewis and Brooks, 1978) suggests that by about 21 to 24 months of age, three-quarters of children tested identify with mirror representations of themselves. These children attempt to touch or clean off a spot previously put on the child's nose by the experimenter when they are able to see it on themselves in the mirror. Moreover, infants at this age begin to label orally their own pictures and differentiate them from the pictures of other infants. By this age, language also becomes increasingly important in communication with others. The child is so different socially at 20 months from the newborn infant that it is difficult to believe that so much change could take place in less than 2 years. However, for some atypical infants the change to a verbally communicative, self-aware individual may not occur easily, if at all. The tendencies of relatively verbal autistic children, for example, to substitute "you" for "I," to not use the word "yes," and to echo the speech of others rather than using language in a self-constructed way (Ricks and Wing, 1976), and the tendency of blind children to be delayed in their self-reference and pretend play (Fraiberg, 1977b) may indicate problems in self-awareness that create powerful barriers to communication with others.

INFANT SOCIAL GAMES

As a reprise of some of the important developmental changes occurring during the period of infancy, we may consider the development of infant-caregiver games. This section represents the summary of a more detailed discussion by Ross and Kay (1980) of infant-caregiver games. In order to consider a social interaction to be a game, Ross and Kay require that two players be involved, that there be alternation of turns with at least one repetition of the acts involved, and that there be nonliterality of action. In Ross and Kay's research and the research of others, infants under the age of about 6 months have been found to play chiefly an appreciative role in these games, with caregivers repeating structured actions such as peekaboo, "gonna get you," or "horsie," and the infant smiling, laughing, and showing motor excitement (Gustafson et al., 1979; Ross and Kay, 1980). By the age of 7 months (Bruner, 1977) infants begin to discover rhythm in games, demonstrated through smiling and laughter in anticipation of the exciting acts performed by the caregiver. At 10 to 11 months children are observed to take turns hesitatingly in object exchange games, and by 12 months they take confident and regular turns. By the age of 14 to 15 months infants initiate game sequences themselves. Later they will invent new games or initiate novel games with their caregivers (Ross and Kay, 1980).

This pattern of social development demonstrates the caregiver's allowing the child to take turns before the child need be aware that turns are being taken. At the same time, the caregiver's presentation of the highly simplified, regular, and predictable events may allow infants a special opportunity for developing expectations. Caregivers also often use language in a repetitive way to mark the end of the caregiver's turn (Ratner and Bruner, 1978), indicating that a reaction from the infant is in order. The increasing role of infants in regulating their game environment parallels increasing infant initiative in other areas of social interaction (e.g., in the attachment relation). Researchers observing infant games report that as the infant's role in game playing increases, mothers decrease playing the games that previously involved the child in a more passive way. By 12 months, the passive younger infant games are no longer played (Gustafson et al., 1979).

Social games may be a topic of special interest to caregivers of atypical infants. First, they possibly can diagnose the social skills available to the infant. Jones (1980) noted problems connected with turn taking when infants with Down syndrome repetitively vocalize without reference (visual regard) to the mother. Social games also allow repetition of short sequences of events in a form that is highly palatable to the caregiver as well as the infant, and may thus be a source of early learning for the atypical child. For example, blind infants are sometimes passive to the external environment and simple parent-child turn taking games may provide their first realization of the predictability of external change and their own ability to effect that change. Bigelow (personal communication, 1982) describes a mother of a blind infant who developed a game of kissing her baby repeatedly on alternate cheeks, pausing momentarily between each kiss. The baby began to turn his cheek in anticipation of the next kiss.

ASSESSMENT OF INFANT CHARACTERISTICS

The general message of this chapter is that a number of major developmental changes take place during the early months of life that affect and are affected by the child's social environment. Assessing an atypical infant's status with respect to these changes will increase our scientific understanding of atypical infants, will help to educate caregivers, and will aid in our choices of remediation for handicapped populations. The developmental changes described involve a number of important psychological variables, and therefore require a multivariate approach to infant assessment. An approach to assessment that is fully congruent with the point of view developed in this chapter is proposed by Simeonsson et al. (1980a, 1980b) for use with severely handicapped infants and young children. Simeonsson et al. suggest the following domains for assessment, all of which are outlined in this chapter as being important to social development and which also allow assessment of children with highly limited repertoires of behavior: characteristic state changes, repetitive rhythmic behavior patterns, temperament, communicative skills, self-recognition, and attachment. Details on specific assessment procedures available for each of these domains are given by Simeonsson et al. Assessments in these areas allow us: 1) to develop expectations about endogenous fluctuations in state of the infant; 2) to clarify our understanding of the infant's signals; 3) to give us an idea about which kinds and levels of stimulation the infant presently does not tolerate, tolerates, or enjoys; and 4) to help us understand the nature of infants' relations with people in comparison with their relations to objects and the child's needs for security. These assessments provide an important first step to understanding, valuing, and remediating the difficulties of atypical infants.

SUMMARY

In this chapter some of the ways in which special characteristics of atypical infants may interact with the early challenges or issues confronting caregiver and infant are considered. The discussion has a strongly developmental perspective, emphasizing the way in which developmental changes in children's capacities influence their social interactions. In achieving satisfactory resolution of these developmental issues, caregivers of atypical infants are seen as making proportionately greater contributions than caregivers of nonhandicapped infants. It is hoped that improved methods for assessment will aid in the achievement of these resolutions.

ACKNOWLEDGMENTS

The author wishes to thank Ann Bigelow, Robert Harmon, Myron Rothbart, and Michael I. Posner for their critical reading of an earlier version of this chapter. Research reported in this chapter was supported in part by NIMH Grant MH26674-04.

Chapter Outline

I. LEARNING APPROACHES TO INFANT SOCIAL DEVELOPMENT
Learning approaches to social development include:

A. Drive reduction theories
B. Operant learning theory
C. Bandura's social learning theory

II. THE CHILD'S CONTRIBUTION TO SOCIAL DEVELOPMENT
Four major influences which precipitated the shift to an investigation of the child's contributions to social development are presented. These influences include:

A. Piaget's studies of cognitive development
B. Work of psychoanalytically oriented investigators (e.g., Escalona, Sanders, and Spitz)
C. Bowlby's writings on attachment
D. Recent infancy research

III. INFANT TEMPERAMENT
Temperament is described as the infant's constitutionally based patterns of reacting to stimulation and the infant's capacities for self-regulation. The role of the caregiver is seen as dependent in part upon the child's temperamental characteristics.

IV. DEVELOPMENTAL ISSUES OF INFANCY

A. Sander's sequence of issues on adaptations typically faced by mother-child pairs during infancy are reviewed. These developmental issues are:
1. Initial regulation
2. Reciprocal exchange
3. Initiative
4. Focalization
5. Self-assertion

B. These issues are discussed as they relate to atypical infants as well as to normal babies.

V. INFANT SOCIAL GAMES
Infant social games are considered as potential situations for assessing atypical infants' social development and as a source of early learning.

VI.   ASSESSMENT OF INFANT CHARACTERISTICS

A multivariate approach to infant assessment is suggested, which includes state, temperament, communicative behavior, and attachment variables.

REFERENCES

Ainsworth, M. D. A. The development of infant-mother interaction. In B. M. Caldwell and H. N. Ricciuti (Eds.), *Review of Child Development Research* (Vol. 3). Chicago: University of Chicago Press, 1973.

Als, H., Tronick, E., and Brazelton, T. B. Stages of early behavioral organization: The study of a sighted infant and a blind infant in interaction with their mothers. In T. F. Field (Ed.), *High-Risk Infants and Children: Adult and Peer Interactions*. New York: Academic Press, 1980.

Bandura, A. *Social Learning Theory*. Englewood Cliffs, NJ: Prentice-Hall, 1977.

Bandura, A., and Walters, R. H. *Social Learning and Personality Development*. New York: Holt, Rinehart & Winston, 1963.

Bates, J. E. The concept of difficult temperament. *Merrill-Palmer Quarterly*, 1980, *26*, 299–319.

Bates, J. E., Freeland, C. A. B., and Lounsbury, M. L. Measurement of infant difficultness. *Child Development*, 1979, *50*, 794–803.

Baumrind, D. Current patterns of parental authority. *Developmental Psychology Monographs*, 1971, *4*, (No. 1, Part 2).

Bigelow, A. *Object Permanence for Sound Producing Objects: Parallels between Blind and Sighted Infants*. Paper presented at the International Conference on Infant Studies, New Haven, CT, 1980.

Bijou, S. W., and Baer, D. M. *Child Development, Volume II*. New York: Appleton-Century-Crofts, 1965.

Bowlby, J. *Attachment and Loss, Volume 1: Attachment*. New York: Basic Books, 1969.

Bowlby, J. *Attachment and Loss, Volume 2: Separation: Anxiety and Anger*. New York: Basic Books, 1973.

Brazelton, T. B., Koslowski, B., and Main, M. The origins of reciprocity: The early mother-infant interaction. In M. Lewis and L. A. Rosenblum (Eds.), *The Effect of the Infant on Its Caregiver*. New York: Wiley, 1974.

Bruner, J. S. Early social interaction and language acquisition. In H. R. Schaffer (Ed.), *Studies in Mother-Infant Interaction*. London: Academic Press, 1977.

Buss, A. H., and Plomin, R. *A Temperament Theory of Personality*. New York: Wiley, 1975.

Carey, W. B., and McDevitt, S. C. Revision of the infant temperament questionnaire. *Pediatrics*, 1978, *61*, 735–739.

Cohen, P. The impact of the handicapped child on the family. *Social Casework*, 1962, *43*, 137–142.

Derryberry, D., and Rothbart, M. K. Emotion, attention, and temperament. In C. E. Izard, J. Kagan, and R. Zajone (Eds.), *Emotion, Cognition, and Behavior*. Cambridge: Cambridge University Press, in press.

Dollard, J., and Miller, N. E. *Personality and Psychotherapy: An Analysis in Terms of Learning, Thinking and Culture*. New York: McGraw-Hill, 1950.

Emde, R. N., and Brown, C. Adaptation to the birth of a Down's syndrome infant: Grieving and maternal attachment. *Journal of the American Academy of Child Psychiatry*, 1978, *17*, 299–324.

Emde, R. N., Katz, E. L., and Thorpe, J. K. Emotional expression in infancy: II. Early deviations in Down's syndrome. In M. Lewis and L. A. Rosenblum (Eds.), *The Development of Affect*. New York: Plenum, 1978.

Escalona, S. K. *The Roots of Individuality: Normal Patterns of Development in Infancy.* Chicago: Aldine, 1968.

Field, T. Interactions of preterm and term infants with their lower- and middle-class teenage and adult mothers. In T. Field (Ed.), *High-Risk Infants and Children.* New York: Academic Press, 1980.

Fraiberg, S. Parallel and divergent patterns in blind and sighted infants. *Psychoanalytical Study of the Child,* 1968, *23,* 264–300.

Fraiberg, S. Blind infants and their mothers: An examination of the sign system. In M. Lewis and L. Rosenblum (Eds.), *The Effect of the Infant on Its Caregiver.* New York: Wiley, 1974.

Fraiberg, S. *Every Child's Birthright: In Defense of Mothering.* New York: Basic Books, 1977a.

Fraiberg, S. *Insights from the Blind.* New York: Basic Books, 1977b.

Gewirtz, J. L. A learning analysis of the effects of normal stimulation, privation and deprivation on the acquisition of social motivation and attachment. In B. M. Foss (Ed.), *Determinants of Infant Behavior.* New York: Wiley, 1961.

Goodenough, F. L. Expressions of emotions in a blind-deaf child. *Journal of Abnormal and Social Psychology,* 1932, *27,* 328–333.

Gottman, J. M., and Ringland, J. T. The analysis of dominance and bi-directionality in social development. *Child Development,* 1981, *52,* 393–412.

Gustafson, G. E., Green, J. A., and West, M. J. The infant's changing role in mother-infant games: The growth of social skills. *Infant Behavior and Development,* 1979, *2,* 301–308.

Hanson, M. J. *Teaching Your Down's Syndrome Infant: A Guide for Parents.* Baltimore: University Park Press, 1977.

Harlow, H. F. The nature of love. *American Psychologist,* 1958, *13,* 673–685.

Jones, G. Prelinguistic communication skills in Down's syndrome and normal infants. In T. Field (Ed.), *High-Risk Infants and Children.* New York: Academic Press, 1980.

Kaye, K. Thickening thin data: The maternal role in developing communication and language. In M. Bullowa (Ed.), *Before Speech: The Beginning of Interpersonal Communication.* Cambridge: Cambridge University Press, 1979.

Landesman-Dwyer, S., and Sackett, G. P. Behavioral changes in nonambulatory, mentally retarded individuals. In C. E. Meyers (Ed.), *Quality of Life in Severely and Profoundly Mentally Retarded People: Research Foundations for Improvement.* Washington, DC: American Association for Mental Deficiency, 1978.

Lewis, M., and Brooks, J. Self-knowledge and emotional development. In M. Lewis and L. A. Rosenblum (Eds.), *The Development of Affect.* New York: Plenum, 1978.

Maccoby, E. E., and Masters, J. C. Attachment and dependency. In P. H. Mussen (Ed.), *Carmichael's Manual of Child Psychology.* New York: Wiley, 1970.

Meadow, K. P. The development of deaf children. In E. M. Hetherington (Ed.), *Review of Child Development Research* (Vol. 5). Chicago: University of Chicago Press, 1975.

Miranda, S. B., and Fantz, R. L. Recognition memory in Down's syndrome and normal infants. *Child Development,* 1974, *45,* 651–660.

Osofsky, J. D. *Handbook of Infant Development.* New York: Wiley, 1979.

Posner, M. I., and Rothbart, M. K. The development of attentional mechanisms. In J. Flowers (Ed.), *Nebraska Symposium on Motivation.* Lincoln: University of Nebraska Press, 1981.

Ratner, N., and Bruner, J. S. Games, social exchange and the acquisition of language. *Journal of Child Language*, 1978, 5, 391–401.

Rheingold, H. K. The effects of environmental stimulation upon social and exploratory behavior in the human infant. In B. M. Foss (Ed.), *Determinants of Infant Behavior I.* London: Methuen, 1961.

Ricks, D. M., and Wing, L. Language, communication and the use of symbols. In L. Wing (Ed.), *Early Childhood Autism* (2nd ed.). Oxford: Pergamon, 1976.

Robson, K. S., and Moss, H. A. Patterns and determinants of maternal attachment. *Journal of Pediatrics*, 1970, 77, 976–985.

Ross, H. S., and Kay, D. A. The origins of social games. In K. Rubin (Ed.), *Children's Play.* San Francisco: Jossey-Bass, 1980.

Rothbart, M. K. *Longitudinal Home Observation of Infant Temperament.* Paper presented at the International Conference on Infant Studies, New Haven, CT, April, 1980.

Rothbart, M. K. Measurement of temperament in infancy. *Child Development*, 1981, 52, 569–578.

Rothbart, M. K., and Derryberry, D. Development of individual differences in temperament. In M. E. Lamb and A. L. Brown (Eds.), *Advances in Developmental Psychology* (Vol. 1). Hillsdale, NJ: Erlbaum, 1981.

Rothbart, M. K., and Derryberry, D. Theoretical issues in temperament. In M. Lewis and L. Taft (Eds.), *Development Disabilities: Theory, Assessment and Intervention.* New York: S. P. Medical and Scientific Books, 1982.

Rothbart, M. K., and Hanson, M. J. A comparison of temperamental characteristics of Down's syndrome and normal infants. *Developmental Psychology*, 1983, 19, 766–769.

Safford, P. L., Gregg, L. A., Schneider, G., and Sewell, J. M. A stimulation program for young sensory-impaired, multihandicapped children. *Education and Training of the Mentally Retarded*, 1976, 11, 12–17.

Sander, L. W. Issues in early mother-child interaction. *Journal of the American Academy of Child Psychiatry*, 1962, 1, 141–166.

Sander, L. W. The longitudinal course of early mother-child interaction: Cross case comparison in a sample of mother-child pairs. In B. M. Foss (Ed.), *Determinants of Infant Behavior IV.* London: Methuen, 1969.

Sander, L. W. The regulation of exchange in the infant-caretaker system and some aspects of the context-content relationship. In M. Lewis and L. Rosenblum (Eds.), *Interaction, Conversation and the Development of Language.* New York: Wiley, 1977.

Sander, L. W., Stechler, G., Burns, P., and Julia, H. Early mother-infant interaction and 240 patterns of activity and sleep. *Journal of the American Academy of Child Psychiatry*, 1970, 9, 103–123.

Schlesinger, H. S., and Meadow, K. P. *Sound and Sign: Childhood Deafness and Mental Health.* Berkeley: University of California Press, 1972.

Sears, R. R. Dependency motivation. In M. Jones (Ed.), *Nebraska Symposium on Motivation.* Lincoln: University of Nebraska Press, 1963, pp. 25–64.

Sears, R. R., Whiting, J. W. M., Nowlis, V., and Sears, P. S. Some child rearing antecedents of dependency and aggression in young children. *Genetic Psychology Monographs*, 1953, XLVII, 135–234.

Serafica, F. C., and Cicchetti, D. Down's syndrome children in a strange situation: Attachment and exploration behaviors. *Merrill-Palmer Quarterly*, 1976, *22*, 137–150.

Simeonsson, R. J., Huntington, G. S., and Parse, S. A. Assessment of children with severe handicaps: Multiple problems-multivariate goals. *Journal of the Association for the Severely Handicapped*, 1980a, *5*, 55–72.

Simeonsson, R. J., Huntington, G. S., and Parse, S. A. Expanding the developmental assessment of young handicapped children. *New Directions for Exceptional Children*, 1980b, *3*, 51–74.

Skinner, B. F. *Science and Human Behavior.* New York: Macmillan, 1953.

Solnit, A. J., and Stark, M. H. Mourning and the birth of a defective child. *The Psychoanalytic Study of the Child*, 1961, *16*, 523–537.

Spitz, R. A. *No and Yes: On the Genesis of Human Communication.* New York: International Universities Press, 1957.

Spitz, R. A. *The First Year of Life.* New York: International Universities Press, 1965.

Sroufe, L., and Waters, E. Attachment as an organizational construct. *Child Development*, 1977, *48*, 1184–1199.

Stern, D. N. A micro-analysis of mother-infant interaction behavior regulating social contact between a mother and her 3½-month-old twins. *Journal of the American Academy of Child Psychiatry*, 1971, *10*, 501–517.

Stern, D. N. Mother and infant at play: The dyadic interaction involving facial, vocal, and gaze behaviors. In M. Lewis and L. A. Rosenblum (Eds.), *The Effect of the Infant on Its Caregiver.* New York: Wiley, 1974.

Stone, L. J., Smith, H. T., and Murphy, L. B. *The Competent Infant.* New York: Basic Books, 1973.

Thoman, E. B., Becker, P. T., and Freese, M. P. Individual patterns of mother-infant interaction. In G. P. Sackett (Ed.), *Observing Behavior (Vol. 1), Theory and Applications in Mental Retardation.* Baltimore: University Park Press, 1978.

Thomas, A., and Chess, S. *Temperament and Development.* New York: Bruner/Mazel, 1977.

Yarrow, L. J. The development of focused relationships during infancy. In J. Hellmuth (Ed.), *Exceptional Infant* (Vol. 1). Seattle: Special Child Publications, 1967.

Zelazo, P. Smiling to social stimuli: Eliciting and conditioning effects. *Developmental Psychology*, 1971, *4*, 32–42.

CHAPTER 8

Learning and Cognition during Infancy

Craig T. Ramey, Bonnie J. Breitmayer,
and Barbara Davis Goldman

Learning is an adaptation of a particular organism to a given context or set of circumstances. Those circumstances may involve forces impinging upon the child from the outside environment or they may involve experientially based adaptations to given attributes and processes within the child. Infancy is a time when learning is rapidly taking place, and it is the purpose of this chapter to review what we know about its many facets and developmental course. Particular emphasis is placed on understanding the similarities and differences in learning processes as they relate to typical and atypical infants.

LEARNING AS ADAPTATION

According to a formulation by the philosopher Ervin Laszlo (1972), learning can be conceptualized as experientially acquired processes of self-stabilization.

> *The common element in all varieties of learning is that learning is obtained by a certain form of activity in which the organism pursues a conscious or unconscious goal and attempts to escape a situation or a problem. Hence, learning is a modification of behavior attained by the solution of a problem posed for the individual by his environmental relations (p. 80).*

Infants typically begin to learn about their world in the everyday experiences that they have with their caregivers in their homes or other caregiving situations. If, indeed, it is in these ordinary, but incredibly rich, environments in which infants acquire their initial knowledge about the world, it is helpful to have some organizing scheme to help us conceptualize that general process. Figure 8.1

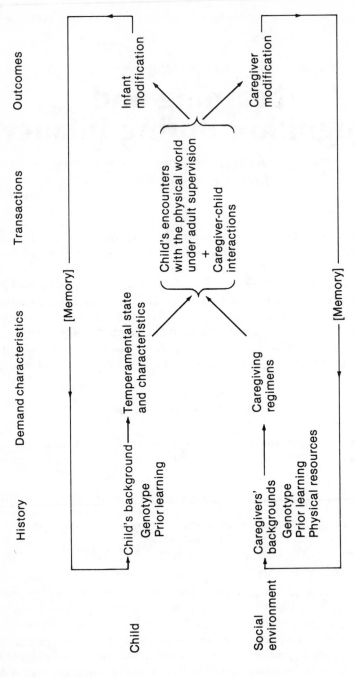

Figure 8.1.   A general systems model of infant learning.

contains a schematic diagram that we have found useful. It is derived from general systems theory and has been described in more detail by Ramey et al. (1982).

THE LEVEL OF ANALYSIS PRINCIPLE

The *level of analysis* principle suggests that a dynamic open-ended system is composed of interacting parts and that these different parts may be construed as levels of influences potentially determining outcomes. With respect to the cognitive development of infants, two levels of analysis seem especially important: 1) analyses at the level of the child's state of knowledge; and 2) analyses at the level of the environments that infants encounter. Four characteristics at each of these levels are particularly germane. We have called these: 1) *historical characteristics*; 2) *demand characteristics*; 3) *transactional characteristics*; and 4) *outcomes*.

By historical characteristics we mean events that have occurred in the past that potentially have relevance to functioning at a given moment. Thus, at the level of the child, we may be concerned with the child's genotype and past learning experiences. At the level of social environment, we may be concerned with the social backgrounds of the child's primary caregivers, their genotypes, their previous learning, or the resources over which they have control. However, for these historical characteristics to have an impact upon the developing child at a given moment they must be translated into variables that have extension in space and time; that is, they must impact upon the child in some physical way. Therefore, the child's prior experiences may become transformed into a propensity for certain behavioral or temperamental characteristics. Similarly, the caregivers' backgrounds might become transformed into particular caregiving regimens or the propensity to create particular learning environments. Given that learning is an interaction between the environment and the child and that the caregivers provide the child's environments (either through the ways they behave toward the child socially or the way that they arrange the physical environment), the child's demand characteristics and the environment's demand characteristics both determine the experiences that a child will have. This co-determination is likely whether it be in the child's encounters with the physical world under adult supervision or the social interchanges in which the child engages with his/her caregivers. Having engaged in an organism-environment transaction of significance, the child will both be altered by that environment (e.g., caregiver) and alter that environment (perhaps changing the caregiver's style). Therefore, it is likely that both actors in a transactional encounter leave that experience as slightly different persons than when they entered it. To the extent that either remembers the outcome of the transaction, future encounters with the same or different environments are modified. Thus, through the operation of experiential feedback and memory, the child's and caregiver's repertoire become shaped and expanded.

Various theoretical schemes have been proposed to describe and explain more precisely how this generic process operates. In the next section we consider the theoretical approaches of psychometrics, constructivism, behaviorism, and information processing as applied to the development of learning and cognition during infancy.

THE PSYCHOMETRIC TRADITION

The psychometric tradition is a normative and comparative approach to development that stems from the pioneering work of Alfred Binet and his colleagues in Paris shortly after the turn of the century. The initial impetus for this now time-honored tradition was the desire to create efficient and effective assessment devices to determine the likelihood of children profiting from available educational services. The essential features of this approach include: 1) the sequencing by age of developmental milestones; 2) the determination of the distribution of variability around the typical age of milestone attainment; 3) the specification of one's performance relative to that of the distribution of representative children; and 4) the validation of performance on these scales relative to performance on other measures thought logically to be related to the test in question. The most widely used psychometric tests in psychology, and certainly the best known, are those that have been concerned with the construct of intelligence, usually expressed as an IQ derived from the administration in a prescribed fashion of a test such as the Stanford-Binet Intelligence Scale or the Weschler Scale of Intelligence for Children.

Following the successful development of standardized tests for intelligence with school-aged children, a variety of tests were developed for use with infants. The scores derived from infant tests (sometimes called developmental indices or developmental quotients), although perhaps not measuring the same aspects of intelligence as those meant for older children, have been nevertheless derived using the same test-construction logic and highly similar empirical methods. In general, raw scores from performance on the tests are converted to mental ages and then an individual's performance is expressed as a number indicating his/her standing relative to age peers. Currently there are three major developmental tests frequently used with infants. The most widely used of these tests is the Bayley Scales of Infant Development (Bayley, 1969). These scales consist of both a mental scale and a psychomotor scale. The two scales yield a Mental Development Index and a Psychomotor Developmental Index, either of which may be converted to age equivalent scores. The scales are well-standardized and adequately reliable.

Another widely used test is the Gesell Developmental Schedules from which one can derive a developmental quotient. Although these scales have recently been revised (Knobloch and Pasamanick, 1974), some questions still remain about the complete adequacy of their standardization. Horowitz (1982), after examining the Gesell Developmental Schedules, has concluded that these tests tend to be more clinically oriented and, as such, more geared to diagnosis. She has also pointed out that the Gesell Scale is probably less related conceptually to the Stanford-Binet Intelligence Scale than is the Bayley Scale.

A third intelligence scale, however, is meant to be a downward extension of the Stanford-Binet Intelligence Scale. It is known as the Cattell Infant Intelligence Scales (Cattell, 1940), and is useful for children who fail to obtain a basal score at the 2-year level on the Stanford-Binet. However, the Cattell norms are based on a small number of children, all of whom were from one geographic area, white, and of similar socioeconomic status. Thus, the adequacy of the available norms for this scale is questionable.

According to Horowitz (1982), the use of infant assessment scales can be thought of as fulfilling one or more of four major purposes: 1) to provide an assessment procedure relevant to diagnosis of cognitive functioning; 2) to identify the specific areas of functioning in which the infant may be developmentally advanced or retarded; 3) to guide the formulation of an early intervention program; and 4) to evaluate the effectiveness of implemented interventions. However, it should be recognized that each of these infant scales assumes intact sensory equipment and functional motoric skills in the young child. To the extent that sensory handicaps or orthopedic handicaps exist, the validity of the resulting developmental quotients or indices are called into question because the mode of presentation of items to individual infants may be inappropriate or severely compromised. At present there do not exist well-standardized

assessment techniques for children with particular sensory handicaps, such as blindness or deafness, or orthopedic handicaps. Therefore, one must interpret the results of the administration of these
infant scales to those populations with extreme caveats and cautions.

Recently, Ramey et al. (1982) reviewed the use of standardized
tests with children who are likely candidates for special education
programs (the interested reader is referred to that article for more
detail and for recommendations of particular tests to be used with
handicapped children). For children for whom the aforementioned
infant tests are appropriate, the tests have served as the primary
classification mechanism for various mental handicaps. The following IQ's or mental quotients have frequently been used to classify
infants: developmental quotient 55 to 70, mildly retarded; developmental quotient 40 to 55, moderately retarded; developmental
quotient 30 to 45, severely retarded; and developmental quotient less
than 30, profoundly retarded.

Several points about performance on these infant scales are particularly noteworthy. First, in general, the performance derived from
infant scales has not been highly correlated with performance much
later in life, but the later in infancy such scales are administered,
the more likely there is to be a correlation with subsequent test performance (Ramey et al., 1973). However, this point should be qualified by noting that there seems to be more consistency in performance across time for infants who score very low on these scales than
for ones who score nearer to the national average of 100 or above.
Thus, these tests might best be construed as providing a useful measure of current functioning, but they should not be thought of as being
highly predictive of subsequent performance.

Second, although children might show mild delays on these
tests associated with such conditions as prematurity, mild birth complications, and congenital anomalies, they frequently have later test
scores that indicate they are performing within the normal range.
Sameroff and Chandler (1975), in a highly influential review on early
childhood handicaps, concluded that the quality of the environments to which children with such handicaps are exposed apparently influences the developmental status that they eventually attain.
Specifically, children from disadvantaged families, presumably with
developmentally nonsupportive environments, seem to retain the
lower levels of performance that they initially exhibited early in
infancy, whereas many children with such anomalies or problems
in more advantaged homes (e.g., higher socioeconomic status) tend
to be indistinguishable developmentally from normal, healthy children by the time that they reach school age. Another major point to

note is that children from severely disadvantaged families, including those from very low socioeconomic status homes, initially obtain developmentally normal scores on infant tests of mental development but frequently show a later developmental decline relative to their more advantaged peers. No organic pathology has been found to account for that decline, which typically begins during the second year of life (see Knobloch and Pasamanick, 1953; Ramey and Haskins, 1981). Because this decline seems to be associated with the period of rapid language acquisition, the relationship between linguistic environments to which children are exposed and subsequent linguistic and intellectual development is a topic that is receiving a great deal of research attention.

Over the past 10 years there has been increasing interest in the failure of infant "mental" tests to predict subsequent mental performance in terms of IQ scores or school achievement. Data have shown that for samples of children with no known handicaps, there is very little correlation between infant test results and later performance. However, there is considerable evidence that infant mental tests are useful in identifying youngsters who are markedly deviant, even as young as 10 months of age. Children who perform significantly below the norm on infant tests generally demonstrate developmental problems throughout the early school years. Yet, the nature of the developmental problem of any particular child is rarely made clear from the score provided by an infant mental test. Although the score may suggest "mental retardation," the child may or may not be retarded; the score may reflect the effects of cerebral palsy, a sensory impairment, a motor handicap, or some form of organic brain dysfunction. Both the difficulty of predicting later IQ in nonimpaired youngsters and the problems inherent in identifying particular disorders in impaired youngsters lie, in part, in the fact that infant mental tests rely heavily on the child's motor responses to make inferences about mental capabilities (see Johnson, 1982).

THE CONSTRUCTIVIST APPROACH

In contrast to assessing milestone attainment, the constructivist approach to cognitive development is concerned with how the infant constructs knowledge of the world. The best known and most influential theorist in this tradition is the Swiss psychologist Jean Piaget.

Piagetian theory starts with the central postulate that all intelligence has at its source the infant's motor actions on the environment. Through such organism-environment exchanges, inborn reflex mechanisms progressively differentiate and become integrated, eventually giving rise to internalized actions called mental operations. Mental operations are the ideas or strategies with which we cope with the world. Piaget, a biologist by training, considered intellectual organization a special case of the general life process of adaptation. It is special in the sense that whereas biological adaptation requires a constant adjacency of the organism to its material surroundings for the organism-environmental interrelationships to occur, mental adaptation, by virtue of its internalized structures, permits a progressive release from this adjacency until at its culmination the intellect can function on its own.

A second central postulate of Piagetian theory is that intellectual operations are acquired in a lawful sequence. Piaget (1970) divided the developmental sequence into three major periods, each divided into a number of stages, or subperiods. Each period represents a qualitatively different mode of thinking, and each is further removed than its predecessor from the requirement of environmental adjacency.

The first of these, called the sensorimotor period, lasts from birth until approximately age 2 (it is important to note that although Piaget provided approximate age boundaries for each stage, they are only approximate; he was not particularly concerned with establishing age norms). It takes the baby from a reflexive, body-centered organism whose world is spaceless, timeless, and objectless to one with acquired behavior patterns and the ability to think, at least in a rudimentary, practical sense, about those objects and everyday events that he/she has directly experienced.

The sensorimotor period is followed by a period of representational intelligence, so named because the child is increasingly able to symbolize or represent objects mentally. This period is divided into two subperiods, one of preoperations and one of concrete operations (in earlier works these were presented as two of four major periods). During the preoperational subperiod, lasting until about age 7, symbolic thought processes become increasingly apparent, particularly in the child's use of language. However, the child still tends to be the focus of his/her own world, and time and space are centered upon the self. When dealing with physical objects and quantities, the child attends to one aspect to the neglect of others. Gradually, the preoperational subperiod gives way, by a process of "decentering," to the subperiod of concrete operations. Now the child becomes less dependent upon his/her own perceptions and motor actions and shows a capacity for reasoning, although still at a concrete level. Stimuli must be immediately before the child in order for problem solving to occur because the capacity to make verbal and mental manipulations is still limited. Given the opportunity to view Tom, Mary, and Alice, the concrete operational child would be able to state how they should stand in order to be positioned according to ascending height, but told that Mary is taller than Tom and Tom is taller than Alice, the child in this stage may have difficulty specifying which child is the shortest.

Finally, beginning at approximately 11 to 13 years, there emerges the third major period, that of propositional, or "formal," operations. The formal operational child or adult is able to deal with abstract relationships instead only with things. For the first time he/she can intellectually manipulate the merely hypothetical and systematically evaluate a lengthy set of alternatives. In other words, the intellect can encompass the universe regardless of spatial or temporal distance; the goal of cognitive adaptation has been achieved. Not everyone reaches the period of formal operations. Some individuals fail to attain them undoubtedly because they are limited with respect to the as yet unidentified biological substrate required. The limiting effect of some social environments on the attainment of formal operations is also evident; in groups that do not emphasize symbolic skills or in which educational experiences are limited, formal operations may be late in developing or may not occur at all.

This chapter deals primarily with that portion of Piaget's theory concerned with infant development, that is, the sensorimotor period. The step-wise achievements of the period are described in some detail; following this description a small sample of the very large volume of research that has been inspired by Piaget's theory is presented. In order to understand the sensorimotor period and related research, however, the reader must have some understanding of selected concepts central to the overall theory.

The developmental changes in cognitive structures were the major object of study for Piaget. *Structure* is Piaget's metaphor for describing the organizational properties of thought. Qualitatively different cognitive structures or ways of viewing the world underlie the varying forms of thought during each of the developmental periods.

Piaget emphasized that cognitive structures are not present at birth, merely to unfold with increasing age. Their source is innate, however, because they develop from reflexes present at birth. Reflexes are behaviors that occur automatically in response to certain stimuli. A few reflexes remain fixed whether or not they are exercised. The majority, however, require stimulation for their stabilization. Moreover, each time a reflex is activated that experience alters each subsequent performance. From these early organism-environment exchanges more complex forms of behavior begin to evolve.

How did Piaget account for this gradual evolution? Corresponding to each innate reflex (e.g., sucking, grasping, and crying) there is assumed to exist a reflex *scheme*. The scheme, which may be thought of as a substructure, is the mental-structural basis for the sensorimotor action sequences that the infant repeatedly carries out in response to a particular class of events. When we say that the infant has a "sucking scheme" we refer to the fact that he/she is disposed to carry out organized sucking movements, a specific class of action sequences, in response to the insertion of something suckable into his/her mouth. A scheme is a kind of sensorimotor level counterpart of a symbolic-representational level concept. An older person represents or thinks of a given object as an instance of a class; a baby acts or behaves toward an object as though it belongs to a particular class, in the present example to the class "something to suck." Throughout life, environmental events may be reacted to only in terms of existing mental structures or organization; during infancy, this means in terms of available schemes.

One important property of schemes is that they become elaborated through practice. We tend to think of the sucking reflex as very basic and innate. However, it is quite clear that a great deal of learning with respect to sucking takes place even within the newborn's first days. At first, the nipple must be thrust into the infant's mouth in order for sucking to begin. Early efforts may be clumsy, and the nipple may very well be lost, in which case it must be thrust in again. Soon, however, the infant becomes more adept; the sucking reflex is adapted to the contours of the nipple, and if the nipple is lost, the infant seems to search for it.

A second very important property of schemes is that various schemes may be combined, or coordinated, to form larger wholes. For example, the previously mentioned sucking scheme is combined with the reaching scheme when the hand is brought to the mouth, or with the visual scheme when the child begins sucking at the sight of the bottle. As these elementary schemes gradually become elaborated and intercoordinated, the infant's behavior begins to look more and more unambiguously intelligent.

It is imporant to realize that according to Piaget's theory, this mode of making cognitive progress is not limited to a single period of development. It is inherited, along with other adaptive processes, as part of our biological endowment. Like other adaptive processes—but unlike cognitive structures, which undergo dramatic changes with development—the fundamental processes of intelligence remain essentially invariant throughout life. They are, therefore, called "functional invariants." The most important invariants are *organization* and *adaptation*.

Organization may be thought of as the internal part of intellectual functioning. It is the tendency for all species to integrate their processes, physiological or psychological, into coherent systems. At a psychological level, infants coordinate various schemes, for example, sucking with grasping, grasping with vision, and so on.

Adaptation refers to the dynamic outer aspect of functioning, that is, the organism-environment exchange. It is made up of two complementary processes, *assimilation* and *accommodation*. Assimilation is the tendency for organisms to incorporate substances and stimuli for which there already exist appropriate internal structures. At a biological level the body assimilates suitable nutrients into its organic structure. At a primitive psychological level, the infant assimilates the attributes of diverse objects into one of its available reflex schemes, for example, the sucking scheme. At a somewhat more advanced cognitive level, the toddler may address all adult males as "daddy." At a still more advanced level, the reader of this text will interpret its contents in accordance with her/her prior knowledge of cognitive development. The important thing to remember is that assimilation essentially means interpreting or construing external objects and events in terms of one's own presently available ways of thinking about things.

Complementary to assimilation is accommodation, the process by which an existing structure *changes* so as to incorporate external reality better. At a physical level, muscle mass increases in response to exercise. At a primitive psychological level, the infant makes certain adjustments when reflex schemes are exercised on various objects; for example, the sensory and motor experiences will be different when sucking on a blanket than while nursing, and these varied experiences will be incorporated into the sucking scheme, forever changing it.

Piaget considered assimilation and accommodation to be two sides of the same coin of adaptation. He believed that the human nervous system has been programmed by evolution to ensure an equilibrium between internal and external factors. When the organism encounters external circumstances, those elements compatible with current schemes are assimilated, ensuring the scheme's basic continuity. Simultaneously, the scheme accommodates or changes in response to those elements that are discrepant. Piaget called this tendency toward active self-regulation *equilibration* and considered the construction of cognitive structures to occur in a gradual fashion primarily as the result of this process.[1] It is important to realize that when external circumstances are very discrepant, that is, too advanced for the individual's current schemes, cognitive adaptation can not occur because assimilation and accommodation only take place in relation to existing cognitive structures.

We have said that by repeated assimilations and accommodations to a given milieu, the cognitive system evolves slightly, each change making possible further assimilations and accommodations. Viewed at close range, for example, from one day to the next, the changes are very slight, if noticeable at all. Viewed from sufficient distance, on the other hand, changes are striking. Contrast, for example, the newborn, whose interactions with the world are centered around very basic reflexes, with the toddler, who possesses a great deal of practical information concerning his/her everyday world of people, objects, and events. There can be no denying that there is considerable qualitative difference in the way that these two individuals relate to the world. One of Piaget's major contributions was to provide a framework for conceptualizing how the quantitative changes from successive assimilations and accommodations gradually give rise to qualitative differences. This framework is, of course, his sequence, or stages, of cognitive development. The following section illustrates how, according to Piaget, the infant's day-to-day interactions with the environment give rise to the qualitative changes that occur during infancy, that is, during the sensorimotor period.

Sensorimotor Period

Piaget referred to the interval between birth and approximately age 2 as the sensorimotor period because the infant, lacking the capacity for mental representation, must construct knowledge based on his/her perceptions and motor actions. The period consists of six stages (sometimes called substages). As the infant traverses these stages, behavior begins to look more intentional and, therefore, more intelligent. One way of conceptualizing the progression through the six stages is in terms of the infant's increasing ability to define practical goals and to proceed systematically to achieve them.

---

[1] It is worth noting that some developmental psychologists who are otherwise sympathetic to Piaget's theory have been critical of his notion of equilibration as an explanation for how change in cognitive structures occurs because they consider the process *itself* to be inadequately explained (e.g., see Block, 1982; Bruner, 1959; Flavell, 1977).

During approximately the first month of life, the *stage of reflex activity*, inborn reflexes such as sucking, swallowing, crying, and others are refined. At the beginning of the period, the reflexes appear rather inflexible. By the end, however, the infant can, to some extent, adapt them to different circumstances, progress that Piaget attributed, at least in part, to experience. Of course much experience or practice occurs through the use of reflexes in the service of utilitarian goals as, for example, when the baby sucks to obtain nourishment. However, Piaget believed that when an organism has available a structure, whether innate or learned, there is a basic tendency to exercise it. Thus, when he observed his own 2-day-old son making sucking-like movements between feedings, Piaget attributed the behavior not to hunger or to the effect of some external excitant that set the reflex in motion but to this tendency to seek stimulation actively. Closely related is the tendency to generalize schemes to a variety of objects, as when the infant exercises the sucking scheme on non-nutritive objects such as blankets and hands. Through these various types of exercises, the infant has occasion to learn about the environment, and hereditary reflexes become progressively more efficient and differentiated. At the end of the stage, in accordance with the principle of organization, some reflex schemes have developed into fairly complex psychological structures that incorporate the results of the infant's experience. Note that although progression in the first stage involves significant learning, change is confined to the reflexes.

The second stage (1 to 4 months) is characterized, first, by the continued perfection of individual schemes and, second, by the gradual coordination or integration of one scheme with another. For example, the hand and whatever it happens to be grasping will be brought to the mouth and sucked, indicating a functional relationship between sucking and prehension. The initial contact between hand and mouth may have begun by accident in the course of the infant's exercising the movement scheme. This fortuitous event has value for the infant as it enables the sucking scheme to be exercised. Should it be interrupted— and that is likely to happen because the infant's movements are not fully coordinated—the infant actively tries to reinsert the hand in the mouth in order to reinstate the pleasurable activity. This sort of behavior gives the stage its name, the stage of *primary circular reactions*; the actions are "primary" in that they are basically reflex responses of the child's own body, and "circular" in that they are repeated.

The process of accommodation is clearly evident in the second stage; in the above example it occurs as the infant gradually modifies initially aimless movements to make them increasingly efficient in bringing the hand to the mouth. The result of this repeated activity is, finally, a smoothly organized set of directed movements—a new, learned scheme. Some other new schemes that involve the coordination of two others are visual and auditory and visual and prehension.

During stage 3 (approximately 4 to 8 months), the attention of the infant begins to shift away from its primary focus on his/her own body and toward objects in the external world. The acquisition, during stage 2, of the ability to coordinate schemes makes possible the new behavior pattern that is the hallmark of stage 3. The pattern is the repetition of behavior that has produced stimulating events. It begins when the infant's action happens to produce some interesting perceptual outcome. For example, in the process of grasping a toy, the infant may shake it a little causing it to make an interesting sound. Perceiving a connection between his/her action and the sound, the infant repeatedly shakes the toy, apparently for the sheer pleasure of producing the sound. Such actions of the body upon the environment give the period its name, the stage of *secondary circular reactions*.

The appearance of secondary circular reactions marks a clear advance in cognitive development; it shows that the infant's horizons have expanded to encompass the external world and, further, that his/her behavior can change under conditions of contingent sensory stimulation (reinforcement). However, the stage 3 infant should not be thought of as having a clear sense of cause and effect relations. At most, secondary circular reactions are only quasi-intentional because the means has only become apparent after the end has been attained. According to Piaget, for behavior to be considered intentional, the goal must be perceived in advance.

Clearly intentional goal-directed behavior emerges in stage 4 (8 to 12 months). As in stage 2, individual schemes are coordinated. However, they are no longer centered on the body; now, during this stage of *coordination of secondary schemes*, they are coordinated and generalized outward to new situations in order to solve problems in the environment. For example, Piaget's son deliberately pushed aside his father's hand in order to grasp a box of matches.

The outstanding characteristic of stage 5 (12 to 18 months) is active exploration. Increasing cognitive extroversion is apparent as the infant, confronted with a novel object, applies a variety of schemes with seemingly endless modifications. The child throws, bats, and drops the object from varying heights, all the while assessing the object's response to these actions. In the course of these "experiments" (*tertiary circular reactions*), the infant comes to appreciate the real properties of objects, and when new problems arise, is able with some trial and error to apply this newfound knowledge to its solution. Tantalized by an attractive object, the strongly accommodative stage 5 child is quite capable of devising a strategy to obtain it; a tablecloth on which the object sits may serve as a vehicle with which to pull the object closer, or an almost-out-of-reach object may be batted with the fist until it is close enough to be grasped. With such planful behavior, no wonder stage 5 is considered the last "pure" sensorimotor stage.

A most important achievement emerges as the sensorimotor period approaches its conclusion during the second half of the second year. That achievement is, of course, the beginning ability to produce and comprehend one thing as standing for or representing another. Now the child can represent the object of his/her cognition internally; no longer must acts of intelligence be bound by external perceptual and motor actions. This important advance makes possible a dramatic change in the infant's adaptive behavior. The 18-month old has the beginning of what Piaget called "pre-vision" or foresight, the ability to solve problems mentally without the need to enact physically a series of experiments. This ability gives the sixth stage its name, the stage of *invention of new means through mental combinations*.

In our brief, general account of the sensorimotor period, we describe cognitive progress in terms of the stages of action, Piaget's account of how the child gradually comes to adapt actions to external circumstances (Piaget, 1952). In other works Piaget (1951, 1954) described infant development from the point of view of the infant's construction of *knowledge* about the world.

Piaget saw the newborn as having no conception of "out there" and, therefore, no awareness of time, of spatial and causal relationships between events and objects, and, in fact, no realization that objects continue to exist when they are not apparent to the senses. He believed that these concepts are gradually constructed as a result of the infant's actions on the environment. Therefore, their ontogeny is structurally connected to the infant's emerging adaptations, and Piaget used the same six-stage framework to describe their appearance.

We will summarize the infant's progressive development in just one domain, that of the object concept. The belief in the continuing existence of objects is fundamental to all mental development, to the ability to use language, and to the development of affective attachments to caregivers. Few concepts have so captured the fancy of American psychologists and inspired such a volume of research.

We take for granted that, appearance notwithstanding, objects do not enlarge as we approach or recede in size as we leave them behind. We know that they may move or be moved from one location to another when out of our presence. Above all, we realize that they continue to exist even when we cannot perceive them. In other words, we take for granted that the identity, behavior, and the very existence of objects is fundamentally independent of our own interaction with them. Basic as this concept is, Piaget claimed that object knowledge or object permanence is not inborn, but must be acquired in a universal, fixed sequence of stages.

Because at the heart of the object concept is the awareness that objects continue to exist when one can no longer see them, Piaget observed and described the infant's reaction to the disappearance of objects, inferring knowledge of the continuing existence of the object from the infant's search behavior. It is quite evident during stages 1 and 2 that the infant notices objects when they are present; even the neonate will reflexively "lock onto" a slowly moving object and follow it until it disappears from sight. Once the object is out of sight, however, the cognitively introverted young infant shows no further interest. By the end of stage 2, the infant continues to stare at the point at which the object disappeared. However, there is no active search behavior that would suggest an awareness that the object continues to exist. Instead, Piaget believed, the stage 2 infant merely pursues an action (looking) that has been interrupted.

Stage 3 marks the beginning of active search behavior. The stage 3 infant will recognize and reach for a familiar toy or bottle even when it is partially covered. If an object falls from the crib, the infant is likely to lean over in an attempt to keep the object in view. However, the search is short-lived if the infant does not immediately find the object. Furthermore, it is confined to the visual modality. Surprisingly, Piaget observed—as have countless investigators since— that the stage 3 infant may watch intently while an adult hides an object underneath or behind something else (a handkerchief or a small screen, perhaps) and yet set aside the obstacle to retrieve the object only if a recognizable part of it visibly protrudes from underneath or behind the barrier. Such behavior suggests that the stage 3 infant is not yet quite aware that the object has an enduring existence of its own.

By stage 4, the child will manually search for and retrieve an object that he/she sees "hidden." However, note the most peculiar limitation evident in Piaget's description of the behavior of his 10½-month-old daughter Jacqueline:

> *Jacqueline is seated on a mattress with nothing to disturb or distract her (no coverlets, etc.). I take her parrot from her hands and hide it twice in succession under the mattress on her left in [point] A. Both times Jacqueline looks for the object immediately and grabs it. Then I take it from her hands and move it very slowly before her eyes to the corresponding place on her right, in [point] B. Jacqueline watches this movement very attentively, but at the moment when the parrot disappears in B, she turns to her left and looks where it was before, in A (Piaget, 1954, p. 51).*

Because it is almost incomprehensible that one would continue to look for the toy at point A, even after having watched it moved to B, countless skeptical researchers have tried to replicate the phenomenon. All have observed this error, called the AB error, in some form. Piaget, of course, attributes the error to the infant's failure to appreciate the object's independent existence in time and space; because stage 4 infants are still tied to a world of practical actions, having acted (searched) successfully at point A, the infant is led to perceive the object as the object of that particular place.

Gradually in stage 5 the child becomes able to cope with what Piaget called a series of visible displacements. Thus, if Piaget had repeated the hiding sequence described above when Jacqueline was 15 months old, she would have gone directly to point B to find her parrot. If Piaget had complicated the experiment by further displacing the parrot to point C, she would have bypassed point B and immediately searched at C, providing that she had seen her father move the toy from B to C. If, however, Piaget had covered the toy in some way, say by placing his handkerchief over it before placing both under the mattress, and then had surreptitiously deposited the toy under the mattress before withdrawing the cover, Jacqueline would have looked only under the handkerchief where she had seen the toy disappear. Under these conditions of "invisible displacement," she would have been unable to infer the unseen toy's location under the mattress because the stage 5 infant cannot yet visualize or represent the toy itself.

During stage 6, the full-blown object concept emerges, and the child gradually overcomes the limitation described above. Consider Jacqueline's behavior at 18 months:

> *Jacqueline watches me when I put a coin in my hand, then put my hand under a coverlet. I withdraw my hand closed; Jacquelines opens it, then searches under the coverlet until she finds the object. I take*

*the coin back, put it in my hand and then slip my closed hand under
a cushion situated at the other side. . .Jacqueline immediately searches
for the object under the cushion. . . .I complicate the test as follows; I
place the coin in my hand under the cushion. I bring it forth closed
and immediately hide it under the coverlet. Finally, I withdraw it and
hold it out, closed, to Jacqueline. Jacqueline then pushes my hand aside
without opening it (she guesses that there is nothing in it, which is
new); she looks under the cushion, then directly under the coverlet,
where she finds the object (Piaget, 1954, p. 79).*

Clearly Jacqueline regards the coin as an entity that, despite her
father's tricks, will continue to exist and can be found with a little
persistent searching. Piaget is now willing to credit her with having
attained the concept of object permanence.

Some 50 years after publication of Piaget's first works on child
development, his theory continues to generate considerable research. A large body of the research on the sensorimotor period has
been directed toward clarifying specific aspects of the theory, especially various questions concerning the development of the object
concept. A second large category of studies centers around the development and use of psychometric measures based on Piaget's theory. Studies using these scales have addressed both theoretical and
more applied questions, many of them directly related to the handicapped infant. Here we can consider only a few of the issues addressed by research in these two categories.

Issues Related to the Construction of the Object Concept

Piaget believed that infants learn about objects, including the fact
that they exist permanently in space, as a result of the actions that
they perform on them during the course of the first 18 months. Recently, a number of investigators have taken issue with this view,
contending that infants come to know objects before they have had
opportunities to construct knowledge through acting upon them.
Reasoning on the basis of evidence, not available when Piaget wrote
his infancy books, that very young infants are capable of perceiving
depth and form (Fantz et al., 1975; Gibson, 1969), some psychologists
have suggested that infants can simply see that objects are solid in
space. In support of this claim, Bower et al. (1970) report that 2-
week-old infants will reach toward objects in a directed manner with
fingers molded to correspond to the size and shape of the object and
will be distressed when their hands contact the empty space where
the object, which was actually a virtual image, was.

A second argument made by those who claim knowledge of objects before the second year of life is that Piaget's requirement that the infant demonstrate object knowledge by actively searching for a hidden object makes unreasonable demands on the child's motor capacities and ability to attend to and remember events. Simpler tasks (e.g., tasks requiring the infant to visually tract the trajectory of, rather than manually search for, a disappearing object) have been devised and claims have been made that they demonstrate object knowledge in infants as young as 5 months. However, many psychologists are unconvinced by the evidence for early competence, and several have presented contradictory evidence (for a brief summary of the claims and their evidence, see Gratch, 1979).

Another focus of research concerning the object concept has been the A$\overline{\text{B}}$ error. There is no question that, just as Piaget claimed, infants of about 8 to 12 months continue to search for objects in a hiding place in which they have searched successfully even though they watched the object being moved to a second hiding place. Searching for an object in one place or another may occur for a variety of reasons, only some of which have to do with object representation. For years, researchers have tried to determine what besides the lack of knowledge that objects continue to exist even when they are not perceptually present would cause the infant to engage in such counterintuitive search behavior. However, a satisfactory alternate interpretation of the phenomenon is yet to be made. In summary, many points concerning how infants come to possess object knowledge await clarification. Although Piaget's belief that the infant must construct the object is not acceptable to all psychologists, this belief and, more generally, his metaphor of the child as "problem solver" have, as pointed out by Gratch (1979), the virtue of focusing attention on the phenomenon to be explained, namely how the infant thinks.

Issues Addressed by Piaget-inspired Psychometric Scales

One focus of studies making use of the Piaget-inspired psychometric scales has been to investigate the influence of varying life circumstances on intellectual development. For example, given Piaget's belief that the object concept is constructed as a result of the coordination and reorganization of schemes that takes place as a consequence of the infant's actions on everyday objects, it is reasonable to ask what effect variations in experiences may have on sensorimotor development.

How will the development of the object concept be affected

when, due to the child's own characteristics or to those of his/her everyday environment, the infant is deprived of opportunities to act on objects? This question underlies a number of studies, two of which we will discuss. The first one concerns the development of children born with severe motor handicaps that curtail the manipulation of objects, and the second compares the development of children raised in environments that would be expected to provide varying amounts of opportunity for interaction with persons and objects.

Decarie (1969) studied the behavioral development of children born with phocomelia, an anomaly in which limbs are missing and feet and hands are attached directly to the torso like flippers. This unfortunate birth defect was one outcome of the ingestion, during the early months of pregnancy, of thalidomide, a sedative and antinausea drug prescribed in the late 1950s and early 1960s. One of Decarie's aims was to determine whether the construction of the object concept in these children lacking opportunities for coordination of initially heterogeneous schemes would be significantly delayed. She administered a scale (Decarie, 1962) based on Piaget's observations of the development of children's search for disappearing objects to 21 children with varying degrees of malformation ranging from malformation of one extremity to quadruple phocomelia, the absence of all four extremities. The children were allowed to use whatever ways they could to convey knowledge of the displaced objects (some children removed the screens with their mouth, others with their toes, and so on). Decarie found that all of the children between 24 and 31 months of age and four below age 2 had reached the sixth stage of object permanence. Recall that normally this stage is reached at between 18 and 24 months of age. At first she was surprised by her findings as she had expected a marked delay. On closer examination, however, her findings were not so startling; it was apparent that most of the children did not, in fact, lack the schemes required for the construction of the object concept; those who were unable to use their hands could use substitute channels that led to such coordinations as toes-mouth, eyes-toes, shoulder-chin-eyes, and so on. Decarie interpreted her results as being in no way contradictory to Piaget's theory; in the normal child, prehension is mostly hand prehension, but the scheme of prehension, like intelligence itself, has many different ways of reaching its goal.

Another study that explored the effect of varying life circumstances on the development of the object concept was conducted in three rearing environments in Greece: an orphanage where the caregiver-infant ratio was 1:10, a baby center with a ratio of 1:3, and the homes of working-class families (Paraskevopoulos and Hunt,

1971). The study compared the means of the infants' ages at various levels of object construction, using the object construct scale of the Uzgiris-Hunt Ordinal Scales of Development (Uzgiris and Hunt, 1975), widely used Piaget-based scales representing various branches of sensorimotor development. The children at the orphanage attained the top level of the object concept—retrieving an object that has undergone a series of three invisible displacements—at 195 weeks; those at the baby center at 154; and the home-reared infants at 130 weeks. This substantial range of 65 weeks, or about a year and a quarter, for achieving the top level of object concept suggests considerable plasticity with respect to the development of the structure of intelligence depending on rearing environment.

A second major question that has been addressed using Piaget-based psychometric scales is whether or not Piaget was correct in his claim that his stages occur universally in an invariant sequence. Progression of individuals in various contexts through the stages in the same orderly sequence is, of course, a basic requirement for any stage theory. Transcontextual validity of the invariance of Piaget's stages has been assessed in a number of ways. One approach that has particular relevance to this chapter is the comparison of mentally retarded with nonretarded individuals. Studies showing that retarded children traverse the developmental stages in the same sequence that nonretarded children do would support the validity of Piaget's account of development. Weisz and Zigler (1979) reviewed 31 such studies, four of which concerned progression through the stages in the sensorimotor period. They concluded that the great preponderance of the evidence supports the hypothesis that retarded and nonretarded persons traverse the same stages of development in the same order, differing only in the rate at which they progress and in the level that they ultimately attain. The hypothesis seems to be generally supported regardless of whether retardation is the result of known biological defects such as brain damage or genetic disorders (e.g., Down syndrome) or whether it is presumed to be the result of cultural-familial factors.

THE BEHAVIORAL TRADITION

The behavioral approach to infant cognition and learning has been presented most systematically in the writings of Bijou and Baer (1961, 1965). Like Piaget, this approach conceptualizes development as the product of interactions between the child and the environment. Behavior is generally divided into two large classes, one of which is called reflex or *respondent behaviors*. Respondents are so named because as a class they are behaviors that are responsive to preceding stimulation. In this sense, they are reflexive, and unlikely to be affected by the stimulation that follows them. Examples of respondent behaviors include pupil constriction in the presence of light and salivation in response to food being placed in the mouth. Preceding stimuli, which give rise to reflexive behaviors in this paradigm, are called *unconditioned stimuli*; development generally proceeds by forming functional associations between unconditioned stimuli and new and previously neutral stimuli called *conditioned stimuli*. In this way a conditioned stimulus gives rise eventually to a response that is highly similar to the reflexive or unconditioned response. This process may be thought of generally as stimulus substitution in that one stimulus (the conditioned one) becomes functionally equivalent through association with another one (the unconditioned stimulus). Typically, this functional equivalence occurs through a repeated series of pairings of the conditioned stimulus and unconditioned stimulus. Through the processes of generalization and discrimination, variations on the conditioned stimulus may also become functionally effective in eliciting respondent behaviors. Classical conditioning has been demonstrated with quite young normal infants in a variety of situations, including the pairing of sounds with food (Marquis, 1931). However, there currently exists a controversy (e.g., see Sameroff and Cavanagh, 1979) concerning whether classical conditioning has, in fact, been demonstrated with neonates or very young infants.

Operant Behaviors

Unlike respondent behaviors, operants are not reflexive behaviors, but tend to be more voluntary in nature. They are controlled primarily by the consequences that occur after the behavior has been emitted. These consequences, or *contingencies* as they are frequently called, are of several varieties, including one class called *positive reinforcers*, which are stimuli that when consistently added to the environment following a response increase the likelihood of that response in the future. *Negative reinforcers*, on the other hand, are stimuli that when consistently subtracted from the environment following a response strengthen that response for the future. *Punishing stimuli* are those that when added to the environment following a response weaken the probability of that response.

It has been well-established that operant conditioning can occur from the first few days of life, and that this form of learning plays an increasingly important role in expanding the infant's behavioral repertoire. It has been shown, for example, that one can modify the sucking behavior of neonates by allowing the infant to receive milk when he/she emits sucks of a predetermined amplitude and only when that occurs (Sameroff, 1968).

To illustrate further the process of inquiry in this paradigm let us choose a response that becomes increasingly differentiated through time and increasingly important for the child—vocalization. Vocalizations begin as complex undifferentiated sounds, and during the course of development become the highly articulate symbolic conveyers of information that we call language. From a behavioristic orientation, we know a great deal about how these responses develop during infancy. For example, Rheingold et al. (1959) demonstrated that when an adult simultaneously and briefly smiled, vocalized, and touched a child after the infant had emitted a vocal sound that was not crying or fussing, the rate of the infant's vocalizations could be increased. Donald Routh (1969) further demonstrated that if one used a reinforcer similar to that used by Rheingold et al. and reinforced either consonant or vowel sounds, but not both, one could increase the probability of the reinforced sound occurring in relation to the kinds of sounds that were not reinforced. It has also been demonstrated by Ramey and Ourth (1971) that this very natural kind of reinforcer must occur almost immediately following the infant's vocalization if it is to have the effect of increasing the rate of that behavior. In fact, if the reinforcer is delayed by as little as 3 seconds following the end of the infant's vocalization, it ceases to be effective. However, not all reinforcers are equally likely to affect behaviors such as vocalization positively. Seligman (1970) has argued that all biological organisms are "prepared" for certain classes of stimuli to be particularly or exclusively functional as reinforcers for certain classes of behaviors. One of the tasks for researchers operating from a behavioristic or operant orientation is, therefore, to determine which classes of behaviors in the everyday lives of children are likely to be affected positively or negatively by the application of naturally occurring stimuli.

Procedures that involve the systematic provision of auditory and/or visual stimulation contingent upon some prior child behavior are frequently mentioned in the small but growing literature concerned with the development of appropriate methods for both the assessment and facilitation of cognitive development in multihandicapped and severely delayed infants and children (Accrino and Zuromski, 1978; Brinker, 1981; Friedlander et al., 1967; Haskett and Hollar, 1978; Ramey et al., 1972; Sokolow and Urwin, 1976; Watson and Hayes, 1981). Confronted with the challenges presented by the restricted repertoire of the motorically involved child, work to date has been primarily devoted to the development of sensitive manipulanda, which would allow even the severely disabled child independently to activate and hence receive reinforcement from such equipment as slide projectors and tape recorders (see especially Accrino and Zuromski, 1978; Friedlander et al., 1967). Because many of the participants in these studies had not previously evidenced any appreciable learning abilities, presentations of the data from such research/intervention projects have primarily consisted of demonstrations that these children could learn; that is, they could recognize and exploit the action-consequent contingencies made available to them.

It appears that researchers have recently begun to go beyond simply ascertaining whether a child did or did not learn, to more thoroughly examining the pattern of responses offered in a contingency situation. This has provided information concerning the relative speed with which effective actions are discriminated from ineffective ones (Brinker, 1981). However, despite the face validity of a procedure that assesses the ability to learn as an indication of a child's inherent learning ability, no evidence has yet been presented that would indicate that the participants who did *not* demonstrate learning, who took longer, or who appeared less sophisticated in their strategies were different in any other way relative to the other participants. Contingency learning situations thus have been useful in revising the impressions of the learning capabilities of some severely impaired young children, but further work is necessary to determine the diagnostic potential of such situations.

THE INFORMATION PROCESSING TRADITION

As one might surmise, the information processing approach focuses upon infants not as they construct their world, not as they learn about the contingencies available, but rather as they "process" the information in their environment. Yet, as information processing involves storage, retrieval, and comparison of stored and currently perceivable stimuli, the congruence between this approach and the Piagetian notions of assimilation/accommodation and schemes should be apparent. Furthermore, because specific experiences affect the contents of the information processes, learning too is integral, if not central, to this approach. In many ways, it is less of a specific theoretical orientation than either of the two preceding; rather, a diverse set of researchers seem to share perspectives and/or paradigms that are concerned very broadly with infants' abilities to remember configurations of stimuli, to develop expectancies of future configurations based on that past experience, and to behave in a variety of ways interpretable by researchers as evidence for a process of active comparison of past with present, and expected with observed.

What information researchers believe that infants know, what they acknowledge as early cognitive competence, has been determined in large part by the cleverness of these researchers in asking questions in ways that preverbal infants can answer. At the moment, researchers seem to be remarkably clever; hence, our understanding of infant cognitive abilities is expanding daily. Because any listing of what we currently know is bound to be outdated even a few months hence, this section focuses upon the kinds of paradigms— the ways of framing questions—that are currently proving so productive. Such a review is illustrative rather than exhaustive, but the interested reader is referred to other sources for more thorough treatments of specific areas.

Probably the most common paradigm for examining the infant's information processing ability is the habituation paradigm. If an infant is repeatedly presented with the same stimulus, the infant's response to that stimulus will decrease or habituate: the infant will get bored. If the stimulus is visual, visual fixation times will decrease as the infant looks less and less at the stimulus each time. Presumably the repeated presentations of a stimulus allow the infant to acquire a neuronal model (Sokolov, 1963, 1969) or schema; to the extent that the schema or model matches the stimulus, the infant "recognizes" the stimulus, there is nothing new to be learned, and attention tapers off. To indicate that such tapering off is not due to fatigue or other factors, a novel stimulus should precipitate dishabituation, or an increase in attention. The habituation phase is thought to index encoding. By systematically varying what is similar and what is different in the dishabituation stimulus, one can discover what features of the original stimulus were encoded, and thereby explore the development of a variety of information processing abilities in typical and atypical infants.

Cohen (1981) examined eight infants with Down syndrome and eight normally developing infants at each of three ages (19, 23, and 28 weeks) in a typical habituation task. Each infant sat in his/her mother's lap, facing a display screen that had a light in its center that blinked on and off at the beginning of each trial, to ensure the infant's attention. As soon as the infant looked at the light, a specific patterned stimulus appeared on the left side. The stimulus remained there until the infant looked away from it. The next trial would then start with the blinking light, the series continuing until an infant's fixation time was half of what it had been at the beginning. Once that criterion of habituation was reached, novel stimuli were then presented.

The infants with Down syndrome differed from the normally developing infants in two ways. First, the infants with Down syndrome in all three age groups had significantly longer fixation times than the normal infants, with mean fixation times being as much as six times longer in the two youngest groups. Second, although all three Down syndrome groups reached the criterion of habituation, and in fact did so in no more trials than the normal infants, true habituation did not seem to have occurred in the two younger age groups. The youngest infants with Down syndrome recovered interest in the previously "habituated" stimulus when it was re-presented after a brief pause and the introduction of another stimulus. Apparently, the previous decrease in looking time, thought to reflect habituation, was due to other factors. The intermediate age infants did not recover interest to the novel stimulus; they may have been tired, or they might have habituated to the whole situation, not to the specific stimulus. Only for the 28-week-old infants did the Down syndrome infants' behavior look like that of their normally developing counterparts.

The finding of a deficit in recovery, rather than in habituation, is consistent with work with infants at high risk due to perinatal trauma (Cohen, 1981) and with the findings of a slightly different habituation study of a group of male infants with five or more minor physical anomalies, a group at risk for attentional deficits in later life (Schexnider et al., 1981). In all these cases, it seems that the infants overgeneralized, or did not differentiate one stimulus from even a quite dissimilar one, just because it appeared in the same place. It is quite possible that such behavior will prove to be a useful index in identifying infants with information processing delays or deficits. However, much of the more recent work with normally developing infants has gone beyond habituating infants to a single redundant stimulus and has instead explored early concept formation and categorical perception. This truly seems a far and creative leap from the early demonstrations that infants could, in fact, habituate, and it is this very recent work that could provide a sensitive assessment tool for the widest range of typically and atypically developing infants.

In the categorical or conceptual habituation paradigm, pioneered by McGurk (1972), the infant is presented with a series of stimuli that are invariant in one way (the category or concept) but differ slightly from each other in other respects; multiple exemplars of a particular "category" are presented until an habituation criterion is reached. In McGurk's first study, the infants were presented with a particular form that varied in orientation from trial to trial. After reaching the habituation criterion, they showed little interest in that same form in yet another orientation, but dishabituated to a new (but actually quite similar) form. In contrast, a group of infants who were always presented with the same form, in the *same* orientation, dishabituated to both the novel form and the novel orientation. Here, as in subsequent work, it seems that young infants can perceive categorically, but that such categorical perception is dependent upon exposure to slightly differing multiple exemplars of a category. Infants who are not exposed to such slight variations may, obviously enough, develop much more "rigid" categories, so rigid that only exact replicas are considered instances of the class or category. Infants may also create categories that are much broader than experimenters intend, as the infants with Down syndrome in Cohen's study might have done when they seemed to form a category of, and habituate to, "visual stimuli presented in this laboratory apparatus." Parenthetically, such phenomena also occur outside the laboratory so that infants in their naturally occurring environments may also create categories from the perceptual array available to them that are more broad or narrow than their caregivers either intend for the infant or possess themselves. Caregivers may well be unaware of such differences before infants learn to talk, but with the advent of single-word speech, over- and undergeneralization become evident.

Some very recent work with other infants at risk for developmental handicaps indicates in a somewhat different way the varying kinds of categorical perception capabilities of very young infants. Caron and Caron (1981) presented infants with a set of stimuli wherein a relational feature (e.g., little shape above identical big shape or a face pattern) was held constant, but the shape of the components was different from trial to trial. Following habituation, a novel set of components was presented both in the familiar, habituated configuration and in a novel configuration. They were specifically interested in seeing if the infants would dishabituate (recover attention) only to the new components in the novel configuration, but not to the new components in the familiar configuration. If that happened, the infants must have been ignoring the specifics of the components because their novelty did not elicit attention. Instead, they must have been attending to the configuration because its novelty evoked increased attention. If the infants were attending to the configuration, then they must have abstracted from the familiarization trials the constant configuration against the changing specifics of the components.

Full-term and preterm infants were presented four problems (face-nonface, above-below, same face-different face, and neutral-smiling face) with four to six exemplars of each concept during habituation trials. A separate control group of full-term infants was habituated to a single exemplar of each concept. The results indicated the importance of both experience and biological status: discriminations (dishabituation) on the basis of the configural relations were significantly above chance for all four problems for the full-term, multiple-exemplar group, whereas the full-term, single-exemplar group infants exceeded chance scores on only one problem (face-nonface). Exactly the reverse was obtained for the component discrimination problems. Here, single-exemplar infants clearly differentiated component changes on three of the four problems, whereas the multiple-exemplar infants did so for only one problem (same face-different face). Depending upon the type of exposure (varying or invariant) infants learn, over the course of four to six trials, to attend to different aspects of a perceptual array, here either to its configuration or to its components. With the preterm infants, however, influences stemming from their status as "at risk" seemed to override the influences of stimulus exposure. Even though they were presented with multiple exemplars, their configural discrimination never exceeded chance (on three of the four problems their scores were significantly below those of term infants); instead they showed dishabituation on a component basis on all four problems. It should be noted that the preterm infants habituated just as quickly as if not more quickly than the term infants; they clearly were attending to and habituating to different aspects. Caron and Caron (1981) interpret these findings as indicating that preterm infants may have difficulty in the processing of particular content, specifically complex content of a configural nature. Here, despite the provision of a cognitively complex, configural "environment," only the less complex componential "environment" was processed.

Similarly, difficulty in conceptual information processing was also evident in a recent study with cerebral-palsied infants. McDonough and Cohen (1982) employed the categorical habituation procedure with 12- to 24-month-old infants with cerebral palsy and normally developing matched control infants. All of the normal infants, all of the older (19 to 24 months) infants with cerebral palsy, but only some of the younger infants with cerebral palsy acquired the concepts. Because this procedure eliminates the need for motoric competence, the failure of some of the younger infants with cerebral palsy to habituate selectively was interpreted as truly reflecting an inability to acquire the concept. Such inability, in turn, was interpreted as reflecting truly delayed cognitive development, separate from motoric disabilities.

Although extensively employed, presenting the same stimulus or category repeatedly until the infant evidences boredom is certainly not the only technique used to study infant information processing capabilities. Related to the habituation-dishabituation procedure, but different in several important aspects, is the recognition memory/paired comparison technique. (See Cohen and Gelber, 1975, for a detailed review.) Here, the infant's ability to remember and discriminate is revealed through the presentation of two identical stimuli, side by side, for a "familiarization" period. Immediately following are brief test periods in which a now familiar stimulus is paired with a novel one, different in one or many respects from the familiar stimulus. Given sufficient familiarization time, infants typically look longer at (prefer) the novel stimulus, indicating that they remember the familiar and can discriminate it from the novel. This paradigm, developed by Fantz and employed by him and his colleagues (see Fantz et al., 1975, for a comprehensive review) has provided much useful information about the capabilities of both typical and atypical infants. For example, given equal familiarization time and moderately difficult problems, (where it was necessary to see the overall configuration), normal infants demonstrated a preference for the novel at an earlier age (approximately 2 months younger) than infants with Down syndrome (Miranda and Fantz, 1974). When the discrimination between novel and familiar was relatively simple, however, no differences were found (Fantz et al., 1975).

A similar pattern of results for Down syndrome versus normally developing infants was found using yet a third technique employed to ascertain information processing abilities in infants. As before, demonstration of a preference for one stimulus over another is used to indicate the ability to discriminate between them; the difference is that the infant is required to perform different operant responses, or the same response in different locations, to produce different stimuli. With a modification of Friedlander's Playtest apparatus, Glenn et al. (1981) investigated differential preference for various kinds of auditory stimulation in infants with Down syndrome and nonhandicapped infants matched for mental age. Touching two different yellow buttons protruding from red boxes produced two different kinds of stimuli; in the first situation, contact with one button produced a song, and the other, a repetitive piano tone. In the second situation, a nursery rhyme was either sung or played on an instrument. Infants with Down syndrome produced the repetitive tone for the same duration and frequency that normal infants did, and the majority of both Down syndrome and normal infants preferred the sound of speech to instruments. However, infants with Down syndrome had much longer response durations for the more complex stimuli (although no differences in frequency), presumably indicating a need/desire for more time to process the more complex stimuli. Similarly, in earlier work using Fantz's visual preference technique, infants with Down syndrome also spent more time overall in looking at the various stimuli, but showed less clear-cut preferences for particular stimuli, especially the more complex stimuli, than did normally developing infants (Miranda and Fantz, 1973). However, infants with Down syndrome are not simply delayed with respect to normally developing infants. Rather, the differences seem to be complex, varying both in degree and in kind over the course of the first year. (See Miranda, 1976, for a review of the extensive Down syndrome-normal infant comparative work using the techniques of visual preference and recognition memory).

Up to this point, the dependent measures used to index information processing have essentially involved changes (or differences) in the duration of some behavior directly related to stimulus, or information, input (e.g., looking). A somewhat different way to index information processing is through affective expressions. The two types most commonly used have been smiling and vocalizing as indicators of recognition, or the congruence between expected and observed (e.g., McCall, 1972), and various expressions of surprise, as indicators of a discrepancy, or incongruence between expected and observed events (Charlesworth, 1969). Kagan and his colleagues (Kagan, 1969, 1971, 1979; Kagan et al., 1978) have used smiling and vocalizing extensively to index perceptual-cognitive processes, especially the process of a successful "match" between the infant's schema (a mental representation that presumably influences or is isomorphic to what he/she expects to perceive) and what he/she actually perceives. The presumption seems to be that infants take a few seconds to recognize that what they currently perceive (e.g., a face) match their schema developed from past experience (with faces), and then when they do so recognize it, they smile.

The "tension-release" hypothesis of Sroufe and Waters (1976) is similar, but much more elaborated. Sroufe and Wunsch (1972) had earlier found a developmental progression in the kinds of events (items) that elicited laughter in infants. Normally developing infants under 6 months usually laughed only in response to intense, intrusive stimulation, such as being bounced vigorously, whereas older infants would laugh instead at incongruity, such as the mother crawling or sucking on a bottle. The tension-release hypothesis postulates that infants laugh when they can rapidly process information, and the differences in the kinds of events that make babies of different ages laugh is due to changes in the infants' information processing capabilities and in the kinds of schemata available to them.

Cicchetti and Sroufe (1976) have used the developmental progression in the expression of laughter previously found with normally developing infants to study the interrelationship of cognition and affect in infants with Down syndrome. Despite marked differences in age of onset and frequency of laughter, the events that produced laughter earliest in normal babies also produced laughter (or, more commonly, smiling) earliest in babies with Down syndrome. The concordance between the affective indices and separate assessments of cognitive development provided further support for the hypothesized affective-cognitive interrelationship, as well as suggesting that assessment via affect might be a fruitful avenue to pursue in the future. Similarly, concordances were found in a separate sample of infants with Down syndrome between Bayley scores and their affective expressions (both positive and negative) to the repeated presentation of a squeaky doll (Gunn et al., 1981). It would seem, then, that affective indices of information processing can differentiate not only typical from atypical infants, but also are sufficiently sensitive to differentiate among a sample of atypical infants with the same syndrome.

Kagan et al. (1978) have developed a procedure that combines features from several of the above information processing approaches. Their procedure employs a modification of the habituation/dishabituation paradigm with multiple indices of processing (attentional, affective, and physiological). An attention getting, sequentially ordered stimulus is repeated over a series of trials, is transformed to create a discrepant stimulus, and then is returned to its original form. Developmental changes in the cardiac and behavioral responses that index assimilation of the stimulus event, surprise at the transformation, and recognition of the original event have been found in extensive work with normally developing children during their first 3 years of life (Kagan et al., 1978; Zelazo and Kearsley, 1982). The consistency of such developmental changes has recently allowed for the creation of a battery for the assessment of cognitive functioning, via information processing, in motorically handicapped infants and young children (Zelazo, 1979), especially those for whom more traditional assessments seem to underestimate their cognitive abilities.

The last information processing procedure we consider circumvents the requirement of behavioral responses entirely. It would seem that these new techniques, event-related brain potentials and averaged evoked potentials, might allow handicapped infants and young children to reveal their information processing abilities directly, unconfounded by their frequently atypical movement patterns and affective responses. Both of these methods, described but briefly below, attempt to tap directly the neurological substrate of the orienting reflex, elicited whenever there is a change in a previously habituated stimulus or when features of the perceivable environment differ from what was expected (Sokolov, 1969).

In the ordinary electroencephalographic recording, one can see that the electrical activity of the brain, recorded from scalp electrodes, changes not only with state (deep sleep, alert and awake, and so forth) but also when various stimuli are presented. However, clear responses to discrete stimuli are often masked by the "background noise." By averaging responses over many presentations of the same stimulus, changes in the electrical activity (potential) that are unrelated to the specific stimulus average out, leaving only the changes evoked by the particular stimulus. One may then see particular patterns in the brain waves, with "peaks and valleys" occurring at specific latencies after the presentation of stimuli. The very early sections (components) of the wave seem related to sensory characteristics, such as color or modality, and the ones that follow seem to vary with the information processing demands of the various stimuli presented, such that the more informative and important the stimulus, the higher the amplitude of the wave form (Courchesne, 1977, 1978a, 1978b). Stimuli presented repeatedly, as in the traditional habituation paradigm, elicit waves that are different from the waves that immediately follow the presentation of the novel or discrepant dishabituation stimulus in older children and adults (Courchesne, 1977, 1978a).

Recent studies now indicate that very young infants, whose behavioral responses (length of fixation, and so forth) differ when they are presented with expected versus discrepant events, also show the particular waveform responses that reflect such a discrimination in older subjects. Courchesne et al. (1981) were primarily concerned with the apparent transition in the forms of these long latency waveforms from infancy to adulthood and in the "maturational roots" of three of the waveforms that seem to occur in response to particular kinds of information processing demands. Not quite half of the normally developing 4- to 7-month-old infants they tested provided sufficient data for analysis; the others fell asleep, cried, pulled off the electrodes, refused to look at the stimuli, or blinked excessively. The 10 infants who cooperated viewed repeated presentations of a slide of a face; another face was the discrepant, or infrequently presented, event. The two faces were presented in random order such that only 12% of the presentations (or at least 70 over a 10-minute period) were of the discrepant slide. Their results indicated that in infants under 6 months, only two of the three waveforms seen in older children were apparent. No P3 waveforms, the type that seems highly related to orienting to discrepancy, were discriminable in this situation. Courchesne et al. considered the absence of P3 waveform as perhaps reflecting lack of sufficient maturation, or as perhaps reflecting only the complexity of the particular task presented.

The latter seems to be more likely, given a recent report by Hoffman et al. (1981). They also were interested in exploring in infants the parameters of event-related potentials, and, like Courchesne et al., used high and low probability visual stimuli, although of a much "simpler" nature, with 3-month-old infants. Similarly, they also retained only about one-third of infants tested, but again, their data are of interest. In brief, when infants were provided with sufficient repeated exposure to develop an expectancy, a clear P3 waveform, called LPC (late positive component), was seen in response to the presentation of an unexpected stimulus. Moreover, a trial-by-trial analysis revealed that this LPC occurred more frequently when a sequence of three or more familiar stimuli, instead of one or two, preceded the "unexpected" stimuli. Of interest also are their data indicating that the LPC, or P3 waveform, occurs at the same latency, approximately 300 to 600 milliseconds after the stimulus, as in adults. Their assumption that it was the extreme simplicity of their visual stimuli that allowed for such rapid processing seems tenable. Even given such simplicitly, the infants in this study evidenced a perhaps surprising rapidity of information processing, especially when one considers that the stimuli were flashed on the projection screen for 500 milliseconds only.

It seems, then, that young infants can process information *very* fast, and can react differentially to novel versus expected events, with differentiation among three well-established components of evoked brain potentials. With sufficient modification to reduce the now considerable subject loss, these procedures hold promise both for the exploration of infant memory and information processing, and as a long-sought-for method to assess cognitive processing free of motoric response limitations. It should be noted that very similar to identical techniques are currently in use in the form of evoked response audiometry, which is used in differential diagnosis in infants and young children in whom hearing loss is suspected. In that procedure, however, the question is whether the infant or child is receiving stimuli. In the work of concern here, the researchers are exploring how (and if) a child "processes" the stimuli, in the sense of forming a model or schema and then "evaluating" whether stimuli are concordant or discrepant with that schema. Although much more normative data are required before such techniques could be used in the assessment of handicapped infants and young children (Barnet, 1971), data from a study of infants with Down syndrome support its utility.

Barnet et al. (1971) presented brief auditory stimuli (clicks) to infants developing normally and infants with Down syndrome approximately 1, 6, and 12 months of age; the infants were asleep. Stimuli were presented repeatedly because a major focus of the study was to determine if a progressive decrease in magnitude (height) of the evoked response, presumed to index habituation, would occur. Results of group comparisons indicated that at none of the three ages did the groups of infants with Down syndrome show a response decrement (habituate), whereas the groups of 6- and 12-month-old normal infants did so. It is important to note, however, that individual infants with Down syndrome did appear to habituate, as indexed by response decrement. Similarly, the component presumed to index orienting to novelty/discrepancy, P3 waveforms, was very clear in the early part of the session, when the stimuli were novel, with the older normal infants, but it was often indistinct in the infants with Down syndrome. Some of the older infants with Down syndrome did have well-developed P3 waveform components, and these tended to be the same infants who also showed response decrement, or habituation.

In sum, there are several different ways to study typical and atypical infants' abilities to perceive, remember, form categories, and compare the stimuli available to them in their environment to the models in their minds. These measures differentiate both between typical and atypical, and among the atypical, in ways that seem understandable if not wholly predictable at the outset. Whether one of the several information processing paradigms reviewed in this section is superior to the others, in sensitivity to subtle differences between individuals concurrently or in its degree of correlation with subsequent outcome measures, remains to be seen. The greatest utility of these various experimentally derived paradigms may come not from the competition of one with another, but instead from their use in concert. To the extent that each provides one small window on the mind, a whole wall of such windows may allow us to see intelligence in action.

CONCLUDING COMMENTS

Each of the four traditions summarized in this chapter has had a long and productive history. The four traditions have generated a considerable amount of research on learning and cognition in infancy; unfortunately, those bodies of research have tended to remain somewhat isolated from one another. To some extent this is understandable because each of the traditions seems to deal primarily with a separate set of questions about early development, rather than representing competing hypotheses about how development occurs.

The *psychometric tradition*, through its individual differences emphasis, is concerned with developing effective and efficient measures by which to rank order individuals relative to their age peers. The *constructivist tradition*, represented best by the theories of Piaget, tends to be primarily descriptive in nature and to focus on the specification of the cognitive structures and their order of emergence. Although often referred to as a system concerned with the process—in contrast to the content—of intelligence, in many ways it has been more successful in building a taxonomy of the components and substrates of intellectual development than in specifying how change occurs. The *behavioral tradition* focuses on understanding behavior primarily through attempts to modify it, by programming a variety of contingencies in well-controlled laboratory settings. Thus, although there has been quite explicit concern with understanding the mechanisms that regulate behavioral development over the short term, this approach tends not to emphasize the typical sequences in which developmental attainments are achieved. Finally, the *information processing tradition* has a great deal in common with the constructivist orientation. It is concerned primarily with assessing what cognitive contents and structures are present in infants at various ages and with various handicaps and with determining the impact of those cognitive structures on the infant's likelihood of processing new information.

Because these four traditions address different facets of development, they might be seen as complementary perspectives with therapeutic implications for handicapped infants. The Piagetian perspective is helpful in sensitizing special educators and other professionals to what cognitive accomplishments to look for in that it provides a rich analytical framework for the stages of development. The behavioral tradition is frequently used as a set of techniques to systematically change deviant behavior toward more normal development. The information processing tradition, particularly with the use of the variants of the habituation paradigm, represents a set of techniques that hold great promise and that might prove to be particularly useful in assessing the cognitive capabilities of severely and profoundly handicapped individuals who frequently have such constricted behavioral repertoires that more traditional assessment techniques are precluded. Moreover, extant and future research on information processing during infancy may be of value therapeutically. For example, given the extreme consistency with which atypical infants have been found to have problems with the processing of complexity, a systematically structured and gradual introduction of complexity in the environment might allow these infants to overcome, at least partially, the difficulties they seem to have. Finally, the psychometric tradition provides a set of techniques that can be used to provide global assessments of children's developmental status which may continue to be appropriate as outcome measures for special education programs designed to enhance the development of at-risk and handicapped children.

A major issue for those who study the development of behavior is that of continuity. For those concerned with the development of cognitive ability, the issue involves the predictability of later cognitive status from assessments made in infancy. Although continuity, and hence predictability, are of interest to researchers within all four traditions, most attempts at prediction have been made by researchers using instruments developed within the psychometric tradition. These attempts have not provided very strong evidence for stability of individual differences in intelligence between infancy and childhood. Many developmental psychologists have pointed out, however, that such long-term stability of intelligence may be too much to expect. First, the nature of what we conceive of as intelligent behavior in infancy is qualitatively distinct from that which will develop during childhood. The cognitive behavior of the infant is, to use Piaget's term, sensorimotor, meaning that it is tied to the infant's perceptual and motoric capabilities. Post-infancy intelligent behavior, on the other hand, is primarily representational or operational. Although the latter form builds upon the former, the two are qualitatively different, and the low correlations between measures of each (i.e., lack of stability of individual differences) may be, in part, a reflection of inherently discontinuous development. Second, if we believe, as argued in the introduction to this chapter, that development is transactional, then a child's developmental status is co-determined by his/her characteristics and the environments to which he/she is exposed. Therefore, we should not expect to predict an individual's long-term accomplishments without simultaneously understanding both his/her capabilities and the environments to which he/she will be exposed through time.

We end this chapter by noting that in the last two decades our knowledge about infant development in general and our knowledge about the ability of infants to learn and think in particular has increased tremendously. As a field of inquiry we have gone from William James' conception of the infant's perception of the world as a "blooming, buzzing confusion" to an appreciation of the enormous complexity and regularity of the infant's understanding of that world. New research is being reported daily, constantly causing us to revise our preconceived notions of the limitations of infants. It is a time of exciting discovery and a time for vigorously pursuing the implications of our expanding knowledge about normal development for the assistance of handicapped and atypical children.

Chapter Outline

OVERVIEW: Learning is described as an adaptation to a given context or set of circumstances. Infants learn about their world primarily through their caregiving environment. The level of analysis principle is introduced as a means of determining developmental outcomes. This process is explained by examining four theoretical approaches—psychometrics, constructivism, behaviorism, and information processing.

I.   THE PSYCHOMETRIC TRADITION
This theoretical approach is concerned primarily with developing effective measures for rank ordering individuals relative to their age peers.

II. THE CONSTRUCTIVIST TRADITION
The constructivist position, represented best by the theories of Piaget, tend to be primarily descriptive in nature and to focus on the specification of the cognitive structures and their order of emergency. Although often referred to as a system concerned with the process, in contrast to the content of intelligence, in many ways it has been more successful in building a taxonomy of the components and substrates of intellectual development than in specifying how change occurs.

III. THE BEHAVIORAL TRADITION
The behavioral tradition focuses on understanding behavior primarily through attempts to modify it by programming a variety of contingencies in well-controlled laboratory settings. Thus, although there has been quite explicit concern with understanding the mechanisms that regulate behavioral development over the short term, this approach tends not to emphasize the typical sequences in which developmental attainments are achieved.

IV. THE INFORMATION PROCESSING TRADITION
The information processing tradition has a great deal in common with the constructivist orientation. It is concerned primarily with assessing what cognitive contents and structures are present in infants at various ages and

with various handicaps and with determining the impact of those cognitive structures on the infant's likelihood of processing new information.

V.   SUMMARY

The four traditions reviewed address different facets of development. They may be seen as complementary perspectives with therapeutic implications for handicapped infants. The continuous research on infant development allows us constantly to revise our preconceived notions of the limitations of infants.

REFERENCES

Accrino, S. P., and Zuromski, E. S. *Simple Discrimination Learning with Sensory Reinforcement by Profoundly Retarded Children.* Paper presented at the annual meeting of the Eastern Psychological Association, Washington, DC, 1978.

Barnet, A. B. Evoked potentials in handicapped children. *Developmental Medicine and Child Neurology,* 1971, *13,* 313–320.

Barnet, A. B., Olrich, E. S., and Shanks, B. L. EEG evoked responses to repetitive auditory stimulation in normal and Down's syndrome infants. *Developmental Medicine and Child Neurology,* 1971, *13,* 321–329.

Bayley, N. *Bayley Scales of Infant Development: Birth to Two Years.* New York: Psychological Corp. 1969.

Bijou, S. W., and Baer, D. M. *Child Development I: A Systematic and Empirical Theory.* New York: Appleton-Century-Crofts, 1961.

Bijou, S. W., and Baer, D. M. *Child Development II: Universal Stage of Infancy.* New York: Appleton-Century-Crofts, 1965.

Block, J. Assimilation, accommodation, and the dynamics of personality development. *Child Development,* 1982, *53,* 281–295.

Bower, T. G. R., Broughton, J. M., and Moore, M. K. Assessment of intention in sensori-motor infants. *Nature,* 1970, *228,* 679–681.

Brinker, R. *Patterns of Learning by Handicapped Infants.* Paper presented at the biennial meeting for the Society for Research in Child Development, Boston, 1981.

Bruner, J. S. Inhelder and Piaget's *The Growth of Logical Thinking:* A psychologist's viewpoint. *British Journal of Psychology,* 1959, *50,* 363–370.

Caron, A. L., and Caron, R. F. Processing of relational information as an index of infant risk. In S. L. Friedman and M. Sigman (Eds.), *Preterm Birth and Psychological Development.* New York: Academic Press, 1981.

Cattell, P. *The Measurement of Intelligence of Infants and Young Children.* New York: Science Press, 1940; Psychological Corp., 1960.

Charlesworth, W. R. The role of surprise in cognitive development. In D. Elkind and J. H. Flavell (Eds.), *Studies in Cognitive Development: Essays in Honour of Jean Piaget.* New York: Oxford University Press, 1969.

Cicchetti, D., and Sroufe, L. A. The relationship between affective and cognitive development in Down's syndrome infants. *Child Development,* 1976, *47,* 920–929.

Cohen, L. B. Examination of habituation as a measure of aberrant infant development. In S. L. Friedman and M. Sigman (Eds.), *Preterm Birth and Psychological Development.* New York: Academic Press, 1981.

Cohen, L. B., and Gelber, E. R. Infant visual memory. In L. B. Cohen and P. Salapatek (Eds.), *Infant Perception: From Sensation to Cognition: Vol. I. Basic Visual Processes.* New York: Academic Press, 1975.

Courchesne, E. Event-related brain potentials: A comparison between children and adults. *Science,* 1977, *197,* 589–592.

Courchesne, E. Neurophysiological correlates of cognitive development: Changes in long-latency event-related potentials from childhood to adulthood. *Electroencephalography and Clinical Neurophysiology,* 1978a, *45,* 468–482.

Courchesne, E. Changes in P3 waves with event repetition: Long-term effects on scalp distribution and amplitude. *Electroencephalography and Clinical Neurophysiology*, 1978b, 45, 754–766.

Courchesne, E., Ganz, L., and Norcia, A. M. Event-related brain potentials to human faces in infants. *Child Development*, 1981, 52, 804–811.

Decarie, T. *Intelligence and Affectivity in Early Childhood*. New York: International Universities Press, 1962.

Decarie, T. G. A study of the mental and emotional development of the thalidomide child. In B. Foss (Ed.), *Determinants of Infant Behavior IV*. London: Methuen, 1969.

Fantz, R. L., Fagan, J. F., and Miranda, S. B. Early visual selectivity as a function of pattern variables, previous exposure, age from birth and conception, and expected cognitive deficit. In L. B. Cohen and P. Salapatek (Eds.), *Infant Perception: From Sensation to Cognition: Vol. I: Basic Visual Processes*. New York: Academic Press, 1975.

Flavell, J. H. *Cognitive Development*. Englewood Cliffs, NJ: Prentice-Hall, 1977.

Friedlander, B. Z., McCarthy, J. J., and Soforenko, A. Z. Automated psychological evaluation with severely retarded institutionalized infants. *American Journal of Mental Deficiency*, 1967, 71, 909–919.

Gibson, E. J. *Principles of Perceptual Learning and Development*. New York: Appleton-Century-Crofts, 1969.

Glenn, S. M., Cunningham, C. C., and Joyce, P. F. A study of auditory preferences in nonhandicapped infants and infants with Down's syndrome. *Child Development*, 1981, 52, 1303–1307.

Gratch, G. The development of thought and language in infancy. In J. Osofsky (Ed.), *Handbook of Infant Development*. New York: Wiley, 1979.

Gunn, P., Berry, P., and Andrews, R. J. The affective response of Down's syndrome infants to a repeated event. *Child Development*, 1981, 52, 745–748.

Haskett, J., and Hollar, W. D. Sensory reinforcement and contingency awareness of profoundly retarded children. *American Journal of Mental Deficiency*, 1978, 83, 60–68.

Hofmann, M. J., Salapatek, P., and Kuskowski, M. Evidence for visual memory in the averaged and single evoked potentials of human infants. *Infant Behavior and Development*, 1981, 4, 401–421.

Horowitz, F. D. Methods of assessment for high-risk and handicapped infants. In C. T. Ramey and P. L. Trohanis (Eds.), *Finding and Educating High-Risk and Handicapped Infants*. Baltimore: University Park Press, 1982.

Johnson, N. Assessment paradigms and atypical infants: An interventionist's perspective. In D. Bricker (Ed.), *The Application of Research Findings to Intervention with At-Risk and Handicapped Infants*. Baltimore: University Park Press, 1982.

Kagan, J. Continuity in cognitive development during the first year. *Merrill-Palmer Quarterly*, 1969, 15, 102–119.

Kagan, J. *Change and Continuity in Infancy*. New York: Wiley, 1971.

Kagan, J. Structure and process in the human infant: The ontogeny of mental representation. In M. H. Bornstein and W. Kessen (Eds.), *Psychological Development from Infancy: Image to Intention*. Hillsdale, NJ: Erlbaum, 1979.

Kagan, J., Kearsley, R., and Zelazo, P. *Infancy: Its Place in Human Development*. Cambridge, MA: Harvard University Press, 1978.

Knobloch, H., and Pasamanick, B. Further observation on the behavioral development of Negro children. *Journal of Genetic Psychology*, 1953, *83*, 137–157.

Knobloch, H., and Pasamanick, B. *Gesell and Amatruda's Developmental Diagnosis: The Evaluation and Management of Normal and Abnormal Neuropsychologic Development in Infancy and Early Childhood* (3rd ed.). New York: Harper and Row, 1974.

Laszlo, E. *Introduction to Systems Philosophy: Toward a New Paradigm of Contemporary Thought*. New York: Gordon and Breach, 1972.

Marquis, D. P. Can conditioned responses be established in the newborn infant? *Journal of Genetic Psychology*, 1931, *39*, 479–492.

McCall, R. B. Smiling and vocalization in infants as indices of perceptual-cognitive processes. *Merrill-Palmer Quarterly*, 1972, *18*, 341–347.

McDonough, S., and Cohen, L. B. *Use of Habituation to Investigate Concept Acquisition in Cerebral Palsied Infants*. Paper presented at the International Conference on Infant Studies (ICIS), Austin, TX, April, 1982.

McGurk, H. Infant discrimination of orientation. *Journal of Experimental Child Psychology*, 1972, *14*, 151–164.

Miranda, S. B. Visual attention in defective and high-risk infants. *Merrill-Palmer Quarterly*, 1976, *22*, 201–228.

Miranda, S. B., and Fantz, R. L. Visual preferences of Down's syndrome and normal infants. *Child Development*, 1973, *44*, 555–561.

Miranda, S. B., and Fantz, R. L. Recognition memory in Down's syndrome and normal infants. *Child Development*, 1974, *45*, 651–660.

Paraskevopoulos, J., and Hunt, J. McV. Object construction and imitation under differing conditions of rearing. *Journal of Genetic Psychology*, 1971, *119*, 301–321.

Piaget, J. *Play, Dreams and Imitation*. New York: Norton, 1951.

Piaget, J. *The Origins of Intelligence in Children*. New York: International Universities Press. 1952.

Piaget, J. *The Construction of Reality in the Child*. New York: Basic Books, 1954.

Piaget, J. Piaget's theory. In P. H. Mussen (Ed.), *Carmichael's Manual of Child Psychology: Vol. 1* (3rd ed.). New York: Wiley, 1970.

Ramey, C. T., Campbell, F. A., and Nicholson, J. The predictive power of the Bayley Scales of Infant Development and the Stanford-Binet Intelligence Test in a relatively constant environment. *Child Development*, 1973, *44*, 790–795.

Ramey, C. T., Campbell, F. A., and Wasik, B. H. Use of standardized tests to evaluate early childhood special education programs. *Topics in Early Childhood Education*, 1982, *1*, 51–60.

Ramey, C. T., and Haskins, R. The modification of intelligence through early experience. *Intelligence*, 1981, *5*, 21–27.

Ramey, C. T., Hieger, L., and Klisz, D. Synchronous reinforcement of vocal responses in failure-to-thrive infants. *Child Development*, 1972, *43*, 1449–1455.

Ramey, C. T., MacPhee, D., and Yeates, K. O. Preventing developmental retardation: A general systems model. In L. A. Bond and J. M. Joffe (Eds.),

Facilitating Infant and Early Childhood Development. Hanover, NH: University Press of New England, 1982.

Ramey, C. T., and Ourth, L. L. Delayed reinforcement and vocalization rates of infants. *Child Development*, 1971, *42*, 291–298.

Rheingold, H. L., Gewirtz, J. L., and Ross, H. W. Social conditioning of vocalization in the infant. *Journal of Comparative and Physiological Psychology*, 1959, *52*, 68–73.

Routh, D. K. Conditioning of vocal response differentiation in infants. *Developmental Psychology*, 1969, *1*, 219–226.

Sameroff, A. J. The components of sucking in the human newborn. *Journal of Experimental Child Psychology*, 1968, *6*, 607–623.

Sameroff, A. J., and Cavanagh, P. J. Learning in infancy: A developmental perspective. In J. Osofsky (Ed.), *Handbook of Infant Development.* New York: Wiley, 1979.

Sameroff, A. J., and Chandler, M. J. Reproductive risk and the continuum of caretaking casualty. In F. D. Horowitz (Eds.), *Review of Child Development Research* (Vol. 4). Chicago: University of Chicago Press, 1975.

Schexnider, V. Y. R., Bell, R. Q., Shebilske, W. L., and Quinn, P. Habituation of visual attention in infants with minor physical anomalies. *Child Development*, 1981, *52*, 812–818.

Seligman, M. E. P. On the generality of the laws of learning. *Psychological Review*, 1970, *77*, 406–418.

Sokolov, E. N. *Perception and the Conditioned Reflex.* New York: Macmillan, 1963.

Sokolov, E. N. The modeling properties of the nervous system. In M. Coles and I. Maltzman (Eds.), *A Handbook of Contemporary Soviet Psychology.* New York: Basic Books, 1969.

Sokolow, A., and Urwin, C. "Playmobile" for blind infants. *Developmental Medicine and Child Neurology*, 1976, *18*, 498–502.

Sroufe, L. A., and Waters, E. The ontogenesis of smiling and laughter: A perspective on the organization of development in infancy. *Psychological Review*, 1976, *83*, 173–189.

Sroufe, L. A., and Wunsch, J. P. The development of laughter in the first year of life. *Child Development*, 1972, *43*, 1326–1344.

Uzgiris, I. C., and Hunt, J. McV. *Assessment in Infancy: Ordinal Scales of Psychological Development.* Urbana: University of Illinois Press, 1975.

Watson, J. S., and Hayes, L. A. *Response-Contingent Stimulation as a Treatment for Developmental Failure in Infancy.* Paper presented at the biennial meeting of the Society for Research in Child Development, Boston, 1981.

Weisz, J., and Zigler, E. Cognitive development in retarded and nonretarded persons: Piagetian tests of the similar sequence hypothesis. *Psychological Bulletin*, 1979, *86*, 831–851.

Zelazo, P. R. Reactivity to perceptual-cognitive events: Application for infant assessment. In R. B. Kearsley and I. E. Sigel (Eds.), *Infants at Risk: Assessment of Cognitive Functioning.* Hillsdale, NJ: Erlbaum, 1979.

Zelazo, P. R., and Kearsley, R. B. *Memory Formation for Visual Sequences: Evidence for Increased Speed of Processing with Age.* Paper presented at the International Conference on Infant Studies, Austin, TX, April, 1982.

CHAPTER 9
Early Language Development

William A. Bricker, Jean A. Levin, and Patrick R. Macke

The acquisition of language by a child is a remarkably complex process, although, as noted by Chomsky (1965), most children master the majority of the complexities of language by the age of 4 and seem to do so without the benefit of instruction. At the other pole are those atypical children who do not acquire language at all, even with extremely precise instruction. Given the thousands of pages that have been written about both sides of the language acquisition process, we can reasonably conclude that there are no final answers as to how one intervenes to improve the language of an atypical infant. At best, we have bits and pieces derived from a number of sources but not one best authoritative position on the most efficient way to proceed. The frustration that this ambiguity generates is shared by all of us who have been professionally involved with attempts at teaching language to atypical infants and young children and to an even greater extent by the parents of the children who feel that we should know more than we do.

The purpose of this chapter is to put several of the major approaches to language intervention into perspective and to provide our own conclusions about how to proceed from this state of relative ignorance with the best possible chances of success. We have attempted to do this by synthesizing information from linguistic, psycholinguistic, sociolinguisitic, cognitive, and behavioral sources. They each contribute to our collective abilities to help children improve in the areas of language and thought. A beginning point of discussion is Chomsky's view of language learning:

> Clearly, a child who has learned a language has developed an internal representation of a system of rules that determine how sentences are to be formed, used, and understood . . . He has done this on the basis of observation of what we may call primary linguistic data. This must include examples of linguistic performance that are taken to be well-formed sentences, and may include also examples designated as non-sentences, and no doubt much other information of the sort that is

required for language learning, whatever this might be . . . On the basis of such data, the child constructs a grammar—that is, a theory of the language of which the well formed sentences constitute a small part. As a precondition for language learning, he must possess, first, a linguistic theory that specifies the form of the grammar of a possible human language, and, second, a strategy for selecting a grammar of the appropriate form that is compatible with the primary linguistic data (Chomsky, 1965, p. 25).

This would seem to be a problem for any child, and, perhaps, an impossibility for a brain-injured child. The important aspect of this description is that it places the burden for language learning entirely on the child, but this is not an unusual case. An examination of many important recent publications on language acquisition (Bates et al., 1979; Bloom and Lahey, 1978; Bowerman, 1978; Leonard, 1978) indicates a reliance on the child to learn, acquire, deduce, comprehend, generate, or invent solutions for the problems associated with acquisition of language. The vast majority of these studies are descriptive. Until scientific inquiry is focused also on the remediation of problems that are found in the communication processes of atypical young children, we have little hope of discovering successful intervention strategies rapidly. The assumption often made is that if children cannot learn language on their own, then they simply cannot learn it at all. This is the attitude that the present chapter was written to overcome. We must intervene actively with atypical infants and young children and do so on the basis of the best information available to us.

An abundance of information depicting early communicative development from both a cognitive and social perspective exists to date (Als, 1979; Bates et al., 1979). Recent clinical and research emphases on the impact of handicapping conditions on developmental outcomes and also on the relationship between parents and infants has provided further information on early communication patterns. The integration of these bodies of knowledge are critical to providing a model of intervention for infants and their families. Thus, it is the parent-infant interactive dyad to which we address our intervention model and to which we advocate application of cognitive and social targets for programming. The provision of direct intervention in the area of communication based on a cognitive-social perspective that utilizes behavioral strategies and acknowledges the impact of the handicapping condition on both the infant's development and the parent's motivation and ability to interact forms the basis for this chapter.

PATTERNS OF EARLY SOCIAL INTERACTION

A first concern about the prerequisite processes of any aspect of development must focus on the early relationship between the atypical infant and the infant's parents. The birth of a handicapped infant brings with it two inevitable states. The first, the reaction of grief and shock by the parents and other members of the family, is described by many writers (Robinson and Robinson, 1976; Wolfensberger, 1972). Professionals have reported visiting families who appeared to be in mourning when the event was, in fact, the birth of a blind infant (Fraiberg et al., 1969). Hayden described some of her initial encounters with parents of infants with Down syndrome in which the parents seemed frightened and awkward. The parents actually had to be taught to cuddle, talk to, and play with their newborn. The parents seemed to consider their infant as someone who had a contagious disease (Hayden and Haring, 1976).

The second state is the discovery by the parents that the agencies and the professionals who are supposed to help them adjust and react to the fact of their infant's disability are inconsistent and contradictory in their recommendations and alternative modes of intervention. The alternatives range from allowing the infant to die to suggesting early intervention as early as the first few weeks after birth (Sherlock, 1979; Wolfensberger, 1980). This latter action is the one that may be critical to subsequent attempts at intervention for a number of reasons outlined below. We must find the means to foster early positive interactions even during the first few days of the infant's life.

An area of considerable emphasis in the study of early communicative development is that of the parent-infant interaction process, and more specifically, the active role of each partner in this process (Als, 1979; Osofsky and Connors, 1979). The body of knowledge currently available in the field of infant development enables the interventionist or parent not only to be aware of patterns of interaction as seen in the normally developing infant but also to identify specific forms of both caregiver and infant behavior that could positively influence subsequent cognitive, social, and linguistic development. Studying the interactional process allows one to observe specific forms of both caregiver and infant behavior as having communicative function, identify possible disruptions in the interactive process upon the birth of a handicapped infant (Ramey et al., 1980; Yarrow et al., 1973), and provide intervention through the parent-infant dyad.

There are several major considerations that are central to understanding the process of parent-infant interaction and its application to intervention with the atypical infant. First is the concept of the dyad as one distinct unit of analysis (Bowlby, 1969; Milenkovic and Uzgiris, 1979). This orientation focuses on the caregiver's and infant's behavior as part of one specific unit of analysis rather than as two separate entities. Each partner is continually modifying the other's behavior and continually adjusting to this partner's behavior as part of a "circular feedback process" (Condon and Sander, 1974; Lewis and Rosenblum, 1974) where the dyadic unit is seen as one set of circular behavior patterns.

A similar issue is that of the reciprocal behavior patterns developed early in the infant's life (Als, 1979). The synchrony or timing of mother responses to the infant's behavior and the infant's responses to the mother are illustrated in several studies that address this issue of synchrony. Stern et al. (1977), for example, refer to the alternating and simultaneous patterns of the dyad as shared mother-infant behavior. An interesting case of synchrony is the one described by Condon and Sander (1974) in which a newborn infant was observed to move systematically first one hand and then the other in synchrony with the sentences being spoken to him. In describing this phenomenon, Als (1979) noted maternal behavior patterns that occur in response to infant states. When the infant's eyes are closed and he/she is not producing vocalizations or movement, the mother tends to withdraw physically by holding the baby away from her body and discontinuing any en *face* interaction or vocalizations. In contrast, when the infant's eyes are open, the mother tends to hold the infant close to her body and interacts through eye contact and vocal behavior. A continuous two-way interactional system or process thus develops early in the infant's life through each partner's active role in the interaction process. Each is continually reestablishing routines and, in turn, actually modifying the other's behavior. Using a behavioral framework, one might state that it is the reinforcement value of interactional patterns that is critical in the process. The infant is reinforced for his/her behavior (i.e., vocalizations and open eyes) by the mother's responses (i.e., physical bonding, en *face* contact, and vocalizations). The mother's behavior, through her eye contact and vocalizations, is instrumental in the infant's earliest development.

These findings are consistent with others that show that adult human speech is an important determiner in an infant's structure. Language can be used to increase the rate of vocal production on the part of the infant (Rheingold et al., 1959) and can be used to increase the amplitude of the sucking response of newborn infants. The recorded voice of an infant's mother, even when it was distorted electronically, was used to quiet the crying infant (Turnure, 1971). In fact, newborns have been shown to discriminate basic speech sounds on a categorical basis, which is an extremely sensitive but flexible capability (Eimas, 1974). However, this effect is seen with only a restricted number of consonants and with a few vowels (Butterfield and Cairns, 1976).

Several investigations showed that the length of feeding was directly related to the modes of stimulation used by the mother. During the suck-pause pattern, mothers that stimulated their infants early in the pause phase prolonged both the pause and the length of feeding, whereas those who stimulated later in the pause produced resumed sucking and shorter feeding times (Kaye and Brazelton, 1971). Thoman et al. (1970, 1972) studied the interaction patterns between primiparous mothers and their infants in feeding situations, and found that the new mothers stimulated their infants more but did so with inconsistent patterns and thereby prolonged the feeding situation and made it less pleasant.

In cases of infants who fail to thrive, evidence was gathered that the mothers became increasingly incompetent and distressed in feeding situations due to the lack of synchrony between the mother and the infant (Leonard et al., 1966). From these studies, we can derive a clear picture of the importance of the feeding situation in the subsequent emotional and social development of the infant.

A second aspect of mother-infant interaction is the effect of infant state changes on caregiver activities. Denenberg and Thoman's (1976) extensive longitudinal study recorded state changes with 10 infants. They found that the infants varied from 2 state changes per hour to more than 10 per hour, and that the frequency of change was persistent across 3-month intervals. In this study, they also identified one infant who was less attentive when being held than when he was awake in the crib. As a consequence, the mother became increasingly less attentive, avoided direct eye-gazing with the infant, and reduced the amount of time she spent holding him over a 7-week period in comparison with six other mothers of more typical babies. This form of asynchrony is frequently reported in the literature on autistic infants (Rimland, 1964).

Beckwith (1976) has provided an excellent review of significant dimensions of caregiver behavior. Although the amount and intensity of stimulation must be carefully graded and controlled by the caregiver, the overall amount and quality is related to infant intellectual development (Clarke-Stewart, 1973) and to greater amounts of activity and exploration (Yarrow et al., 1973). One aspect of stimulation is through the vestibular system, which is viewed as an important aspect of balance, arousal, and ability to coordinate movements in later infancy and early childhood. This system is best stimulated through picking up and holding the infant in a variety of positions (Ainsworth, 1973; Bell and Ainsworth, 1972). In addition, the more responsive the caregiver is to infant sensitivities and responses, the more adjusted and socially effective the child will be several years later (Yarrow et al., 1973).

PARENTAL PATTERNS WITH ATYPICAL INFANTS

The evidence for maternal effect on infant development in nonhandicapped populations suggests that the need for early detection and early intervention with handicapped and at-risk infants is of particular significance. Hayden (1979) makes this clear:

> Some people believe that the problems of the birth to age three group are only in the health and medical realms. Indeed, many of these children desperately need health and medical care early, but they and their families also need early educational intervention. While nonhandicapped young children may make acceptable progress without early educational interventions, handicapped or at risk children do not. To deny them the attention that might increase their chances for improved functioning is not only wasteful, it is ethically indefensible (p. 510).

The challenges presented by the effects of having a handicapped infant on maternal behavior must not be overlooked. Recent research has begun to address this topic. A critical study in this regard indicated that handicapped infants were difficult to soothe when crying, rarely smiled, and vocalized infrequently in response to comforting or vocalization by the parent (Stone and Chesney, 1978). In a more recent study, handicapped infants were found to cry more frequently and louder, were difficult to console, were obviously slower in development, engaged in less eye contact, and, in general, did little that reinforced the actions of the caregiver (Ramey et al., 1980). In a study of autistic children and their interactions with their mothers, approximately 75% of the variance in predicting family and parental stress was related to specific degrees of dependency and lack of appropriate response patterns. The key factor was the amount of the mother's time that was consumed in meeting the child's needs and the prognosis concerning the ultimate state of dependency when the child became an adult (Bristol, 1980). In other words, the more needs that a child had and the longer the parents were going to have to provide for those needs, the greater the stress. This finding was replicated with severely handicapped young children with caregiving demands being the single most important factor in parental stress reactions to their handicapped child. Lack of social responsiveness and repetitive forms of behavior also contributed to stress (Bell, 1980).

Wolff (1969, 1971) studied the early vocal development of infants and young children and found differences between maternal responses to handicapped and nonhandicapped children's vocalizations. Mothers of normally developing infants were able to identify certain cries and vocalizations to signify specific needs across a group, whereas mothers of autistic children were unable to attach these meanings or respond differentially to their children's cries and vocal behavior. This, in particular, illustrates the potential for an upset to reciprocal interactions.

The importance of positive early parent-infant interaction must not be minimized. These interactive processes are an integral component, but alone are not sufficient for the acquisition of a communicative system in the young infant.

PRELINGUISTIC DEVELOPMENT: COGNITION AND LANGUAGE

The development of cognitive prerequisites during the first 2 years of life, or sensorimotor bases of language, are a critical instructional domain for anyone working with infants and their families. Whereas interactive processes form the bases for having a purpose to communicate, or for the functions of language, cognitive prerequisites provide the content, or "what to talk about," in the child's language system.

One reason for minimal accepted models of infant communication programming is the lack of theoretical agreement regarding the relationship of early cognitive, or sensorimotor, development and communication. This relationship has been of a controversial nature based on two general theoretical foundations, those of Piaget (1954) and Vygotsky (1962).

Piaget assumed language develops through successive stages, which reflect the development of cognitive processes. The child's sensorimotor action schemes upon objects form the basis for conceptual classes of behavior (e.g., climbing and hitting), which are later replaced and represented by symbolic linguistic units (i.e., words to represent the actions). Language use, according to Piaget, develops as the child's cognitive processes become more complex through his/her defined successive hierarchial stages (Piaget, 1962, 1980). Egocentric speech, one phase in that development, is a non-social form that reflects the child's current cognitive level of development. In contrast, Vygotsky believed that the infant's early language is social and communicative, but is not based upon egocentric speech, and that the child begins to use language as a directive tool to cognition or to provide a symbolic means to direct his/her behavior upon the presence of obstacles.

For Vygotsky, egocentric speech was a change in the function of speech, from being social communication to its use as self-regulating behavior. In contrast to Piaget, Vygotsky saw language at this stage as a tool to thought: ". . . thought development is determined by language, i.e., by the linguistic tools of thought and by the sociocultural experience of the child" (1962, p. 51). Vygotsky assumed that language and thought develop from separate roots and act upon each other; the prespeech intellectual development and preintellectual speech develop separately and function for each other at the stage in which children begin to inquire about the means of objects. Vygotsky found language to serve as a tool to direct action and plan future action.

Although there is a general agreement that a relationship exists, there are currently three controversial hypotheses regarding the degree and nature of that relationship. These form the three versions of the "Cognition Hypothesis" (Cromer, 1976; Miller et al., 1980). One version holds that specific sensorimotor attainments are necessary and sufficient to the acquisition of corresponding language milestones. Another version hypothesizes that these cognitive attainments are necessary, but not sufficient to the development of language. The third, the correlational version, assumes a close temporal association between cognitive and linguistic attainments, but not a causal relationship. Recent studies of the relationship between specific sensorimotor attainments and early communicative behavior in normally developing infants implied a correlational relationship (Bates, et al., 1977). To date, however, there is still a lack of agreement among theorists.

Although this relationship is unresolved, there is still considerable information based on theory and research describing the sequence of early communicative development. The pragmatics movement of the communication field is probably the most relevant body of literature. This movement refers to the social aspects of communication, and has redirected language research of the past decade to study an infant's meaning within a contextual framework, including both vocal and nonvocal behavior. Piagetian theory is embedded in this movement, providing the cognitive content of the infant's early interactions (Bates, 1976; Bates et al., 1975; Bloom, 1974; Bowerman, 1973a, 1973b, 1973c). The pragmatics approach is discussed in length in a separate section of this chapter.

Piaget's theory of cognitive development, specifically sensorimotor behavior during the first 2 years of life, is based on the infant's earliest interactions with his/her environment. It is these interactions with the environment and the differentiated responses of the environment upon the child's actions that form the foundation for later language development. For instance, the infant's actions upon objects before acquisition of speech, through motor schemes, form the basis for later and more complex behavior.

Piaget divides the first 2 years of life, or sensorimotor development, into six substages, each a precursor and building block for the next. He defines this period in the development of a child as the "origins of intelligence" (1952), or the basis for future adaptive success. The actual areas, or content areas of Piaget's sensorimotor stages include the object permanence concept, use of tools, or means-end behavior, spatial and temporal relationships, physical cause-effect, and imitation. His theory assumes a vertical representation of these five areas as they develop in complexity through six substages from birth to 24 months. Simultaneously, there is a horizontal orientation, where the relationship of the child's skills in each of the five general areas develop. Piaget's theoretical assumption is that the child develops cognitively in these five domains through his/her early interactions with objects and people in the environment. The infant learns to detour physical barriers in the home, use tools to obtain out of reach objects, learn that objects have differentiated uses and functions, and search for missing objects when they are not in view. All of these represent preverbal interactions with the world, and all are developed through continuous interactions with the environment.

Central to our inclusion of Piagetian assumptions is not to trace his developmental model, but to emphasize its role in the issue of infant communicative development. Piaget's sensorimotor domains and hierarchial sequence provide the content of the infant's world, or "what to talk about," and a developmental guideline to examine the infant's "understanding" of the world in an operationalized manner. Two examples may assist in applying this perspective for programming objectives.

First is the concept of object permanence, which basically states that an object still exists even though it may be out of sight. Early in an infant's development, his/her level of the "permanent object" concept is not permanent; when a person or object disappears, it is essentially "out of sight, out of mind." Through continued inter-actions with the environment and the processes of adaptation, the child eventually learns that there is still a "mother" or "ball" in his/her life even if she or it is not in his/her visual presence. Before that stage of development, infants can only acknowledge their affirmation of or request for that object if it is in their view. As the object per-manence concept becomes more complex, children learn that the object still exists, and they can either physically search for it or use language to obtain it. The use of language in this symbolic form is a critical development in the infant's linguistic and cognitive ac-quisition and allows for more adaptive intelligent behavior. How-ever, if a handicapped infant displays significant cognitive delays in this domain, his/her subsequent language will be significantly limited. Rather than to "wait and hope," we advocate early pro-gramming in this area by direct systematic intervention with the child and his/her parents in order to maximize this development.

The second example is the area of means-end. Again, this do-main is one that becomes clearly more complex throughout the in-fant's development. Initially, the infant's use of means to obtain a goal, or end, is extremely limited. The infant may use a basic cry or vocalization, which may be interpreted as being a request, or a signal for assistance or interaction. As his/her sensorimotor development becomes more complex, he/she uses differentiated cries or vocali-zations as means of communication and even uses tools, such as objects or a parent's arm, to acquire needs and wants. Naturally, the desired most functional set of means is the linguistic set, a lexicon that will allow the child to obtain needs and wants. Again, many children with significant delays may not develop according to the normal timelines or milestones. It is our responsibility to address this type of development through necessary training objectives fol-lowing as closely as possible the normal developmental sequence and its framework.

The concept of intentionality is a central consideration in the field of early communication and cognitive development during the first 2 years of life (Bates, 1976; Bloom, 1974; Bricker et al., 1981; Lock, 1980). Its basic definition and explanations are frequently de-veloped through a "homunculus" belief that the development of in-tentional or purposeful behavior is from within the infant's internal processes. This mentalistic view assumes that the infant actively processes information and makes critical decisions that determine the course of his/her development (Bates et al., 1977; Bowerman, 1973c). This implies a discrimination made by the infant through

his/her decisions, rather than through control of external environmental events. In normal development this is not a critical factor if
conditions are neurologically and environmentally set so that normal
development results (Bricker and Campbell, 1980). This implication
is critical to the development of children with handicapping conditions, for such a homunculus belief places the responsibility for
development on the child, rather than on the interventionist and
selection of strategies to be used.

Intentionality is seen as critical to language acquisition and is
generally viewed as a "product" or developmental attainment that
occurs early in life. It is treated within a Piagetian framework of
cognitive development (Brainerd, 1978; Moerk, 1977; Piaget, 1952,
1954) from the aspect of prelinguistic intent (Bates, 1976, Bates et
al., 1979; Dore, 1977; Halliday, 1975). Bates has completed a series
of longitudinal studies to investigate the development of communicative prelinguistic intent, and others, such as Halliday, Dore, and
Steckol and Leonard (1981), have based their research investigations
on her framework. They describe intention as the basis of behavior
and subsequent communicative development. Bates' work on the
development of prelinguistic performatives, or early nonverbal functions of communication, places intentionality within a sequence of
development commensurate with the Piagetian sequence.

Bates' (1976) model of intentional development addresses both
the cognitive and social prerequisites for language. The phases of
this model signify three levels, the perlocutionary, illocutionary, and
locutionary stages of development. The term *perlocutionary* refers
to stages 1 to 3 of Piaget's sensorimotor development, from birth to
8 months of age. During this phase, unintentional signals through
movements and/or vocalizations are made by the infant. Although
they are not purposeful, they often seem to be intentional to the
caregiver or other observer. Illocutionary behavior, corresponding to
the sensorimotor stages 4 and 5, or 8 to 18 months, includes conventional signals produced for intentional reasons such as waving,
vocalizing to gain the attention of others, or throwing a kiss to greet.
Locutions, the third phase delineated by Bates, occurs during stage
6, the final sensorimotor stage, 18 to 24 months, and consists of
conventional verbal utterances, such as single words or phrases, to
communicate here and now referents and persons. It is the illocutionary phase and those forms of behavior that are especially critical
to the study of intentional behavior and early language acquisition.
The acquisition of behavior depicted in substage 4, or coordination
of secondary circular reactions (combined use of previously acquired
schemes), is depicted by Piaget as the onset of intentional behavior.

How does one, then, operationally determine that an infant "has the desire" to do something or that the infant in fact is communicating intention? The role of context in the study of infant communication is a first means of describing a specific behavior as having purpose. A second means is to regard the parent and infant's behavior as one set of interactions and use not only the infant's behavior but the parent's initiations and responses in defining the communicative act. These are two means probably most used in current practice today, supported through videotaped data collection of interaction patterns of parent-infant dyads.

THE PRAGMATIC AND SOCIAL PERSPECTIVE

The pragmatic approach to language refers to the central role of context in both the acquisition of infant communicative behavior and in subsequent language use. The recent pragmatic focus on the social bases of language has redirected research and speech/language therapy to a study of meaning within its contextual framework. Bates (1976) has defined this pragmatics approach as a study of "the rules governing the use of language in context" (p. 420). A brief introduction to the development of this approach illustrates the influence of Piagetian theory on the study of language, an aspect evident within the pragmatics literature (Bates, 1976; Bowerman, 1978; Dunst, 1978; Morehead and Morehead, 1974; Rees, 1978). Also significant to us, although not addressed within the pragmatics research, is the concept of functional reinforcement and, more importantly, the role of reinforcement theory in language intervention for the atypical infant. It is within this framework of underlying cognitive and reinforcement theories that we wish to expand the pragmatics approach in respect to the intervention needs of infants.

The semantic-based approaches of language, developed in the late 1960s and early 1970s, rejected Chomsky's innatist views toward language and its syntactic base by attributing cognitive and social environmental factors to the development of word meaning. Empirical studies supporting the constancy of semantic meaning across diverse languages (Bowerman, 1973a, 1973b; Brown, 1973; Schlesinger, 1974; Slobin, 1970) and semantic case relations among varied syntactic structures (Fillmore, 1968; Ingram, 1971) led to an emphasis on early word meaning and a semantic model of language development. The relationship of early cognitive development to language meaning was introduced within the semantic model by such researchers as Schlesinger (1971) and Sinclair (1971). The semantic literature, however, focused on language development at the two-word level of semantic relations generally emerging at 24 months, precluding any regard of infant language behavior. Antinucci and Parisi (1973, 1975) initiated the study of language prior to the 2-year level through their concept of "deep structure trees." This model was based on the study of early word meaning within the infant's single-word productions in order to capture the intent of an utterance. For the first time in language research, social nonverbal aspects of context were addressed surrounding the first verbal forms at the 10- to 12-month age level. This essentially is the basis for the pragmatics movement—the study of actual utterances as they are used in context.

There have been various approaches to language acquisition and use in context, but certainly the rebirth of the topic was predicated on the extensive review of language provided by Bloom and Lahey (1978). Bloom (1973, 1974) was among the first to challenge the linguistic models that had dominated the field of language research for a decade, which were based on the mentalistic syntactic structure approach espoused by Chomsky and others. Bloom demonstrated that any given utterance used by a young child could not be interpreted by either its structure or its specific verbal content, but rather through the intersection of the spoken content, and the context in which the utterance was used. Her model of language development (1973) divides language into three dimensions: content, form, and use. This model, based indirectly on Piagetian theory, emphasizes the child's development of sensorimotor schemes in relation to objects as the bases for subsequent development of content or meaning. Thus, these earlier interactions with the environment are the foundation for language content, whereas form describes the means in which it is expressed, as in gesture, vocalization, or verbalizations. Use, or the functions of language in social context, is the basis for pragmatics.

Bloom's position acknowledges the importance of early interactions with the environment, both with objects and people, and establishes the active characteristics of that interaction as the foundation for later language. Others have supported this model by studying the child's early prelinguistic behavior, both in actions toward objects and social vocal/gestural responses in relation to people (Morehead and Morehead, 1974). Whereas the child's action schemes upon objects may be the basis for Bloom's dimension of language content, Bates (1976) identifies the social interaction, or action upon social agents in the environment, as the basis for language use.

Halliday (1975), in his study of the prelinguistic verbal and gestural behavior of his son, Nigel, during the first 2 years, demonstrated the significance of contextual analyses in defining early communicative intent. He called his contextual approach "socio-semiotics" to signify the social interactive nature of initial language use by young children. This approach has also been used in a concurrent set of literature, that of parent-infant interaction research, which analyzes prelinguistic behavior in both the normal developing and the atypical infant within the dyadic context. Bruner (1975) has noted that the shared action experiences of mother-infant dyads during the prelinguistic period are the primary bases for language. He acknowledges cognitive bases of this early behavior in respect to reciprocal, or give-take interaction: ". . . cognitive development before the use of speech is considered the major source of continuity between prespeech communication and language" (p. 3). Bruner also acknowledges the social components, or directive function, of communication developed during the sensorimotor period. The earliest interactions between parent and child include joint action and attention toward objects which are prerequisite to later joint referencing and subsequent object naming. As early as 3 months the infant will follow the line of the mother's gaze, resulting in the shared attention toward objects. It is this give-take behavior, or early synchronous communicative games, that led Bruner (1973, 1975), Condon and Sander (1974), Lewis (1977), Lewis and Brooks-Gunn (1979), and others to emphasize the early social bases of later language use. In addition, Sugarman (1973) describes the early cognitive-social aspects of parent-infant interaction as an elaborate system for socialization later in life.

Bates et al. (1979) describe the protoimperative that involves the use of a social agent in order to overcome the limited physical abilities of the young child in an effort to achieve a nonsocial outcome. For example, an infant sees and wants a cookie that is on a low table. The infant moves to the table, reaches, fails to touch the cookie, moves to another position, reaches, and fails again. By then turning in the direction of a social agent and emitting particular vocal productions while simultaneously producing some of the actions necessary to acquire the cookie (i.e., reaching toward it), the infant can sometimes receive assistance from an adult and obtain the goal. Bates views this as a process similar to that used by the infant who obtains a rake of some sort as a tool or intermediary, and thereby pulls the cookie into reach. For this reason, she acknowledges the similarity of developmental process between tool use at the cognitive level of coordination of schemes with the use of social communication as a tool.

In the opposite direction, Bates has recognized that imitation can be a productive means for helping the child become more efficient in the communicative process. For example, in the situation above, the adult would have a high probability of saying, "Oh! You want a cookie! Can you say cookie?" If the child imitates without undue hesitation, the adult may go on to say, "Say 'want cookie,'" and thereby help the child expand the utterance toward even greater efficiency. Of this process, Bates says, ". . . imitation permits the reproduction of arbitrarily linked or poorly understood relations." She adds the following to this:

> This does not mean, however, that imitation involves no analysis. There are at least two levels of analysis required for imitation to take place:
>
> a. First, the "selection of models" is an active process, one that is almost always initiated by the organism rather than the human model. Like the selection of symbols, the selection of objective vehicles for imitation depends much more on the internal stage of the knower than on the properties of the environment. Uzgiris and Hunt (1975) stress the difficulty of eliciting imitation if the child is not "in the mood."
>
> b. Second, the "creation of the match" (or partial match) between the objective and the subjective vehicle is certainly a process requiring some very sophisticated perceptual-motor analysis. We have evidence that the child is carrying out such an analysis from the gradual selection of certain properties or features of the model for his first approximation in matching, the correction procedures he employs in perfecting his match, the sequence in which the features are selected.
>
> In short, the study of imitation does not signal a return to Behaviorism, nor to any other empiricist theory of knowledge. A good theory of imitation will be crucial to any complete, rationalist account of human cognitive development. . . . The capacities underlying imitation are clearly part of our innate apparatus for the acquisition of culture (Bates, et al., 1979, pp. 332–333).

As we have stated, the term *intention* is continually used as a central theme in descriptions of early communicative behavior such as that written by Bates. We, too, have identified the emergence of intention to be a critical component of language acquisition, but are cautious in our account of its development. To view intention as a "mental act" or internal process places the action in unobservable neural organizations rather than as a behavior occurring in direct relationship with external environmental events (Skinner, 1957).

When dealing with Piagetian terminology, psychologists and teachers tend to neglect behavioral terms and rely on descriptions of mental processes. The pragmatics research tends to assume a mentalistic view commensurate with Piagetian theory of the "mind." As interventionists who believe that behavioral repertoires can be taught—and intelligence in fact can be modified—we must use the cognitive developmental progression as content of instruction within a framework where the history of environmental control and our systematic engineering of that environment are part of the construct "intention" (Bricker et al., 1981). Robinson and Robinson (1978) have noted that nearly every component of Piagetian sensorimotor development can be defined in behavioral terminology, and more importantly, is modifiable through contingency management strategies.

However, we can address the early social functions of language within Piagetian sensorimotor development by turning away from the mentalistic view of intention and toward that of functional reinforcement. The literature generally assumes intentional behavior to emerge upon use of coordinated secondary schemes when previously acquired action schemes are used in new combinations in order to obtain a goal (Levin, 1982). We borrow Bates' concepts of the protoimperative and protodeclarative functions within our definition to include the use of objects and social agents as tools to obtain goals. The goal must be preexisting and be reliably identifiable by two or more observers, and the actions of the infant must be directed away from that goal in order to obtain the tools (object or social) necessary for the chained means-end sequence, and return to the goal. Two alternative forms of behavior may result at the end of the chain. First, the infant may complete the chain and not obtain his/her goal. Here, the act has been under the control of the means, and the act itself has been reinforcing to the infant. Our second result is that the infant obtains his/her goal and, upon a set of similar antecedent events, will again complete the chain and obtain the goal. This is essentially the definition of functional reinforcement. Motivation is thus defined by examining the consequences of an action. Bricker and Campbell's (1978) description of the "is-does language of reinforcement" addresses this issue:

> . . . a consequence is reinforcing to a given child when and only when it has the desired effect of improving the child's motivation to learn or to continue to respond correctly . . . A consequence IS what consequence DOES to a child's motivation (p. 12).

Halliday (1975) supports this view in his analysis of social intentional development:

> The child knows what language is because he knows what language does. The determining elements in the young child's experience are the successful demands on language that he himself has made, the particular needs that have been satisfied by language for him. He has used language in many ways—for the satisfaction of material and intellectual needs, for the mediation of personal relationships, the expression of feelings and so on. Language in all these uses has come within his own direct experience and because of this, he is subconsciously aware that language has many functions that affect him personally. Language is, for the child, a rich and adaptable instrument for his realization of his intentions; there is hardly any limit to what he can do with it (p. 55).

The pragmatics approach regards the earliest interactions with social agents, from birth, as critical to the further development of intention. The concept of intention can be examined in the pragmatic literature through its various accounts of the "social functions of language," as provided by Dore (1977), Halliday (1975), and Rees (1978).

The most widely regarded concept of social functions is that developed by Halliday in the observations of his son. He notes the first model or function of language to be the instrumental. This serves as a means to "get things done" or as the "I want" function. Here the infant satisfies basic material needs through action schemes, vocalizations and gestures, and, later, words. An example may be that of an infant vocalizing to gain his/her mother's attention, and in turn, receiving more food. The point that must be made here is that with this and all other language functions, the infant's earliest behavioral forms are shaped by the caregiver and thus develop a purpose. An infant may initially cry, and this behavior is typically consequated by being fondled or fed. The behavior is a primary circular reaction (substage 1) or under the control of the consequence: I cry, I get picked up. Upon repetition and variations, the infant may vocalize rather loudly (i.e., screaming) and be picked up immediately, yet in contrast, be vocalizing softly in the form of vocal play (i.e., cooing) and be consequated by the mother softly cooing back. This leads to secondary circular behavior, or substage 2, where the infant's behavior shifts under the control of the antecedent conditions. It is these early interactions with the environment, shaped through consequences, that form the basis for subsequent communicative functions.

The next function, delineated by Halliday and similar to the instrumental outcome, is the regulatory function. This refers to the use of communication to regulate or control the behavior of others. Again, this is produced by the infant through the form of vocalization movements and gestures and later replaced by more complex forms of conventional language (i.e., words and sentences). Halliday (1975) refers to this development as a function of the environment:

> . . . such general types of regulatory behavior, through repetition and reinforcement, determine the child's specific awareness of language as a means of behavioral control. The child applies this awareness, in his own attempts to control his peers and siblings, and this in turn provides the basis for an essential component in his range of linguistic skills, the language of rules and instructions. Whereas at first he can make only simple unstructured demands, he learns as time goes on to give ordered sequences of instructions, and then progresses to the further stage where he can convert sets of instructions into rules . . . thus his regulatory model of language continues to be elaborated, and his experience of the potentialities of language in this use further increases the value of the model (p. 56).

While there are ten basic functions that enter into adult language, we only describe the first five because of our focus on young atypical children. The first two functions, the instrumental and regulatory, are critical prerequisites for subsequent use of language. They are essentially serving the most basic "performative" functions. The others are also important to the development of social language use. The interactional, or "me and you" function, relates to early social interaction and subsequent development. The personal function, an extension of the interactional, serves the "here I come" function and relationship of self and others (Lewis, 1977; Lewis and Brooks-Gunn, 1979; Lewis and Cherry, 1977). Halliday's fifth function relates to the heuristic role—the use of language to explore reality and gain knowledge through interactions.

Halliday saw evidence of these five functions occurring during the first 18 months of life, with the first four evidenced by 12 months. The primary emphasis should be toward the continual modification of these functions in both content and form, beginning with simple unconventional signals and continuing through the development of symbolic conventional utterances.

However, the critical aspect of the early emergence of language pertains to the relationship between cognitive processes and early language. Our data to date indicate clearly that certain developments are critical before language can be learned even in its most rudimentary form. We have sufficient evidence to indicate that the formation of some secondary schemes and their "intentional" coordinations must be present for language to be learned. These schemes are generally in the domains of special foods, social interactive play with adults, and certain forms of isolated play. Language is generally learned most quickly within these contexts, which preexist as complex forms of nonverbal behavior. From this beginning, language begins to act back on behavior in terms of allowing for the more rapid acquisition of subsequent coordinations of new secondary schemes (Luria, 1981; Vygotsky, 1962).

A MODE OF EARLY INTERVENTION WITH FAMILIES

The basis for a language intervention program centers on the child's parents. This focus is found in our Early Intervention Program, which is being utilized in a cooperative effort by Kent State University and Children's Hospital and Medical Center of Akron. Our intervention system is based on a test-teach format that follows the strong inference model initially proposed by John Platt (1964) and incorporated into the field of special education by Bricker (1976). Specific interventions are based on Bricker's (1981) explication of Constructed Interaction Adaptation Theory (CIAT), which is a synthesis of operant and cognitive positions. Areas of instruction are selected from the Index of Qualification for Specialized Services (Bricker and Campbell, 1980). The index consists of between 12 and 20 dimensions, depending on the level of competence of the children being assessed. Each dimension was selected because of the basic nature of its definition in that each dimension was considered to be a basic prerequisite to all subsequent behavioral development. Thus, vision, hearing, tonicity, and quantity and quality of motor movement are considered to be the most basic levels to be assessed. Such dimensions as motor and verbal imitation, receptive language, expressive language, and the use of coordinated secondary schemes represent the highest levels for the groups being assessed. Not only are these dimensions selected considered to be prerequisite to the usual domains such as fine and gross motor competencies, self-help skills, social development, and the pervasive definition of language, but each also is considered to be modifiable through either instruction or therapy.

Translating Index Scores into Individual Programs

The Index of Qualification for Specialized Services has three subgroups of dimensions that pertain directly to language training. The first is in the domain of motivation and includes consequence preferences, compliance, social responsiveness, and primary circular reactions. Consequence preference can be evaluated by determining the range and type of events that operate to motivate a child.

The dimension of compliance is used to rate degree of resistance or acceptance of instructional routines. A child who scores toward the high (5) end would be one who resists instruction through temper tantrums, crying, "turning off," or "tuning out" instructional attempts. Many of the children who have severe motor disabilities have a striking tendency to wait out situations for long periods of time in a manner that we have come to refer to as learned helplessness (Seligman, 1975). Children toward the one (1) end of the scale are quick to cooperate in instructional activities and perform willingly for periods of 10 to 15 minutes.

Primary circular reactions are basic behavioral responses controlled solely by consequent events and existing for only brief periods of time. They are one of the first indications of infant learning. Primary circular reactions are related to motivation in that the required response is already in the repertoire of the child and only needs to be changed either in terms of rate or probability. Social responsiveness relates to such factors as recognition of parents and friends as differentiated from relative strangers.

The second set of variables relates to cognitive actions and includes motor imitation, secondary circular reactions, and use of coordinated secondary schemes. Scores on these dimensions are taken from the Uzgiris-Hunt Scales (1975) as well as from a set of criterion-referenced measures that are used in the Early Intervention Program. We define secondary circular reactions as preverbal or operative concepts in that the child is under the control of objects or events on a conceptual basis. One example is in functional classification in which spheres are acted upon as balls by being rolled, thrown, bounced, hit, or kicked; hat-like objects are placed on the head; and cup-like objects are brought to the mouth in pretend (or real) drinking. In other words, the properties of the object prime the child to behave toward that object in a particular way and to behave differently in the presence of objects having other properties. In addition, the child must respond to groups of such objects that share certain relevant properties but differ on other nonrelevant properties. This basis for grouping objects is critical to language learning (Bricker, 1976). Investigators have demonstrated that initial verbal concepts could be more rapidly taught if the preverbal secondary circular schemes were used as the targets for the instruction (Guess et al., 1978).

The coordination of secondary schemes is more complex in that a chain cf individual action schemes are used as an intentional means for achieving a given end. For example, a ball as a secondary scheme can be acted upon by throwing, catching, kicking, or bouncing it. However, in a game of kickball, when a child is playing defense (in the field), the schemes that must be used include catching the ball and then throwing it to another person. When the child is playing offense (the side doing the kicking), the goal is to kick the ball and then run to a designated base. All children participate in both sets of schemes, and, to play properly, they must alternate the strategies of catch-throw and kick-run, depending on where they are in the game. Most complex human behavior is of the type involving the coordination of secondary schemes. Important aspects of human language reflect these structures in terms of talking about cause and effect as the product of specific chains of such action schemes (Bricker et al., 1981).

The final set of dimensions on the Index that relate to language are the more obvious ones of oral-motor vocal skill, verbal imitation, receptive and expressive language, and conversational use of language. Oral-motor vocal processes are the most overlooked and underrated aspects of language intervention programs. The ability to coordinate the articulators and to sustain exhaled breath while vocalizing are two of the major language problems of both Down syndrome and cerebral-palsied young children. Early intervention can be done with great success in the oral-motor vocal domain (Bricker and Bricker, 1976), and it must be a primary consideration for all children in the process of attempting to teach them verbal language. The final dimension on this particular scale is conversational use of language. This process is what we define verbal production to be before it can be considered language. A child must be able to talk interactively with an adult or other child about matters that are "not here" or "not now" and be able to do so in a flexible manner before we would attribute language use to the child.

Through the use of these dimensions, one can establish a clear heirarchy of educational objectives. All objectives emphasize active parental involvement.

The conclusion that one reaches using the sources cited in this chapter is that language occurs throughout the daily life of the child and effective interventions occur best during times when the child is most likely to be at home rather than in the therapy room. For this reason, the parents are important partners in all aspects of language training. They must know about the sensorimotor developments on which language seems to rest and should know how to arrange the home environment to facilitate the development of each of these forms of behavior. The parent must also be able to identify the speech sound errors in the expressive language of their child and have a basic ability to change some or all of these faulty productions. Thus, the school and the therapy rooms become only a stage on which the processes of intervention are played for the benefit of the parents.

CONCLUSIONS

The period of sensorimotor development, or the first 2 years of life, represents a time of active exploration and learning. Experiences based upon the infant's earliest interactions with his/her environment are the key to subsequent communicative development. It is not from "within" that the infant learns and grows; it is the interaction with parents and the activities, events, and objects in the environment that serve to facilitate this growth. Communication evolves from the infant's earliest behavior, which, although not intentional, comes to have an effect on the parent and in turn begins to convey "meanings." The reciprocal interaction process between infant and parent is that vehicle from which a communicative system develops.

The available literature supports the significance of the early parent-infant interaction process on development of both a child's cognitive and communication systems. The issues that are most important for early communication programming evolve around these assumptions:

1. Intervention should be targeted toward the parent-infant dyad, not solely the infant. Programming is aimed at developing positive interactive patterns and teaching parents to use their behavior most effectively and to react to their infant's behavior systematically.
2. The infant's earliest behavior is not purposeful; however, it is this nonintentional communication that serves to form later intentional communication. Parents' responses to infant behavior set the base for the infant's differentiated responses, and in turn a communicative system can develop.
3. Sensorimotor, or cognitive, development during infancy is a critical component of infant communication programming. Cognition during this period is the foundation of the child's content for language. Parents must be educated and included in their child's cognitive development in order for this process to be facilitated within the home environment.
4. Pragmatics, or the study of social aspects of language, provide a starting point for communicative development. The use of social context in offering the infant a variety of learning experi-

ences and interpreting/reinforcing the infant's communication is central to the acquisition of a *functional* language system.

Only with and through the parent-infant dyad can we provide the context, content, and functions of communication, and make these truly meaningful for the developing infant. It is the daily life routines of the infant that are most salient for the infant and that are most effective for the development of sensorimotor and pragmatic bases of language.

DEVELOPMENTAL SEQUENCE OF INFANT COMMUNICATION

The following outline provides a general descriptive sequence of early communicative development. It is meant to provide the reader with a cursory overview of the child's social communicative accomplishments during the first 2 years. More in-depth descriptions and discussions may be found in the works of Bates, Halliday, and Lewis as cited in the references.

Birth to Nine Months

Communication is not purposeful, or intentional.
The infant produces signals that may be interpreted by the parents and others as conveying meaning.
The parent assumes communicative intent and begins to respond systematically to the infant's behavior.
Gestures, through grasping, shaking, and waving, are interpreted as communicative signals.
Vocalizations, through cries, fussing, and cooing, are used both in solitary settings and in interaction. Intonational changes begin.

Nine to Fifteen Months

Communication becomes intentional.
The infant uses people as social agents to obtain needs and wants.
Objects become tools to obtain needs.
Gestures, vocalizations, and first words are used as means to obtain ends intentionally as communicative acts.
The infant's communicative functions, according to Halliday's hierarchy (1975), during this period include:

Instrumental   the "I want" function

Regulatory   the "control other's behavior" function
Interactional the "you and me" function
Personal   the "here I am, look at me" function

Communication is not yet truly "conventional"; the infant uses a
variety of signals to convey meaning. These may be similar to
adult communication (waving bye-bye) or not yet conventional
(using a specific sound "uh" to mean "pick me up," "mommy,
I want you," "get me away from him," or "I want to play on the
sofa"). Parents begin to recognize consistent signals as intentional communication.

Sixteen to Twenty-four Months

Communication becomes "conventional."
The infant uses communication to express more complex communicative functions (Halliday, 1975):

1. Heuristic   "Tell me why" function or "What's that?"
2. Imaginative "Let's pretend and play" function
3. Informative "I'll tell you" function

The infant's vocabulary expands dramatically; conventional words
now replace previous signals.
The transition from single words to two-word phrases may begin;
these phrases generally express one meaning or action (e.g.,
"doggie go," "eat cookie," "mommy, up"). The infant now has
the relational meanings expressed within his/her two-word
phrases with such functions as:

Negation   No _____
Rejection   No _____
Possession   My _____
Locative   Here _____
Action   Go _____
Attributes   Big _____
Denial   That not _____
Reoccurrence More _____

Chapter Outline

OVERVIEW: Prelinguistic developmental processes are described. Issues related to facilitating early language development in atypical infants are examined.

I. PATTERNS OF EARLY SOCIAL INTERACTION
The literature on parent-infant social interaction affirms the importance of this early relationship to the infant's development of communication skills.

II. PARENTAL PATTERNS WITH ATYPICAL INFANTS
The effects of an infant's handicapping condition on the parent-child relationship may influence reciprocal interaction and thus, the acquisition of a communicative system for the young infant.

III. PRELINGUISTIC DEVELOPMENT: COGNITION AND LANGUAGE

   A. The relationship between early cognition and language development is presented from two major theoretical perspectives:
      1. Piaget's theory
      2. Vygotsky's theory

   B. A model of the development of intention addresses both cognitive and social prerequisites for language.

IV. THE PRAGMATIC AND SOCIAL PERSPECTIVE

   A. Early interactions with the environment are significant in the infant's development of communication behavior.
   B. Major research, such as the investigations by Bloom, Halliday, and Bates, describe developmental processes. Bloom's model divides language into:
      1. Content—derived from early interactions with the environment.
      2. Form—means by which language is expressed.
      3. Use—function of language in a social context.

V. A MODE OF EARLY INTERVENTION WITH FAMILIES

A language intervention program, a component of the Kent State Early Intervention Program, is based on a test-teach format. The Index of Qualification for Specialized Services is utilized to determine needed areas of instruction. The reciprocal interaction process between infant and parent is that vehicle from which a communicative system develops.

REFERENCES

Ainsworth, M. D. S. The development of infant-mother attachment. In B. M. Caldwell and H. N. Ricciuti (Eds.), *Review of Child Development Research* (Vol. 3). Chicago: University of Chicago Press, 1973.

Als, H. Social interaction: Dynamic matrix for developing behavioral organization. In I. Uzgiris (Ed.), *New Directions for Child Development: Social Interaction and Communication during Infancy*. San Francisco: Jossey-Bass, 1979.

Antinucci, F., and Parisi, D. Early language acquisition: A model and some data. In C. A. Ferguson and D. I. Slobin (Eds.), *Studies of Child Language Development*. New York: Holt, Rinehart and Winston, 1973.

Antinucci, F., and Parisi, D. Early semantic development in child language. In E. Lenneberg and E. Lenneberg (Eds.), *Foundations of Language Development: A Multidisciplinary Approach* (Vol. 1). New York: Academic Press, 1975.

Bates, E. *Language and Context: The Acquisition of Pragmatics*. New York: Academic Press, 1976.

Bates, E., Benigni, L., Bretherton, I., Camaioni, L., and Voterra, V. From gesture to the first word: On cognitive and social prerequisites. In M. Lewis and L. Rosenblum (Eds.), *Interaction, Conversation, and the Development of Language*. New York: Wiley, 1977.

Bates, E., Benigni, L., Bretherton, I., Camaioni, L., and Volterra, V. *The Emergence of Symbols: Cognition and Communications in Infancy*. New York: Academic Press, 1979.

Bates, E., Camaioni, L., and Volterra, V. The acquisition of performatives prior to speech. *Merrill-Palmer Quarterly*, 1975, *21*, 205–226.

Beckwith, L. Caregiver-infant interaction and the development of the high risk infant. In T. D. Tjossem (Ed.), *Intervention Strategies for High Risk Infants and Young Children*. Baltimore: University Park Press, 1976.

Bell, P. J. Characteristics of handicapped infants: A study of the relationship between child characteristics and stress as reported by mothers (Doctoral dissertation, University of North Carolina, 1980). *Dissertation Abstracts International*, 1980, *41*, 4356A–4357A (University Microfilms No. 8104366).

Bell, S. M., and Ainsworth, M. D. S. Infant crying and maternal responsiveness. *Child Development*, 1972, *43*, 1171–1190.

Bloom, L. *One Word at a Time: The Use of Single-word Utterances before Syntax*. The Hague: Mouton, 1973.

Bloom, L. Talking, understanding, and thinking. In R. L. Schiefelbusch and L. Lloyd (Eds.), *Language Perspectives—Acquisition, Retardation, and Intervention*. Baltimore: University Park Press, 1974.

Bloom, L., and Lahey, M. *Language development and language disorders*. New York: Wiley, 1978.

Bowerman, M. *Early Syntactic Development: A Cross-linguistic Study with Special Reference to Finnish*. Cambridge, England: Cambridge University Press, 1973a.

Bowerman, M. Structural relationships in children's utterances: Syntactic or semantic? In T. E. Moore (Ed.), *Cognitive Development and the Acquisition of Language*. New York: Academic Press, 1973b.

Bowerman, M. *Structural Relationships in Children's Utterances: Syntactic Acquisition of Language*. New York: Academic Press, 1973c.

Bowerman, M. Semantic and syntactic development: A review of what, when, and how in language acquisition. In R. Schiefelbusch (Ed.), *Bases of Language Intervention*. Baltimore: University Park Press, 1978.

Bowlby, J. *Attachment and Loss*. New York: Basic Books, 1969.

Brainerd, C. *Piaget's Theory of Intelligence*. Englewood Cliffs, NJ: Prentice-Hall, 1978.

Bricker, W. A. Service of research. In M. A. Thomas (Ed.), *Hey, Don't Forget about Me!* Reston, VA: Council for Exceptional Children, 1976.

Bricker, W. *Constructed Interaction Adaptation Theory*. Unpublished manuscript, Kent, OH: Kent State University, 1981.

Bricker, W. A., and Bricker, D. D. The infant, toddler, and preschool research and intervention project. In T. D. Tjossem (Ed.), *Intervention Strategies for High-Risk Infants and Young Children*. Baltimore: University Park Press, 1976.

Bricker, W. A., and Campbell, P. H. *Motivating Behavioral Change*. Canton, OH: Lincoln Way Special Education Regional Resource Center, 1978.

Bricker, W. A., and Campbell, P. H. Interdisciplinary assessment and programming for multihandicapped students. In W. Sailor, B. Wilcox, and L. Brown (Eds.), *Methods of Instruction for Severely Handicapped Students*. Baltimore: Paul H. Brookes, 1980.

Bricker, W. A., Macke, P. R., Levin, J. A., and Campbell, P. H. The modifiability of intelligent behavior. *Journal of Special Education*, 1981, *15*, 145–163.

Bristol, M. M. Maternal coping with autistic children: Adequacy of interpersonal support and effects of child's characteristics (Doctoral dissertation, University of North Carolina, 1980). *Dissertation Abstracts International*, 1980, *40*, 3943A–3944A (University Microfilms No. 7925890).

Brown, R. *A First Language: The Early Stages*. Cambridge, MA: Harvard University Press, 1973.

Bruner, J. S. Organization of early skilled action. *Child Development*, 1973, *44*, 1–11.

Bruner, J. The ontogenesis of speech acts. *Journal of Child Language*, 1975, *2*, 1–19.

Butterfield, E. C., and Cairns, G. F. The infant's auditory environment. In T. D. Tjossem (Ed.), *Intervention Strategies for High-Risk Infants and Young Children*. Baltimore: University Park Press, 1976.

Chomsky, N. *Aspects of the Theory of Syntax*. Cambridge, MA: MIT Press, 1965.

Clarke-Stewart, K. A. Interactions between mothers and their young children: Characteristics and consequences. *Monographs of the Society for Research in Child Development*, 1973, *38* (6–7, Serial No. 153).

Condon, W. S., and Sander, L. Neonate movement is synchronized with adult speech: Interactional participation and language acquisition. *Science*, 1974, *183*, 99–101.

Cromer, R. Cognitive hypothesis of language acquisition and implications for child language deficiency. In Morehead and Morehead (Eds.), *Normal and Deficient Child Language*. Baltimore: University Park Press, 1976.

Denenberg, V. H., and Thoman, E. B. From animal to infant research. In T. D. Tjossem (Ed.), *Intervention Strategies for High-Risk Infants and Young Children*. Baltimore: University Park Press, 1976.

Dore, J. "Oh them sheriff": A pragmatic analysis of children's responses to questions. In S. Ervin-Tripp and C. Mitchell-Kernan (Eds.), *Child Discourse*. New York: Academic Press, 1977.

Dunst, C. J. A cognitive-social approach for assessment of early nonverbal communicative behavior. *Journal of Childhood Communication Disorders*, 1978, *2*, 110–123.

Eimas, P. D. Linguistic processing of speech by young infants. In R. L. Schiefelbusch and L. L. Lloyd (Eds.), *Language Perspectives—Acquisition, Retardation, and Intervention*. Baltimore: University Park Press, 1974.

Fillmore, C. J. The case for case. In E. Bach and R. T. Harms (Eds.), *Universals in Linguistic Theory*. New York: Holt, Rinehart & Winston, 1968.

Fraiberg, S., Smith, M., and Adelson, M. A. An educational program for blind infants. *Journal of Special Education*, 1969, *3*, 121–139.

Guess, D., Keogh, W., and Sailor, W. Generalization of speech and language behavior. In R. L. Schiefelbusch (Ed.), *Bases of Language Intervention*. Baltimore: University Park Press, 1978.

Halliday, M. Learning how to mean. In E. Lenneberg and E. Lenneberg (Eds.), *Foundations of Language Development: A Multidisciplinary Approach* (Vol. 1). New York: Academic Press, 1975.

Hayden, A. H. Handicapped children, birth to age 3. *Exceptional Children*, 1979, *45*, 510–516.

Hayden, A. H., and Haring, N. G. Early intervention for high risk infants and young children: Programs for Down's syndrome children. In T. D. Tjossem (Ed.), *Intervention Strategies for High-Risk Infants and Young Children*. Baltimore: University Park Press, 1976.

Ingram, D. Transitivity in child language. *Language*, 1971, *47*, 888–909.

Kaye, K., and Brazelton, T. B. *Mother-infant Interaction in the Organization of Sucking.* Paper presented at the Society for Research in Child Development, Minneapolis, 1971.

Leonard, L. B. Cognitive factors in early linguistic development. In R. L. Schiefelbusch (Ed.), *Bases of Language Intervention*. Baltimore: University Park Press, 1978.

Leonard, M. F., Rhymes, J. P., and Solnit, A. J. Failure to thrive in infants. *American Journal of Diseases of Children*, 1966, *111*, 600–612.

Levin, J. A. *The Acquisition of Intentional Communication in Young Children with Down syndrome through Maternal Interaction.* Unpublished doctoral dissertation, Kent, OH: Kent State University 1982.

Lewis, M. *The Infant and Its Caregiver: The Role of Contingency.* Paper presented at a Conference of Infant Intervention Programs, Milwaukee, June, 1977.

Lewis, M., and Brooks-Gunn, J. Toward a theory of social cognition: The development of self. In I. C. Uzgiris (Ed.), *Social Interaction and Communication during Infancy*. San Francisco: Jossey-Bass, 1979.

Lewis, M., and Cherry, L. Social behavior and language acquisition. In M. Lewis and L. Rosenblum (Eds.), *Interaction, Conservation, and the Development of Language: The Origins of Behavior* (Vol. 5). New York: Wiley, 1977.

Lewis, M., and Rosenblum, L. (Eds.). *The Effect of the Infant on Its Caregiver.* New York: Wiley, 1974.

Lock, A. *The Guided Reinvention of Language*. London: Academic Press, 1980.

Luria, A. R. *Language and Cognition*. New York: Wiley, 1981.

Milenkovic, M. F., and Uzgiris, I. C. The mother-infant communication system. In I. Uzgiris (Ed.), *New Directions in Child Development, Social Interaction, and Communication during Infancy.* San Francisco: Jossey-Bass, 1979.

Miller, J. F., Chapman, R. S., Branston, M. B., and Reichle, J. Language comprehension in sensorimotor stages 5 and 6. *Journal of Speech and Hearing Research,* 1980, *23,* 284–311.

Moerk, E. *Pragmatic and Semantic Aspects of Early Language Development.* Baltimore: University Park Press, 1977.

Morehead, D., and Morehead, A. From signal to sign: A Piagetian view of thought and language during the first two years. In R. Schiefelbusch and L. Lloyd (Eds.), *Language Perspectives—Acquisition, Retardation, and Intervention.* Baltimore: University Park Press, 1974.

Osofsky, J. D., and Connors, K. Mother-infant interaction: An integrative view of a complex system. In J. D. Osofsky (Ed.), *Handbook of Infant Development.* New York: Wiley, 1979.

Piaget, J. *The Construction of Reality in the Child.* New York: Basic Books, 1954.

Piaget, J. *The Origins of Intelligence in Children.* New York: International Universities Press, 1952.

Piaget, J. *Play, Dreams and Imitation in Childhood.* New York: Norton, 1962.

Piaget, J. The psychogenesis of knowledge and its epistemological significance. In M. Piattelli-Palmarini (Ed.), *Language and Learning: The Debate between Jean Piaget and Noam Chomsky.* Cambridge, MA: Harvard University Press, 1980.

Platt, J. R. Strong inference. *Science,* 1964, *146,* 36–42.

Ramey, C. T., Beckman-Bell, P., and Gowen, J. W. Infant characteristics and infant-caregiver interactions. In J. J. Gallagher (Ed.), *New Directions for Exceptional Children: Parents and Families of Handicapped Children.* San Francisco: Jossey-Bass, 1980.

Rees, N. Pragmatics of language. In R. L. Schiefelbusch (Ed.), *Bases of Language Intervention.* Baltimore: University Park Press, 1978.

Rheingold, H., Gewirtz, J., and Ross H. Social conditioning of vocalization in the infant. *Journal of Comparative and Physiological Psychology,* 1959, *52,* 68–73.

Rimland, B. *Infantile Autism.* New York: Appleton-Century-Crofts, 1964.

Robinson, C., and Robinson, J. H. Sensorimotor function and cognitive development. In M. Snell (Ed.), *Systematic Instruction of the Moderately and Severely Handicapped.* Columbus, OH: Charles E. Merrill, 1978.

Robinson, N. M., and Robinson, H. B. *The Mentally Retarded Child* (2nd ed.). New York: McGraw-Hill, 1976.

Schlesinger, I. M. The production of utterances and language acquisition. In D. I. Slobin (Ed.), *The Ontogenesis of Grammar.* New York: Academic Press, 1971.

Schlesinger, I. M. Relational concepts underlying language. In R. L. Schiefelbush and L. L. Lloyd (Eds.), *Language Perspectives—Acquisition, Retardation, and Intervention.* Baltimore: University Park Press, 1974.

Seligman, M. E. *Helplessness: On Depression, Death and Development.* San Francisco: W. H. Freeman, 1975.

Sherlock, R. Selective non-treatment of newborns. *Journal of Medical Ethics,* 1979, *5,* 139–140.

Sinclair–de Zwart, H. Sensorimotor action patterns as a condition for the acquisition of syntax. In R. Huxley and E. Ingram (Eds.), *Language Acquisition: Models and Methods*. New York: Academic Press, 1971.

Skinner, B. F. *Verbal Behavior*. New York: Appleton-Century-Crofts, 1957.

Slobin, D. I. Universals of grammatical development in children. In G. B. Flores d'Arcais and W. J. M. Levelt (Eds.), *Advances in Psycholinguistics*. Amsterdam, Holland: North-Holland Publishing Co., 1970.

Steckol, K. F., and Leonard, L. B. Sensorimotor development and the use of prelinguistic performatives. *Journal of Speech and Hearing Research*, 1981, *24*, 262–269.

Stern, D., Beebe, B., Jaffe, J., and Bennett, S. The infant's stimulus word during social interaction. In H. R. Schaffer (Ed.), *Studies in Mother-infant Interaction*. New York: Wiley, 1977.

Stone, N. W., and Chesney, B. H. Attachment behaviors in handicapped infants. *Mental Retardation*, 1978, *16*, 8–12.

Sugarman, S. *Description of Communicative Development in the Prelanguage Child*. Unpublished master's thesis, Amherst, MA: Hampshire College, 1973.

Thoman, E. B., Leiderman, P. H., and Olson, J. P. Neonate-mother interaction during breast feeding. *Developmental Psychology*, 1972, *6*, 110–118.

Thoman, E. B., Turner, A. M., Leiderman, P. H., and Barnett, C. R. Neonate-mother interaction: Effects of parity on feeding behavior. *Child Development*, 1970, *41*, 1103–1111.

Turnure, C. Response to voice of mother and stranger by babies in the first year. *Developmental Psychology*, 1971, *4*, 182–190.

Uzgiris, I., and Hunt, J. McV. *Assessment in Infancy: Ordinal Scales of Psychological Development*. Urbana: University of Illinois Press, 1975.

Vygotsky, L. S. *Thought and Language*. (E. Hanfmann, trans.). Cambridge, MA: MIT Press, 1962.

Wolfensberger, W. *The Principle of Normalization in Human Services*. Toronto: National Institute of Mental Retardation, 1972.

Wolfensberger, W. A call to wake up to the beginning of a new wave of "euthanasia" of severely impaired people. *Education and Training of the Mentally Retarded*, 1980, *15*, 171–173.

Wolff, P. H. The natural history of crying and other vocalizations in early infancy. In B. M. Foss (Ed.), *Determinants of Infant Behavior IV*. London: Methuen, 1969.

Wolff, P. H. Mother-infant relations at birth. In J. G. Howells (Ed.), *Modern Perspectives in International Child Psychiatry*. New York: Brunner/Mazel, 1971.

Yarrow, L. J., Goodwin, M. S., Manheimer, H., & Milowe, I. D. Infancy experiences and cognitive and personality development at ten years. In L. J. Stone, H. T. Smith, and L. B. Murphy (Eds.), *The Competent Infant: Research and Commentary*. New York: Basic Books, 1973.

CHAPTER 10
Motor Development
Linda Fetters

THE IMPORTANCE OF MOTOR DEVELOPMENT

Each of us has been amused by the struggling infant who, with legs spread, huffs and puffs to a standing position, only to teeter momentarily, topple over, and begin the arduous process of standing all over again. The months preceding this event have been filled with similar struggles. Rolling, sitting, and crawling have all been mastered in the process of developing independent movement. These struggles dominate infancy. Movement and postural control enable the infant to explore and gain mastery over the environment. Playing with toys, feeding, and even the ability to speak all require movement. The Swiss developmental psychologist Jean Piaget described infancy as a time when sensorimotor abilities represent the very origins of intelligence. According to Piaget (1952), the infant's ability to physically manipulate and explore the environment provides the experience necessary to acquire knowledge about how the world operates. For example, the 3-month-old infant brings a brightly colored toy to his/her face for visual and oral exploration. In this way, the properties of the object can be seen and felt. The texture, temperature, taste, and size of the object can all be explored through the movement pattern of reach, grasp, and bring to the face. The older infant can bang, shake, and drop objects. The properties of the object and the consequences of acting on that object are experienced through movement. Although the relationship of cognition and motor abilities remains controversial (Kagan, 1979; Kopp, 1974), infancy is the time when developing motor abilities pervade every aspect of development.

Before the middle of the second year, infants communicate primarily with movement. Pointing to the refrigerator, turning away from food, or thrusting both arms in the air indicates "I'm hungry," "I'm full," or "pick me up" for the nonverbal infant. Movement be-

comes the means for communication, and parents begin to understand their infant's needs and desires by observing and interpreting
actions.

The development of independent movement frees parents from
carrying, physically supporting, or wheeling their infant. The crawling infant can move out into the world to explore under the table
and behind the chair. The walking toddler can choose to play downstairs or climb the stairs to his/her room. Choosing is an important
aspect of motor development. As independent movement is acquired, choices present themselves. Exercising choices informs the
infant that he/she has control over at least some aspects of the world.

Infants with motor problems have difficulty acquiring these
same satisfying experiences. They may need more help for a longer
time than normal infants. The experiences gained by their motorically competent peers may need to be provided for them. The essence
of intervention programs for infants with motor problems includes
not only helping the infant acquire independent movement, but
teaching parents how to provide experience for their infant that a
motorically normal infant could gain independently. For example,
the infant who is not able to reach and grasp an object to bring to
his/her face may need work on developing these abilities through
specific exercises. Placing objects in the infant's hand and mouth
and holding them for visual exploration ensures the infant of experience before the motor control necessary for this ability is available. Parents can provide experience for their infant that simultaneously facilitates normal motor and cognitive development.

Parents may need to carry or physically support the infant with
motor problems for a longer period of time than is necessary for the
normal infant. This means parents continue to make the choices
about when and how movement takes place. Faced with this inability
to make choices, the infant with motor problems may attempt to exert
control over the environment in other ways. Fussing, crying, and
temper tantrums may all produce responses from parents giving the
infant control of others even though the interactions are negative.
This negative preverbal communication between parent and child
may replace the more positive interaction possible with more independent movement. The child who cannot reach out to parents
may not be picked up as often. The cerebral-palsied child who
stiffens when held may not be able to communicate how much he/she
wants to be held. The message the parents receive is "Put me down"
or "Don't cuddle me," which may be the opposite of the child's
intention. Unable to make specific desires and needs known, the

child with motor handicaps has many activities done *to* him rather than *with* him. Parental praise, which flows spontaneously in acknowledgment of new motor achievements, may not occur for the child incapable of these achievements.

THE IMPORTANCE OF KNOWLEDGE OF MOTOR DEVELOPMENT

Motor abilities affect all aspects of infant development. Consequently, it is essential for professionals working with infants to have knowledge of normal motor development. The quality of movement or the age of achieving certain motor skills may vary extensively among infants. A thorough understanding of motor development is needed to distinguish normal variation in ability or style from abnormal development. Physical and occupational therapists are educated to analyze movement. They can discern normal from abnormal development and develop programs to promote normal sensorimotor abilities. In addition, therapists can assist other members of an interdisciplinary team in assessing the contribution of the motor problem to other aspects of development. For example, the psychologist testing infants must realize that psychomotor assessments like the Bayley Scales of Infant Development (Bayley; 1969) are potentially biased in that they require precise fine motor control. Passing an item such as putting pegs in a board may be more a test of motor coordination than cognitive ability. Fetters (1981) found that infants with motor problems frequently failed the classic test for object permanence, which requires the motor response of searching for a hidden object under a cloth. When these same infants were tested with an alternative method requiring only a visual search response, they had age appropriate development of this concept. Thus, infants with potentially normal mental skills may seem delayed because of motor problems.

The following sections of this chapter describe the sequence of normal motor development. The relationship of reflexes to movement is stressed. The reader should gain a basic understanding of how the ability to move changes as the infant matures and what accounts for these changes. The remainder of the chapter describes motor abilities of atypical infants, some selected assessment tools and the currently used therapeutic approaches for intervention. The chapter concludes with a review of research on the efficacy of motor intervention and suggestions for future work.

NORMAL MOTOR DEVELOPMENT

Principles of Motor Development

Motor development progresses in a cephalocaudal (head to toe) and proximal-distal (from close to the midline of the body to away from midline) direction. For example, the infant gains head control before trunk control and arm control before hand control. Although this sequence is generally followed, all parts of the body develop simultaneously. Complete control tends to occur first in proximal parts; however, distal parts begin development before full proximal control is evident.

Control of the body occurs first in the horizontal and then the vertical position. Infants master head control on their stomachs (prone) and backs (supine). Gradually, control is evident in the more upright (vertical) positions of sitting and standing. There is a strong, inherent urge for the infant to be upright. Anyone who has attempted to diaper an 8 month old supine infant has confronted this urgency as the baby struggles to be upright. This urgency represents the infant's struggle against the forces of gravity, a struggle that occurs automatically with the development of the reflexive abilities described in the following section.

Reflexive Development

Gross Motor Development   All volitional movements have as their substrata an elaborate mechanism of reflex action. This reflex mechanism develops automatically during infancy, and is probably preprogrammed in the central nervous system (Evarts et al., 1971). Preprogrammed implies that the reflex mechanism for movement is transmitted genetically, is shared by the human species, and is elaborated with maturation of the central nervous system. Most of our basic motor patterns are preprogrammed and controlled by mechanisms referred to as central programs. Motor abilities develop as a result of the interaction between innate abilities controlled by central programs and experience gained in the environment. For example, recent research suggests that infants even in the first days of life reach out to objects they are viewing (Bower, 1974; Hofsten, 1979). Because this ability occurs soon after birth, it is thought to be centrally programmed. This ballistic newborn pattern, however, is modified and elaborated with experience as the infant matures.

Central programs govern the development of the reflex mechanism that underlies all movement. This mechanism includes the *primary reflexes* of the newborn, such as sucking, and the later acquired postural responses, such as thrusting the hands out to prevent a fall. Because infants with motor problems frequently have abnormal reflexive development, it is essential to appreciate the relationship of reflexes to motor development.

Primary Reflexes   A reflex may be defined as a predictable motor response that follows some specific sensory input. The motor response is predictable in a general sense, but not stereotyped. Newborn reflexes are referred to as primary or primitive reflexes. The primary reflexes that are most important for motor development are included in Table 10.1.

Controversy exists as to the significance of primary reflexes in human development. There are currently at least three interpretations of these reflexes. First, primary reflexes are viewed as behaviors that link humans to their animal ancestors. The phrase "ontogeny recapitulates phylogeny" suggests that human development follows the course of animal-human evolution. Behaviors of the immature human are seen as vestiges of animal heredity. Phylogenetically older behaviors are replaced by newer abilities as the infant matures. According to this interpretation, primary reflexes are integrated by the central nervous system because they have lost functional significance through evolution.

An alternative to this view suggests that because primary reflexes have remained through evolution, they must serve some purpose in human development. Proponents of the view that human development is a continuous process suggest that infant behaviors are antecedents to behaviors of the older child and adult. Lipsitt (1976) suggests that primary reflexes provide the substrata for function that may not be obvious until much later in development. For example, primary stepping (see Table 10.1) is regarded as the reflexive antecedent to the walking pattern developed by the older infant. In order to demonstrate this developmental link, Zelazo and Kolb (1972) designed an experiment in which parents attempted to maintain primary stepping past the time of normal inhibition by practicing the reflex with their infants. The group of infants receiving practice not only maintained primary walking when it should have been inhibited, they also walked sooner than the unpracticed group. Zelazo and Kolb suggest that these results demonstrate continuity in human development from primary reflexes to functional movement. Oppenheim (1981) offers an alternative interpretation of these results and the third interpretation of the role of primary reflexes. He suggests that although maintenance of a reflex like primary stepping is possible, it does not imply, in a teleological sense, that this

Table 10.1. Primitive reflexes related to gross motor skills

Reflex	Starting position	Stimulus	Response	Integration	Retention
Moro	Infant upright or semi-upright	Head is dropped back suddenly giving a quick stretch to the anterior neck muscles (flexors)	First, the infant extends the arms up and out with hands open, infant cries; second, arms cross chest in an embrace; legs extend	By 6 months	Interferes with head control; sitting balance. If arms and legs extend when the head drops, it is difficult to gain control of the body
Asymmetrical tonic neck reflex (ATNR)	Infant supine	Passive, infant's head turned 90° to each side. Active, examiner elicits head turning with visual pursuit. Both stimuli stretch the neck musculature	Fencing posture; face side, arm and leg extend; occipital side, arm and leg flex	By 6 months	Interferes with hand to mouth, hands together, crossing midline of the body and rolling. Position of the head affects muscle tone in arms and legs
Traction	Infant supine	Infant pulled to sitting forearms; stimulus is stretch to shoulder muscles	Flexion of arm shoulder, hand, and whole body follows	By 5 months	Difficulty with reach and grasp

Reflex	Position	Stimulus	Response	Integration	Significance
Neck righting	Infant supine, head in middle	Turn head 90° to each side	Whole body rolls to side, head is turned toward body; log rolling rather than segmental	By 5 months	Interferes with ability to move upper and lower body separately
Palmer grasp should appear with traction	Infant supine	Pressure in palm from ulnar side	All fingers flex around stimulus	By 5 months	Fisted hands and a lack of coordinated grasp and release
Plantar grasp	Infant supine	Pressure on ball of foot at base of toes	All toes flex around stimulus	By time of full weightbearing	Interferes with standing balance
Symmetrical tonic neck reflex (STNR)[a]	Prone or hands and feet	Flexion and extension of head and neck	Head flexed, arms flex, and legs extend; head extended, arms extend and legs flex	Appears at 6 months integrated by 12 months	All movements may be affected if they are initiated with head movements
Primary stepping	Infant held standing	Move infant forward	Rhythmical walking with exaggerated flexion of legs and feet	By 2 months	Unclear

[a] Note: The STNR is not present in the newborn; it appears later. However, it is considered a primitive reflex because it is modified and incorporated into controlled movement.

reflex is the antecedent to human walking. Primary stepping is normally not practiced, and it disappears long before later walking occurs. If the two behaviors were tightly linked, this disappearance would not be likely. Oppenheim (1981) suggests that primary reflexes are examples of what he terms "ontogenetic adaptations" (p. 74). These reflexes are functional for the fetus and newborn for brief periods during development. They then become integrated by the central nervous system as their usefulness wanes. He suggests that primary stepping is useful for the fetus to "walk" into the head down position in utero (in the uterus) in preparation for birth. Because the reflex loses its functional significance after this achievement, it is soon integrated by the newborn and disappears. Oppenheim suggests that development may be characterized by these discontinuous events as well as by continuous abilities. Behavior seen during infancy may be continuously elaborated through childhood or it may serve a purpose and then disappear.

Infants with motor problems may retain primitive reflexes past the normal time of integration. Some infants use their reflexes adaptively for movement; however, frequently this abnormal retention interferes with normal movement. For example, rolling will be difficult for the infant with an obligatory asymmetrical tonic neck reflex (ATNR) (see Table 10.1). Obligatory implies that every time an infant's head is turned, the arm and leg on the face side extend. This extension prevents rolling. Even an increased tendency to this reflex may interfere with rolling. The infant may extend his/her arm at the initiation of the roll, but be unable to flex it close to the body in order to complete the roll. In the former case, movement is prevented, in the latter, the speed and quality of the movement are affected. In both cases integration of the ATNR is necessary for normal movement.

Postural Responses   In addition to the integration of primitive reflexes, the development of *postural responses* is necessary for normal movement. Postural responses include righting, equilibrium, and protective reactions. These reactions maintain the head in an upright position and ensure alignment of body parts for normal movement.

Vestibular and optical righting reactions maintain the head in an upright position. Both reactions are elicited as the head is displaced, as in bending forward or walking. If a seated person is pushed forward or to the side, the person's head is automatically maintained in an upright position and does not follow the trunk. The vestibular apparatus housed in the inner ear is sensitive to head displacement; therefore, as the person is pushed forward, a portion of the vestibular apparatus relays information about head position to networks in the brain that control muscles in the head and neck (Wilson and Peterson, 1978). Visual information is used in conjunction with vestibular input to monitor and control head position. Information from the eyes is also relayed to the brain with subsequent influence on the contraction of head and neck muscles (Cohen, 1974). Righting reactions mature first in the forward and backward direction and then from side to side.

Body righting reactions ensure alignment of body parts for normal movement. For example, if a newborn's head is rotated to the side, the body follows automatically and the infant rolls as a unit (neck righting). This is often referred to as log rolling because the infant moves as a whole. Later, as the body righting reactions develop, the infant's head rotates and there is a latency before the upper trunk and then the pelvis rotate. This ability to move the body segmentally allows the infant to roll. The body righting reactions, which act to allow segmental rolling, are elicited by the stretch placed on muscles as the head rotates on the shoulders and the shoulders on the pelvis (Barnes et al., 1979; Magnus, 1926; Twitchell, 1965).

Equilibrium responses are also automatic and assist us in maintaining an upright position against the forces of gravity. Again, if a seated person is tipped to the side, not only will the head right, but the trunk will curve with the shoulder moving toward the displacing force. This curve of the trunk is an equilibrium or tilt reaction (Milani-Comparetti and Giodoni, 1967). If shifting is continued, the arm and leg will extend in order to provide more body mass against falling. The participation of trunk and limbs is a complete equilibrium reaction. Equilibrium responses are elicited when the vestibular apparatus is stimulated. The appropriate muscles are activated via the vestibular nuclei in the brain, which in turn activate the trunk and limbs to prevent falling (Martin, 1967).

Equilibrium responses develop sequentially. They first appear in the prone and supine positions followed by sitting, hands and knees position, and standing. The responses are elicited most easily by placing a person on a movable surface and slowly tipping the surface, although in reality they function when the body is moving and the supporting surface is stationary.

If a person is rapidly tilted from a sitting or standing position, *protective* reactions are elicited from the arms. The arms are thrust into space whenever the displacing force is too rapid or too forceful for the body to be controlled by righting or equilibrium responses. Protective reactions develop first in the forward direction, followed by sideways and finally backward. Input through vestibular, joint, and muscle (proprioception) and visual channels can all elicit protective responses.

Relationship of Primary and Postural Responses   Normal motor abilities develop from an elaborate reflexive mechanism. Primary reflexes are integrated and postural responses emerge as the infant progresses through the first year of life. Many authors have suggested that primary reflexes must be integrated before postural responses will occur (Bobath, 1971; Milani-Comparetti and Giodoni, 1967). They imply that the acquisition of postural responses in part assists in the integration of primitive reflexes, although the exact mechanism of this interaction is not specified. This cause-effect model may not be accurate. Although a sequential relationship exists of postural responses following primary reflexes, the two reflexive sets may develop independently.

Evidence for this independent development comes from a longitudinal study by Molnar (1978) of 53 mentally retarded infants and young children. All subjects had delayed motor development. In spite of normally integrated primary reflexes, these children showed delays in the appearance of postural responses, specifically, protective extension and equilibrium responses. The inhibition of primary reflexes, then, was not contingent upon the development of postural responses.

Fine Motor Development   The ability to grasp and manipulate objects has an analogous reflexive background. Prechtl and Beintema (1975) describe primitive newborn palmar grasping (hand) (see Table 10.1) as a response to touch in the palm. This can be observed by placing a finger into a newborn's hand. The infant's response is to immediately flex and grasp the stimulus. The newborn will continue grasping often until the stimulus is removed. Twitchell (1970) describes this localized hand response as only a portion of a larger reflexive response called the traction response. This response is elicited by slightly pulling on the newborn's arm, thus stretching the shoulder muscles. The infant responds by flexing the entire arm and hand, often pulling up into a sitting position. According to Twitchell, hand grasp is first elicited by stretch to shoulder muscles and only occurs as part of a total flexor pattern of the arm. He suggests that this total response is fractionated so that eventually only the hand will flex. Later, merely touching the palm elicits grasping. This touch-elicited grasping fractionates even further into what Twitchell describes as the instinctive grasp response. Now, if a part of the hand is touched, only that portion flexes rather than the entire hand. These localized responses occur first at the radial (thumb) side of the hand

and develop toward the ulnar (little finger) side of the hand. They also progress from the palm distally to the fingertips. This reflexive ability is then elaborated with further maturation and experience into precise control of the hand.

   Characteristics of Muscle   In addition to the normal integration of primitive reflexes and the development of postural responses, normal *muscle tone* and *strength* are necessary for movement. These two terms are not synonymous; however, defining them in mutually exclusive categories is difficult. Although oversimplified, *muscle strength* involves properties of muscles, the nerves that cause them to contract, and specific paths or areas in the brain that affect specific muscles. A cut nerve or lack of exercise can produce muscle weakness. Certain chemical changes in muscle, as in muscular dystrophy, also produce weakness. The strength of muscles is evaluated by increasing the amount of resistance (weight or load) on the muscle while the muscle is contracting. Because this type of voluntary contraction is difficult to elicit in infants, estimates of muscle strength (rather than measurement) are usually made. Exercises that increase the amount of weight, the number of times a particular weight can be lifted, or both of these are used to improve muscle strength.

   Muscle tone is defined by the degree of resistance felt by the examiner while a part of the body is taken through a range of movements (Lance and McLeod, 1977). It is the response of a muscle to passive movement. Because muscles develop tone in order to adopt postures for movement, muscle tone is also referred to as postural tone. Various networks in the brain and spinal cord control postural tone.

   Normal tone includes a wide variety of tension. Postural tone can be viewed as a continuum with decreased tone (hypotonia) at one end and increased tone (hypertonia) at the other. The demarcations between normal and abnormal tone are not always precise, and because tone is subjectively assessed, multiple indicators of postural tone are useful. In addition to resistance to passive movement, another indicator of postural tone is an observation of body parts at rest and in motion. The brain organizes muscle action in groups of muscles (synergies) rather than by isolated muscles. As a result, postural tone abnormalities are seen by looking at the body posture as it is affected by particular patterns of muscles. For instance, hypertonia may be seen only in those muscles that extend the body (extensors) or only in those that bend it (flexors). Sometimes both groups are involved. The child with hypertonus, such as the child with spastic cerebral palsy, may walk on his/her toes with legs crossed.

This pattern is due to extensor hypertonus. The muscles that cross the legs (adductors) are activated in conjunction with those that extend the knee and point the toe. These extensor muscles are normally opposed by flexor muscles. The lack of this normal flexor opposition results in abnormal patterns of movement. Hypotonia is usually seen in several muscle groups simultaneously. The child with hypotonia, such as a child with Down syndrome, may sit on the floor with a rounded back and legs spread far apart. The hypotonia may also be evident when this same child stands with the same pattern of widely spread legs.

Postural tone is not a static phenomenon. It is as dynamic as human movement requires it to be. Various factors affect postural tone including fatigue, temperature, speed of movement, difficulty of the task, and the position of the infant at the start of as well as during movement.

The extremes of fatigue and temperature increase abnormal tone. The speed of the moving part also affects the tone. If an examiner moves a limb slowly, muscle tone may feel normal. If the same part is moved rapidly, the tonus in the muscles might increase or be overpowered and decrease. Muscle tone also changes with the speed of active motion. The child with hypertonicity may have normal tone while reaching for a toy, but have increased tone when this action is performed rapidly. This increased tone may prevent a successful reach.

The position of the child also affects postural tone. The prone position tends to facilitate the flexor muscles in the body, whereas the extensor muscles are facilitated in the supine position. If muscle tone abnormalities are present, this tendency may be exaggerated. The child with hypertonus in the flexor group may not be able to right his/her head, because as the prone position is approached (as in being pushed forward), her flexor muscle tone is facilitated. Because all the flexors may be activated simultaneously, the child may flex forward and be unable to maintain balance. The supine infant with extensor hypertonus may not be able to roll because rolling from supine requires activation of flexor muscles. Supine may provide such strong activation of extensor muscles that the flexors are overpowered and unable to function.

Exercises that increase muscle strength are not helpful when treating problems of muscle tone. Adding a load to hyper- or hypotonic muscles usually makes movement more difficult and should be avoided. Exercises and activities designed to minimize effects of position and maximize the control of normal tone are the most appropriate.

In summary, reflexes provide the substrata for all volitional movement. The temporal sequence of appearance from integration of primitive reflexes, maturation of postural responses, and development of volitional movement is similar in all humans. Normal variation in chronology of these events, quality, speed, and skill of movement all make for uniqueness in physical ability. Children with motor problems may have abnormally retained primitive reflexes, delayed or abnormal postural responses, abnormal muscle tone or muscle strength, or deficits of speed, accuracy, or timing of movement.

SEQUENCE OF MOTOR SKILLS

Gross Motor

The following sequential description is an overview of the general progression of gross motor milestones from the newborn period through the time at which the infant stands and walks. Early researchers observed large numbers of infants and recorded the ages at which particular abilities such as head control, sitting, crawling, and walking were achieved (Gesell and Amatruda, 1947; McGraw, 1963). The concept of age norms or motor milestones that developed from these observations has provided a basis for many standardized assessments of gross motor abilities (Bayley, 1969; Frankenberg and Dodds, 1967). Although describing motor development by milestones ignores the essential components of movement (e.g., reflexes, muscle tone, and strength), it does provide an additional framework for observing movement. Specific ages at which these abilities are achieved have purposely been omitted from the following descriptions in order to give the reader an appreciation of the general sequence of motor development and possible variation without stressing a chronological sequence. The reader should consult Chapter 5 for specific ages at which motor milestones are achieved. Motor development is described here according to the infant's behavior in the prone, supine, sitting, and standing positions. In this way the reader may appreciate the effects of position on the infant's developing skills.

Prone   Head control develops in prone as infants begin to lift their heads, usually in pursuit of visual stimulation (Figure 10.1A). Blind infants are delayed in the development of head control in prone (Fraiberg, 1971) suggesting that vision plays an important role

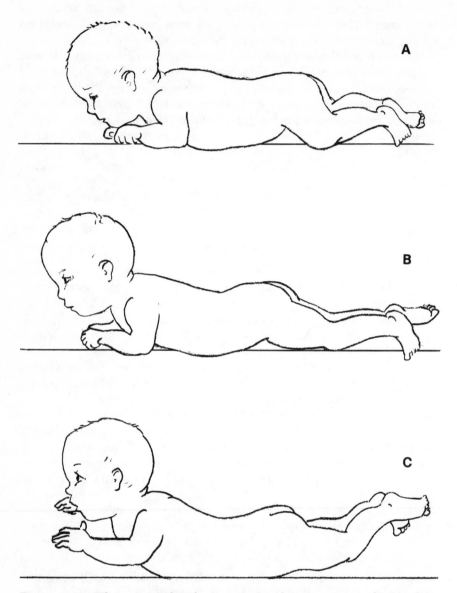

Figure 10.1.   The prone infant begins to extend against gravity by first lifting the head (A), then bearing weight on the forearms (B), then lifting the head, arms, and legs at the same time (C).

in the acquisition of this skill. As the ability to extend against gravity continues, infants lift their upper trunk and begin to bear weight on their forearms. At first forearms are held tightly against the body with hands fisted (Figure 10.1B). As equilibrium responses improve in the trunk and head control is mastered, infants move their arms away from this tightly flexed position. This bilateral (both sides of the body) ability soon gives way to unilateral (one side) activity. Now the infant can lean on one arm and reach out with the other (Figure 10.2). During this phase of development, infants may kick their legs (usually symmetrically), but increasing control is most evident in the upper body. Extensor abilities continue to improve, and pushing up on extended arms with hands open becomes possible. It is common to see infants flipping onto their backs from this position. Parents often believe their infant is initiating rolling. True rolling, however, involves moving the upper and lower trunk separately and does not develop until later. This back flipping often stops as the infant gains control of the extended position, and parents may be concerned that their infant has stopped rolling. This apparent regression is really a progression of control, and true segmental rolling will soon develop. The legs become more controlled at this time, and they assist the arms in pivoting the body in a circle. Some infants may become upset that this newly found movement merely moves them

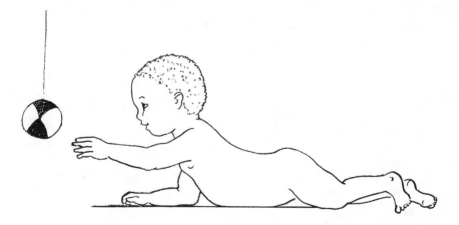

Figure 10.2.   Development in prone continues as the infant now bears weight on one arm while reaching with the other.

in circles, but others seem to enjoy the pivoting maneuver for its own sake. Infants then may begin belly crawling (combat crawl) (Figure 10.3). Some infants use both arms and legs for this crawling, whereas others drag their bodies by pulling forward only with their arms. Next, the lower trunk and legs assume weight, and infants push up from the fully extended position up onto hands and knees (quadruped). They will first hold this position, and later, as postural stability improves, they become mobile and rock back and forth. Although infants can remain sitting if placed at this time, they usually do not independently push into a sitting position until they can maintain the quadruped position. Once the infant can assume a sitting position, he/she is free to move from sitting to hands and knees. Crawling begins and the environment becomes accessible to the curious infant.

Prone Variation   Creeping and crawling patterns are extremely variable. Some infants only belly crawl, whereas others omit any type of crawling altogether. The weightbearing and reciprocal movement abilities acquired during crawling are important components of later movement, however noncrawlers apparently acquire these same components by alternate means. Robson (1970) has described a group of infants who "seat scoot" rather than crawl. Although this is a pattern of movement children with Down syndrome frequently use, it is also seen in normal children. Robson suggests a familial tendency when seat scooting occurs in normal children.

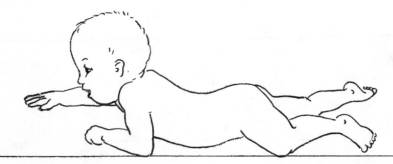

Figure 10.3.   *Some infants begin forward progression by pulling their bodies along the ground with just their arms.*

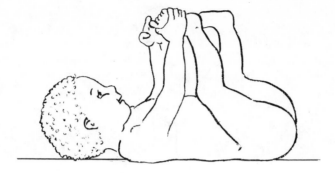

Figure 10.4.   *Supine development includes exploring objects and parts of the body with hands and eyes.*

Supine   Motor abilities develop simultaneously in prone and supine positions. Waving and kicking are the predominant early motor patterns in the supine positions. Infants move their heads in all directions to follow people and objects moving through their world. Controlled movement in the arms often begins in the supine position. The infant is fully supported in this position, thus freeing the arms for activity. Hand watching frequently precedes hand to mouth activity. As the ATNR becomes fully integrated, the head and hands can move in any combination. Lying and watching objects is quickly replaced with reaching out, grasping, and bringing objects to the mouth or eyes for exploration (Figure 10.4).

Rolling from the supine position occurs during the second half of the first year of life. This ability follows the appearance of the body derotative reflex described by Milani-Comparetti and Giodoni (1967). In attempting to right themselves against gravity, infants roll to the prone position and assume quadruped or sitting, depending on their ability. Until abdominal muscles are strong enough to enable sitting up directly from the supine position, rolling to the prone position or side lying (transitional sitting) remains the most effective way of achieving a sitting position.

Supine Variation   Early control of the body in the supine position may not be as evident as prone abilities. Vision is a powerful facilitator of motor development. Infants can see the world from the supine position, and in this position, adults tend automatically to bring visual stimuli into the infant's field of vision. The prone infant

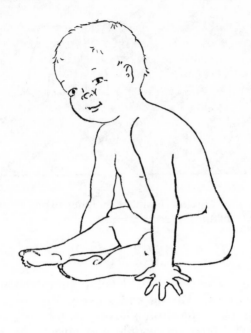

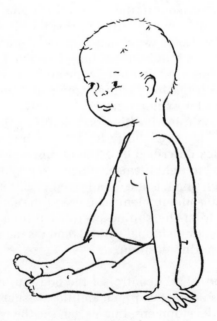

Figure 10.5.   Sitting is first possible only with the use of the arms for support.

often has to search for this stimulation, and consequently, head lifting develops. Supine infants turn their heads in all directions, but the head remains supported and less control is necessary. Some infants prefer to be supine, and as a consequence, head control may develop more slowly in these infants. Infants primarily positioned in the prone position tend to develop head lifting earlier than those infants positioned in the supine position (Holt, 1960; Shea, 1971).

Patterns of rolling are often variable. The body part initiating the roll may vary between head, shoulder, hip, leg, or any combination of these. The onset of rolling, just as any means of moving about, is affected in part by the infant's desire for movement. Thus, infants acquire movement patterns at variable ages as a function of neuromotor maturation, experience, and desire to move.

Sitting   When placed in a sitting position, newborns may lift their heads and even briefly extend their backs. However, most newborns slump into flexion due to undeveloped head and trunk control. As body control begins to develop in prone and supine positions, infants placed in the sitting position are able to lift their heads and extend their trunks, although still in need of full support. As head righting, equilibrium, and protective responses mature, independent sitting becomes possible. First infants support their whole weight on arms propped in front of the body (forward protection or parachute) (Figure 10.5). As equilibrium responses improve, the trunk can control sitting and the arms and hands are free for exploration. The fully independent sitter can escape most falls with the use of equilibrium responses in the trunk, and only the most violent or sudden displacement requires use of the arms for protection.

Sitting Variation   Normally, children use a variety of sitting postures. Sitting with legs out in front (long sitting), with both feet to one side (side sitting), or with feet at the hip on the same side (reverse tailor sitting or "W" sitting) (Figure 10.6) are the most common. Some children use all these positions, whereas others prefer one or two. Children with hypertonus frequently sit in a tailor or W position exclusively. These positions (particularly W sitting) need to be discouraged as they tend to facilitate abnormal patterns of hypertonus.

Standing   Newborns may automatically or reflexively take weight on their feet if supported, and, if propelled, may even take steps (automatic or primary walking). This initial ability is followed by a time of non-weightbearing (astasia). During this phase, infants

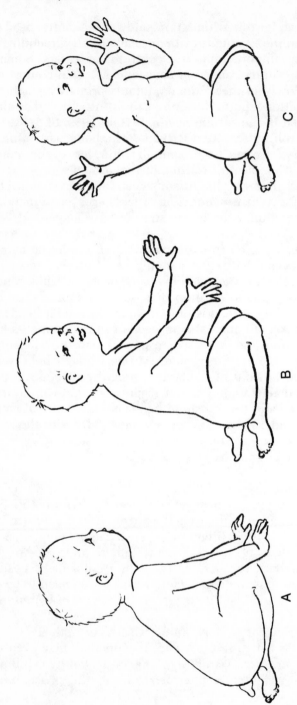

Figure 10.6.   The sitting position referred to as "W" sitting or reverse tailor sitting is used by many infants. The feet are at the side of the body along the point of the hip joint.

will not assume weight on their legs. Only after mastering the body in prone, supine, and sitting positions, and all the gradations in between, can the infant attain control of the fully upright position. This upright control usually begins with kneeling. The infant may move into a kneeling position from a quadruped or sitting position. Balance and mobility are achieved first in kneeling and only later in standing. Infants may pull themselves to standing with legs somewhat passive. Later pulling to stand is accomplished by first half-kneeling and pushing to stand. The infant shifts to one knee, freeing the opposite leg from weight. This leg is then free to be placed and have weight shifted onto it as the infant comes to a standing position with extended legs. This struggle is soon replaced with a fluid, effortless movement from kneeling to standing. In fact, infants who have achieved independent standing can assume this position from a prone or supine position often faster than hands can reach out to stop them.

The infant is becoming a toddler. Walking is first attempted in bursts of a few steps and a fall. Infants spread their feet far apart and hold their arms up and out above their head (high guard). The former position minimizes falling; the latter maximizes protection when the inevitable fall occurs. The base of support narrows, and the arms are lowered as walking develops. At first, the trunk is held stiffly and feet slap the surface as the infant toddles from place to place. Mature walking emerges from this toddling gait as balance and strength improve. Trunk and knees are flexed slightly rather than rigidly extended and a heel-to-toe pattern develops. That tiny infant with wobbling head and thrashing limbs has struggled against the forces of gravity, assumed the upright, and is off.

Standing Variation   There is wide variation in the amount of time infants want to be in a standing position, either supported or unsupported. Some infants want to be held on their feet almost from birth. They have extensor tone that enables them to continue to bear weight even through the normal phase of astasia. Other infants crumple into flexion as newborns and continue to do so for many months. Both patterns can be normal. Either pattern, however, might mean abnormal tone. A single finding such as this is never cause for alarm. However, if it is accompanied by other atypical movements or abilities, an evaluation might be recommended. The age at which a child walks is an important milestone for families. Indeed, it marks autonomy in a concrete form. There is a wide variation in the age at which toddlers walk, it occurs as early as 8 months and as late as 24. A child who has normal movement, tone, and strength but is not walking alone at 18 months will accomplish this, he/she just needs more time. Infants may have all the motoric prerequisites but remain crawling or need one-hand support for weeks past the time when parents believe they should be on their own. Even coaxing does not seem to help. Parents often try sturdier support shoes, although a recent report by Staheli and Griffin (1980) confirms that supportive shoes are unnecessary for normal foot development. Time seems to be the best remedy—if motor development is normal, every child walks.

Fine Motor

Precise use of the hands for reaching, grasping, and manipulation is one of the major accomplishments of infancy. Arm and hand skills develop through differentiation from gross to precise patterns. The following description of the development of hand and arm skills is aimed at giving the reader a general outline of fine motor development.

Arms and hands are used for exploration, self-care, and postural control. The infant must be supported or have developed postural control before the arms and hands are free for activity. The prone infant will use arms and hands for movement or support. An infant placed in a sitting position may need his/her arms for support, whereas this same infant on the mother's lap will be able to use his/her hands freely to play. Thus, the infant's position may affect the functional use of arm and hands.

Reaching   Reaching is first observed when infants are supine. Instead of reaching directly for an object by moving in a straight line, the infant first reaches using an arc pattern. The arm moves out to the side and then to the object (Hofsten, 1979). This circumventive pattern is often accompanied by missing the object so that swipes occur rather than successful reaches. Swiping and circumventive reaching are replaced with accurate, directed reach as the infant matures. The speed of this ability increases along with its precision.

Grasping   The purpose of reaching is to move the hand to an object or person. As reaching develops so does the hand's ability to grasp, hold, and manipulate objects. Early researchers described the ontogeny of voluntary grasp using the same observational techniques developed for description of gross motor abilities (Castner, 1932; Gesell and Amatruda, 1947; Halverson, 1931; McGraw, 1941). At first, the hand is fisted when objects are contacted. Hitting or batting objects is prevalent. If toys are placed in an infant's hand, they are held by the reflexive hand grasp, but the infant cannot yet let go. As hand grasp becomes integrated, extension of the wrist and fingers facilitates releasing. The improved modulation of flexor and extensor abilities is necessary in order to grasp and manipulate objects.

Mature grasping, just like more reflexive grasping, is first performed with the whole hand. Total patterns of flexion and extension are used to close on an object, hold it, and release it. In contrast to the radial ulnar direction seen in the reflexive development of grasping described by Twitchell (1965, 1970), development of mature grasping progresses from the ulnar to the radial side of the hand. An object is first held in the palm by all fingers flexing. Later, this same object is apprehended with the ulnar side of the palm and held securely with the ulnar three fingers. This marks a fractionalization in control, which is more fully elaborated as the radial side of the hand begins to be used preferentially. In addition to this ulnar-to-radial shift, control shifts from the palm and proximal fingers to the distal fingertips for fine manipulation. Objects are first grasped between the base of the index finger and thumb (inferior pincer), and later at the tips of these fingers (superior, distal, or neat pincer). This ulnar-to-radial, proximal-distal pattern is observed developmentally regardless of the object being grasped.

Reaching and Grasping Variation   Research by Kopp (1974) suggests that infants show variation in the development of speed and accuracy of reach and grasp. We know intuitively that some infants have better fine motor skills than others, however normal variation in the patterns used for reaching, grasping, and manipulation has not been systematically described.

MOTOR DEVELOPMENT OF ATYPICAL INFANTS

Infants with motor problems form a heterogeneous group. Some have a diagnosis such as cerebral palsy in which a precise description of the motor problems can be made, whereas many others may be described as developmentally delayed or atypical. Problems that present during infancy may disappear over time or they may become more serious. It is often difficult for a clinician to predict the outcome of a motor problem because developmental change during the first years of life can be so dramatic. Infants may be evaluated over a period of months before the full extent of the motor problems becomes evident. The following description of the motor development of atypical infants is presented in three sections; *normal variation, abnormal variation*, and *pathology*. This categorization of the problem is not meant to provide labels for infants. Rather, it exemplifies a process utilized clinically to understand the motor problem and make appropriate recommendations to families. Examples of infant problems that fit the categores are offered at the end of each section.

Normal Variation

Variation in motor development is common. The sequence, pattern, or adeptness of motor abilities may all vary. The motor development of infants with normal variation may be atypical but not abnormal. Parents need to be assured that their child is normal, and the variation should be described and discussed. For example, as described previously, infants crawl using a variety of patterns. One variation is plantigrade, or bear, crawling in which only hands and feet touch the ground during movement. Although this movement pattern is functional, it looks awkward, and parents may worry that this pattern is in some way abnormal. They need assurance that this is normal variation.

Abnormal Variation

Infants in this group show clear signs of abnormal development. It is difficult to know if these problems are transient or are early signs of lasting pathology. For example, a 6 month old may have mild hypertonia with delayed motor skills. These symptoms may disappear by 10 months without any intervention. These same symptoms, however, may be early signs of cerebral palsy, and by 10 months of age the hypertonicity may have increased with more marked motor delays. Early identification and intervention may have aided the infant's development. An incorrect diagnosis of deviancy, however, unnecessarily alarms families and may alter perceptions of their child's competency. These perceptions may be difficult to change if the infant later develops normally. The risk of falsely identifying a problem must be weighed against the consequences of waiting for more definitive signs. Sequential evaluations spanning a few months may aid in differentiating transient from lasting abnormality. Specific motor concerns may be described and demonstrated for parents, and although the abnormal symptoms should never be hidden or denied, parents must be assured that only time and repeated observations will yield answers regarding the implications of current abnormal symptoms.

This lack of certainty is disquieting for professionals and possibly agonizing for parents. Motor intervention in the form of physical or occupational therapy may be recommended for an infant even though a specific diagnosis has not been made. Parents often want to do something directly for their infant during this waiting time and exercises give them this concreteness. Abnormal muscle tone, delayed motor abilities, and other abnormal variations in motor development may be helped with exercises and activities even if the precise etiology is unknown. Parents should understand that intervention may be temporary and that it may not be essential to the developmental outcome of their infant.

Recommending intervention in situations in which a precise developmental diagnosis is not possible, however, may have a negative consequence for the family. They may believe that more is wrong with their child than they are being told, or, as mentioned previously, they may develop perceptions of their child that are or will become inaccurate. To define a motor problem and decide whether to recommend intervention, the following questions should be considered.

1. Does the infant have problems in other areas of development? (This might suggest a more general problem.)
2. Would the suggestion of intervention be helpful, or could it have negative consequences for a particular family?
3. Do facilities exist for frequent evaluation of the infant in order to observe development over time?

The decision to recommend therapy is an important one, and should be made by a team of developmental specialists or, at a minimum, a therapist and physician. If therapy is recommended to parents of an infant who may have transient motor problems, they should be assured that they are being told all the known facts about their infant's condition. They must be informed that no empirical evidence exists suggesting that therapy for infants with transient motor problems is beneficial. Rather, the decision is being made based on the clinical impressions of their infant.

Prematurity   Infants born prematurely provide an example of a group of infants who may have abnormal variation in motor development. As described in Chapter 3, premature infants are at risk for developmental problems; however, the majority of infants born prematurely develop normally (Parmelee, 1981). Early abnormal signs may be transient, making it difficult to predict the outcome for a particular infant based on early medical or behavioral sequelae (Sameroff, 1975). As a consequence, sequential evaluations of prematurely born infants are necessary to follow developmental changes closely.

Premature infants are normally hypotonic at birth. The less mature the infant, the greater the hypotonia (Saint-Anne Dargassies, 1966). Muscle tone and motor activity develop first in the legs and progress toward the head. In contrast, postural control later proceeds in a cephalocaudal direction just as in full-term infants. The premature infant at full-term equivalency (40 weeks gestation) does not have the motor skills or postural tone of the infant born at term (Carter and Campbell, 1975; Howard et al., 1976). In addition, primitive reflexes are weaker and preferential body postures are absent (i.e., holding the head to the right as seen in full-term infants) (Prechtl et al., 1979). Elaborate documentation exists for the development of muscle tone, reflexes, and mobility of preterm infants until they reach term equivalency. Follow-up assessments during the first 2 years of life, however, have primarily included motor milestones and ignored assessing the components of motor ability.

What is normal versus abnormal progression for a premature infant? Do premature infants merely "catch up" to their full-term peers, or is their motor development in some way unique? At what point is "catch up" development completed? Longitudinal research should provide answers to these questions; however, findings have been equivocal. Research by Field et al. (1978) suggests that preterm infants have motor delays through the first year of life as measured by the Bayley Scales of Infant Development. Sigman and Parmelee (1979) found similar delays with preterm infants followed through the second year. A more optimistic viewpoint is supported by the research of Fetters and Goldberg (1981). Preterm infants in their sample showed significant delay at 6 months on the Bayley Motor Scale; however, on a variety of other motor tests, the preterm infants were not delayed. Fine motor skills accounted for the delays on the Bayley. Twelve of the 14 preterm infants, however, had normal Bayley Motor scores at 1 year. The two infants with continued delay at 1 year had demonstrated marked hypotonia at 6 months in comparison to the other infants. The research suggests that premature infants may have transient delays in motor development.

A recent review of the effects of developmental intervention offered to preterm infants during their hospitalization or as follow-up suggests that motor development is generally not improved by the types of programs used (Campbell, in press). The programs described, however, were not based on the specific motor problems of premature infants. The various forms of sensory stimulation used, including massage, rocking, and use of water beds, may not be useful in facilitating motor abilities. Intervention is a heterogeneous term. If improvement in motor skills is the expected outcome of intervention, then a program must be designed that specifically addresses this outcome.

Pathology

Infants in this group have readily identifiable motor problems such as those associated with Down syndrome or cerebral palsy. Although specific symptoms may change with development and intervention, these infants have long-term motor disability. Infants with a pathological motor problem are usually referred for therapy as soon as a diagnosis is made.

Cerebral Palsy   Cerebral palsy is a general disability with variations in symptoms. Infants with cerebral palsy have motor problems as a result of a deficit in the brain. The deficit is incurred in utero or during early infancy. Thus, a 5 year old who suffers meningitis or head trauma may have a motor problem, but it would not be described as cerebral palsy even though the symptoms may be the same. The term *cerebral palsy* does not imply that an infant is mentally retarded; it refers only to the motor impairment. Infants with cerebral palsy may be mentally retarded, they may develop learning problems, or they may have normal intellectual abilities. The motor problem in cerebral palsy includes postural tone abnormalities. These include hyper- or hypotonus or a fluctuation of tone. Spasticity, for example, is severe hypertonus. The type of cerebral palsy is described by the quality of muscle tone and the areas of the body involved in the disability. For example, an infant with spastic quadriplegic cerebral palsy has increased postural tone and motor impairment throughout the body and limbs. The infant with spastic diplegia has involvement primarily in the lower trunk and legs. A complete classification is offered in Bobath and Bobath (1972).

Muscle tone may change during infancy, thus, the descriptive diagnosis may change. An infant may be hypotonic during the early months and gradually develop increased postural tone. By age 2 increased tone and athetosis may be present. Athetotic movements are slow, writhing movements; the athetotic child is in constant motion (Bobath and Bobath, 1972; Lance and McLeod, 1977). The diagnosis of this infant changes from hypotonic to hypertonic to athetoid cerebral palsy.

The infant with hypertonic or spastic cerebral palsy has a paucity of movement patterns. Movement is usually slow and limited in range. Primitive reflexes may be retained past their normal time of integration and the postural responses may be delayed (Bobath, 1969; Bobath and Bobath, 1975). Spastic muscles hold joints and body parts in abnormal and frequently stressful positions. Muscles may develop contractures (abnormal shortening of muscle) resulting in abnormal joint positions. Common sites for contractures are ankles, hips, knees, and elbows. Joints may also subluxate (slip from normal alignment). Hips are the most likely joints to subluxate. Goals of an intervention program include reducing the hypertonicity and improving the amount, quality, and range of movement. These infants need increased mobility. Improving mobility usually helps in preventing contractures and subluxations.

Infants with hypotonicity have very different problems. Although they also may have a paucity of movement patterns, the excursion of the movements is increased compared to normal. They are less likely to retain primitive reflexes, but postural responses may be delayed. These infants have difficulty maintaining stability against gravity as their muscles do not develop adequate postural tone to hold them. Contractures are rare in this group, but hip subluxations are not because the muscles have difficulty holding the joint intact against external forces. Goals of intervention for infants with hypotonus include improving stability by increasing muscle tone. In addition, movement patterns need to be facilitated and subluxation prevented.

Down Syndrome   Infants with Down syndrome generally are delayed in motor development, although just like any other group of infants, there is a wide variation in abilities (Hanson, 1981; Share, 1975; Zausmer, 1978). Delays may be attributed to a number of problems shared by infants with Down syndrome. Hypotonia and muscle weakness contribute to slow achievement of motor skills, joint instability, and increased flexibility. Patterns requiring joint stability such as lifting the head in the prone position, weightbearing on forearms, or holding the quadruped position may be particularly difficult for an infant with Down syndrome.

Motor intervention is routinely suggested for these infants (Hanson, 1977; Zausmer, 1978). A major goal of intervention is to promote normal patterns of motor development. Improving muscle tone and strength also aides in preventing joint problems due to hyperflexibility.

Congenital Blindness   Early researchers suggested that the sequence of gross motor development was the same for blind and sighted infants (Gesell and Amatruda, 1947). Blind infants, however, were often delayed by many months in their achievement of gross motor abilities. Recent research has qualified this general conclusion (Adelson and Fraiberg, 1974; Fraiberg, 1971; Freedman and Cannady, 1971). Blind infants develop stability patterns (e.g., sitting or standing in the same sequence) within the same age range as sighted infants (Adelson and Fraiberg, 1974). Mobility patterns (e.g., reaching, crawling, and walking), however, are delayed in blind infants (Fraiberg, 1971; Parmelee et al., 1959). According to Fraiberg (1971), patterns of mobility require visual elicitation. Blind infants who are offered sound cues to replace vision still do not reach toward the sound. Fraiberg proposes that sound alone does not inform the blind infant about the physical properties of the object. The infant may not know if the object is graspable or not, and lacking this information may not be induced to reach.

Fraiberg (1971) stresses the importance of intervention with blind infants and their parents to aid in facilitating the mobility patterns that are normally delayed. She submits that audition and tactile sensation do not completely replace vision and that parents need to know when and how to use these alternate sensory systems to promote normal sensorimotor abilities.

ASSESSMENT OF MOTOR DEVELOPMENT

Accurate assessment of infant development requires skill and knowledge. Many assessment tools exist for collecting and recording motor development, but the usefulness of these tools depends on the competency of the evaluator. Much can be learned about motor development from observation of the infant and talking to the parents. A thorough motor exam requires minimal handling; this is important because typical abilities may be difficult to elicit when infants are handled by strangers. The clinician needs to know the infant's typical behavior. Parents can supply information regarding the infant's preferred positions for sleeping and playing and typical patterns of movement. Clinicians must also listen carefully to the *parents'* major concerns about their infant's motor development. While talking with parents the following observations can be made:

Independent control
   Observe the infant's ability for independent control of his/her body. Is the amount of physical support appropriate for the infant's age?
Movement patterns
   Is there evidence that abnormal tone exists? Is abnormal tone

interfering with normal movement? Are movement patterns as well as the speed, accuracy, and coordination of movement appropriate for the infant's chronological age?

Primitive reflexes

Are nonintegrated primitive reflexes interfering with spontaneous movement? Eliciting primitive reflexes is individually less important than observing their role in functional movement.

Some responses may need to be elicited by handling the infant. Whenever possible parents should be asked to elicit the needed observation. It is often easier for the examiner to assess abilities accurately when freed from the responsibility of handling an infant. Parents should not feel that their handling is being evaluated, rather they should be assured that their infant will be happiest and respond more reliably when handled by his parents. The following responses should be elicited by the parents:

Effect of position on muscle tone and movement

Infants should be moved through prone, supine, sitting, and standing positions. The effects of position and movement from one to the other should be noted. Does muscle tone change or spontaneous movement change with a change in position?

Postural responses

The righting, equilibrium and protective responses appropriate for a particular infant should be elicited. These may be evident when changing the infant's position.

Assessment of primitive reflexes, muscle tone, and muscle strength may be unpleasant for the infant and are best done by the examiner.

Primitive reflexes

The reflexes most important for motor abilities (see Table 10.1) may be assessed individually. The importance of these reflexes, however, is in their relationship to functional movement.

Muscle tone

In addition to observing movement patterns, muscle tone should be assessed as a response to passive movement. The examiner can only describe muscle tone if it has been felt.

Muscle strength

Muscle strength is estimated by the examiner based on the force of *active* contraction produced by the infant.

The method of recording motor assessments depends, in part, on the function of the record. Standardized assessment of gross and fine motor abilities have been developed that enable the examiner to compare a particular infant with a large sample of normal infants

(Bayley, 1969; Frankenburg and Dodds, 1967; Gesell and Amatruda, 1947; Wolanski and Zdanska-Bricken, 1975). Results on these assessments tell the examiner whether the infant is delayed, normal, or advanced in motor development relative to norms, but they do not take into account the quality of movement, etiology of problems, or functional abilities of the infant. For example, the Motor Scale of the Bayley Scales of Infant Development is a standardized assessment used frequently in research with atypical infants (Campbell and Wilhelm, 1979; Fetters and Goldberg, 1981; Field, et al., 1978; Sigman and Parmelee, 1979). Items are scored pass/fail with an age range given for each item. For instance, one item, "elevates self by arms, prone" is given an age range for achievement between .7–5 months, with an average age of 2.1 months. All infants in a standardization sample passed this item by 5 months of age. Failure on this item may indicate a delay, but the examiner has no information regarding the reason for failure. Abnormal muscle tone, absence of righting reflexes, or poor vision could all contribute to an inability to lift the head and chest in the prone position. Standardized tests are most useful as screening assessments or research tools.

Other assessments have been designed that relate primitive and postural reflexes to gross motor ability (Hoskins and Squires, 1973; Milani-Comparetti and Giodoni, 1967). Although these tests aid in detecting possible reasons for motor problems (e.g., retained primitive reflexes or delayed postural responses), they do not take into account quality of movement, muscle tone or strength, or functional abilities. They, too, are best used as screening assessments.

Another form of motor assessment is the developmental profile. Many profiles have been developed by personnel working in comprehensive developmental programs (D'Eugenio and Rogers, 1976; Sanford, 1974). The motor section of these profiles includes selected items from standardized assessments, functional and qualitative descriptions of movement, and primitive and postural reflex assessments. Profiles are often time-consuming to collect, but may be helpful in fully describing motor abilities of an infant with pathological motor development. Specific programs of intervention can be designed from these profiles.

INTERVENTION

Nature/Nurture

Does environmental input in the form of motor intervention improve the motor abilities of atypical infants? This remains an essential but incompletely answered question. In order to appreciate the controversy over intervention, it is important to ask an even more basic question. Does the environment contribute to the motor development of normal infants, or is motor development simply an unfolding of genetically determined neuromuscular development?

The latter viewpoint, that the environment contributes little to motor development, is supported by Gesell and Thompson's (1929) research with a pair of identical twins. Because identical twins have identical genetic endowments, any difference in motor abilities would be attributed to environmental influences. Stair climbing was one motor skill studied in these twins. Gesell and Thompson gave only one twin special stair climbing practice. The practice, however, was apparently unnecessary because the unpracticed twin could climb stairs immediately upon introduction. In a critique of this study, however, Bower (1974) points out that practice consisted of passively moving the infant on the stairs. As Bower suggests, this may be an inappropriate technique to accelerate stair climbing. Hein and Diamond's (1972) research with kittens supports Bower's criticism. They found that active practice was required for kittens to develop independent movement. Kittens restrained from self-produced movements did not develop active locomotion.

Dennis' (1940) research with Hopi Indians is often cited as evidence that the environment contributes little to the ability to walk. One group of Hopi's swaddle their infants and carry them upright, secured to a board. Movement is impossible except for infrequent times when clothes are changed. This restriction had no apparent effect on independent walking, as both the restricted group and a control group of unrestricted Hopi infants walked independently at 15 months. The restricted group, however, had constant practice in the upright position. Because infants automatically strive for the upright posture, early practice in this position may be facilitatory to early standing.

The importance of the environment for motor development is supported by the research of White et al. (1964) with institutionalized infants and the work of Adelson and Fraiberg (1974) with congenitally blind infants. White et al. (1964) enriched the environment of one group of institutionalized infants with visual stimulation and extra handling by ward personnel. A control group of infants received routine stimulation and care. The enriched group of infants developed visually guided reaching earlier than the control group.

Adelson and Fraiberg (1974) designed a program of auditory-tactile stimulation for blind infants to facilitate those aspects of motor development normally influenced by vision (e.g., coming to sit and independent walking). They were able to decrease the delays in motor development for the group receiving stimulation.

Focusing on the nature versus nurture controversy may prove moot when atypical children are concerned. For the normal infant, certain aspects of motor development may be acquired through neuromaturation, whereas others are more dependent on environmental facilitation. There is probably one set of developmental rules or guidelines that normal development follows; however, these guidelines may be very different for atypical infants.

Theoretical Assumptions
Influencing Programs of Motor Intervention

The rules that govern development when the brain has been damaged are unknown. They depend in part on the areas and the extent of damage.

Current programs of motor intervention are based on assumptions about the brain's ability to recover from damage or insult. One common assumption is that damage to the young brain has less deleterious effects than similar damage to an older brain. The immature brain is thought to be more "plastic" than the mature brain. This assumption, which originated from the work of Kennard (1936), has been challenged by Goldman (1971, 1974, 1976). Kennard proposed that infant monkeys performed better than older monkeys (on cognitive/perceptual tasks) following surgical oblation (destruction of tissue) to areas of the brain. In similar research, Goldman (1974) suggested that if infant monkeys were tested 2 to 3 years after surgical oblation rather than within the first 2 years, they were impaired to the same extent as the older monkeys. The infant monkeys then eventually developed the same disabilities as the older monkeys. Although research involving the motor system generally is more consistent with the model that the immature brain is more resilient after oblation, this research is also equivocal. Fine motor skills are particularly vulnerable in both young and old. Lawrence and Hopkins (1976) have demonstrated increased fine motor disability with age in monkeys with infantile pyramidal tract lesions. The assumption that the damaged young brain will generally show better recovery than the damaged older brain should be seriously questioned.

A second assumption at the basis of motor intervention programs is that experience, in the form of exercises and activities, will alter the brain so that normal motor function will ensure. The exact nature of this alteration is not specified; however, St. James-Roberts (1979) suggests that the sparing of function after damage to motor areas in the brain occurs as a result of redundancy of motor systems. Motor abilities seem to be controlled by multiple networks in the brain. These networks overlap in function, and if one network is damaged, other networks take over its function. This redundancy of control networks may not be available for other abilities (i.e., perceptual or cognitive tasks). The importance of experience within this model of redundancy is unclear. The brain may be independently capable of this network change or experience may play some specific role. Experience may need to have specific characteristics and be available at certain times during development to be most effective.

Approaches to Developmental Motor Intervention

Programs of motor intervention provide specific environmental input in order to facilitate normal motor development and discourage aberrant movement. Programs are usually developed by physical and occupational therapists who have been trained in developmental therapy and child development. These programs may be implemented by therapists, family members, or personnel involved in early intervention.

A variety of therapeutic approaches to developmental motor impairment are available. The more traditional approaches to motor problems stressed passive exercise to maintain joint mobility. Adaptive equipment and braces were used frequently to assist the child in standing (Deaver 1956; Phelps 1940). Contemporary approaches to intervention stress active movement on the part of the child. Braces for cerebral-palsied children have been replaced by lightweight plastic orthoses (similar to splints) that help hold joints in good alignment for movement. These newer approaches also emphasize family management of the infant with motor problems. Suggestions on carrying, holding, feeding, and dressing may be given, which all tend to optimize motor development (Finnie, 1975).

The two most common approaches used by therapists are neurodevelopmental treatment, developed by Bobath and Bobath (1972) and the neurophysiological approach of Rood (Stockmeyer, 1967, 1972). Other developmental approaches such as proprioceptive neuromuscular facilitation (Knott and Voss, 1968) are more appropriate for adults. The patterning approach suggested by Doman and Delacato (Doman, 1974) has been discouraged by the medical profession (Cohen et al., 1970; Sparrow and Zigler, 1978; Zigler, 1981).

Neurodevelopment treatment and the Rood approach have similarities. Both view the motor development of normal and motorically impaired infants as emerging sequentially. They stress the relationship of reflexes and movement and the importance of sensory input for the modification and facilitation of motor development. They differ in their description of motor development, the specific use of reflexes and the sensory techniques used to facilitate movement. The following synopses of the two theoretical approaches provide an overview of each approach.

Neurodevelopmental Treatment   Neurodevelopmental treatment was developed by Bobath and Bobath (1972) for the treatment of cerebral palsy. It has been used with infants with other diagnoses (Harris, 1981), and the basic concepts and techniques are appropriate for any developmental motor problem (Ellis, 1967). An infant's developmental level is described, and a program is designed to aid the infant in sequential progression through the remaining motor skills developed ontogenetically by the normal infant.

Goals of therapy include obtaining normal muscle tone and facilitating coordinated movement. Both of these goals are achieved with the use of handling. Appropriate handling of the infant can minimize abnormal tone and movement while simultaneously promoting normalcy. For example, a 10-month-old infant with spastic quadriplegic cerebral palsy may not have developed· rolling. Treatment might include placing the child in a sidelying position and then rolling him/her back and forth toward prone and supine position. Facilitating rolling might be done by holding one hip and moving the pelvis back and forth, waiting for the infant to derotate the upper body. This simulates normal rolling, but requires the infant to perform only part of the movement. This rolling exercise is practiced allowing the infant to perform actively as much of the movement as possible. After continued practice the infant should be able to initiate and complete the movement independently. Slow, rotational movement also tends to decrease spasticity. The rolling exercise, thus, promotes more normal tone and coordinated movement, the two goals of neurodevelopmental treatment. Increasing the speed of rotational movements tends to facilitate muscle tone; consequently, this same exercise could be used to help an infant who has hypotonia (such as in Down syndrome) roll.

In the exercise just described the hip serves as a key point of control. Key points are proximal body parts used in handling to promote normal tone and movement. Learning neurodevelopmental theory requires developing skill in facilitating movement from key points. Programs include a variety of movement exercises so that the infant who is not rolling may also work on sitting balance and other activities. Family members and other professionals working with the infant are encouraged to acquire skills in handling the infant so that normal tone and movement are reinforced throughout the day. Principles of neurodevelopmental therapy have been applied to feeding and other self-care abilities (Finnie, 1975; Mueller, 1972). Assisting the family with total management of the child with motor problems is an important aspect of neurodevelopmental therapy, and parent education is essential.

Rood Approach   The developmental approach of Rood (Stockmeyer, 1967) suggests that the neuromuscular system serves two separate biological functions. The first is a mobilizing function, which enables fast and protective movements. The second is a stabilizing function, which provides support and control of the individual. The interactions of these dual functions of mobility and stability result in coordinated movement. Bearing weight on forearms in the prone position is a stability pattern, whereas rolling is a mobility pattern. The physiology and neurophysiology of muscles that mobilize are different from those that stabilize, although most muscles combine functions and are not purely mobilizers or stabilizers. As a result, muscles are differentially responsive to the sensory stimuli that augment this treatment. For instance, mobilizing muscles may be facilitated with quick stretch while increasing load (resistance) improves stabilizing function.

Rood describes two sequences of motor development. The skeletal sequence involves posture and movement, whereas the vital sequence involves food intake, respiration, and speech. Both sequences include mobility and stability patterns. The developmental sequence described by Rood emphasizes different aspects in comparison to the sequence of Bobath (1972). Both approaches, however, assess the infant's functional level. Treatment includes activities that promote the infant through the normal sequence of motor development. Rood encourages the use of various sensory techniques such as mechanical vibration of muscles, ice brushing, and manual techniques. These techniques augment but do not solely comprise therapy. It is necessary for the therapist using the Rood approach to know the neurophysiology these techniques employ as well as the exact function of the muscles exercised (mobilizer versus stabilizer). Although the literature describing this approach does not specifically state the family's role in therapy, most clinicians using the Rood approach involve the family in a home program.

Intervention Research

During the last 25 years specific philosophies and techniques of treatment have been developed to meet the needs of infants with developmental motor problems. The main goal of treatment has been to improve the motor performance of infants. Clinical evidence of individual success and the sincere desire to offer help to families has provided sufficient reason for physicians to continue referring infants to therapy. Although treatment lacks sufficient empirical support, medical opinion seems to favor intervention because of the "it probably doesn't hurt even if it doesn't help" attitude. Taft (1981) and Denhoff (1981) both state that although empirical evidence is scant, offering motor intervention through physical and occupational therapy provides support for families in managing the problems of the handicapped infant. But is therapy successful in achieving the primary goal of improving the motor performance of infants with developmental problems? Only recently have attempts been made through clinical research to answer this question.

Henderson (1981) offers a complete review of research in physical and occupational therapy with children. From her review of research with cerebral-palsied infants she suggests that methodological problems pervaded all research attempts in the 1950s and 1960s. As a consequence, results must be regarded as suggestive but inconclusive. She adds that although recent researchers have acknowledged the earlier methodological problems, they have not been able to eliminate them. Difficulties remain because of the nature of the problem and the subjects under study. It is difficult to know the exact nature of the central nervous system deficit in a child with cerebral palsy. In addition, the obvious disability may be extremely variable from child to child. These two factors make matching of groups for research extremely difficult. Single-subject designs may offer an alternative method for research (Goodisman, 1982).

Research on motor intervention with Down syndrome infants is more conclusive. Improved sensorimotor abilities have been demonstrated by infants with Down syndrome participating in intense, long-term programs (Hanson, 1981; Zausmer, 1978). Infants involved in short-term, less intense therapy, however, do not demonstrate significant change (Harris, 1981). The amount of time in therapy may be an important factor.

An exhaustive review of the intervention literature is beyond the scope of this chapter. However, two points are of importance. First, research on motor intervention has been scant, although programs offering intervention have multiplied during the last decade. An assumption seems to have been made that motor intervention is good, although empirical support and evaluation are needed to test this assumption. More precise information is also needed regarding what type of intervention is best for a particular child. In what intensity should therapy occur, and who should be involved in its delivery?

Does therapy benefit the social-interactional health of the family or the infant's ability to move? The answers to both of these questions are important goals and may be achieved in therapy.

Second, future research must include sophisticated research design and analysis. Campbell and Wilhelm (1979) offer an excellent account of the problems and some solutions to research with developmentally handicapped infants. The following caveats must guide future research.

1. Motor intervention is not a unitary entity. Research reports must include specific techniques used, in addition to the amount of time spent in treatment.
2. Infants with a particular diagnosis (e.g., cerebral palsy or Down syndrome) form a heterogeneous group. Consequently, groups must be matched with equal numbers of infants with comparable problems. For instance, infants with spastic quadriplegia should not be compared to infants with spastic hemiplegia. In addition, subjects must be matched on variables that affect motor performance such as intelligence and perceptual abilities.
3. Comparisons of treatment philosophies and techniques must be made. After careful matching of groups, treatment offered to each group should reflect these comparisons.

SUMMARY

The characteristics and assumptions of motor intervention with atypical infants needs further research. While this research continues, however, families continue to need professional support and assistance in caring for their infant with motor problems. Transdisciplinary teams of professionals, together with families, should design specific programs of intervention that meet the multiple needs of atypical infants.

Clinicians must not fear research. Continually evaluating the results of motor intervention will clarify how we can benefit infants with atypical motor development.

Chapter Outline

OVERVIEW: The importance of motor development to
the young infant is described, and normal developmental processes are reviewed. Specific problems and
treatments for atypical infants are presented.

I. THE IMPORTANCE OF MOTOR DEVELOPMENT
Movement is used by infants for all aspects of development. Infants communicate with movement as well
as learn about the environment through motor abilities.

II. THE IMPORTANCE OF KNOWLEDGE OF MOTOR DEVELOPMENT
Professionals working with atypical infants should have
an appreciation of motor development and a general
knowledge of normal motor development sequences.

III. NORMAL MOTOR DEVELOPMENT

A. *Principles of motor development*
Control of the body begins in the head and progresses toward the toes. In addition, control begins
in the head, trunk, and pelvis and moves out toward
the limbs.

B. *Reflexive development*

1. *Gross motor development*
All volitional movements have as their substrata an elaborate mechanism of reflex action.

a. *Primary reflexes*
The reflexes of the newborn are a part of
this mechanism.

b. *Postural responses*
Righting, equilibrium, and protective responses all mature as the infant gains control of her body.

c. *Relationship of primary and postural responses*
Primary reflexes are integrated and postural responses emerge as the infant progresses through the first year of life.

2. *Fine motor development*
The ability to grasp and manipulate develops
from a reflexive background.

3. *Characteristics of muscle*
    Normal movement requires normal muscle tone and strength.

IV. SEQUENCE OF MOTOR SKILLS

A. *Gross motor*
    Infants develop postural control in a specific sequence. This sequence is described in detail with a description of possible variations which normally occur.
B. *Fine motor*
    The sequential development of fine motor skill and variation is described.

V. MOTOR DEVELOPMENT OF ATYPICAL INFANTS
Infants with motor problems may have normal variation, abnormal variation, or pathology of motor development. Each of these categories is described. Specific problems for each category include:

A. Prematurity
B. Cerebral palsy
C. Down syndrome
D. Congenital blindness

VI. ASSESSMENT OF MOTOR DEVELOPMENT

A. Guidelines for clinical assessment of motor problems are given.
B. Specific motor assessments and their limitations are described.

VII. INTERVENTION

A. *Nature/Nurture*
    Motor development represents a combination of maturation and experience.
B. *Theoretical assumptions influencing programs of motor intervention*
    Current assumptions and research in the area of brain recovery from insult are described and questioned.
C. *Approaches to developmental motor intervention*

Current therapeutic approaches for motor problems are described. These include:

1. Neurodevelopment treatment
2. The Rood approach

D. *Intervention Research*

Little empirical evidence is available on the question of the efficacy of motor intervention programs. Recommendations for future research are included.

REFERENCES

Adelson, E., and Fraiberg, S. Gross motor development in infants blind from birth. *Child Development*, 1974, *45*, 114–126.

Barnes, M. R., Crutchfield, C. A., and Heriza, C. B. *The Neurophysiological Basis of Patient Treatment, Vol. II: Reflexes in Motor Development*. Morgantown, WV: Stokesville Publishing, 1979.

Bayley, N. *Manual for the Bayley Scales of Infant Development*. New York: Psychological Corporation, 1969.

Bobath, K. *The Motor Deficit in Patients with Cerebral Palsy*. Clinics in Developmental Medicine, No. 23. Philadelphia: J. B. Lippincott, 1969.

Bobath, B. *Abnormal Postural Reflex Activity Caused by Brain Lesions* (2nd ed.). London: William Heinemann, 1971.

Bobath, K., and Bobath, B. Cerebral Palsy. In. P. Pearson & C. Williams (Eds.), *Physical Therapy Services in the Developmental Disabilities*. Springfield, IL: Charles C Thomas, 1972.

Bobath, B., and Bobath, K. *Motor Development in the Different Types of Cerebral Palsy*. London: William Heinemann, 1975.

Bower, T. G. R. *Development in Infancy*. San Francisco: W. H. Freeman, 1974.

Campbell, S. Effects of intervention in the special care nursery. In D. Routh and M. Woolraich (Eds.) *Advances in Behavioral Pediatrics* (Vol. 4). Greenwich, CT: Jai Press, in press.

Campbell, S. K. and Wilheim, I. J. *Developmental Sequences in Infants at High Risk for Central Nervous System Dysfunction: The Recovery Process in the First Year of Life*. Paper presented at the 3rd Annual Conference of the Michigan Association for Infant Mental Health, Ann Arbor, April, 1979.

Carter, R., and Campbell, S. Early neuromuscular development of the premature infant. *Physical Therapy*, 1975, *55*, 1333–1343.

Castner, B. M. The development of fine prehension in infancy. *Genetic Psychology Monographs*, 1932, *12*, 105–193.

Cohen, B. The vestibular-ocular reflex arc. In H. H. Hornhuber (Ed.), *Handbook of Sensory Physiology Vestibular System* (Vol. 6). Berlin: Springer, 1974.

Cohen, H. J., Birch, H. G., and Taft, L. F. Some considerations for evaluating the Doman-Delacato "patterning" method. *Pediatrics*, 1970, *45*, 302–314.

Deaver, G. G. Methods of treating the neuromuscular disabilities. *Archives of Physical Medicine*, 1956, *37*, 363–366.

D'Eugenio, D. B., and Rogers, S. J. *Early Intervention Developmental Profile.* Ann Arbor: University of Michigan, 1976.

Denhoff, E. A sensory-motor enrichment program. In C. C. Brown (Ed.), *Infants at Risk: Assessment and Intervention*. New Brunswick, NJ: Johnson & Johnson Pediatric Roundtable, 1981.

Dennis, W. The effect of cradling practices upon the onset of walking in Hopi children. *Journal of Genetic Psychology*, 1940, *56*, 77–86.

Doman, G. *What To Do about Your Brain-injured Child*. New York: Doubleday, 1974.

Ellis, E. *Physical Management of Developmental Disorders*. Clinics in Developmental Medicine, No. 26. London: William Heinemann, 1967.

Evarts, E. V., Bizzi, E., Burke, R. E., DeLong, M., and Thach, W. T. Central control of movement. *Neuroscience Research Program Bulletin*, 1971, 9, 1–170.

Fetters, L. Object permanence development in infants with motor handicaps. *Physical Therapy*, 1981, 61, 327–333.

Fetters, L., and Goldberg, S. Motor development of the premature infant. Paper presented at the International Conference on Infant Studies, Austin, March, 1981.

Field, T., Hallock, N., Ting, G., Dempsey, J., Dabiri, C., and Shuman, H. A first year follow-up of high-risk infants: Formulating a cumulative risk index. *Child Development*, 1978, 49, 119–131.

Finnie, N. *Handling the Young Cerebral Palsied Child at Home*. New York: Dutton, 1975.

Fraiberg, S. Intervention in infancy: A program for blind infants. *The Journal of the American Academy of Child Psychiatry*, 1971, 10, 381–405.

Frankenberg, W. K., and Dodds, J. B. The Denver Developmental Screening Test. *Journal of Pediatrics*, 1967, 71, 181–185.

Freedman, D. A., and Cannady, C. Delayed emergency of prone locomotion. *Journal of Nervous and Mental Disease*, 1971, 153, 108–117.

Gesell, A., and Amatruda, C. S. *Developmental Diagnosis*. New York: Haber, 1947.

Gesell, A., and Thompson, H. Learning and growth in identical infant twins: An experimental study by the method of co-twin control. *Genetic Psychology Monographs*, 1929, 6, 1–124.

Goldman, P. S. Functional development of the pre-frontal cortex in early life and the problem of neuronal plasticity. *Experimental Neurology*, 1971, 32, 366–387.

Goldman, P. S. Plasticity of function in the CNS. In D. G. Stein, J. J. Rosen, and N. Butters (Eds.), *Plasticity and Recovery of Function in the Central Nervous System*. New York: Academic Press, 1974.

Goldman, P. S. The role of experience in recovery of function following orbital prefrontal lesions in infant monkeys. *Neuropsychologic*, 1976, 32, 366–387.

Goodisman, L. D. A manipulation-free design for single-subject cerebral palsy research. *Physical Therapy*, 1982, 62, 284–289.

Griffin, P. M., and Sanford, A. R. *Learning Accomplishment Profile for Infants (LAP-I)*. Winston-Salem, NC: Kaplan School Supply Corp., 1975.

Halverson, H. M. An experimental study of prehension in infants by means of systematic cinema records. *Genetic Psychology Monographs*, 1931, 10, 107–286.

Halverson, H. M. A further study of grasping. *Journal of Genetic Psychology*, 1932, 7, 34–64.

Halverson, H. M. Studies of the grasping responses of each infancy: I. *Journal of Genetic Psychology*, 1937, 50–51, 371–392.

Hanson, M. J. Down's syndrome children: Characteristics and intervention research. In M. Lewis and L. Rosenblum (Eds.), *Genesis of Behavior (Vol. 3): The Uncommon Child*. New York: Plenum, 1981.

Hanson, M. J. *Teaching Your Down's Syndrome Infant: A Guide for Parents*. Baltimore: University Park Press, 1977.

Harris, S. R. Effects of neurodevelopmental therapy on motor performance of infants with Down's syndrome. *Developmental Medicine and Child Neurology*, 1981, 23, 477–483.

Hein, A., and Diamond, R. M. Locomotory space as a prerequisite for acquiring visually guided reaching in kittens. *Journal of Comparative and Physiological Psychology*, 1972, *81*, 394–398.

Henderson, A. Research in occupational therapy and physical therapy with children. In B. W. Camp (Ed.), *Advances in Behavioral Pediatrics* (Vol. II). Greenwich, CT.: Jai Press, 1981.

Hofsten, C. Observations on the development of reaching for moving objects. *Journal of Experimental Child Psychology*, 1979, *28*, 158–173.

Holt, K. S. Effects of positioning on motor development. *Journal of Pediatrics*, 1960, *57*, 571–575.

Hoskins, T. A., and Squires, J. E. Developmental assessment: A test for gross motor and reflex development. *Physical Therapy*, 1973, *53*, 117–126.

Howard, J., Parmelee, A. H., Kopp, C. B., and Littman, B. A neurologic comparison of pre-term and full-term infants at term conceptional age. *The Journal of Pediatrics*, 1976, *88*, 995–1002.

Kagan, J., Kearsley, R. B., and Zelazo, P. R. *Infancy*. Cambridge, MA: Harvard University Press, 1979.

Kennard, M. A. Age and other factors in motor recovery from precentral lesions in monkeys. *American Journal of Physiology*, 1936, *115*, 138–146.

Knott, M., and Voss, D. E. *Proprioceptive Neuromuscular Facilitation*. New York: Harper & Row, 1968.

Kopp, C. B. Fine motor abilities of infants. *Developmental Medicine and Child Neurology*, 1974, *16*, 629–636.

Lance, J. W., and McLeod, J. G. The mechanism of muscle tone and movement. In *A Physiological Approach to Clinical Neurology*. London: Butterworths, 1977.

Lawrence, D. G., and Hopkins, D. A. The development of motor control in the rhesus monkey: Evidence concerning the role of corticomotoneuronal connections. *Brain*, 1976, *99*, 235–254.

Lipsitt, L. P. Developmental psychobiology comes of age: A discussion. In L. P. Lipsitt (Ed.), *Developmental Psychobiology, The Significance of Infancy*. New York: Wiley, 1976.

Magnus, R. On cooperation and interference of reflexes from other sense organs with those of the labyrinths. *Laryngoscope*, 1926, *36*, 701–712.

Martin, J. P. *The Basal Ganglia and Posture*. Philadelphia: J. B. Lippincott, 1967.

McGraw, M. B. Neural maturation as exemplified in the reaching-prehensile behavior of the human infant. *The Journal of Psychology*, 1941, *11*, 127–141.

McGraw, M. B., *The Neuromuscular Maturation of the Human Infant*. New York: Hafner, 1963.

Milani-Comparetti, A., and Giodoni, E. A. Routine developmental examination in normal and retarded children. *Developmental Medicine and Child Neurology*, 1967, *9*, 631–638.

Molnar, G. E. Analysis of motor divides in retarded infants and young child. *American Journal of Mental Deficiency*, 1978, *83*, 213–222.

Mueller, H. A. Facilitating feeding and prespeech. In P. H. Pearson and C. E. Williams (Eds.). *Physical Therapy Services in the Developmental Disabilities*. Springfield, IL: Charles C Thomas, 1972.

Oppenheim, R. W. Ontogentic adaptations and retrogressive processes in the development of the nervous system and behavior: A neuroembryological perspective. In K. Connolly and H. F. R. Prechtl (Eds.), *Maturation and Development: Biological and Psychological Perspectives*. Clinics in Developmental Medicine. Philadelphia: J. B. Lippincott Co., 1981.

Parmelee, A. H. Early intervention for preterm infants. In C. C. Brown (Ed.), *Infants at Risk: Assessment and Intervention*. New Brunswick, NJ: Johnson & Johnson Pediatric Roundtable, 1981.

Parmelee, A., Fiske, C., and Wright, R. The development of ten children with blindness as a result of retrolental fibroplasia. *A. M. A. Journal of Diseases of Children*, 1959, *98*, 198–200.

Phelps, W. M. The treatment of the cerebral palsies. *Journal of Bone and Joint Surgery*, 1940, *22*, 1004–1012.

Piaget, J. *The Origins of Intelligence in Children*. New York: International Universities, 1952.

Prechtl, H. F. R., and Beintema, D. *The Neurological Examination of the Full Term Newborn Infant*. Clinics in Developmental Medicine, No. 12, Philadelphia: J. B. Lippincott, 1975.

Prechtl, H. F. R., Fargel, J. W., Weinmann, H. M., and Bakker, H. H. Postures, motibility and respiration of low-risk pre-term infants. *Developmental Medicine and Child Neurology*, 1979, *21*, 3–27.

Robson, P. Shuffling, hitching, scooting or sliding: Some observations in 30 otherwise normal children. *Developmental Medicine and Child Neurology*, 1970, *12*, 608–618.

Saint-Anne Dargassies, S. Neurological maturation of the premature infant 28 to 41 weeks gestational age. In F. Falkner (Ed.), *Human Development*. Philadelphia: W. B. Saunders, 1966.

Sanford, A. *Learning Accomplishment Profile (LAP)*. Winston-Salem, NC: Kaplan Press, 1974.

Sameroff, A. J. Early influences on development: Fact or fancy? *Merrill-Palmer Quarterly*, 1975, *21*, 267–294.

Share, J. B. Developmental progress in Down's syndrome. In R. Koch and F. F. de la Cruz (Eds.), *Down's Syndrome (Mongolism): Research, Prevention and Management*. New York: Bruner/Mazel, 1975.

Shea, A. M. Positioning in infancy possible effects on early motor development. Unpublished masters thesis, Boston: Tufts University, 1971.

Sigman, M., and Parmelee, A. H. Longitudinal evaluation of the pre-term infant. In T. M. Field, A. M. Sostek, S. Goldberg, and H. H. Shuman (Eds.). *Infants Born at Risk*. New York: Spectrum, 1979.

Sparrow, S., and Zigler, E. Evaluation of a patterning treatment for retarded children. *Pediatrics*, 1978, *62*, 137–150.

St. James-Roberts, I. Neurological plasticity, recovery from brain insult, and child development. *Advances in Child Development and Behavior*, 1979, *14*, 253–319.

Staheli, L. T., and Griffin, L., Corrective shoes for children: A survey of current practice. *Pediatrics*, 1980, *65*, 13–17.

Stockmeyer, S. A. An interpretation of the approach of Rood to the treatment of neuromuscular dysfunction. *American Journal of Physical Medicine*, 1967, *46*, 900–956.

Stockmeyer, S. A. A sensorimotor approach to treatment. In P. H. Pearson and C. E. Williams (Eds.), *Physical Therapy Services in the Developmental Disabilities*. Springfield, IL: Charles C Thomas, 1972.

Taft, L. F. Intervention programs for infants with cerebral palsy: A clinician's view. In C. C. Brown (Ed.), *Infants at Risk: Assessment and Intervention.* New Brunswick, NJ: Johnson & Johnson Pediatric Roundtable, 1981.

Twitchell, T. E. Normal motor development. *Physical Therapy*, 1965, 45, 411–418.

Twitchell, T. E. Reflex mechanism and the development of prehension. In K. J. Connolly (Ed.), *Mechanisms of Motor Skill Development.* New York: Academic Press, 1970.

White, B. L., Castle, P., and Held, R. Observation on the development of visually directed reaching. *Child Development*, 1964, 35, 349–364.

Wilson, V. J., and Peterson, B. W. Peripheral and central substrates of vestibulospinal reflexes. *Physiological Review*, 1978, 58, 80–105.

Wolanski, N., and Zdanska-Brincken, M. A. A new method for the evaluation of motor development of infants. *Polish Psychological Bulletin*, 1975, 4, 116–120.

Zausmer, E. Early developmental stimulation in Down's syndrome. In S. M. Pueschel (Ed.), *Down Syndrome.* Kansas City: Sheed Andrews & McMeel, 1978.

Zelazo, N., and Kolb, S. Walking in the newborn. *Science*, 1972, 176, 1058–1059.

Zigler, E. A plea to end the use of the patterning treatment for retarded children. *American Journal of Orthopsychiatry*, 1981, 51, 388–390.

SECTION IV
EARLY
INTERVENTION

Over the past decade considerable information has been amassed defining early intervention service delivery models and documenting the short- and long-term effects of these programs. In the final section Hanson defines exemplary practices in the field in light of this experience (Chapter 11) and reviews studies on the efficacy of early intervention (Chapter 12). The primary focus is from an educational model, which emphasizes coordinated health, so-

cial, and educational services to meet the comprehensive needs of the atypical infant population.

The provision of services to young atypical children and their families necessitates coordinated planning and implementation efforts across fields. The success of these efforts can be ensured only through the continuous exchange of information and collaboration among those charged with care and services for young children.

CHAPTER 11

Early Intervention
Models and Practices

Marci J. Hanson

> *We have learned the answers to three important questions that we asked and that we have been asked many times: (a) What does a baby do? (b) What can you do with a handicapped baby? (c) How do you get a baby to do things? We have learned there is a great deal of work involved with a handicapped child, but also the rewards of the hard work are well worth it.*
>
> *This program has helped us first to get to know Tony better and to know him as an individual with a great deal of potential. I think it has helped me personally to know that I am capable of helping both my child and other children. Most of all it has helped us to hang in there and not give up on Tony or give up hope.*
>
> Kathy Graville
> Parent
> (Hanson, 1977, p. 5)

Social, political, and scientific factors have converged in recent years to support the need for early intervention services for children who are developmentally at risk. The movement fostered in the 1960s to enhance the development of socially disadvantaged children has been extended in more recent years to a broader spectrum of children including those at biological risk. This shift is reflected by legislation in many states to provide early education to children with special needs beginning at birth, concern from public agencies over the need to fund services for infants, and the demand and needs expressed by parents for support and assistance soon after the child's birth. It is unlikely that this demand will subside given the increasing survival rate of large numbers of infants who are disabled or obviously at risk. Additionally, factors such as child abuse and teenage pregnancies contribute to a heightened incidence of handicaps in young children (Hayden, 1979). These social and political concerns have been paralleled by documentation of the importance of early experiences on later intellectual development (Hunt, 1961) and by a flood of basic research in the last 10 to 15 years on infant development.

This work has led to a view of the infant's competence from birth (Stone et al., 1973). Thus, both scientific and social-political variables have created a focus on intervening in the life of the young child who is at risk or disabled. This focus has produced the need for comprehensive and effective early intervention services.

The term *intervention* implies several assumptions. First, it connotes the design and implementation of a plan of action. Intervenors must have expertise in the areas of infant development, disabling conditions, and teaching strategies in order to develop this plan. In addition, they must be sensitive to and considerate of the social issues that may arise, particularly with families who are culturally different or problem laden. Second, the term *intervention* assumes that some degree of change is possible. Change may mean that the child's development progresses to meet normal developmental expectations, or change may mean that families adapt to the fact that the child will not develop normally (e.g., the child will never walk). Each is important.

Decision making regarding the design and matching of appropriate services to given children and families remains a difficult and complex task. Clinical experience and research findings, however, provide us with guides and identifiable components that must be considered in the design of intervention services. These components are reviewed in this chapter, and those factors that contribute to exemplary practices in early intervention services for children from birth to 3 years and their families are outlined. Intervention is used here generically to encompass all services from health care to psychological and educational support. The bulk of the discussion, however, is directed toward educational concerns.

WHY INTERVENE?

Provision of services to families of children at risk for developmental disability is a thoroughly defensible notion. Common sense and empirical evidence (reviewed in Chapter 12) dictate that attention be given to children early in life to sustain their development and ensure optimal growth. Without special, comprehensive interventions, children with known disability and those at high risk for developing problems may not develop early skills and relationships needed in order to lead productive lives. The aim of early intervention programs is to prevent disorders that may arise from pre- or perinatal trauma or impairments and/or remediate the effects of identified disabilities.

Despite the possible benefits of these services, many children are not referred to such programs at early ages. The "wait and see" and "perhaps the child will outgrow this" attitudes remain pervasive. Sound reasons may exist for this caution in referring children for intervention services. Services may not be available in a given location, or available services may be so diverse, untested, and/or controversial that responsible referrals to them cannot be made. Undoubtedly the referring professional also may be concerned about the potential deleterious effect of mislabeling a child. Given the inability of current infant screening and assessment devices to predict which children will be delayed at a later age and to determine which children will benefit from particular treatments, the decision to refer becomes difficult. These concerns however must be weighed against the effects of withholding opportunity for treatment. Parents are typically the first persons to recognize a developmental problem with their child. Failure to discuss honestly the issues and services available to them is professionally inexcusable. Additionally, precluding early services may render a child irreversibly handicapped. For example, a child with spasticity who does not receive appropriate therapeutic treatment, handling, and positioning may be in jeopardy of developing irreversible contractures. Providing parents with accurate information both on what is and is not known about the child's disorder and guiding them through the referral and treatment process undoubtedly alleviates many of the potential effects of "labeling" the child.

As Denhoff (1981) relates, one out of every ten families includes a child with a developmental disability. He maintains that although the effects of early enrichment regimens are often difficult to assess, there is evidence that the benefits of such services outweigh potential drawbacks. These benefits cited include the following:

> (1) They provide the infant and his/her parents with opportunities for both to develop to full potential. (2) Strengthening of the natural interactions between infant and parents that these programs provide is fundamental to good family development. (3) Various and numerous problems that produce parent guilt, anger, and frustration are lessened in a supportive milieu. (4) Constant reinforcement between infant and parents during the almost three-year program may lay the groundwork for the eventual emergence of positive developmental patterns (1981, p. 35).

As Denhoff suggests, the effects of early intervention, however difficult to document, are multifaceted and extensive.

COMPONENTS OF EXEMPLARY MODELS

In the last decade programs for infants and toddlers have prolifer-
ated. Such programs include both home- and center-based interventions located in schools, hospitals, and private facilities. The federal
government, through its Handicapped Children's Early Education
Program network (Office of Special Education Programs, U.S. Department of Education, formerly the Bureau of Education for the
Handicapped), has provided the leadership nationally to develop
and evaluate early intervention service models. Many of the demonstration projects funded through this network have supplied the
descriptive and empirical information necessary to ascertain which
model components are essential for exemplary services. The components reviewed in this chapter include the following: 1) target
populations; 2) philosophical approaches; 3) staffing patterns; 4) services for infants; 5) services for families; 6) coordination with other
agencies; and 7) provision of integrated (disabled and nondisabled)
services.

Target Populations

Assessing the needs of a geographical area and devising a clear definition of the target population to be served is the first step in the
development of a service approach. This definition dictates further
plans for referral and curriculum development. Currently, most infant programs serve the full range of infants from those with no
known disability but who, because of congenital problems, may be
at risk, to those babies with severe and multiple handicapping conditions.

Tjossem (1976) classifies "vulnerable" infants into three categories: infants with established risk, infants at environmental risk,
and infants at biological risk. Babies with *established risks* are defined as "those whose early appearing aberrant development is related to medical disorders of known etiology bearing well known
expectancies for developmental outcome within specific ranges of
developmental delay" (p. 5). The child with Down syndrome is an
example of a child in this risk category.

Tjossem (1976) defines infants at *environmental risk* as "biologically sound infants for whom life experiences including maternal
and family care, health care, opportunities for expression of adaptive
behaviors, and patterns of physical and social stimulation are sufficiently limiting to the extent that, without corrective intervention,
they impart high probability for delayed development" (p. 5). These

children are those raised in deprived settings for a significant portion of their infancy period.

The final type of risk is that of *biological risk*. Those at biological risk are defined as "infants presenting a history of prenatal, perinatal, neonatal, and early development events suggestive of biological insults to the developing central nervous system and which, either singly or collectively, increase the probability of later appearing aberrant development" (Tjossem, 1976, p. 5). Gorski (Chapter 3) discussed the difficulties in determining which of these infants will have later delays and also the issues of providing appropriate treatment, especially during the early weeks or months in the intensive care nursery.

Regardless of which factors render the infant vulnerable to developmental delay, the scope or target of intervention approaches must be not only the child but also the child's family. Assisting the infant's caregivers to understand his/her unique signals and behavior, to facilitate the baby's development, and to appraise the baby's status realistically over time are goals that dictate that family members be actively involved in any intervention effort.

Philosophical Approaches

Programs for children of preschool age and older can typically be categorized according to the theoretical approach adopted such as Piagetian, Behavioral, or Montessori. Such theories provide the undergirding for the development of curricula, instructional methods, role of the teacher, environmental setting, and view of the child's learning process.

In practice, most infant programs do not derive their procedures from such a single, clear theoretical perspective. Rather, programs typically combine elements of several models (Friedlander et al., 1975; Mittler, 1977; Tjossem, 1976). This practice risks providing obstacles or confusion for program implementation, more specifically with respect to curriculum design (Dunst, 1981).

Almost without exception, though, programs do define their approach as "developmental," and curricula generally focus on assisting the child to meet developmental milestones. The selection of these developmental targets, the sequences for teaching, and the means of training them differ from program to program. Therefore, given the lack of theoretical guidance reflected by current practices, philosophical approaches are discussed along the following dimensions rather than from a purely theoretically based perspective: 1) view of the infant; 2) purpose; 3) service delivery personnel; 4) curriculum; 5) instructional method; and 6) intervention setting.

View of the Infant   The view of the infant's roles and abilities in the interactional and educational process provides the overlay for the approach selected. The two extremes of the continuum are the view of the infant as a passive recipient and the view of the infant as an active learner. Programs adopting the former view focus primarily on stimulating the infant's senses and moving the child through exercises. Those viewing infants as active learners, on the other hand, base learning experiences on the individual child's initiations and responses to environmental stimuli, whether they be the mother's touch or the infant's play with a *Busy Box* toy.

Purpose   The purpose of the intervention is determined by the population served. Options range from programs providing day care to those systematically training parents as the primary teachers of their infants. Day care alternatives are obviously needed for families where both parents work and also are desirable options for environmentally at-risk children (Heber and Garber, 1975; Ramey et al., 1976). For other programs, training parents to teach their children is the primary purpose, whether the program be home-based, center-based, or a combination thereof (Lillie and Trohanis, 1976)

Service Delivery Personnel   Approaches also vary with regard to staffing patterns and the role of staff. Center-based programs often have a team of staff members representative of health care, psychological, and educational professionals (Haynes, 1976). Team members may function autonomously, providing specific treatments to children each in their own area of expertise, or they may jointly perform child assessments and develop treatment programs. Parents may or may not be actively included as team members. At the other end of the spectrum are home-based programs where a staff member serves as a consultant to parents, thereby assisting them to become the primary teachers of their children (Hanson, 1977; Shearer and Shearer, 1976). Such programs are particularly appropriate for families located in rural environments or for those with children with a specific disability or developmental need.

Curriculum   Dunst (1981) defines a curriculum as:

> *. . . a series of carefully planned and designed activities, events, and experiences intentionally organized and implemented to reach specified objectives and goals, and which adhere and ascribe to a particular philosophical and theoretical position, and whose methods and mode*

of instruction and curriculum content are logically consistent with the psychological perspective from which it has been derived (p. 9).

As was previously discussed, strict theoretical underpinnings are seldom found in practice for curricular designs, and contrasts between curricular orientations can be made on a variety of dimensions. Curricula may be *developmental* (e.g., Portage Project, Shearer and Shearer, 1976) in focus and aimed at teaching children developmental milestones in a sequential fashion, or they may be primarily concerned with training functional skills, such as the preschool "survival skill" of completing tasks without teacher direction (Vincent et al., 1980). Additionally, a number of exemplary intervention program curricula combine elements from several major theoretical perspectives such as the behavioral and Piagetian approaches (Bricker and Bricker, 1976; Johnson et al., 1979; Robinson and Robinson, 1978). They utilize developmental theory as a guide to curriculum content and a behavioral theoretical approach for determining how to structure, teach, and modify goals. Curricula also can be contrasted as to their orientation toward *product* or *process* learning. Most curricula have lists of target skills arranged in sequential order for training. More recently attention has been given to training process learning, that is, developing a "learning to learn" curriculum (Brinker and Lewis, 1982; Hanson, 1978). This orientation is based on the premise that infants are active learners who develop an awareness of causal relationships between their actions and environmental consequences ("contingency awareness") (Watson, 1966, 1972).

Instructional Methods   Methods of teaching infants vary along the continuum from directed to nondirected instruction. Many programs provide an enriched environment (e.g., toys and equipment to stimulate infants' movements and senses) and allow the infant to learn by selecting various activities and experiences. At the other end of the continuum are programs that teach a child selected target skills under highly structured circumstances. This type of program is characterized by identification of preselected goals, the conditions under which responses occur, and the consequation provided the infant for correct or incorrect responding.

Intervention Setting   Infant programs today are located in the full spectrum of settings—public and private schools, hospitals, homes and mental health and social service clinics. As such, they embody the full range of settings for service delivery. Some programs are exclusively home-based, others are center-based, and still others combine both approaches. Research on the efficacy of early intervention reveals that the setting is not the crucial variable but rather parental involvement (Bronfenbrenner, 1975). Analyses demonstrate that both home and center-based programs can positively influence child development.

Summary   This brief discussion of the various philosophical approaches employed by early intervention programs discloses the diversity of service models and also the difficulty in making comparative evaluations or judgments regarding the efficacy or appropriateness of any given regimen. However, a few major points can be underscored. Current research in infancy (Osofsky, 1979; Stone et al., 1973) highlights the importance of approaching the infant, even the disabled infant, as a competent, active learner capable of initiating and responding to the environment, no matter how handicapped the child may be. Second, decisions regarding the purpose, educational settings, curricula, and instructional methods must stem from identified theoretical models and the needs of the target population. Theoretical structure is essential to provide the framework for all intervention content and strategy and the needs of the particular population served dictates the format (e.g., day care, center based, or home based). [The reader is directed to Dunst (1981) for a discussion of major theoretical approaches and the design of infant curricula.] Furthermore, insofar as possible children should be provided experiential opportunities to utilize and expand upon their skills in all areas of development. Learning opportunities ideally combine various developmental domains (e.g., fine motor and communication) and focus on teaching children functional and naturally reinforcing skills (e.g., pulling to stand to get into the toy box, reaching for a toy, and making a sound to gain the attention of mother or father). Attention to the *process* of learning is needed as well as teaching infants to become mobile, explore their environment, and communicate with others. Finally, the one factor above all others that seems to be crucial is that of parent involvement. Research reports have indicated that those programs that actively involved parents were responsible for the most enduring and impressive gains (Bronfenbrenner, 1975).

Staffing Patterns

With no other age group is it so apparent that a range of disciplines must be represented in the delivery of services. Infants at risk typically must be closely monitored and/or treated for health concerns.

Parents of these infants often need emotional support and practical information for dealing with their children, and the infants must be provided opportunities for optimal growth and development. These needs have given rise to the *team* approach to service delivery.

The use of an interdisciplinary team to screen, assess, and provide educational and medical treatments to the young child is described in a number of publications (Allen et al., 1978; Bricker and Campbell, 1980; Haynes, 1976; Lyon and Lyon, 1980; McCormack and Goldman, 1979). These reports discuss the techniques used by team members and describe team coordination systems.

Early intervention programs typically employ professionals from the health care, psychological, and educational fields. Team members may include a special education teacher, clinical psychologist, social worker, physical therapist, occupational therapist, communication (speech and language) therapist, physician (generally a pediatrician and/or neurologist), nutritionist, and nurse. A few or all of these members may staff a center and work on a full-time, part-time, or consultant basis. Few programs, however, have the funding base to support such an extensive staff, particularly on a full-time basis. The degree to which team members coordinate activities is similarly diverse. Members may perform separate assessments and treatments with children and share information (interdisciplinary) or meet as a group having performed these services to jointly discuss and identify intervention goals (multidisciplinary). More recently, the approach termed *transdisciplinary* has been advocated. The transdisciplinary team approach, according to Lyon and Lyon (1980), is characterized by *joint team* effort, *staff development,* and *role release.* This approach necessitates that team members work together on assessing and treating children and train one another in their areas of expertise (while maintaining primary responsibility for their area). The role release strategy implies that members implement treatment facets that have traditionally been the domain of the "expert" in that area. As such each member is able to treat the "whole" child. For example, a physical therapist may utilize a "cognitive" activity such as a child playing with a puzzle or form board to motivate the child to perform a motor activity like reaching; the speech therapist similarly would ensure that the infant is appropriately positioned before engaging in speech facilitation activities. The parent is an important member of the team as well, and is given training (e.g., positioning and handling, facilitating communication, and structuring a learning task) on how to provide services for the child; the parent in turn instructs team members on the best procedures to use in interacting with and motivating the child and also on which goals to set. Team members may be designated as case managers for specific children or one member may be assigned the facilitator role to carry out a variety of interventions as is the case of a home visitor. This is similar to the role of "educational synthesizer" as described by Bricker (1976).

Current early intervention practice necessitates the involvement of professionals from a variety of disciplines and parents in the development of therapeutic strategies. The composition of the team, level of involvement, and implementation of services will vary, of course, depending on program purpose and needs. However, those models that emphasize coordinated services across disciplines generally are judged to be most effective and desirable by parents and practitioners in infant care settings. Denhoff (1981) relates that currently there is "a refocusing of the traditional medical role away from a disease model to a more comprehensive one"—a model that encourages collaborative efforts between all infant care and service providers.

Services for Infants

Coming from a developmental perspective infant programs often have based intervention efforts on an additive notion—teaching children milestone after milestone up the chart to higher order performance levels. Milestones selected are typically derived from infant assessment scales. This approach ignores attention to the process of learning as well as factors that include the importance of: 1) identifying the infant as an active learner; 2) determining and understanding the infant's individual signals and interactional style; 3) teaching the infant functional skills; 4) recognizing the interrelatedness of behaviors across developmental areas; and 5) facilitating the infant's motivation and ability to learn.

The case for viewing the infant as a competent and active learner is well-documented in this volume. Virtually every discussion starts with the premise that the infant from birth is capable of initiating and responding to the environment. The task for parents and infant service providers, thus, becomes understanding each individual infant's signals and style of interacting so that these skills can be developed into more complex and functional behavior for the infant. Even the most handicapped infant is capable of signaling the caregiver; the difficulty is in helping caregivers to learn to identify and "read" the signals. Two infants provide examples of unique signaling systems. One infant was born with no oral cavity, missing limbs, and limited vision; the other infant because of birth injuries was born deaf-blind with severe hypertonicity. Both babies were fed through gastrostomy tubes (tubes into their stomachs). The parents of each faced many difficult challenges in caring for their infants, not the least of which was developing a relationship with the child and understanding what the child needed at any point in time. The parents of both babies developed highly sophisticated means for communicating with their infants. The first baby learned to make differentiated whines for 'I'm hungry," "I'm wet," "I have dirty diapers"—whines that could be reliably "read" by her mother and father. The second baby and her mother communicated through body movements; for example, the baby moved her torso slightly to indicate when she wanted to be picked up. These cases represent dramatic examples of the individual infants' special means of interacting with the environment. Furthermore, as the research on infant temperament so clearly points out, even nondisabled infants exhibit tremendous variability on dimensions such as responsivity, distractibility, activity level, and mood (Carey, 1972; Rothbart, 1981; Thomas and Chess, 1977).

The selection of educational activities for infants at risk or disabled is governed by the infant's developmental level and needs. An underlying principle for decision making should be the selection of goals (in conjunction with the child's parents) that provide functional skills for the child upon which more complex skills can be built. In teaching a child to label objects, the first objects selected may include those related to foods or toys (e.g., cup, bottle, and ball). Armed with the skills to communicate, the child can begin to use sounds or words to produce desirable events (e.g., eating and playing). Labels taught in isolated circumstances are less likely to be generalizable to new settings or motivating or useful to the child. Intervenors, likewise, should avoid the pitfall of selecting goals from developmental assessments. Although "stacking eight blocks" and "demonstrating stranger anxiety" may be useful in comparing the developmental levels of children, it does not follow that they necessarily must be training goals.

Infants should be assessed in all areas of development (motor—fine and gross, cognitive, social, speech and language, and self-help) and goals should be established where treatment needs are identified. The team approach to infant services facilitates combining treatment programs, and as such underscores the importance of recognizing that infant behaviors are interrelated. Rather than the physical therapist positioning a child at one time and the teacher working with the child at another time on a goal related to manipulating a toy, a more efficient and beneficial approach is the combination of both programs so that the child is appropriately positioned to manipulate the toy and, thus, receives reinforcement for being in the proper position and playing with the toy. Such a training approach builds on the skills in the infant's repertoire, acknowledges the interrelatedness of skills, and capitalizes on the advantage of the natural reinforcement value of the situation.

Finally, the body of research substantiating infant competence (Stone et al., 1973) has been paralleled by investigations of the young infant's learning processes. The role of response contingent experiences in facilitating "feelings of efficacy" (White, 1959), social competence (Goldberg, 1977; Watson, 1972), and cognitive development (Lewis and Goldberg, 1969) has been documented. In this learning paradigm the infant exercises control over his/her environment and is able to produce predictable outcomes. If infant behavior is responded to consistently, infants learn that their actions affect the environment. This process is accepted as essential to learning, affective and cognitive development, and motivation. Studies by Watson (Watson, 1971, 1972; Watson and Ramey, 1972) on contingent learning suggested that infants receiving contingent experiences (as contrasted to noncontingent control group infants) not only learned target motor behavior but also exhibited positive affective responses. Other investigations established that "contingency" experiences have a generalized facilitory effect on retention and learning of other unrelated responses (Finkelstein and Ramey, 1977; Rovee and Fagan, 1976). This research raises implications for developing process-oriented curricula designed to teach children to "learn to learn" (Brinker and Lewis, 1982; Hanson, 1978; Lewis, 1978). Furthermore, it leads one to question the incorporation of noncontingent stimulation toys and activities in an infant training program. The use of toys, such as wind-up mobiles, in which the feedback the infant receives is *noncontingent* (not contingent on the infant's response) may in fact prove detrimental. Watson's (1971, 1972) studies, for example, suggest this may be the case. Rather, the bulk of the evidence shows that curricula should focus on the provision of response-contingent experiences for the infant.

The emphasis of this discussion is on educational services for infants. The assumption is made that health care is conducted by trained medical personnel. It should be noted, however, that the infant "teacher" can be an important assistant to health care providers. By providing general health care surveillance and referring parents to proper services when disorders arise or when further evaluations (e.g., ophthalmological, audiological, and so forth) are warranted, the infant interventionist can ensure that infants receive the coordinated range of services necessary for optimal development.

Services for Families

Bronfenbrenner's (1975) review of early education programs led him to conclude strongly that the most successful interventions actively involved parents. The rationale for involving parents is extensive and centers on issues such as the amount of time spent with the child, the need for consistent child care, the quality of parent-child interactions, the reinforcing value of the parent, the cost-effectiveness of parent-delivered services, and the success of parents in producing child change through their teaching efforts (Bricker and Bricker, 1976; Lillie and Trohanis, 1976; Vincent and Broome, 1977).

Today parents are faced with a range of program options and responsibilities. On one hand, the staff members of early intervention programs seek to increase parents' active participation in their children's education; yet, on the other hand, they must recognize the limits parents often face. As with direct services to infants, the various needs of the parent population served demand flexible program options.

The range of roles and responsibilities available to parents extend from that of teacher to advocate to staff member. These roles are extensively outlined in a number of publications (Lillie and Trohanis, 1976; Shearer and Shearer, 1977; Turnbull, 1978; Wiegerink et al., 1980).

The needs of parents are similarly diverse. This discussion highlights four major need areas: 1) general information; 2) support and counseling, 3) education/training, and 4) parent-infant interaction.

Information When parents of a young infant are first referred to an intervention program they often come filled with questions—questions about the child's disorder or special need, questions about prognosis, questions about services available now and in the future, questions about the effects of intervention, and questions about basic caregiving. The list of issues faced by families seems endless. Often the meeting with intervention program staff provides the first opportunity to discuss these issues extensively. Over time through discussions, parent meetings, interviews, and/or perhaps a formal parent needs assessment process (e.g., Parent Needs Assessment, Project KIDS, Department of Special Education, Dallas Independent School District, Dallas, Texas) the parents' goals and needs are identified.

Infant intervenors, thus, are charged with the task of synthesizing information from many resources in order to assist parents; they must also refer parents to other agencies when necessary.

A useful method for determining appropriate early intervention services in a manner requiring shared input from professional staff members and parents is the adoption of an individualized plan for the family. This plan is much like the individualized education program (IEP) for the child. One such example is the parent involvement plan (PIP), which lists parent needs ranging from medical and transportation services to instructional needs relating to a child's educational program (Brackman et al., 1977; Filler and Kasari, 1981; Hanson, 1981). Bricker and Casuso (1979) describe a similar plan, the individual parent plan, which incorporates identification of objectives for family involvement and evaluation activities related to meeting those objectives. Methods such as these provide a basis for gathering information about families' needs and designing appropriate strategies in order to furnish parents with the information and services they seek.

Support and Counseling   All parents face a never ending series of decisions and adjustments surrounding child rearing. For parents of children at risk these decisions and adjustments may constitute major stresses and disruptions to family dynamics. These parents are not only faced with the emotional loss of the expected child (Solnit and Stark, 1961), but also acceptance of the diagnosis and special needs of the child. This adjustment process does not stop. As one mother recently expressed in a parent meeting, "People need to understand that having a handicapped child goes on all day. I have to dress him differently, feed him differently; he's handicapped when we go to the grocery store, when we come to school, when we visit relatives. It's a part of everything we do *all the time.*"

To the specific needs of the child may be added concomitant or related stresses—financial concerns, marital problems, medical needs. These stresses must be addressed and alleviated before the family can become fully involved in the child teaching process.

Early intervention programs can assist by referring parents to mental health and social service agencies when available. Additionally, program options that include opportunities for parents to talk with one another or with professionals trained in counseling are deemed useful by participating parents (Hanson, 1981). The position, thus, advocated for staff members is that of coordinator or broker of services; they are charged with devising services or referring parents to services as needed.

Education/Training   The parent role most often discussed in the literature is that of the child's teacher. Although parents vary as to the degree to which they wish to take on teaching responsibilities, most want at least basic information on how to care for the baby, how to hold and feed the baby, and how to play with the baby. All these activities can be utilized, of course, to facilitate the infant's development. A variety of training options can be used to dispense this information to parents, the most common of which are group meetings, training in the classroom, or individual sessions. Although all options are useful for different goals, programs should develop a plan for communicating with the child's parent on a regular basis. This communication may range from a note sent home with the child to a structured program, planning and data collection system between parent and professional (Hanson, 1977). It must be remembered, however, that the effects of any treatment activities are limited to that 1 to 2 hours per day or week that the infant attends a program unless parents are providing follow-through activities at home.

Parent-Infant Interaction   Understanding the unique behavior of the child at risk often poses special problems to parents—the baby may not be as responsive as a normal child, may not make eye contact or display facial expressions as readily as a normal child, or may become rigid when held. These characteristics tax the relationship between parent and child and highlight an important intervention need. As Fraiberg and colleagues indicated (Fraiberg, 1974), a major intervention goal became assisting parents to recognize and understand their infants' cues so that they could establish a mutually beneficial relationship with their babies.

Goldberg (1977) notes that parents typically monitor their infant's behavior and decide when and how to intervene. Parents' feelings of competence as parents undoubtedly are linked to the subsequent infant responsiveness. If parents—particularly parents of children at risk or disabled—are not assisted in this interactional process, they may experience great difficulty with their babies. Continued interactions between parent and child may be jeopardized.

Three characteristics of individual differences among infants are considered by Goldberg (1977). They include: 1) *readability*, "the extent to which an infant's behaviors are clearly defined and provide distinctive signals and cues for adults" (p. 171); 2) *predictability*, "the extent to which an adult can reliably anticipate behavior from contextual events and/or immediately preceding behaviors" (p. 172); and 3) *responsiveness*, "the quality and extent of infant reactions to stimulation" (p. 172).

These characteristics provide a guide for identifying issues faced by parents of babies at risk in establishing relationships with their infants. Fraiberg (1974), for example, found that parents of blind babies needed to learn to read their babies' hand signals in the absence of normal facial expressions. Likewise, the baby with an irregular schedule and unpredictable state changes has been shown to produce distress for the caregiver (Thoman et al., 1978). Similarly, the nonresponsive severely handicapped infant may "turn off" the parent's ministrations or, as in the case of preterm babies, necessitate shifts in parent behavior to arouse the child (Field et al., 1979). Assisting parents to understand their infants' cues and learn to modify their infants' behaviors (e.g., soothe) promotes interest in the infant and feelings of parenting competence, thus stimulating mutually effective and satisfying interactions. Guidelines and practices such as those proposed by Bromwich (1981) provide a model for such intervention efforts. Additionally, analysis of parent-child interaction "styles" provides the intervenor with information with which to communicate with parents and also the basis for devising individualized education/treatment strategies (Vietze and Anderson, 1981).

The provision of services to families must include all family members, be adaptable to different family constellations, and consider cultural variability. This discussion uses the term *parent* throughout. In most programs *parent* is synonomous with *mother*. Often mothers are primarily involved in their child's education program, with fathers, siblings, and other family members receiving less responsibility for support and services. Although difficult to achieve, early intervention programs must strive to meet the needs of *all* family members. At the same time programs must be providing services appropriate for the variety of family constellations found in American families today—two-parent families, single-parent families, extended families, foster families. Furthermore, disabilities strike across all groups; programs must be geared to provide service to the range of cultures in our society. A case in point is that of a toddler in an early intervention program. The child was clumsy at school, often tripping and falling, although no physiological reasons for this behavior were found. When staff members visited this Samoan child's home they realized that the child had been raised in a home environment consisting largely of low mats; the furniture at school constituted obstacles never before encountered by the child. Additionally, across cultures the roles of mothers and fathers are defined quite differently; intervention programs must be cautious so that services do not conflict with family patterns and values. Last, making information available in various languages facilitates adequate communication between the home and intervention program.

Coordination with Other Agencies

Most parents of a child at risk are involved with a myriad of agencies. The infant's health must be monitored closely, special tests may need to be conducted (e.g., ophthalmological and audiological), the family may be assigned to agencies that determine benefits (e.g., insurance) and services available (e.g., psychotherapy)—the list goes on and on. A mother in an intervention program recently remarked that she was "on her fourteenth social worker in 3 years." The appointment calendars of many of these parents as they shuffle from agency to agency often match those of a business executive's for complexity. Parents are faced, therefore, with determining the needs of their children, identifying services that are available, and ensuring that the children receive these services. In the process they must synthesize the various professional opinions given in order to make decisions for their child. The burden can be tremendous.

Infant intervention programs are in the unique position of gathering information from all these agencies because it is essential to the early intervention process that the child's medical concerns are identified, special test reports are provided, and family involvement with social service agencies is defined. This position provides program staff members with the unique opportunity and responsibility of coordinating services. This coordination is crucial to ensure adequate child care and consistent service provision.

Integrated Services

Most early intervention programs, although located in schools, hospitals, and homes, do not have access to groups of nondisabled children, which could serve as normal age peer models for the disabled youngsters. The research on early integrated services (Guralnick, 1977, 1978) and the spirit of Public Law 94-142, the Education for All Handicapped Children Act (although not applicable to children below age 3), however, indicate that the provision of services to young children in integrated (disabled and nondisabled) settings is desirable. Children are benefited by learning from one another, and parents of both disabled and nondisabled children learn that they often share more similarities than differences. Thus, integrating children at early ages ensures that children at risk and their families are not relegated to an isolated status within the community. Although often difficult from a practical standpoint to achieve (i.e., locating groups of nondisabled young children), integrated services nevertheless are a noteworthy goal.

SUMMARY

The question of early intervention has been moved from *whether* to provide services to *how* best to provide services. No trends in our society indicate that the need for early support and training activities will subside. Rather it is likely that families in increasing numbers will continue to seek out such services. The challenge before us, thus, is to exercise a vigilant watch over these services to ensure that parents are actively involved in the planning and evaluation process so that programs meet the consumer's needs, and to ensure that the most effective practices are empirically identified and professional and program standards are fully defined and met. This challenge remains.

Chapter Outline

Overview: The case for early intervention is presented. Exemplary service delivery components are identified and discussed.

I. Why Intervene?
Social, political, and scientific findings have converged in recent years to provide the rationale for early intervention.

II. Components of Exemplary Models
Major program components include:

A. Definition of target populations:
1. Infants with established risks
2. Infants at environmental risk
3. Infants at biological risk

B. Philosophical approaches:
1. View of the infant
2. Program purpose
3. Service delivery personnel
4. Curriculum
5. Instructional methods
6. Intervention setting

C. Staffing patterns:
1. Interdisciplinary team
2. Transdisciplinary model (this model is advocated)

D. Services for infants are derived from considerations of the following:
1. Identifying the infant as an active learner
2. Determining and understanding the infant's individual signals and interactional style
3. Teaching the infant functional skills
4. Recognizing the interrelatedness of behaviors across developmental areas
5. Facilitating the infant's motivation and ability to learn

E. Services for families are centered around four major need areas:

    1.   General information
    2.   Support and counseling
    3.   Education/training
    4.   Parent-infant interactions

F.   Coordination with other agencies is an essential component for early intervention programs.

G.   Integrated service delivery, a service delivery approach that includes nondisabled as well as disabled children, is advocated.

III. SUMMARY

The question of defining the most *appropriate* and *best* services for young children remains. Intervenors are challenged to contribute to this knowledge base.

REFERENCES

Allen, K. E., Holm, V. A., and Schiefelbusch, R. L. (Eds.). *Early Interven-tion—A Team Approach.* Baltimore: University Park Press, 1978.

Brackman, B., Fundakowski, G., Filler, J. W., Jr., and Peterson, C. Total pro-gramming for severely/profoundly handicapped young children. In B. Wil-cox (Ed.), *Proceedings of the Illinois Institute for Educators of the Se-verely/Profoundly Handicapped.* Springfield: Illinois Office of Education, 1977.

Bricker, D. Educational synthesizer. In M. A. Thomas (Ed.), *Hey, Don't Forget About Me!* Reston, VA: The Council for Exceptional Children, 1976.

Bricker, W. A., and Bricker, D. D. The infant, toddler, and preschool research and intervention project. In T. D. Tjossem (Ed.), *Intervention Strategies for High-Risk Infants and Young Children.* Baltimore: University Park Press, 1976.

Bricker, W. A., and Campbell, P. H. Interdisciplinary assessment and pro-gramming for multihandicapped students. In W. Sailor, B. Wilcox, and L. Brown (Eds.), *Methods of Instruction for Severely Handicapped Students.* Baltimore: Paul H. Brookes, 1980.

Bricker, D., and Casuso, V. Family involvement: A critical component of early intervention. *Exceptional Children,* 1979, *46,* 108–116.

Brinker, R. and Lewis, M. Discovering the competent handicapped infant: A process approach to assessment and intervention. *Topics in Early Child-hood Special Education,* 1982, *2*(2), 1–16.

Bromwich, R. M. *Working with Parents and Infants: An Interactional Ap-proach.* Baltimore: University Park Press, 1981.

Bronfenbrenner, U. Is early intervention effective? In B. Z. Friedlander, G. M. Sterritt, and G. E. Kirk (Eds.), *Exceptional Infant, (Vol. 3): Assessment and Intervention.* New York: Bruner/Mazel, 1975.

Carey, W. B. Clinical applications of infant temperament. *Journal of Pedi-atrics,* 1972, *81,* 823–828.

Denhoff, E. Current status of infant stimulation or enrichment programs for children with developmental disabilities, *Pediatrics,* 1981, *67* (1), 32–46.

Dunst, C. J. *Infant Learning: A Cognitive-Linguistic Intervention Strategy.* Hingham, MA: Teaching Resources, 1981.

Field, T. M., Sostek, A. M., Goldberg, S., and Shuman, H. H. (Eds.). *Infants Born at Risk: Behavior and Development.* New York: Spectrum, 1979.

Filler, J. W., Jr., and Kasari, C. Acquisition, maintenance and generalization of parent-skills taught with two severely handicapped infants. *Journal of the Association for the Severely Handicapped,* 1981, *6,* 30–38.

Finkelstein, N. W., and Ramey, C. T. Learning to control the environment in infancy. *Child Development,* 1977, *48,* 806–819.

Fraiberg, S. Blind infants and their mothers: An examination of the sign system. In M. Lewis and L. A. Rosenblum (Eds.), *The Effect of the Infant on Its Caregiver.* New York: Wiley, 1974.

Friedlander, B. Z., Sterritt, G. M., and Kirk, G. E. (Eds.). *Exceptional Infant (Vol. 3): Assessment and Intervention.* New York: Brunner/Mazel, 1975.

Goldberg, S. Social competence in infancy: A model of parent-infant inter-action. *Merrill-Palmer Quarterly,* 1977, *23,* 163–177.

Guralnick, M. J. Nonhandicapped peers as educational and therapeutic re-

sources. In P. Mittler (Ed.), *Research to Practice in Mental Retardation*
(Vol. I): Care and Intervention. Baltimore: University Park Press, 1977.

Guralnick, M. J. (Ed.). *Early Intervention and the Integration of Handicapped*
and Nonhandicapped Children. Baltimore: University Park Press, 1978.

Hanson, M. J. *Teaching Your Down's Syndrome Infant: A Guide for Parents.*
Baltimore: University Park Press, 1977.

Hanson, M. J. *Curriculum Development and Related Research with Mod-*
erately and Severely Handicapped Infants. Paper presented at the Fifth
Annual American Association for the Education of the Severely/
Profoundly Handicapped Conference, Baltimore, October, 1978.

Hanson, M. J. A model for early intervention with culturally diverse single
and multi-parent families. *Topics in Early Childhood Special Education,*
1981, 1(3), 37–44.

Hayden, A. H. Handicapped children birth to age 3. *Exceptional Children,*
1979, 45, 510–516.

Haynes, V. B. The National Collaborative Infant Project. In T. D. Tjossem
(Ed.), *Intervention Strategies for High-Risk Infants and Young Children.*
Baltimore: University Park Press, 1976.

Heber, R., and Garber, H. The Milwaukee Project: A study of the use of family
intervention to prevent cultural-familial mental retardation. In B. Z. Friedlander, G. M. Sterritt, and G. E. Kirk (Eds.), *Exceptional Infant (Vol. 3):*
Assessment and Intervention. New York: Brunner/Mazel, 1975.

Hunt, J. McV. *Intelligence and Experience.* New York: Ronald Press, 1961.

Johnson, N. M., Jens, K. G., and Attermeier, S. M. *Carolina Curriculum for*
Handicapped Infants (Field Test Edition). Chapel Hill, NC: Carolina Institute for Research on Early Education for the Handicapped, 1979.

Lewis, M. *Institute for the Study of Exceptional Children: Research Plan.*
Princeton, NJ: Educational Testing Service, 1978.

Lewis, M., and Goldberg, S. Perceptual-cognitive development in infancy:
A generalized expectancy model as a function of the mother-infant interaction. *Merrill-Palmer Quarterly of Behavior and Development,* 1969,
15, 81–100.

Lillie, D. L., and Trohanis, P. L. (Eds.). *Teaching Parents to Teach.* New
York: Walker, 1976.

Lyon, S., and Lyon, G. Team functioning and staff development: A role release approach to providing integrated educational services for severely
handicapped students. *Journal of the Association for the Severely Hand-*
icapped, 1980, 5(3), 250–263.

McCormick, L., and Goldman, R. The transdisciplinary model: Implications
for service delivery and personnel preparation for the severely and profoundly handicapped. *AAESPH Review,* 1979, 4, 152–161.

Mittler, P. (Ed.). *Research to Practice in Mental Retardation (Vol. I): Care*
and Intervention. Baltimore: University Park Press, 1977.

Osofsky, J. D. (Ed.). *Handbook of Infant Development.* New York: Wiley,
1979.

Ramey, C. T., Collier, A. M., Sparling, J. J., et al. The Carolina Abecedarian
Project: A longitudinal and multidisciplinary approach to the prevention
of developmental retardation. In T. D. Tjossem (Ed.), *Intervention Stra-*
tegies for High-Risk Infants and Young Children. Baltimore: University
Park Press, 1976.

Robinson, C. C. and Robinson, J. H. Sensorimotor functions and cognitive development. In M. E. Snell (Ed.)., *Systematic Instruction of the Moderately and Severely Handicapped*. Columbus, OH: Charles E. Merrill, 1978.

Rothbart, M. K. Measurement of temperament in infancy. *Child Development*, 1981, *52*, 569–578.

Rovee, C. K., and Fagan, J. W. Extended conditioning and 24-hour retention in infants. *Journal of Experimental Child Psychology*, 1976. *21* 1–11.

Shearer, D. E., and Shearer, M. S. The Portage Project: A model for early childhood intervention. In T. D. Tjossem (Ed.), *Intervention Strategies for High-Risk Infants and Young Children*. Baltimore: University Park Press, 1976.

Shearer, M. S., and Shearer, D. E. Parent involvement. In J. B. Jordan, A. H. Hayden, M. B. Karnes, and M. M. Wood (Eds.), *Early Childhood Education for Exceptional Children*. Reston: VA: The Council for Exceptional Children, 1977.

Solnit, A. J., and Stark, M. H. Mourning and the birth of a defective child, *Psychoanalytic Study of the Child*, 1961, *16*, 523–537.

Stone, J. L., Smith, H. T., and Murphy, L. B. (Eds.). *The Competent Infant*. New York: Basic Books, 1973.

Thoman, E. B., Becker, P. T., and Freese, M. P. Individual patterns in mother-infant interactions. In G. P. Sackett (Ed.), *Observing Behavior (Vol. 1): Theory and Applications in Mental Retardation*. Baltimore: University Park Press, 1978.

Thomas, A., and Chess, S. *Temperament and Development*. New York: Brunner/Mazel, 1977.

Tjossem, T. D. (Ed.). *Intervention Strategies for High-Risk Infants and Young Children*. Baltimore: University Park Press, 1976.

Turnbull, A. P. Parent-professional interactions. In M. E. Snell (Ed.), *Systematic Instruction of the Moderately and Severely Handicapped*. Columbus, OH: Charles E. Merrill, 1978.

Vietze, P. M., and Anderson, B. J. Styles of parent-child interaction. In M. Begab, C. Haywood, and H. Garber (Eds.), *Psychosocial Influences in Retarded Performance* (Vol. I). Baltimore: University Park Press, 1981.

Vincent, L. J., and Broome, K. A public school service delivery model for handicapped children between birth and five years of age. In E. Sontag, J. Smith, and N. Certo (Eds.), *Educational Programming for the Severely and Profoundly Handicapped*. Reston, VA: The Council for Exceptional Children, 1977.

Vincent, L. J., Salisbury, C., Walter, G., et al. Program evaluation and curriculum development in early childhood special education: Criteria of the next environment. In W. Sailor, B. Wilcox, and L. Brown (Eds.), *Methods of Instruction for Severely Handicapped Students*. Baltimore: Paul H. Brookes, 1980.

Watson, J. S. The development and generalization of "contingency awareness" in early infancy: Some hypotheses. *Merrill-Palmer Quarterly*, 1966, *12*, 123.

Watson, J. S. Cognitive-perceptual development in fancy: Setting for the seventies. *Merrill-Palmer Quarterly*, 1971, *17*, 139–152.

Watson, J. S. Smiling, cooing, and "the game." *Merrill-Palmer Quarterly*, 1972, *18*, 323–339.

Watson, J. S., and Ramey, C. T. Reactions to response-contingent stimulation in early infancy. *Merrill-Palmer Quarterly*, 1972, *18*, 219–227.

White, R. W. Motivation reconsidered: The concept of competence. *Psychological Review,* 1959, *66,* 297–333.

Wiegerink, R., Hocutt, A., Posante-Loro, R., and Bristol, M. M. Parent involvement in early education programs for handicapped children. *New Directions for Exceptional Children,* 1980, 1(4), 67–85.

CHAPTER 12
The Effects of
Early Intervention

Marci J. Hanson

Some people believe that the problems of the birth to age 3 group are only in the health and medical realms. Indeed, many of these children desperately need health and medical care early, but they and their families also need early educational intervention. While nonhandicapped young children may make acceptable progress without early educational interventions, handicapped or at risk children do not. To deny them the attention that might increase their chances for improved functioning is not only wasteful, it is ethically indefensible
(Hayden, 1979, p. 510).

Several extensive literature reviews have been conducted related to the question: Is early intervention effective? Without exception these reviews have concluded that early services for children from birth through preschool years, particularly those services which actively involve parents, constitute an effective means of facilitating child development and remediating the effects of early environmental risks (Beller, 1979; Bronfenbrenner, 1975; Haskins et al., 1978; Lazar and Darlington, 1982; McCluskey and Arco, 1979). Notable programs among those reviewed included home-based programs with a primary focus on parent education (Gordon, 1969, 1972; Gray and Klaus, 1970; Karnes et al., 1970; Lally and Honzig, 1977; Levenstein, 1970; Lambie et al., 1974), child-oriented programs utilizing home-based models (Painter, 1969; Schaefer and Aaronson, 1972), and child-oriented programs with center-based models (Beller, 1974; Heber and Garber, 1975; Palmer, 1972; Ramey et al., 1976; Weikart et al., 1978a). These programs shared a focus on the disadvantaged or environmentally at-risk child, and all demonstrated developmental gains for experimental (treatment) groups of children. Additionally, as Lazar and Darlington (1982) reported, the impact of early education from follow-up studies revealed extensive changes; children in these programs were more likely to meet their school's basic requirements, outperformed control group children on intelligence test measures, and were more likely to provide achievement-related reasons (e.g., school accomplishments) for being proud of themselves. The mothers of these children also were more positive regarding school and vocational issues related to the children. Thus, these evaluation studies on early education disclose a variety of effects primarily related to improved child performance outcomes. At the same time they leave other questions unanswered: 1) Are programs for the biologically impaired infant equally as effective as those for the environmentally at risk/disadvantaged; and 2) What is the range of program effects?

The case for program effectiveness is less clearly established with infants who are biologically at risk or for infants with an established risk than are program effects for children at risk due to sociocultural factors. As Gorski (Chapter 3) indicated in his review of intervention/stimulation programs for biologically at-risk neonates, although studies show promising results for facilitating infant development, the design and implementation of such programs must be carefully considered in light of effects on individual infants both behaviorally and physiologically and on the child's interaction with his/her caregivers.

Current practice in many parts of the U.S. is that children under age 3 born with an established risk (e.g., Down syndrome or blind) factor will be referred for medical and educational treatments (where available). However, given the limited financial and personnel resources in most of these early education programs, only a few systematic attempts to document the effects of these programs have been made. Published reports that present summative data on program effects, thus, are reviewed briefly in this section.

DOCUMENTED EFFECTS FOR CHILDREN AT ESTABLISHED RISK

Down Syndrome

The group of children for which the most information on early intervention effects exists is that of Down syndrome. A number of investigations have produced evidence that infants with Down syndrome benefit from early educational services. One of the major programs studied in this area is that of the Down's Syndrome Program in the Model Preschool Center for Handicapped Children, University of Washington (Hayden and Dmitriev, 1975; Hayden and Haring, 1976). The objectives of that program were to develop and apply sequential teaching to increase the child's rate of development in motor, communication, social, cognitive, and self-help skills (Hayden and Haring, 1977). Emphasis was placed on involving parents as their child's teacher, as liaison agents with classroom teachers, in parent-to-parent programs, and as participants in clinic activities such as conducting site-visitor interviews (Hayden, 1976). Classes included an infant learning class, an early preschool, and a kindergarten class. Results of the early and advanced preschool programs (Hayden and Dmitriev, 1975) indicated that all children in the early preschool programs met self-help objectives to the 85 to 100% competency level, and other skills in gross-motor, language, and concept development ranged from 39 to 100% competency levels. In a later report, Hayden and Haring (1977) stated that children in the Model Preschool Center increased in developmental level and progress rates as they grew older and had longer exposure to the preschool program. The Model Preschool children leveled off at approximately 95% of normal development (measured by Model Preschool Down's Syndrome Inventory), whereas a contrast group that did not attend the Model Preschool leveled off at about 61% of normal development. Follow-up studies of these youngsters (Hayden and Haring, 1979) underscore the effects of this early and continuous training. Children who received early education in the Model Preschool Center continue to outperform other children with Down syndrome and other handicapped children who did not receive the early training as measured on the Vineland Social Maturity Scale and Stanford-Binet. Furthermore, these preschool graduates required fewer special education placements at school age.

Recently Clunies-Ross (1979) studied 36 children with Down syndrome ranging in age from 3 to 37 months who participated in a combination center- and home-based program. Children received structured programs in language, social, self-care, cognitive, fine perceptual motor, and gross motor development. Results from the assessments of these children using the Early Intervention Developmental Profile (D'Eugenio and Rogers, 1976) indicated that children made progressive developmental achievements over the course of the intervention and that their rate of progress was inversely related to the age at which the program was begun.

Hanson and Schwarz (1978) compared the developmental achievements of 15 children with Down syndrome who were participants in an intensive home-based program with developmental data on home-reared Down syndrome children who had not received early intervention. Intervention services focused on assisting parents to "teach" their infants in all areas of development. Findings showed that the development of infants with Down syndrome was accelerated across developmental areas beyond expectations based on descriptive information on children for whom early educational services were not available and as measured on criterion referenced tests and by the Bayley Scales of Infant Development (Hanson, 1981).

Similarly, Ludlow and Allen (1979) compared three groups of children with Down syndrome. One group attended a developmental clinic playgroup or nursery school and their parents received counseling. In a second group the children were home reared but received no special sessions, and a third group of children had been placed in residential care before their second birthday. Developmental assessments were conducted on all children; children in the first group who had received early intervention outperformed the other groups on the Griffiths Mental Development Scales, the Stanford-Binet, Personal Social Development Scale, and Speech Development measures. Likewise, more children from that group were later placed in ordinary school placements than were children from the other two groups.

The effects of early intervention for children with Down syndrome are supported also by several other studies. Connolly and Russell (1976) demonstrated that 40 children with Down syndrome receiving early intervention services attained gross motor, fine motor, feeding, and social skills at earlier ages than children not receiving intervention. Additionally, Connolly et al. (1980) compared 20 children from the previous study who had received early intervention focusing on the family with 53 noninstitutionalized children who had not. The former showed higher intellectual and social quotients at 3 to 6 years of age and earlier acquisition of motor and self-help skills. Results of a study by Bidder et al. (1975) also confirm that a parent-implemented treatment program for home-reared young children with Down syndrome can effectively produce gains in target children as contrasted to children not participating in a treatment program. Similar effects were noted by Aronson and Fällström (1977) in their study of 16 children with Down syndrome between 21 and 69 months of age living in a residential care facility. Children were divided into two groups: one that received preschool training and one that did not. Children in the training group showed a greater increase in mental age than control group children as measured on the Griffiths Mental Developmental Scales.

Finally, several investigations have focused on specific treatment approaches. Harris (1981), for instance, studied the effects of neurodevelopmental therapy on the development of infants with Down syndrome. Twenty infants were divided into two groups—a treatment group receiving therapy sessions and a control group—

and were tested on a pre- and post-test basis on the Bayley Scales of Infant Development and Peabody Developmental Motor Scales. Differences between groups were not found on these measures. It is important to note that all infants were involved in an early intervention program and that the therapy sessions were conducted on a supplemental basis. Differences between groups were noted, however, in favor of the experimental group on attainment of predetermined individual motor treatment objectives. Other intervention efforts have focused on speech and language training. Project EDGE, the University of Minnesota's Communication Stimulation Program for infants with Down syndrome (Rynders and Horrobin, 1975), focused on the use of maternal tutoring to develop receptive and expressive language skills in project children. Children (20 experimental subjects and 20 control subjects) were enrolled between 3 and 9 months of age. Experimental infant group mothers were given 6 weeks of training on instructional methods and materials, followed by semiweekly home visits and monthly group meetings; parents provided daily home instruction to their children. At 3 years of age (after approximately 2½ years in the program), the group that received the training scored higher than the control group on measures of intellectual and receptive-language development (Rynders, 1973).

In the past the prevailing attitude regarding the developmental potential for individuals with Down syndrome has been largely pessimistic. Descriptive studies have documented the developmental delays in these children and progressive developmental decline over the early years (Carr, 1970, 1975; Dameron, 1963; Dicks-Mireaux, 1966, 1972; Share, 1975; Share and Veale, 1974). However, an examination of the early intervention literature reveals a vastly different prognosis for these children. Children with Down syndrome who receive early, systematic training do achieve developmental goals at earlier ages than expected and do outperform groups of children not receiving such services. The fact that a number of different educational approaches throughout the world have demonstrated this phenomenon further strengthens this claim. Thus, the outlook for the development of individuals with Down syndrome who receive specialized training seems more hopeful than previous descriptive research suggested.

Physically/Neurologically Impaired

Physical and occupational therapies are typically included in most early intervention curricula. Yet, few investigations of their effectiveness have been conducted. Numerous factors contribute to this dearth of information, among them difficulties in early diagnosis, in matching subjects for assignment to experimental and control groups, in procurement of a sufficient number of subjects at a given site, and in implementation of the experimental procedures over a sufficient length of time to yield meaningful information. Several clinical researchers, however, have attempted to test the effectiveness of various procedures with children with neuromotor abnormalities; these studies are reviewed in this section.

Carlsen (1975) compared two types of occupational therapy approaches as to their treatment potential with young children with cerebral palsy. Twelve children, ages 1 to 5 years, were assigned randomly to one of two treatment groups for 6 weeks. One group received a "facilitation" approach concentrated on gross sensorimotor activities; the other group received a "functional" therapeutic approach focused on fine motor adaptive and self-care skills. Results of assessments using the motor sections of the Denver Developmental Screening Test and the Bayley Scales of Infant Development favored the group receiving the facilitation approach.

Scherzer et al. (1976) in a similar study compared children with cerebral palsy (all under 18 months of age) using a double-blind study design. An experimental group of children received a minimum of 6 months of neurophysiological physical therapy. The control group of children received traditional passive range of motion exercises. Evaluation revealed definite change for the experimental group on motor (Gesell Developmental Schedules) and social (Vineland Social Maturity Scale) measures.

Vestibular stimulation treatments were examined in several investigations also. Chee et al. (1978) reported that evaluations of the reflex and gross motor skills of cerebral-palsied children, ages 2 to 6 years, demonstrated improvement for experimental group children who received 4 weeks of horizontal and vertical semicircular canal stimulation. The 12 treatment subjects were compared to 11 control subjects (six of whom were in a handled subgroup and five of whom were in a nonhandled subgroup). Sellick and Over (1980), however, using a similar treatment procedure, failed to attribute gains to the vestibular stimulation therapy. In their study, 20 children with cerebral palsy ranging from 8 to 56 months of age were randomly assigned to a control or treatment group where they received 4 weeks of vestibular stimulation. Tests utilizing the Bayley Scales of Infant Development showed improvements for both groups and nonsignificant differences between groups.

These studies paint a mixed picture of the effects of various physical therapies in remediating the developmental delay of children with neuromotor disabilities. Nevertheless, some approaches do seem beneficial and others await further testing. The task becomes determining which therapies "work" and with what type of disability.

Sensory Impaired

Few systematic investigations of intervention effectiveness in programs for sensory impaired infants are available. However, the limited evaluation studies in this area do suggest that interventions can be designed to remediate or alleviate the effects of early sensory impairments. Adelson and Fraiberg (1974) conducted a longitudinal study of the gross motor development of 10 blind infants who were enrolled in an early intervention program. The development of these children (ages at which they attained developmental milestones) was compared with norms for sighted infants and also with a comparable group of blind infants from another larger study sample. Results indicated that the children in the Adelson and Fraiberg sample achieved gross motor milestones at earlier ages than did the blind comparison group. Furthermore, their developmental attainments in the areas of neuromuscular maturation and postural achievements corresponded to those within the normal "sighted" infants' range. Delays, however, were noted in the areas of self-initiated mobility and locomotion, delays the investigators attributed to the normally later substitution of sound for sight as motivation for mobility.

Hearing-impaired infants and young children were the subjects for an investigation of the effectiveness of a program at the Bill Wilkerson Hearing and Speech Center in Nashville (Horton, 1976). The intervention program consisted of home training for parents of children under 3 years of age and an acoustic preschool for children ages 3 to 6. Both the language competence and educational achievement of these children were examined. Results revealed that the language competence of children receiving the early training (before age 3) closely resembled that of a normal-hearing group and that their competencies were superior to a later (after age 3, median 4 years) treatment group of hearing-impaired children. Similar findings were noted on educational achievement measures.

Multiply and Severely Handicapped

Attempts to determine the effectiveness of interventions for multiply and severely handicapped infants face serious limitations. Formal assessment instruments are inappropriate due to the sensory and motor impairments of the children; children often have few typical response systems available to them, subject procurement is difficult given the small numbers and heterogeneity of the population, and given the children's diverse needs, intervention packages must include a variety of therapeutic treatments—physical, communication, cognitive, self-help—making assessment of any given approach difficult. Nevertheless, several investigators have attempted to define and evaluate treatment approaches for this group of children.

Haavik and Altman (1977) reported the successful implementation of a training regimen designed to facilitate walking in severely retarded children (ages 2½ to 3 years). The behavioral changes of 20 multiply handicapped children (ranging from 18 to 36 months of age) participating in an intensive, early educational program were documented (Shapiro et al., 1977). These children were observed across eight dimensions (interaction with materials, social interaction, awareness of environment, expressive language, affect, gross motor skills, fine motor skills, and sensory responsiveness) by their teachers. Comparison of the children's performance at the beginning of the school program (pretest) with performance at the time of discharge (post-test) showed that at discharge children were more responsive and functioning at higher levels on all dimensions than they were at entrance to the program.

The effectiveness of the data-based early childhood classroom model serving moderately to profoundly handicapped children was evaluated using a multiple-baseline design by Fredericks et al. (1980). This study showed that children in the Teaching Research Class acquired an average of 6.44 skills per month and children at replication sites acquired a mean of 9.01 skills per month. These gains were significantly greater than gains made by students when they did not receive instruction (.91 skills per month at Teaching Research and .79 skills per month at replication sites). Thus, the educational procedures that included instruction in the area of self-help, motor development, language, and cognitive skills seemed to produce an accelerated learning rate in program children. The use of the multiple-baseline design allowed control for the effects of chance and maturation.

Another recent study by Bricker and Dow (1980) demonstrated that a group of 50 moderately to severely handicapped children made significant developmental progress over the course of participation in an early intervention program. The federally funded program at the Mailman Center for Child Development, University of Miami, was described as a center-based intervention program that focused on five components: classroom or direct intervention, parent involvement, ancillary or support services, instructional content and procedures, and evaluation. Analyses of program results included analyses of child progress, parent involvement, and the use of regression analysis to isolate possible improvement predictors. First, child progress as measured on the Uniform Performance Assessment System (White et al., 1978) revealed statistically significant pre/post-test changes on mean percent of items passed in the areas of preacademic, communication, gross motor, and social/self-help skills. Second, the mean rating of parent involvement as measured by a 4-point scale (1 = high involvement, 4 = low involvement) was 2.11. Finally, regression analyses revealed that the child's pretest score and age at pretest were the best predictors of improvement.

A similar group of 31 moderately and severely handicapped children ranging from birth to 3 years were studied by Hanson (1982). Children also participated in a 3-year federally funded model demonstration educational program, which focused on a combination home- and school-based service delivery system, a transdisciplinary team approach, data-based decision making, and active parent involvement. Children received training across all areas of development—gross and fine motor, cognition, speech and language, self-help, and social. Parents actively participated in goal setting, child teaching, and support meetings with one another. Both child and parent change were measured. Child progress was assessed utilizing the Bayley Scales of Infant Development, the Uniform Performance Assessment System, and the Project Curriculum Objectives Checklist. Results indicated that in both years 2 and 3 when these data were analyzed the groups of children made statistically significant test gains from pre- to post-testing periods on these measures. Parent behavior was assessed using the Parent Behavior Progression Scale (Bromwich, 1981). Analyses also revealed statistically significant pre/post-test differences indicating that parenting behavior became increasingly more adaptive and geared to the children's developmental levels and needs. Finally, a measure of parent satisfaction, a "consumer" reaction questionnaire, revealed that parents were overwhelmingly satisfied with services they received.

These investigations suggest that intensive early educational services for young severely handicapped children can facilitate the development of these youngsters. Demonstration of this progress seems particularly significant in light of the extensive needs and lack of services available to this population in the past (Sontag et al., 1977).

Summary

It is evident from this review that early intervention programs encompass a wide range of treatment approaches, populations served, and evaluation procedures. The focus particularly for programs oriented toward children with established biological risks is diverse. Taken individually each of the studies reviewed reported positive effects of their educational/treatment procedures. However, many studies fail to meet standards for rigorous experimental design. Most, for instance, for ethical reasons were unable to include a control group, most were unable to assign children randomly to groups, and most treated a heterogeneous group of children, making subject matching procedures difficult or impossible to exercise. Furthermore, programs varied with respect to size, service delivery model and setting, degree of parent involvement, staffing, age of children served, and frequency, duration, and type of treatment sessions. The complexity of this evaluation problem thus makes a conclusive overview of this research difficult to draw. However, in a review of 27 studies (many of which were previously described), Simeonsson et al. (1982) reported that:

> Although only 48% of all studies yielded statistical evidence for effectiveness, this figure increases to 81% when the analysis is restricted to those studies that incorporated statistical procedures. . . . In spite of limitations from the standpoint of scientific criteria, research does provide qualified support for the effectiveness of early intervention (p. 638).

RANGE OF INTERVENTION EFFECTS

Multiple Outcome Measures

The evaluation studies reviewed centered primarily on child performance measures, particularly measures of cognitive ability. Typically, programs are considered successful if: 1) children receiving the treatment outperform a control group of children to whom no treatment or another treatment was provided; 2) children in the treatment program demonstrate gains at or above a level relative to developmental expectations (when this descriptive information is available) in the absence of treatment; and/or 3) children receiving the treatment develop skills at a rate at or above a predetermined program standard for rate of development. The potential outcomes of any early intervention effort, however, may range far beyond the immediate effects on the child. As Simeonsson et al. (1980) suggest, assessment approaches should be expanded to include a broader range of behavioral domains including communication, temperament, affect, and behavioral style.

Ramey (1977) proposed five levels of consequences of early educational interventions. These levels are: 1) effects on the child; 2) effects on the child's relationships; 3) effects on the family as a unit; 4) effects on the family's relationship with social units; and 5) effects on social and cultural institutions. Research findings and observations have provided evidence of these broad effects on infants both biologically and/or environmentally at risk who are enrolled in early educational programs.

The effects on the child have been most well-established because attempts to evaluate the efficacy of early intervention typically have utilized measures of child developmental change to document program effects. For example, programs that focus on a particular group of children, such as those with Down syndrome, have documented child progress on developmental assessments as a result of the educational program (Clunies-Ross, 1979; Hanson and Schwarz, 1978; Hayden and Haring, 1976). As previously discussed, even those programs whose population included severely and multiply handicapped infants and toddlers have provided evidence that specific early interventions were effective in facilitating the children's development relative to normative data (Bricker and Dow, 1980; Fredericks et al., 1980; Hanson, 1982).

The *effects on the child's relationship to family members* has received less evaluative attention, perhaps because of the difficulties of measurement. Several studies, however, have examined parent-infant interaction variables. Ramey et al. (1981), for example, found that early intervention services with families of environmentally high-risk children produced greater dyadic involvement (e.g., mother and infant playing together). Widmayer and Field (1980) showed with teenage mothers of preterm infants that providing them with a demonstration of an assessment of their infant (using the Brazelton Neonatal Behavioral Assessment Scale) and a questionnaire on their assessment of their infant's behavior was effective at increasing more optimal interactive practices. Therefore, even relatively indirect interventions may produce powerful effects.

Effects on the family as a unit and the family relationship with other social units are more difficult to identify. An example of these effects, however, is available from a study of parent training with teenage mothers (Field et al., 1982). These researchers reported that mothers who received training showed higher return to work or school rates and lower repeat pregnancy rates. Finally, the *effects on social and cultural institutions* are even more indirectly measured. The increase in magazine articles and television programs on the capabilities of young disabled children certainly indicates that the presence of more competent and "integrated" children in the society is changing societal outlooks and practices toward the disabled. Furthermore, studies such as that by Weikart et al., (1978b) document that providing early services reduces the likelihood of special service needs or more intense special needs at a later point in time. An adoption of quality early services on a widespread basis, therefore, undoubtedly would change the programs and practices in public schools.

This discussion highlights the magnitude of the effects possible when early services are provided. Most of these effects, because of the difficulty in data gathering, however, remain undocumented.

Program Goals

The effectiveness of early intervention also can be studied on the basis of whether or not program goals or purposes are achieved. Sheehan and Gallagher (1982, p. 507) provide samples of possible intervention purposes:

For Infants
1. To maintain normal developmental functioning in all areas
2. To maintain normal functioning in most areas and improve one or more areas to a point of normal development
3. To prevent an increase in developmental delay in one or more areas
4. To demonstrate progress in one or more developmental areas.

For Parents and Other Family Members
5. To reduce stress and anxiety associated with parenting a handicapped infant
6. To increase the verbal and visual interaction between a parent or family member and a handicapped infant
7. To increase the responsibility that a parent takes for educating the handicapped infant
8. To increase parents' ability to use service systems to satisfy needs of families.

Any early intervention effort may include one or more of these program goals. The range of purposes again underscores the diverse nature of intervention goals both across and within programs.

Modification of Risk or Vulnerability

Early intervention outcomes also may be examined by returning to the concept of risk. As Beckwith's (1976) review of the effects of postnatal environment on the infant at risk indicates, early experiences may drastically alter the course of development for these infants. She states, "postnatal experience may amplify or diminish the probability of deficits" (p. 277). This assertion is amply supported by research literature (Drillien, 1964; Sameroff and Chandler, 1975; Werner et al., 1971), which indicates that the infant's transactions with the environment play a crucial role in the child's developmental outcome. For instance, a more severely biologically impaired infant may actually fare better than a less impaired infant if provided with a more supportive and enriching environment. The infant whose parents are supported to retain, teach, and enjoy the baby are likely to feel and have more success at parenting. Thus, "intervention" may be synonomous with "modifying the child's vulnerability" to environmental trauma. By teaching infants new and functional ways of interacting with their environment and by providing support services (informational, emotional, and educational) to families, early intervention programs help families construct environments whereby the children's disorders may be alleviated or diminished rather than compounded.

Cost-Effectiveness

The provision of educational services for infants and toddlers identified as handicapped or at risk for developmental delay represents a considerable financial commitment. Although such services can readily be justified on humanitarian grounds, are these services cost-effective? The evaluation and accounting systems necessary to document service costs are not available or feasible for most individual programs, nor have such systems where available been utilized on a statewide or national level. However, a few major investigative efforts have directly addressed the cost-effectiveness question.

Several of these efforts are described in detail and utilized by Garland et al. (1981) to calculate cost data. Briefly, their calculations suggest clear savings when intervention is begun in the first few years of life. Total educational costs per child were projected as $37,273 for intervention beginning at birth; $37,600 beginning at 2 years of age; $46,816 beginning at 6 years (with attrition and entrance to regular education), and $53,340 at age 6 without attrition to regular education (Garland et al., 1981). The magnitude of potential savings when services are begun early as indicated by these figures is marked.

Follow-up studies of early intervention program "graduates" also provide valuable information on cost-effectiveness. DeWeerd (reported in Garland et al., 1981) indicated that 55.8% of the graduates of early intervention demonstration projects funded through the Handicapped Children's Early Education Program (HCEEP) of the U.S. Department of Education were able to enroll in regular education programs in the first grade. Approximately 44% enrolled in special education programs. Similar findings were reported by a third-party evaluation of HCEEP projects (Stock et al. 1976). These data indicated that nearly two-thirds of the graduates were placed in regular education programs.

Perhaps the most extensive economic analysis of an early education program is that done by Weber et al. (1978). This analysis documents the costs of a compensory education preschool, the Ypsilanti Perry Preschool Project. Children (ages 3 to 4 years) participating in the project were considered "economically disadvantaged" and initially tested in the "educable mentally retarded" range (IQ's from 50 to 85). The development of these children was compared to a randomly assigned group of control children (no preschool experience). Findings from longitudinal studies revealed that project children outperformed control children on measures of cognitive ability, achievement tests, and teacher's ratings of the children's academic, emotional, and social development in the early elementary years. Not only were these developmental gains noted but also noted were significant cost savings for preschool children. Cost benefits were examined in terms of reduction in cost of subsequent education attributable to the preschool experience, benefits from an increase in projected lifetime earnings, and the value of the parents' release time while children attended preschool. Cost analyses produced the following cost and economic benefit figures (expressed in 1979 dollars). For each child the projected benefits were:

Savings from lowered cost for education	$ 3,353
Benefits from increase in lifetime earnings	10,798
Value of parent's release time	668
	$14,819

Costs for operating the program were $2,992 per year per child, or $5,984 for the 2-year preschool program (Schweinhart and Weikart, 1980).

Although these projections cannot be generalized to other projects, they do support the premise that early education services can provide significant educational savings and cost benefits to individuals when viewed on a long-range basis. The investigations reviewed, thus, provide a beginning for analyzing the cost effects of early service. In addition to offering clear positive impact on the development of atypical children and their families, they offer the possibility of significant long-term cost savings to the public.

Community Impact and Outreach

A measure of the worth of any service to the consumer is whether or not the consumer continues to demand and utilize the service. As such, the limited data available in the continuation of early intervention programs document the impact of these service programs.

The group of programs for which such documentation exists is that of the Handicapped Children's Early Education Program (HCEEP), a federal program providing seed money for the development of exemplary early intervention service models. An initial follow-up study of 21 of these demonstration projects revealed that 86% of the projects were continued through other funding sources after the 3-year "seed money" funding was completed (Swan, 1980). A more recent study of 126 HCEEP demonstration projects found that 90 projects, or 71%, are continuing all or some portion of their services after completing the 3-year funding cycle (Cox and Taylor-Hershel, 1982). These continuation funding sources came primarily from local education or government agencies (49%), state education or other agencies (27%), or private sources (foundations, fee for services, and fund raising) (17%). A continuation rate of this level during economically troubled times signals the parent needs and community support associated with these programs.

SUMMARY

Is early intervention effective? A rigorous comparison and analysis of service delivery models throughout the country for disabled and at-risk children has not been conducted. However, these facts remain:

1. Programs for young children at environmental risk produced long-lasting positive effects on child school competence and abilities, children's attitudes, and family attitudes (Lazar and Darlington, 1982).
2. The infant born at high risk for biological damage may benefit from early physical and educational therapies, but attention must be given to the individual infant's needs and responses and to supporting early caregiver infant interactions (see Chapter 3).
3. Early intervention services provided to infants born with established risks (e.g., Down syndrome or sensory impairments) and their families have been shown to be effective at remediating the effects of the disability, accelerating the child's development, and enhancing the child's ability to interact competently with the environment.

4. Family members are affected by the birth of a disabled or at-risk infant and often seek out and benefit from early intervention services.
5. Early intervention services produce a variety of effects—effects on the child, family, and community.
6. Beginning studies of early intervention cost-effectiveness suggest significant savings may be derived from the provision of these services.
7. Reviews suggest that programs that are the most effective at facilitating children's development are those with the following components:
    a. active parent involvement
    b. systematic early educational services
    c. developmentally based curricula
    d. individualized goal setting and frequent assessment and updating of child programs
    e. follow-through activities when the infants leave the program
    f. intervention beginning at as early an age as possible.

The importance of experiences in the early years is seldom questioned in contemporary society. When a child is born with a disability or at risk for later developmental delay, these early experiences may assume even more weight. The foundations of social relationships, basic skills, and learning processes can either be supported or ignored. The weight of the evidence available today suggests the former. The question becomes not "Is early intervention effective?" but "How can we make early interventions more effective?"

Chapter Outline

OVERVIEW: Supporting documentation for the efficacy of early educational and therapeutic efforts is reviewed. Conclusions are drawn that this early education and support is essential to achieve optimal developmental outcomes.

I. IS EARLY INTERVENTION EFFECTIVE?
Literature reviews describing educational program effects for young children environmentally at risk provide evidence for the effectiveness of early intervention.

II. DOCUMENTED EFFECTS FOR THE CHILDREN AT ESTABLISHED RISK
Investigations of programmatic attempts to facilitate the development of children in specific risk categories support the needs for early intervention.
Risk categories include:

A. Down syndrome
B. Physically/neurologically impaired
C. Sensory impaired
D. Multiply and severely handicapped

III. RANGE OF INTERVENTION EFFECTS

A. The range of early intervention program effects are examined with regard to the multiple levels of outcomes, including:
1. Effects on the child
2. Family and community
3. Meeting identified program goals
4. Modifying the child's risk or vulnerability to trauma
5. Cost-effectiveness and program continuation
B. These factors suggest the myriad of variables that must be considered in any attempt to truly document early intervention effectiveness.

REFERENCES

Adelson, E., and Fraiberg, S. Gross motor development in infants blind from birth. *Child Development*, 1974, *45*, 114–126.

Aronson, M., and Fällström, K. Immediate and long-term effects of developmental training in children with Down's syndrome. *Developmental Medicine and Child Neurology*, 1977, *19*, 489–494.

Beckwith, L. Caregiver-infant interaction as a focus for therapeutic intervention with human infants. In R. N. Walsh and W. T. Greenough (Eds.), *Environments as Therapy for Brain Dysfunction*. New York: Plenum Press, 1976.

Beller, E. K. Early intervention programs. In J. D. Osofsky (Ed.), *Handbook of Infant Development*. New York: Wiley, 1979.

Beller, E. K. Impact of early education on disadvantaged children. In S. Ryan (Ed.), *A Report on Longitudinal Evaluations of Preschool Programs*. Washington, DC: Office of Child Development, 1974.

Bidder, R. T., Bryant, G., and Gray, O. P. Benefits to Down's syndrome children through training their mothers. *Archives of Disease in Childhood*, 1975, *50*, 383–386.

Bricker, D. D., and Dow, M. G. Early intervention with the young severely handicapped child. *Journal of the Association for the Severely Handicapped*, 1980, *5*(2), 130–142.

Bromwich, R. M. *Working with Parents and Infants: An Interactional Approach*. Baltimore: University Park Press, 1981.

Bronfenbrenner, U. Is early intervention effective? In B. Z. Friedlander, G. M. Sterritt, and G. E. Kirk (Eds.), *Exceptional Infant (Vol. 3): Assessment and Intervention*. New York: Brunner/Mazel, 1975.

Carlsen, P. N. Comparison of two occupational therapy approaches for treating the young cerebral-palsied child. *The American Journal of Occupational Therapy*, 1975, *29*(5), 267–272.

Carr, J. Mental and motor development in young mongol children. *Journal of Mental Deficiency Research*, 1970, *14*, 205–220.

Carr, J. *Young Children with Down's Syndrome: Their Development, Upbringing, and Effect on Their Families*. London: Butterworths, 1975.

Chee, F. K. W., Kreutzberg, J. R., and Clark, D. L. Semicircular canal stimulation in cerebral palsied children. *Physical Therapy*, 1978, *58*(9), 1071–1075.

Clunies-Ross, G. G. Accelerating the development of Down's syndrome infants and young children. *The Journal of Special Education*, 1979, *13*(2), 169–177.

Connolly, B., and Russell, F. Interdisciplinary early intervention program. *Physical Therapy*, 1976, *56*(2), 155–158.

Connolly, B., Morgan, S., Russell, F. F., and Richardson, B. Early intervention with Down syndrome children. *Physical Therapy*, 1980, *60*(11), 1405–1408.

Cox, J. O., and Taylor-Hershel, D. After HCEEP-demonstration projects continue services. *Emphasis*, 1982, *5*(3), 3–5.

Dameron, L. E. Development of intelligence of infants with mongolism. *Child Development*, 1963, *34*, 733–738.

D'Eugenio, D. B., and Rogers, S. J. *Developmental Screening of Handicapped Infants: A Manual*. Ann Arbor: University of Michigan, 1976.

Dicks-Mireaux, M. J. Development of intelligence of children with Down's syndrome: Preliminary report. *Journal of Mental Deficiency Research,* 1966, *10,* 89–93.

Dicks-Mireaux, M. J. Mental development of infants with Down's syndrome. *American Journal of Mental Deficiency,* 1972, *77*(1), 26–32.

Drillien, C. M. *The Growth and Development of the Prematurely Born Infant.* Baltimore: Williams & Wilkins, 1964.

Field, T., Widmayer, S., Greenberg, R., and Stoller, S. Effects of parent training on teenage mothers and their infants. *Pediatrics,* 1982, *69*(6), 703–707.

Fredericks, B., Baldwin, V., Moore, W., et al. The teaching research data-based classroom model. *Journal of the Association for the Severely Handicapped,* 1980, *5*(3), 211–223.

Garland, C., Stone, N. W., Swanson, J., and Woodruff, G. *Early Intervention for Children with Special Needs and Their Families.* Monmouth, OR: Western States Technical Assistance Resource (WESTAR), 1981.

Gordon, I. J. *Early Childhood Stimulation through Parent Education.* Final report to the Children's Bureau, Social and Rehabilitation Service, Department of Health, Education, and Welfare. Gainesville: Institute for Development of Human Resources, University of Florida, 1969.

Gordon, I. J. *A Home Learning Center Approach to Early Stimulation.* Gainesville: Institute for Development of Human Resources, University of Florida, 1972.

Gray, S. W., and Klaus, R. A. The early training project. The seventh year report. *Child Development,* 1970, *41,* 909–924.

Haavik, S., and Altman, K. Establishing walking by severely retarded children. *Perceptual and Motor Skills,* 1977, *44,* 1107–1114.

Hanson, M. J. Down's syndrome children: Characteristics and intervention research. In M. Lewis and L. Rosenblum (Eds.), *The Uncommon Child.* New York: Plenum Press, 1981.

Hanson, M. J. *Results of the San Francisco Infant Program.* Final report to Special Education Programs, Washington, DC: U.S. Department of Education, 1982.

Hanson, M. J., and Schwarz, R. H. Results of a longitudinal intervention program for Down's syndrome infants and their families. *Education and Training of the Mentally Retarded,* 1978, *13*(4), 403–407.

Harris, S. R. Effects of neurodevelopmental therapy on motor performance of infants with Down's syndrome. *Developmental Medicine & Child Neurology,* 1981, *23,* 477–483.

Haskins, R., Finkelstein, N. W., and Stedman, D. J. Infant-stimulation programs and their effects. *Pediatric Annals,* 1978, *7,* 123–144.

Hayden, A. H. A center-based parent-training model. In D. L. Lillie and P. L. Trohanis (Eds.), *Teaching Parents to Teach.* New York: Walker, 1976.

Hayden, A. H. Handicapped children, birth to age 3. *Exceptional Children,* 1979, *45,* 510–516.

Hayden, A. H., and Dmitriev, V. The multidisciplinary preschool program for Down's syndrome children at the University of Washington Model Preschool Center. In B. Z. Friedlander, B. M. Sterritt, and G. E. Kirk (Eds.), *Exceptional Infant: Assessment and Intervention* (Vol. 3). New York: Brunner/Mazel, 1975.

Hayden, A. H., and Haring, N. G. Programs for Down's syndrome children at the University of Washington. In T. D. Tjossem (Ed.), *Intervention Strategies for High-Risk Infants and Young Children*. Baltimore: University Park Press, 1976.

Hayden, A. H., and Haring, N. G. The acceleration and maintenance of developmental gains in Down's syndrome school-age children. In P. Mittler (ed.), *Research to Practice in Mental Retardation: Care and Intervention* (Vol. 1). Baltimore: University Park Press, 1977.

Hayden, A. H., and Haring, N. G. *The Acceleration and Maintenance of Developmental Gains in School-aged Down's Syndrome Children*. Annual Report to Bureau of Education for the Handicapped, University of Washington, 1979.

Heber, R., and Garber, H. The Milwaukee Project: A study of the use of family intervention to prevent cultural-familial mental retardation. In B. Z. Friedlander, G. M. Sterritt, and G. E. Kirk (Eds.), *Exceptional Infant: Assessment and Intervention* (Vol. 3). New York: Brunner/Mazel, 1975.

Horton, K. B. Early intervention for hearing-impaired infants and young children. In T. D. Tjossem (Ed.), *Intervention Strategies for High-Risk Infants and Young Children*. Baltimore: University Park Press, 1976.

Karnes, M. B., Teska, J. A., Hodgins, A. S., and Badger, E. D. Educational intervention at home by mothers of disadvantaged infants. *Child Development*, 1970, *41*, 925–935.

Lally, J. R., and Honzig, A. S. The family development research program. In M. C. Day and R. K. Parker (Eds.), *The Preschool in Action*. Boston: Allyn & Bacon, 1977.

Lambie, D. Z., Bond, J. T., and Weikart, D. P. *Home Teaching with Mothers and Infants*. Ypsilanti, MI: High/Scope Educational Research Foundation, 1974.

Lazar, I., and Darlington, R. Lasting effects of early education: A report from the Consortium for Longitudinal Studies. *Monographs of the Society for Research in Child Development*, 1982, *47*(2–3, Serial No. 195).

Levenstein, P. Cognitive growth in preschoolers through verbal interaction with mothers. *American Journal of Orthopsychiatry*, 1970, *40*, 426–432.

Ludlow, J. R., and Allen, L. M. The effect of early intervention and preschool stimulus on the development of the Down's syndrome child. *Journal of Mental Deficiency Research*, 1979, *23*, 29–44.

McCluskey, K. A., and Arco, C. M. B. Stimulation and infant development. In J. G. Howells (Ed.), *Modern Perspectives in the Psychiatry of Infancy*. New York: Brunner/Mazel, 1979.

Painter, G. The effect of a structured tutorial program on the cognitive and language development of culturally disadvantaged infants. *Merrill-Palmer Quarterly*, 1969, *15*, 279.

Palmer, F. H. Minimal interaction at age two and three and subsequent intellectual changes. In R. K. Parker (Ed.), *The Preschool in Action*. Boston: Allyn & Bacon, 1972.

Ramey, C. T. *The social consequences of early intervention*. Paper presented at the American Association on Mental Deficiency, New Orleans, June, 1977.

Ramey, C. T., Collier, A. M., Sparling, J. J., et al. The Carolina Abecedarian Project: A longitudinal and multidisciplinary approach to the prevention of developmental retardation. In T. D. Tjossem (Ed.), *Intervention Strategies for High-Risk Infants and Young Children*. Baltimore: University Park Press, 1976.

Ramey, C. T., Sparling, J. J., and Wasik, B. Creating social environments to facilitate language development. In R. Schiefelbusch and D. Bricker (Eds.), *Early Language Intervention*. Baltimore: University Park Press, 1981.

Rynders, J. *Two Basic Considerations in Utilizing Mothers as Tutors of Their Very Young Retarded or Potentially Retarded Children*. Washington, DC: Department of Health, Education and Welfare, U.S. Office of Education, Bureau of Education for the Handicapped (ERIC Document Reproduction #ED 079908), 1973.

Rynders, J. E., and Horrobin, J. M. Project EDGE: The University of Minnesota's communication stimulation program for Down's syndrome infants. In B. Z. Friedlander, G. M. Sterritt, and G. E. Kirk (Eds.), *Exceptional Infant: Assessment and Intervention* (Vol. 3). New York: Brunner/Mazel, 1975.

Sameroff, A., and Chandler, M. Reproductive risk and the continuum of caretaking casuality. In F. Horowitz (Ed.), *Review of Child Development Research* (Vol. 4). Chicago: University of Chicago Press, 1975.

Schaefer, E. S., and Aaronson, M. Infant education research project: Implementation and implications of the home-tutoring program. In R. W. Parker (Ed.), *The Preschool in Action*. Boston: Allyn & Bacon, 1972.

Scherzer, A. L., Mike, V., and Ilson, J. Physical therapy as a determinant of change in the cerebral palsied infant. *Pediatrics*, 1976, 58(1), 47–52.

Schweinhart, L. J., and Weikart, D. P. *Effects of the Perry Preschool Program on Youths through Age 15*. Paper presented at the conference of the Handicapped Children's Early Education Program, Washington, DC, December, 1980.

Sellick, K. J., and Over, R. Effects of vestibular stimulation on motor development of cerebral-palsied children. *Developmental Medicine and Child Neurology*, 1980, 22, 476–483.

Shapiro, L. P., Gordon, R., and Neiditch, C. Documenting change in young multiply handicapped children in a rehabilitation center. *The Journal of Special Education*, 1977, 11, 243–257.

Share, J. B. Developmental progress in Down's syndrome. In R. Koch and F. F. de la Cruz (Eds.), *Down's Syndrome (Mongolism): Research, Prevention, and Management*. New York: Brunner/Mazel, 1975.

Share, J. B., and Veale, A. M. *Developmental Landmarks for Children with Down's Syndrome (Mongolism)*. Dunedin, New Zealand: The University of Otago Press, 1974.

Sheehan, R., and Gallagher, R. J. Conducting evaluations of infant intervention programs. In S. G. Garwood and R. Fewell (Eds.), *Educating Handicapped Infants*. Rockville, MD: Aspen Systems, 1982.

Simeonsson, R. J., Cooper, D. H., and Scheiner, A. P. A review and analysis of the effectiveness of early intervention programs. *Pediatrics*, 1982, 69(5), 635–641.

Simeonsson, R. J., Huntington, G. S., and Parse, S. A. Expanding the developmental assessment of young handicapped children. *New Directions for Exceptional Children*, 1980, 3, 51.

Sontag, E., Smith, J., and Certo, N. (Eds.). *Educational Programming for the Severely and Profoundly Handicapped*. Reston, VA: The Council for Exceptional Children, 1977.

Stock, J. R., Newborg, J., Wnek, L. L., et al. *Evaluation of Handicapped Children's Early Education Program(HCEEP). Final Report*. Columbus, OH: Battelle Center for Improved Education, 1976.

Swan, W. The Handicapped Children's Early Education Program. *Exceptional Children*, 1980, 47, 12–16.

Weber, C. V., Foster, P. W., and Weikart, D. P. *An Economic Analysis of the Ypsilanti Perry Preschool Project*. Ypsilanti, MI: High/Scope Educational Research Foundation, 1978.

Weikart, D. P., Bond, J. T., and McNeil, J. T. *The Ypsilanti Perry Preschool Project: Preschool Years and Longitudinal Results through Fourth Grade*. Ypsilanti, MI: High/Scope Educational Research Foundation, 1978a.

Weikart, D. P., Epstein, A. S., Schweinhart, L., and Bond, L. T. *The Ypsilanti Preschool Curriculum Demonstration Project: Preschool Years and Longitudinal Results*. Ypsilanti, MI: High/Scope Educational Research Foundation, 1978b.

Werner, E. E., Bierman, J. M., and French, F. E. *The Children of Kauai*. Honolulu: University of Hawaii Press, 1971.

White, O., Edgar, E., and Haring, N. G. *Uniform Performance Assessment System*. Seattle: College of Education, Experimental Education Unit, Child Development and Mental Retardation Center, University of Washington, 1978.

Widmayer, S. M., and Field, T. M. Effects of Brazelton demonstrations on early interactions of preterm infants and their teenage mothers. *Infant Behavior and Development*, 1980, 3, 79–89.

Index